FORTY-EIGHT SELECT SERMONS,

PREACHED BY

THAT EMINENT AND FAITHFUL SERVANT
OF JESUS CHRIST,

MR. JOHN WELCH,

SOMETIME MINISTER OF THE GOSPEL IN AIR.

THE TWO LAST OF THEM
WERE DELIVERED AS

HIS FAREWELL SERMONS,

IMMEDIATELY BEFORE
HE WAS APPREHENDED AND MADE A PRISONER
FOR THE
CAUSE AND GOSPEL OF JESUS CHRIST.

TO WHICH IS PREFIXED
THE HISTORY OF

HIS LIFE AND SUFFERINGS,

WITH
SOME PROPHETICAL LETTERS.

The righteous shall be in everlasting remembrance.   Psal. cxii. 6.
Save that the Holy Ghost witnesseth, saying, That Bonds and Afflictions abide me.   Acts xx. 23.
And others had trial of cruel mockings and scourgings, yea moreover, of bonds and imprisonment.   Heb. xi. 36.
Many are the afflictions of the righteous: But the Lord delivereth him out of them all.   Psal. xxxiv. 36.

WIPF & STOCK · Eugene, Oregon

Wipf and Stock Publishers
199 W 8th Ave, Suite 3
Eugene, OR 97401

Forty-Eight Select Sermons
Preached by that Eminent and Faithful Servant of Jesus Christ,
Mr. John Welch, Sometime Minister of the Gospel in Ayre
By Welch, John
ISBN 13: 978-1-60608-594-3
Publication date 1/7/2010
Previously published by George Kenton Harper, 1807

THE CONTENTS.

THE Publisher to the Reader. - - - - 7
An account of Mr. Welch's life. - - - - - 11
Serm. I. On the general judgment.—Rev. xx. 12. *And I saw a great white throne, and him that sat on it, from whose face the earth and the heaven fled away.* - - - - - - 47
Serm. II. On the same subject. - - - - - 64
Serm. III. On repentance.—Rev. ii. 5. *Remember therefore from whence thou art fallen, and do thy first works: or else I will come to thee quickly, and will remove thy candlestick out of his place except thou repent.* - - - 81
Serm. IV. On the same subject. - - - - - 97
Serm. V. On the same subject. - - - - - 113
Serm. VI. On the same subject. - - - - 126
Serm. VII. The same subject continued. - - 137
Serm. VIII. The same subject continued. - - 149
Serm. IX. The same subject continued. - - 160
Serm. X. The same subject continued. - - - 176
Serm. XI. Of the Christian warfare.—Ephes. vi. 10—21. *Finally, my brethren, be strong in the Lord, and in the power of his might. Put on the whole armour of God, &c.* - - 185
Serm. XII. The same subject continued. - - 204
Serm. XIII. The same subject continued. - - 213
Serm. XIV. The same subject continued. - 228
Serm. XV. The same subject continued. - - 237
Serm. XVI. The same subject continued. - - 246
Serm. XVII. The same subject continued. - 257
Serm. XVIII. The same subject continued. - 267
Serm. XIX. The subject finished. - - - - 277
Serm. XX. Upon divers points of religion.—1 John iv. 7, 8. *Beloved, let us love one another, for love comes of God, and every one that loveth is born of God, and knoweth God.* - - 297

CONTENTS.

Serm. XXI. Upon divers points of religion.—2 Cor. iv. 8. *But we are troubled on every side, &c.* - - - - - - - - - 309

Serm. XXII. Psal. lxxxviii. 1. *O Lord God of my salvation, I have cried day and night before thee.* - - - - - - - - - 320

Serm. XXIII. Psal. xlii. 1, 2, 3. *As the hart panteth after the water brooks, so panteth my soul after thee, O God.* - - - - - - - 333

Serm. XXIV. Isaiah xlii. 1. *Behold my servant whom I uphold, mine elect in whom my soul delighteth.* - - - - - - - - - 339

Serm. XXV. John xi. 3, 4, 11, &c. *Therefore his sisters sent unto him, saying, Lord, behold he whom thou lovest is sick, &c.* - - - 347

Serm. XXVI. Upon faith.—Heb. xi. 1. *Now faith is the substance of things hoped for, and the evidence of things not seen.* - - - - 352

Serm. XXVII. The same subject continued. - 356
Serm. XXVIII. The same subject continued. - 366
Serm. XXIX. Upon divers points of religion.—Mat. xxvii. 40. *After he came to his disciples he found them asleep.* - - - - - - 375

Serm. XXX. 2 Cor. v. 14. *For the love of Christ constraineth us, &c.* - - - - - - - 381

Serm. XXXI. Exod. xx. 4, 5, 6. *Thou shalt not make unto thee any graven image, &c.* - 389

Serm. XXXII. Deut. xii. 18. *But thou must eat them before the Lord thy God, in the place which the Lord thy God shall chuse, &c.* - 398

Serm. XXXIII. Upon the freedom of the saints.— Luke i. 74, 75. *That he would grant unto us, that we being delivered out of the hands of our enemies, might serve him without fear, in holiness and righteousness before him all the days of our life.* - - - - - - - - 404

Serm. XXXIV. Upon the same subject. - - 416
Serm. XXXV. Upon the same subject. - - 423
Serm. XXXVI. The same subject continued. - 429
Serm. XXXVII. The same subject continued. 437

CONTENTS.

Serm. XXXVIII. Upon the believer's privilege.—
1 Pet. ii, 8. *But ye are a chosen generation, a royal priesthood, a holy nation, a peculiar people, &c.* - - - - - - - - 443
Serm. XXXIX. Upon the believer's security.—John x. 27, 28. *My sheep hear my voice, and I know them, and they follow me; and I give unto them eternal life, &c.* - - - - 452
Serm. XL. Upon the same subject. - - - 457
Serm. XLI. Upon the same subject. - - - 463
Serm. XLII. Upon God's everlasting love.—John iii. 16, 17. *For God so loved the world, that he gave his only begotten Son, that whosoever believeth in him should not perish, but have everlasting life.* - - - - - - - - 470
Serm. XLIII. Upon the same subject. - - - 484
Serm. XLIV. The Unbeliever condemned.—John. iii. 17. *For God sent not his Son into the world to condemn the world; but that the world through him might be saved.* - - - 492
Serm. XLV. Upon the same subject. - - - 501
Serm. XLVI. Of a happy resurrection.—Philip. iii. 11, 12. *If by any means I may attain unto the resurrection of the dead, &c.* - - - 509

The two following sermons were preached by the author immediately before his imprisonment.
Serm. XLVII. No condemnation to God's elect.— Rom. viii. 1, 2. *Now therefore there is no condemnation to them that are in Christ Jesus, &c.* - - - - - - - - - 515
Serm. XLVIII. Upon the same subject. - - 531

THE PUBLISHER TO THE READER.

Christian Reader,

HERE is presented to your view a few sermons, being part of the labours of that great man of God, Mr. John Welch : one who had more than an ordinary measure of the Spirit of God given to him, evidently known to many, who were so happily blessed as to be under his ministry, and enjoy fellowship and communion with him in the ordinances of the gospel. Of which there is an account of many extraordinary things in the history of his life annexed to this book.

The candid reader will see, by the following sermons, that he hath been mightily impressed with a deep sense of the degeneracy of the age he lived in, especially with the ignorance and wickedness of the people in the several congregations, that the Lord was pleased to call him to preach the gospel amongst ; which doth appear by the many bitter lamentations that the following sermons are filled with ; wherein he labours with all earnestness of spirit, to set home upon their spirits the evil of sin, and the great danger of their eternal ruin by the same ; in opening up our lost and ruined state by Adam, and the miseries that follow thereupon, both in this life, and more especially that eternal misery that abides every soul that dies in an unregenerate state.

Again, it hath been his great work to unfold unto his people the mysteries of the great salvation through Jesus Christ, the Saviour of sinners ; which should be the study of all who profess themselves to be the ministers of the gospel of the blessed Jesus ; to open up, and unfold those great mysteries of salvation *hid from ages and generations* ; but are now made manifest to us in these last days of the world.

The doctrine of a crucified Christ hath been the study of faithful ministers in former ages, and it will yet be the work of all those who labour to be faithful to their Lord and Master in the work of the gospel. It is the work of angels and glorified spirits above to be looking into this great mystery, and will be the work of men and angels to be looking into it for ever through eternity, and will never be able to wade through the depths of that unsearchable treasure of mysteries that are hid in our Immanuel, *God with us*. O ! it is pleasant work, and will be a pleasant exercise to every one that is exercised therein. What is all the work about the throne of God and the Lamb in the upper house above, but just to be looking into these mysteries, and admiring the glorious beauties and excellencies that appear in the face of our Immanuel ; and the more they look, the more wonders will they see for ever through eternity. O then, how well does it become all that are ambassadors for Christ to proclaim these glad tidings of salvation to lost sinners ! It was our Lord's own work immediately after the fall : " Though he was in the form of God, and thought it no robbery to be equal with God," yet he did not think it below him to come down (from his royal throne, where he dwelt from everlasting) with the glad news of salvation to poor trembling Adam, who had ruined himself and all his posterity, when under the awful apprehensions of divine wrath, and vainly thinking to hide himself from the presence of the Lord amongst the thickets of the garden : but behold how everlasting love prevents his fearful thoughts, and O how good news must these be, to hear out of the mouth of a Saviour himself, " That the seed of the woman should bruise the head of the serpent !" Gen. iii. 15.

Again, it was the work of angels to proclaim these news to the poor *shepherds of Bethlehem*, Luke ii. 9. at the birth of our Lord, when he actually came down into our world, in our nature, and vailed himself with our flesh, to tabernacle with us, that he might perform the work the Father had put into his hand to do. Again, it was the work of the blessed apostles, after his resurrection, to spread the doctrine amongst all the nations they had access unto. Paul could say, "I desire to know nothing amongst you but Christ, and him crucified." And Oh! how well then doth it become all who are employed as ambassadors for Christ, to be employed in the same doctrine to the end of the world. But O! how lamentable is it, that so little of that doctrine is to be heard in this land, in the day we now live in; it is amongst one of the greatest signs of the Lord's anger against this land, that this doctrine is like to wear out of the pulpits of many in Scotland; this doctrine is become nauseous to many; yea, the name of Jesus is so unsavoury to many in this age, that when they hear of it in a sermon, they will laugh and flout at it. But O how will they laugh at that day, when he comes "in the clouds of heaven, with power and great glory, attended with an innumerable company of angels, and the spirits of just men made perfect, to take vengeance on all the workers of iniquity;" when they will be forced to "cry to the hills and mountains to fall upon them, and cover them from the face of him that sits upon the throne, and from the wrath of the Lamb." O poor shift to cry to the creature to hide them from the face of the Creator, whose presence fills heaven and earth. "He that sits in heaven will then laugh at them, and the Lord will have them in derision." Psal. ii. 4. I also will laugh at your calamity, and mock when your fear cometh, Prov. i. 26. Fear and trembling will then seize multitudes of men and women, that now look upon all revealed religion as a mere jest and idle stories; but there will be no mocking at the bar of God's judgment, when the secrets of all hearts will be tried, and the sentence come forth, "Go, ye cursed, into everlasting fire, prepared for the devil and his angels." Therefore, O how good were it now for poor sinners to *kiss the Son, lest he be angry*; and make peace with him, while he is making offers of peace to us, and using all possible means to reconcile sinners to him, by the offers of the gospel of peace; therefore, O let us obey his voice, *while it is called to-day.* It is now our happy day of the offers of life and salvation through Jesus Christ; but if we despise such a day of grace as this is, it will not be long till God's day of vengeance come, when he will say to such as despise his offers, " Behold, ye despisers, wonder and perish. Oh that we were wise, that we understood this, that we would consider our latter end," O how happy for ever should we be!

The following sermons are all of them filled with earnest exhortations for the awakening of a secure generation, as we are, at this day. The serious reader will find they are not delivered in a neat and fine dress, to please the fine taste of the age we now live in, who love more to hear a sermon neatly dressed in a fine style of curious learning, than to hear an awakening sermon concerning our own personal sins, and the sins of the generation we live in: but the following are plain to the meanest capacity, " not in the inticing words of man's wisdom, but in demonstration of the Spirit, and of power." And oh! that the Lord himself may give his Spirit to every one, into whose hands they shall come, that they may read the same with faith and love, that they may gain the desired end, is the earnest prayer of him who is your well wisher,

THE LIFE

OF THE REVEREND
Mr. JOHN WELCH,

MINISTER OF THE GOSPEL AT AIR.

MR. JOHN WELCH was born a gentleman, his father being laird of Coliestoun (an estate rather competent than large, in the shire of Nithsdale) about the year 1570, the dawning of our reformation being then but dark. He was a rich example of grace and mercy; but the night went before the day, being a most hopeless extravagant boy: it was not enough to him, frequently, when he was a young stripling, to run away from the school, and play the truant; but, after he had past his grammar, and was come to be a youth, he left the school and his father's house, and went and joined himself to the thieves on the English border, who lived by robbing the two nations, and amongst them he stayed till he spent a suit of clothes. Then, when he was cloathed only with rags, the prodigal's misery brought him to the prodigal's resolution, so he resolved to return to his father's house; but durst not adventure, till he should interpose a reconciler. So, in his return homeward, he took Dumfries in his way, where he had a friend, one Agnes Forsyth, and with her he diverted some days, earnestly intreating her to reconcile him to his father. While he lurked in her house, his father came providentially to the house to salute his cousin, Mrs. Forsyth; and after they had talked a while, she asked him, whether ever he had heard any news of his son John? To her he replied, with great grief, "Oh cruel woman how can you name his name to me; the first news I expect to hear of him is, that he is hanged for a thief." She answered, "Many a profligate boy has become a virtuous man," and comforted him. He insisted upon his sad complaint, but asked whether she knew his lost son was yet alive? She answered yes, he was; and she hoped he should prove a better man than he was a boy: and with that she called upon him to come to his father. He came weeping, and kneeled, beseeching his father for Christ's sake, to pardon his misbehaviour, and deeply engaged to be a new man. His father reproached him and threatened him: yet, at length, by the boy's tears and Mrs. Forsyth's importunities, he was persuaded to a reconciliation. The boy intreated his father to put him to the college, and there to try his behaviour, and if ever thereafter he should break, he said he should be content his father should disclaim him forever. So his father carried him home, and put him to the college, and there he became a diligent student of great expectation, and shewed himself a sincere convert: and so he proceeded to the ministry.

His first post in the ministry was at Selkirk, while he was yet very young, and the country rude. While he was there, his ministry was rather admired by some than received by many; for he was always attended with the prophet's shadow, the hatred of the wicked; yea, even the ministers of that country were more ready to pick a quarrel with his person than to follow his doctrine, as may appear to this day in their synodal records, wherein we find he had many to censure him, and only some to defend him: yet it was thought his ministry in that place was not without fruit, though he stayed but a short time there. Being a young man unmarried, he tabled himself in the house of one Mitchel, and took a young boy of his to be his bed-fellow, who, to his dying day, retained both a respect for Mr. Welch and his ministry, from the impression Mr. Welch's behaviour made upon his apprehension, though but a child. His custom was, when he went to bed at night, to lay a Scots plaid above his bed cloathes, and when he went to his night-prayers, to sit up and cover himself negligently therewith, and so to continue: for, from the beginning of his ministry to his death, he reckoned the day ill spent, if he stayed not seven or eight hours in prayer; and this the boy would never forget till hoary hairs.

I had once the curiosity, travelling through the town, to call for an old man, his name was Ewart, who remembered upon Mr. Welch his being in that place; and after other discourses enquired of him, what sort of a man Mr. Welch was? His answer was, "O Sir! he was a type of Christ." An expression more significant than proper, for his meaning was, that he was an example that imitated Christ: as indeed in many things he did. He told me also, that his custom was, to preach publicly once every day, and to spend his whole time in spiritual exercises! that some in that place waited well upon his ministry with great tenderness, but that he was constrained to leave that place because of the malice of the wicked.

The special cause of his departure was a prophane gentleman in the country, one Scot of Hawickschaw, whose family is now extinct; but because Mr. Welch had either reproved him, or, merely out of hatred, Mr. Welch was most unworthily abused by the unhappy man; and, among the rest of the injuries he did him, this was one; Mr. Welch kept always two good horses for his use, and the wicked gentleman, when he could do no more, either with his own hand, or his servants, cut off the rumps of the two innocent beasts, upon which followed such effusion of blood that they both died; which Mr. Welch did much resent, and such base usage as this persuaded him to listen to a call to the ministry at Kirkcudbright, which was his next post.

But when he was to leave Selkirk, he could not find a man in all the town to transport his furniture, except only Ewart, who was at that time a poor young man, but master of two horses, with which he transported

Mr. Welch, his goods, and so left him; but as he took his leave, Mr. Welch gave him his blessing, and a piece of gold for a token, exhorting him to fear God, and promised he should never want; which promise providence made good through the whole course of the man's life, as was observed by all his neighbours.

At Kirkcudbright he stayed not long, but there he reaped a good harvest of converts, which subsisted long after his departure, and were a part of Mr. Samuel Rutherford's flock, though not his parish, while he was minister at Anwoth; yet when his call to Air came to him, the people of the parish of Kirkcudbright never offered to detain him; so his transportation to Air was the more easy.

While he was in Kirkcudbright, he met with a young gallant in scarlet and silver lace, the gentleman's name was Mr. Robert Glendoning, new come home from his travels, and much surprised the young man, by telling him he behooved to change his garb and way of life, and betake himself to the study of the scriptures (which at that time was not his business) for he should be his successor in the ministry at Kirkcudbright; which accordingly came to pass some time thereafter.

Mr. Welch was transported to Air in the year 1590, and there he continued till he was banished. There he had a very hard beginning, but a very sweet end: for when he came first to the town, the country was so wicked, and the hatred of godliness so great, that there could not one in all the town be found to let him a house to dwell in, so he was constrained to accommodate himself the best he might in a part of a gentleman's house for a time; the gentleman's name was John Stewart, merchant, and sometime provost of Air, an eminent Christian, and great assistant of Mr. Welch.

And when he had first taken up his residence in that town, the place was divided into factions, and so filled with bloody conflicts, that a man could hardly walk the streets with safety. Mr. Welch made it his first undertaking to remove the bloody quarrellings; but found it very difficult work: yet such was his earnestness to pursue his design, that many times he would rush betwixt two parties of men fighting, even in the midst of blood and wounds ; he used to cover his head with a head-piece, before he went to separate these bloody enemies, but never used a sword, that they might see he came for peace, and not for war ; and so, by little and little, he made the town a peaceable habitation.

His manner was, after he had ended a skirmish amongst his neighbours, and reconciled these bitter enemies, to cause a covered table upon the street, and there brought the enemies together, and, beginning with prayer, he persuaded them to profess themselves friends and then to eat and drink together : then, last of all, he ended the work with singing a psalm. So, after the rude people began to observe his example, and listen to his heavenly doctrine, he came quickly to that respect amongst them, that he became not only a necessary counsellor, without whose counsel they would do nothing, but an example to imitate, and so he buried the bloody quarrels.

He gave himself wholly to ministerial exercises ; he preached once every day ; he prayed the third part of his time ; he was unwearied in his studies ; and for a proof of this, it was found amongst his other papers, that he had abridged Suarez his Metaphysics when they came first to his hand, even when he was well stricken in years. By all which it appears that he was not only a man of great diligence, but also of a strong and robust natural constitution, otherwise he had never endured the fatigue.

But if his diligence was great, so it is doubted whether his sowing in painfulness, or his harvest in success, was greater ; for if either his spiritual experiences in seeking the Lord, or his fruitfulness in converting souls, be considered, they will be found unparalleled in Scotland. And many years after Mr. Welch's death, Mr. David Dickson, at that time a flourishing minister at Irvine, was frequently heard to say, when people talked to him of the success of his ministry, that the grape gleanings in Air, in Mr. Welch's time, were far above the vintage of Irvine in his own. Mr. Welch's preaching was spiritual and searching; his utterance tender and moving; he did not much insist upon scholastic purposes; he made no show of his learning. I heard once one of his hearers (who was afterwards minister at Moorkirk in Kyle) say, that a man could hardly hear him and forbear weeping, his conveyance was so affecting. There is a large volume of his sermons now in Scotland; but never any of them came to the press*, nor did he ever appear in print, except in his dispute with Abbot Brown the Papist wherein he makes it appear his learning was not behind his other virtues; and in another piece, called Dr. Welch's Armageddon, printed, I suppose in France, wherein he gives his meditation upon the enemies of the church, and their destruction: but the piece itself is rarely to be found.

Sometimes, before he went to sermon he would send for his elders and tell them, he was afraid to go to pulpit, because he found himself sore deserted; and thereafter desire one or more of them to pray, and then he would venture to the pulpit: but, it was observed, this humbling exercise used ordinarily to be followed with a flame of extraordinary assistance; so near neighbours are many times contrary dispositions and frames. He would many times retire to the church of Air, which was at some distance from the town, and there spend the whole night in prayer; for he used to allow his affections full expression, and prayed not only with an audible, but sometimes a loud voice; nor did he irk in that solitude all the night over; which hath, it may be, occasioned the contemptible slander of some malicious enemies, who were so bold as to call him no less than a wizard.

There was in Air, before he came to it, an aged man, a minister of the town, called Porterfield, the man was judged no bad man, for his personal inclinations;

---

* Mr. Welch's life was published before the following sermons were printed, which were selected from that volume.

but of so easy a disposition, that he used many times to go too great a length with his neighbours in many dangerous practices ; amongst the rest, he used to go to the bow-buts and archery on sabbath afternoon, to Mr. Welch's great dissatisfaction. But the way he used to reclaim him was not bitter severity, but this gentle policy : Mr. Welch, together with John Stewart, and Hugh Kennedy, his two intimate friends, used to spend the sabbath afternoon in religious conference and prayer ; and to this exercise they invited Mr. Porterfield, which he could not well refuse ; by which means, he was not only diverted from his former sinful practice, but likewise brought to a more watchful and edifying behaviour in his course of life.

He married Elizabeth Knox, daughter to the famous Mr. John Knox, minister at Edinburgh, the apostle of Scotland, and she lived with him from his youth till his death. By her, I have heard, he had three sons. The first was called Dr. Welch, a doctor of medicine, who was unhappily killed, upon an innocent mistake, in the Low Countries, and of him I never heard more. Another son he had most lamentably lost at sea ; for when the ship, in which he was, sunk, he swam to a rock in the sea, but starved there for want of necessary food and refreshment ; and when sometime afterwards his body was found upon the rock, they found him dead in a praying posture, upon his bended knees, with his hands stretched out ; and this was all the satisfaction his friends and the world had upon his lamentable death, so bitter to his friends. Another son he had, who was heir to his father's graces and blessings, and this was Mr. Josias Welch, minister at Temple-Patrick, in the North of Ireland, commonly called the *Cock of the Conscience*, by the people of the country, because of his extraordinary wakening and rousing gift. He was one of that blest society of ministers, which wrought that unparalleled work in the North of Ireland, about the year 1639, but was himself a man most sadly exercised with doubts about his own salvation all his time, and would ordinarily say, " That ministers was much to be pitied, who was called to comfort weak saints, and had no comfort himself." He died in his youth, and left for his successor Mr. John Welch, minister at Iron-Gray in Galloway, the place of his grandfather's nativity. What work he did in Scotland, in the time of the late Episcopal persecution for the space of twenty years, is known to all Scotland. He maintained his dangerous post of preaching the gospel upon the mountains of Scotland, notwithstanding of the threatenings of the state, the hatred of the bishops, the price set upon his head, and all the fierce industry of his cruel enemies. It is well known, that bloody Claverhouse, upon secret information from his spies, that Mr. Welch was to be found in some lurking place, at forty miles distance, would make all that long journey in one winter's night, that he might catch him; but when he came he missed always his prey. I never heard of a man who endured more toil, adventured upon more hazard, escaped so much hazard, in the world. He used to tell his friends who counselled him to be more cautious, and not to hazard himself so much, " That he firmly believed dangerous undertakings would be his security, and that whenever he should give over that course, and retire himself, his ministry should come to an end :" which accordingly came to pass; for when, after Bothwell Bridge, he retired to London, the Lord called him by death, and there he was honourably buried, not far from the king's palace.

But to return to old Mr. Welch. As the duty wherein he abounded and excelled most was prayer, so his greatest attainments fell that way; he used to say, " he wondered how a christian could lie in bed all night, and not rise to pray." And many times he rose; and many times he watched. One night he rose from his wife, and went into the next room, where he stayed so long at secret prayer, that his wife fearing he might catch cold, was constrained to rise and follow him, and as she hearkened, she heard him speak as by interrupted sentences, " Lord, wilt thou not grant me Scotland," and after a pause, " Enough Lord, enough," and so she returned to her bed, and he followed her, not knowing she had heard him; but when he was by her, she asked him what he meant by saying, "Enough, Lord, enough." He shewed himself dissatisfied with her curiosity, but told her, "he had been wrestling with the Lord for Scotland, and found there was a sad time at hand, but that the Lord would be gracious to a remnant. This was about the time when bishops first over-spread the land, and corrupted the church. This is more wonderful I am to relate: I heard once an honest minister who was a parishioner of Mr. Welch's many a day, say, "That one night as he watched in his garden very late, and some friends waiting upon him in the house, and wearying because of his long stay, one of them chanced to open a window towards the place where he walked, and saw clearly a light surround him; and heard him speak strange words about his spiritual joy." I do neither add nor alter; I am the more induced to believe this, having heard it from as good a man as any in Scotland, that a very godly man, though not a minister, declared confidently, "that (after he had spent a whole night in a country house of his, at the house-in-the-Muir) he saw such an extraordinary light as this himself, which was to him both matter of wonder and astonishment." But though Mr. Welch had, upon the account of his holiness, abilities, and success, acquired among his subdued people a very great respect, yet was I never in such admiration, as after the great plague which raged in Scotland in his time.

And one cause was this: The magistrates of Air, "forasmuch as this alone town was free, and the country about infected, thought fit to guard the ports with centinels and watchmen; and one day two travelling merchants, each with a pack of cloth upon a horse, came to the town desiring entrance, that they might sell their goods, producing a pass from the magistrates of the town whence they came, which was at that time sound and free; yet, notwithstanding all, the centinels stopped them till the magistrates were called; and when they came they would do nothing without their minister's advice: so Mr. Welch was called, and his opinion asked: he demurred, and put off his hat, with his eyes towards heaven for a pretty space, though he uttered no audible words, yet continued in a praying gesture; and after a little space, told the magistrates they would do well to discharge these travellers their town, affirming, with great asseveration, the plague was in these packs: so the magistrates commanded them to be gone, and they went to Cumnock, a town some ten miles distant, and there sold their goods, which kindled such an infection in that place, that the living were hardly able to bury their dead. This made the people begin to think Mr. Welch an oracle. Yet as he walked with God, and kept close with him, so he forgot not man: for he used frequently to dine abroad with such of his friends as he thought were persons with whom he might maintain the communion of the saints; and once in the year, he used always to invite all his familiars in the town to a treat in his house, where there was a banquet of holiness and sobriety."

He continued the course of his ministry in Air, till king James's purpose of destroying the church of Scotland, by establishing bishops, was ripe; and then it fell to be his duty to edify the church by his sufferings, as formerly he had by his doctrine.

The reason why king James was so violent for bishops, was neither their divine institution, which he denied they had, nor yet the profit the church should reap by them, for he knew well both the men and their communications; but merely because he believed they were useful instruments to turn a limited monarchy into absolute dominion, and subjects into slaves; the design in the world he minded most. Always in the pursuit of his design he followed this method: In the first place, he resolved to destroy a general assembly; knowing well that so long as assemblies might convene in freedom, bishops could never get their designed authority in Scotland; and the dissolution of assemblies he brought about in this manner.

The general assembly at Holy-Rood House, in the year 1602, with the king's consent, indict their next meeting to be kept at Aberdeen, the last Tuesday of July, in the year 1604; and before that day came, the king by his commissioner the laird of Laurieston, discharged them to meet. Mr. Patrick Galloway, moderator of the last assembly, in a letter directed to the several Presbyteries, continued the meeting till the first Tuesday of July 1605, at the same place. Last of all, in June 1605, the expected meeting to have been kept in July following, is by a new letter from the King's commissioner, and the commissioners of the general assembly, discharged and prohibited; but without naming any day or place for any other assembly absolutely; and so the series of our assemblies expired, never to revive again in due form, till the covenant was renewed in the year 1638. However many of the godly ministers in Scotland, knowing well, if once the hedge of the government was broken the corruption of the doctrine would soon follow, resolved not to quit their assembly so. And therefore, a number of them convened at Aberdeen, upon the first Tuesday of July 1605, being the last day that was distinctly appointed by authority; and when they had met, did no more but constitute themselves, and dissolve, and this was all. Amongst those was Mr. Welch, who though he had not been present upon that precise day, yet because he came to the place, and approved what his brethren had done, he was accused as guilty of the treasonable fact committed by his brethren. So dangerous a point was the name of a general assembly, in King James's jealous judgment.

Within a month after this meeting, many of these godly men were incarcerate, some in one prison, some in another; Mr. Welch was sent first to Edinburgh Tolbooth, and then to Blackness, and so from prison to prison, till he was banished to France, never to see Scotland again.

And now the scene of his life begins to alter; but, before his blessed sufferings, he had this strange warning:

After the meeting at Aberdeen was over, he retired immediately to Air; and one night he rose from his wife, and went into his garden (as his custom was) but staid longer than ordinary, which troubled his wife, who when he returned, expostulated with him very hard, for his staying so long to wrong his health: he bid her be quiet, for it should be well with them; but he knew well, he should never preach more in Air. And accordingly, before the next sabbath, he was carried prisoner to Blackness castle. After that, he, with many others, who had met at Aberdeen, were brought before the council of Scotland, at Edinburgh, to answer for their rebellion and contempt, in holding a general assembly, not authorized by the king; and because they declined the secret council, as judges competent in causes purely spiritual, such as the nature and constitution of a general assembly is, they were first remitted to the prison of Blackness, and other places; and thereafter, six of the most considerable of them were brought, under night, from Blackness to Linlithgow, before the criminal judges, to answer an accusation of high treason, at the instance of sir Thomas Hamilton, the king's advocate, for declining, as he alledged, the king's lawful authority; in refusing to admit the council judges competent in the cause of the nature of church judicatories. And after their accusation, and answer was read, by the verdict of a jury of very considerable gentlemen, they were condemned as guilty of high treason.* The punishment continued till the king's pleasure should be known; and thereafter their punishment was made banishment, that the sentence might someway seem to soften their severe punishment, as the king had contrived it.

* So averse were the judges and jury to Mr. Welch's trial, that lord Dunbar, then prime minister for Scotland, in order to obtain a sentence agreeable to the king, addressed the judges with promises and threats, packed the jury, and then dealt with them without scruple or ceremony. *See note on letter first of a collection of letters and memorials, published by sir David Darymple.*

While he was in Blackness, he wrote his famous letter to Dame Lillias Graham, countess of Wigtoun, which here I have inserted.

The consolation of the Holy Ghost be multiplied unto you by Jesus Christ.

OFTEN and many times, christian and elect lady, I have desired the opportunity to be comforted with that consolation wherewith it hath pleased God, of his free grace and mercy, to fill and furnish you. Your remembrance is very sweet aud comfortable to my very soul: since the time I knew you in Christ Jesus, I have ever been mindful of you unto the Lord, and now, not being able to refrain any longer, I could not omit this occasion, not knowing how long it may please the lord to continue my being in this tabernacle, or give me further occasion of writing to any.

Although I have not great matter at this time, yet, in remembrance of your labour of love, hope and patience, I must needs salute your ladyship, knowing assuredly, you are the chosen of God, set apart before ever the world was, to that glorious and eternal inheritance. Being thus comforted in your faith and hope, I am fully assured, though we never have the occasion of meeting here, yet we shall reign together in the world to come.

My desire to remain here is not great, knowing, that so long as I am in this house of clay, I am absent from God; and if it were dissolved, I look for a building, not made with hands, eternal in the heavens. In this I groan, desiring to be cloathed upon, with my house which is in heaven, if so that being cloathed, I shall not be found naked: for I that am within this tabernacle do often groan and sigh within myself, being often times burdened: not that I would be uncloathed, but cloathed upon, that mortality might be swallowed up of life. I long to eat of that tree which is planted in the midst of the paradise of God, and to drink of the pure river, clear as crystal, that runs through the streets of the new Jerusalem. I know that my Redeemer liveth, and that he shall stand at the last day upon the earth. And though after my skin worms destroy my body, yet in my flesh shall I see God; whom I shall see for myself and not another for me; and mine eyes shall behold him, though my reins be consumed within me. I long to be refreshed with the souls of them that are under the altar, who were slain for the word of God, and the testimony they held, and to have these long white robes given me, that I may walk in white raiment, with those glorious saints who have washed their garments, and have made them white in the blood of the Lamb. Why should I think it a strange thing to be removed from this place to that, wherein my hope, my joy, my crown, my elder brother, my head, my Father, my comforter, and all the glorious saints are; and where the songs of Moses and the Lamb are sung joyfully; where we shall not be compelled to sit by the rivers of Babylon, and to hang our harps upon the willow-trees; but shall take them up, and sing the hallelujah, blessing, honour, glory, and power, to him that sits upon the throne, and to the Lamb for ever and ever; What is there under the old vault of the heavens, and in this old worn earth, which is under the bondage of corruption, groaning and travelling in pain, and shooting out the head, looking, waiting and longing for the redemption of the sons of God? What is there, I say, that should make me desire to remain here? I expect that new heavens, and that new earth, wherein righteousness dwelleth, wherein I shall rest for evermore. I look to get entrance into the new Jerusalem, at one of these twelve gates, whereupon are written the names of the twelve tribes of the children of Israel. I know that Christ Jesus hath prepared them for me. Why may I not then, with boldness in his blood, step into that glory, where my head and Lord hath gone before me? Jesus Christ is the door, and the porter; who then shall hold me out? Will he let them perish for whom he died? Will he let them poor sheep be plucked out of his hand for whom he hath laid down his life? Who shall lay any thing to the charge of the man for whom Christ hath died, or rather risen again? I know I have grievously transgressed, but where sin abounded, grace will superabound. I know my sins are red as scarlet and crimson, yet the red blood of Christ my Lord can make them as white as snow or wool: Whom have I in heaven but him, or whom desire I in the earth besides him? Psal. lxxiii. 25. O thou the fairest among the children of men, Psal. xlv. 2. The light of the Gentiles, the glory of the Jews, the life of the dead, the joy of angels and saints, my soul panteth to be with thee; I will put my spirit into thy hands, and thou wilt not put me out of thy presence; I will come unto thee, for thou casteth none away that come unto thee, O thou the delight of mankind! Thou comest to seek and save that which was lost, thou seeking me hast found me, and now being found by thee, I hope, O Lord, thou wilt not let me perish. I desire to be with thee, and do long for the fruition of thy blessed presence, and joy of thy countenance: Thou, the only good Shepherd, art full of grace and truth; therefore I trust thou wilt not thrust me out of the door of grace: The law was given by Moses, but grace and truth came by thee: Who shall separate me from thy love? Shall tribulation, or distress, or persecution or famine, or nakedness, or peril, or sword? Nay, in all these things I am more than conqueror, through thy Majesty, who hast loved me; for I am persuaded, that neither death, nor life, nor principalities, nor powers, nor any other creature, is able to separate me from the love of the Majesty which is in Christ Jesus my Lord. I refuse not to die with thee, that I may live with thee: I refuse not to suffer with thee, that I may rejoice with thee. Shall not all things be pleasant to me, which may be the last step by which, and upon which, I may come unto thee? When shall I be satisfied with thy face? When shall I be drunk with thy pleasures? Come, Lord Jesus, and tarry not.

The Spirit says, Come; the Bride says, Come; even so, Lord Jesus, come quickly, and tarry not.

Why should the multitude of my iniquities, or greatness of them, affright me? Why should I faint in this my desire to be with thee? The greater sinner I have been, the greater glory will thy grace be to thee unto all eternity. O unspeakable joy, endless, infinite and bottomless compassion! O sea of never fading pleasures! O love of loves! O the breadth, and heighth, and depth, and length of that love of thine, that passeth all knowledge! The love of Jonathan was great indeed to David; it passed the love of women; but thy love, O Lord, passeth all created love! O uncreated love! beginning without beginning, and ending without end. Thou art my glory, my joy, and my gain, and my crown; thou hast set me under thy shadow with great delight, and thy fruit is sweet unto my taste: Thou hast brought me unto thy banqueting-house, and placed me in thy orchard: Stay me with flagons, and comfort me with apples; for I am sick and my soul is wounded with love. Behold thou art fair, my love; behold thou art fair, thou hast doves eyes; behold thou art fair, my beloved, yea pleasant: also our bed is green; the beams of our house are cedars, and our rafters are of fir: how fair and how pleasant art thou, O full of all delights! my heart is ravished with thee; O when shall I see thy face! how long wilt thou delay to be with me as a roe, or a young hart leaping upon the mountains, and skipping upon the hills: as a bundle of myrrh be thou to me and lie all night betwixt my breasts; because of the savour of thy good ointments; Thy name is as ointment poured forth: therefore desire I to go out of this desart, and to come to the place where thou sittest at thy repast, and where thou makest thy flocks to rest at noon. When shall I be filled with his love? Surely, if a man knew how precious it were, he would count all things dross and dung to gain it: Truly I would long for that scaffold, or that axe, or that cord, that might be to me that last step of this my wearisome journey, to go to thee, my Lord.

Thou who knowest the meaning of the spirit, give answer to the speaking, sighing, and groaning of the spirit: Thou who hast enflamed my heart to speak unto thee in this silent, yet lovely language of ardent and fervent desires, speak again unto my heart, and answer my desires, which thou hast made me speak to thee. 1 Cor. xv. 55. O death, where is thy sting? O grave where is thy victory? The sting of death is sin; the strength of sin is the law. But thanks be to God, who giveth me the victory through Jesus Christ. What can be troublesome unto me, since my Lord looks upon me with so loving and amiable a countenance? And how greatly do I long for these embracements of my Lord? O that he would kiss me with the kisses of his mouth, Cant. i. 2. for his love is better than wine! O that my soul were the throne wherein he might dwell eternally! O that my heart were the temple wherein he might be magnified, and dwell for ever! All glory be unto my God; angels and saints, praise ye him: O thou earth, yea hills and mountains, be glad; you shall not be wearied any more with the burden of corruption, whereunto you have been subject through the wickedness of mankind. Lift up your heads and be glad, for a fire shall make you clean from all your corruption and vanity, wherewith for many years you have been infected. Let the bride rejoice, let all the saints rejoice, for the day of the marriage with the bridegroom (even the Lamb of God) is at hand, and his fair white robes shall be given her; she shall be arrayed with the golden vestry and needlework of his manifold graces, that shall be put upon her; he, who is her life, shall quickly appear, and he shall quickly appear with him in the glory and happiness of a consummate marriage. But I must remember myself, I know I have been greatly strengthened and sustained by your prayers, (honourable lady, and dearly beloved in our Lord Jesus) continue, I pray you, as you have begun, in wrestling with the Lord for me, that Christ may be magnified in my mortal body, whether living or dead, that my soul may be lifted up to the third heavens, that I may taste of these joys that are at the right hand of my heavenly Father, and that with gladness I may let my spirit go thither where my body shall shortly follow. Who am I, that he should first have called me, and then constitute me a minister of the glad tidings of the gospel of salvation these years already, and now, last of all, to be a sufferer for his cause and kingdom? Now let it be so, that I have fought my fight and run my race, and now from henceforth is laid up for me that crown of righteousness, which the Lord, that righteous God, will give, and not to me only, but to all that love his appearance; and chuse to witness this, that Jesus Christ is the King of saints, and that his church is a most free kingdom, yea, as free as any kingdom under heaven, not only to convocate, hold and keep her meetings, and conventions and assemblies, but also to judge of all her affairs, in all her meetings, and conventions amongst her members and subjects. These two points, *first*, That Christ is the head of his church. *Secondly*, That she is free in her government from all other jurisdiction except Christ's: these two points, I say, are the special causes of our imprisonment, being now convict as traitors for maintaining thereof: we have been ever waiting with joyfulness to give the last testimony of our blood in confirmation thereof, if it should please our God to be so favourable as to honour us with this dignity; yea, I do affirm, that these two points above written, and all other things which belong to Christ's crown, sceptre, and kingdom, are not subject, nor cannot be, to any other authority, but to his own altogether. So that I would be most glad to be offered up a sacrifice for so glorious a truth: but, alas! I fear that my sins, and the abuse of so glorious things as I have found, deprive me of so fair a crown; yet my Lord doth know, if he would call me to it, and strengthen me in it, it would be to me the most glorious day, and gladdest hour, I ever saw in this life; but I am in his hand, to do with me whatever shall please his majesty. It may suffice me, I have had so long a time in the knowledge of the gospel; and that I have seen the things that I have seen, and heard the things that I have heard, and through the grace of God I have been so long a witness of these glorious and good news, in my weak ministry, and that my witnessing hath not been altogether without fruit and blessing; so that I hope at that day, I shall have him to be my crown, my glory, my joy, and reward, and therefore, boldly, I say with Simeon, Lord, now lettest thou thy servant depart in peace, (not in a peaceable dying in my body) but by rendering up to him my spirit, and the sealing and stamping this truth with my blood. I desire not to have it remedied ; but let my Lord's will be done.

Now that prophecy is at hand, which these two worthy servants of the Lord, Mr. George Wiseheart, and Mr. John Knox, my father-in-law, spake ; which was that Christ should be crucified in this kingdom, but glorious should be his resurrection, as Mr. Knox with his own hand upon the margin of Calvin's *Harmony upon the Passion* did write, which is yet extant ; but alas ! for this kingdom. My testimony now doth not differ from that of many before this time, who said, that the kingdom of Scotland should be blood, the kingdom shall be drenched in blood, a forbished and glittering sword is already drawn out of the scabbard, which shall not return until it be made drunk with the blood of the men of this land ; first, the heavy intestine sword, and then the sword of the stranger. O doleful Scotland ! well were he that were removed from thee, that his eyes might not see, nor his ears hear all the evils that are to come upon thee ; neither the strong man by his strength, nor the rich man by his riches, nor the nobleman by blood, shall be delivered from the judgments. There is a great sacrifice to be made in Bozrah, in thee, O Scotland, of the blood of all sorts in the land ; Ephraim shall consume Manasseh, and Manasseh Ephraim ; brother against brother, and every man in the judgment of the Lord shall be armed, to thrust his sword in the side of his neighbour, and all for the contempt of the glorious gospel: and that blood which was offered to thee, O Scotland, in so plenteous a manner, that the like hath not been offered to any nation ; therefore thy judgment shall be greater : but the sanctuary must be begun at, and the measure is not fulfilled, till the blood of the saints be shed ; then the cries will be great, and will not stay, till they bring down the Lord from heaven his throne, to see if the sins of Scotland be according to the cry thereof ; neither shall there be any subject in the land from the greatest to the meanest guiltless. The guilt of our blood shall not only lie upon our prince, but also upon our own brethren, bishops, counsellors, and commissioners ; it is they, even they that have stired up our prince against us : we must therefore lay the blame, and burden of our blood upon them especially, however the rest above written be partakers of their sins with them : and as to the rest of our brethren, who either by silence approve, or by crying peace, peace, strengthen the arm of the wicked, that they cannot return ; in the mean time make the hearts of the righteous sad ; they shall all in like manner be guilty of high treason against the King of kings, the Lord Jesus Christ, his crown and kingdom.

Next unto them all our commissioners, chancellor, president, comptroller, advocate ; and next unto them, all that first or last sat in the council, and did not bear plain testimony for Jesus Christ and his kingdom, for which we do suffer : And next unto them, all those who should have at present, and who should at such times have come, and made open testimony of Christ faithfully, although it had been contrary to plain law, and with the hazard of their lives. When the poor Jews were in such danger, that nothing was expected but utter destruction, queen Esther, after three days fasting, concluded thus with herself, " I will, said she, go into the King, though it be not according to law ; and if I perish, I perish," Esther iv. 16. With this resolution, such as are born counsellors should have said, Christ's kingdom is now at hand, and I am bound also, and sworn, by a special covenant, to maintain the doctrine and discipline thereof, according to my vocation and power, all the days of my life ; under all the pains contained in the book of God, and danger of body and soul, in the day of God's fearful judgment, and therefore, though I shall perish in the cause, yet will I speak for it, and to my power defend it, according to my vocation. *Finally*, all those that counsel, command, consent, and allow, are guilty in the sight of our God : but the mourners for these evils, and the faithful of the land, and those who are unfeignedly grieved in heart for all these abominations, those shall be marked as not guilty, Ezek. ix.

I know not, whether I shall have occasion to write again ; and therefore, by this letter, as my latter will and testament, I give testimony, warning and knowledge of these things to all men, according to the Lord's direction to the prophet, " son of man, I have made thee a watch-man," Ezek. xxxiii. 7, &c. Therefore I give warning to all men hereby, that no man's blood be required at my hands. Thus desiring the help of your prayers, with my humble commendations, and service in Christ, to my Lord, your husband, and all the saints there : the messenger of peace be with you all for evermore. *Amen.*

Yours, to my full power, for
the time Christ's prisoner.
JOHN WELCH.

Blackness, January 6th, 1606.

This is my copy of this prophetical letter ; and it is a question, whether the great prophecy concerning Scotland be yet fulfilled, or to receive its accomplishment ? So there is no doubt part of it is fulfilled. For of all those, who were false judges in that cruel sentence, there is now no remnant, nor memory, as is commonly observed.

Another famous prophetical letter he wrote to Sir William Livingston of Kilfyrth, one of the lords of the College of Justice, whereof this is my copy.

D

Right Honorable, my hearty salutations remembered in the Lord:

YOUR love and care many times have certainly comforted me. And having no other thing to require, I shall, as I may, desire him, who is able to do, and hath undertaken it, to meet you and yours with consolation in his good time.

As for the matter itself, the bearer will shew you, that what is required is such a thing as, in the sight of our Lord, we may not do, without both the hazard of our conscience, and liberty of Christ's kingdom, which should be dearer to us than any thing else. What a slavery were it to us to bind our conscience in the service of our God, in the meanest point of our callings, to the will of men or angels ; and we are fully resolved, that what we did was acceptable service to our God, who hath put it up as service done to him, and has allowed and sealed it to us by many tokens : so that it were more than high impiety and apostacy, to testify the ruin or undoing of any thing, which our God hath ordained to be done. We, sir, if the Lord will, are yet ready to do more in our calling, and to suffer more for the same, if so be it will please our God to call us to it, and strengthen us in it ; for of ourselves we dare promise nothing ; but, in our God, all things.

As for that instrument Spotiswood, we are sure the Lord will never bless that man, but a malediction lies upon him, and shall accompany all his doings ; and it may be, sir, your eyes shall see as great confusion covering him, ere he go to his grave, as ever did his predecessors. Now surely, sir, I am far from bitterness ; but here I denounce the wrath of an everlasting God against him, which assuredly shall fall, except it be prevented. Sir, Dagon shall not stand before the ark of the Lord ; and these names of blasphemy that he wears of lord bishop and archbishop will have a fearful end. Not one beck is to be given to Haman, suppose he were as great a courtier as ever he was, suppose the decree were given out, and sealed with the king's ring; deliverance will come to us elsewhere, and not by him, who has been so sore an instrument, not against our persons, that were nothing (for I protest to you, sir, in the sight of my God, I forgive him all the evil he has done, or can do, to me) but unto Christ's poor kirk, in stamping under foot so glorious a kingdom and beauty as was once in this land; he was helped to cut Sampson's hair, and to expose him to mocking, but the Lord will not be mocked: he shall be cast away as a stone out of a sling; his name shall rot, and a malediction shall fall upon his posterity after he is gone. Let this, sir, be a monument of it, that it was told before, that when it shall come to pass, it may be seen there was warning given him. And therefore, sir seeing I have not the access myself, if it would please God to move you, I wish you did deliver this hard message to him, not as from me, but from the Lord.

JOHN WELCH.

Blackness, 1605.

The man upon whom he complains, and threatens so sore, was bishop Spotiswood, at that time designed archbishop of Glasgow: and this prophecy was punctually accomplished, though after the space of forty years: for, first, the bishop himself died in a strange land, and as many say, in misery: next, his son, sir Robert Spotiswood, some time president of the session, was beheaded by the Parliament of Scotland, at the market-cross of St. Andrews, in the winter, after the battle of Philliphaugh, to which I myself with many thousands were witnesses. And as soon as ever he came to the scaffold, Mr. Blair, the minister of the town, told him that now Mr. Welch's prophecy was fulfilled upon him; to which he replied in anger, that Mr. Welch and he both were false prophets.

But after he left Scotland, some remarkable passages in his behaviour are to be remembered. And, first, when the dispute about church government began to warm, as he was walking upon the street of Edinburgh, betwixt two honest citizens, he told them, they had in their town two great ministers, who were no great friends to Christ's cause, presently in controversy, but it should be seen, the world should never hear of their repentance: (the two men were Mr. Patrick Galloway, and Mr. John Hall;) and accordingly it came to pass; for Mr. Patrick Galloway died easing himself upon his stool; and Mr. John being at that time at Leith, and his servant-woman having left him alone in his house while she went to the market, he was found dead all alone at her return.

He was some time prisoner in Edinburgh castle before he went into exile, where one night sitting at supper with the Lord Ochiltree, who was unclean to Mr. Welch's wife, as his manner was, he entertained the company with godly and edifying discourse, which was well received by all the company, save only one debauched Popish young gentleman, who sometimes laughed, and sometimes mocked and made faces; whereupon Mr. Welch brake out into a sad abrupt charge upon all the company to be silent, and observe the work of the Lord upon that profane mocker, which they should presently behold; upon which immediately the profane wretch fell down and died beneath the table, and never returned to life again, to the great astonishment of all the company.

Another wonderful story they tell of him at the same time. The Lord Ochiltree, the captain of the castle of Edinburgh, and son to the good Lord Ochiltree who was Mr. Welch's uncle-in-law, was indeed very civil to Mr. Welch, but being for a long time, through the multitude of affairs, kept from visiting Mr. Welch in his chamber, as he was one day walking in the court and espying Mr. Welch at his chamber-window, asked him kindly how he did, and if in any case he could serve him? Mr. Welch answered him, he would earnestly intreat his lordship, being at that time to go to court, to petition king James, in his name, that he might have liberty to preach the gospel; which my lord promised to do. Mr. Welch answered, " My lord, both because you are my kinsman, and for other reasons, I would earnestly intreat and obtest you not to promise, except you faithfully perform." My lord answered, he would faithfully perform his promise; and so went for London: but though, at his first arrival, he was really purposed to present the petition to the king; yet when he found the king in such a rage against the godly ministers, that he durst not at that time present it, he therefore thought fit to delay it, and thereafter fully forgot it.

The first time Mr. Welch saw his face after his return from court, he asked him, what he had done with his petition? My lord answered, he had presented it to the king; but that the king was in so great a rage against the ministers at that time, he believed it had been forgotten, for he had gotten no answer. "Nay, said Mr. Welch to him, my lord, you should not lie to God and to me, for I know you never delivered it, though I warned you to take heed not to undertake it, except you would perform it; but because you have dealt so unfaithfully, remember, God shall take from you both estate and honours, and give them to your neighbour in your own time," which accordingly came to pass: for both his estate and honours were, in his own time, translated upon James Stuart, son to captain James, who was indeed a cadet, but not the lineal heir of the family.

While he was detained prisoner in Edinburgh castle, his wife used, for the most part, to stay in his company; but, upon a time, fell a longing to see her family in Air, to which with some difficulty he yielded; but when she was to take her journey, he strictly charged her not to take the ordinary way to her house when she came to Air, nor to pass by the bridge through the town, but to pass the river above the bridge, and so to get the way to her own house, and not to come into the town; for he said, " before you come thither, you shall find the plague broken out in Air:" which accordingly came to pass.

The plague was, at that time, very terrible, and he being necessarily separate from his people, it was to him the more grievous. But when the people of Air come to him to bemoan themselves, his answer was, that Hugh Kennedy, a godly gentleman in their town, should pray for them, and God should hear him. This counsel they accepted, and the gentleman, convening a number of the honest citizens, prayed fervently for the town, as he was a mighty wrestler with God, and accordingly after that the plague decreased.

Now the time is come he must leave Scotland, and never to see it again; so, upon the seventh day of November, 1606, in the morning, he, with his neighbours took ship at Leith; and though it was but two o'clock in the morning, many were waiting with their afflicted families to bid them farewell. After prayer, they sang the twenty-third Psalm, and so, with the great grief of the spectators, set sail for the south of France, and landed in the river of Bordeaux. Within fourteen weeks after his arrival, such was the Lord's blessing on his diligence, he was able to preach in French, and accordingly was speedily called to the ministry, first in one village, then in another; one of them was Nerac, and thereafter was settled in Saint Jean d'Angely, a considerable walled town, and there he continued the rest of the time he sojourned in France, which was about sixteen years. When he began first to preach, it was observed by some of his hearers, that while he continued in the doctrinal part of his sermon, he spoke very correct French, but when he came to his application, and when his affections kindled, his fervour made him sometimes neglect the accuracy of the French construction: but there were godly young men, who admonished him of this, which he took in very good part: so, for the preventing mistakes of that kind, he desired the young gentlemen, when they perceived him beginning to decline, to give him a sign, and the sign was, they were both to stand up upon their feet, and thereafter he was more exact in his expressions through his whole sermon; so desirous was he not only to deliver good matter, but to recommend it in neat expression.

There were many times persons of great quality in his auditory, before whom he was just as bold as ever he had been in a Scots village; which moved Mr. Boyd of Trochrig once to ask him, (after he had preached before the university of Saumur, with such boldness and authority as if he had been before the meanest congregation) how he could be so confident among strangers, and persons of such quality? To which he answered, that he was so filled with the dread of God, he had no apprehension from men at all: and " this answer, said Mr. Boyd, did not remove my admiration, but rather increased it."

There was in his house, among many others who tabled with him for good education, a young gentleman of great quality, and suitable expectations, and this was the heir of the Lord Ochiltree, who was captain of the castle of Edinburgh. This young nobleman, after he had gained very much upon Mr. Welch's affections, fell sick of a grievous sickness, and after he had been long wasted with it, closed his eyes, and expired, as dying men use to do; so, to the apprehension and sense of all spectators, he was no more but a carcase; and was therefore taken out of his bed, and laid upon a pallet on the floor, that his body might be the more conveniently dressed, as dead bodies use to be. This was to Mr. Welch a very great grief, and therefore he stayed with the young man's dead body full three hours, lamenting over him with great tenderness. After twelve hours, the friends brought a coffin, where into they desired the corps to be put, as the custom is; but Mr. Welch desired, that, for the satisfaction of his affections, they would forbear the youth for a time; which they granted and returned not till twenty-four hours after his breath was expired; then they returned, desiring with great importunity the corps might be speedily buried, the weather being extremely hot; yet he persisted in his request, earnestly begging them to excuse him for once more. So they left the youth upon his pallet for full thirty-six hours; but even after all that, though he was urged, not only with great earnestness, but displeasure, they were constrained to forbear for twelve hours yet more. After forty-eight hours were past, Mr. Welch was still where he was, and then his friends perceived he believed the young man was not really dead, but under some apoplectic fit; and therefore proposed to him, for his satisfaction, that trial should be made upon his body by doctors and surgeons, if possibly any spark of life might be found in him; and with this he was content. So the physicians were set at work, who pinched him with pincers in the fleshy parts of his body, and twisted a bow-string about his head with great force, but no sign of life appeared in him; so the physicians pronounced him stark dead, and then there was no more delay to be desired; yet Mr. Welch begged of them once more, that they would but step into the next room for an hour or two, and leave him with the dead youth; and this they granted. Then Mr. Welch fell down before the pallet, and cried unto the Lord with all his might for the last time, and sometimes looking upon the dead body, continuing in wrestling with the Lord, till at length the dead youth opened his eyes, and cried out to Mr. Welch, whom he distinctly knew, "O sir, I am all whole but my head and legs;" and these were the places they had sore hurt with their pinching.

When Mr. Welch perceived this, he called upon his friends and shewed the dead young man restored to life again, to their great astonishment. And this young nobleman, though his father lost the estate of Ochiltree, lived to acquire a great estate in Ireland, and was Lord Castlestuart, and a man of such excellent parts, that he was courted by the earl of Strafford to be a counsellor in Ireland, which he refused to be, until the godly silenced Scottish ministers, who suffered under the bishops in the north of Ireland, were restored to the exercise of their ministry; and then he engaged, and so continued for all his life, not only in honour and power, but in the profession and practice of godliness, to the great comfort of the country where he lived. This story the nobleman communicated to his friends in Ireland, and from them I had it.

While Mr. Welch was minister in one of these French villages, upon an evening a certain Popish friar travelling through the country, because he could not find lodging in the whole village, addressed himself to Mr. Welch to lodge in his house for one night. The servants acquainted their master, and he was content to receive this guest. The family had supped before he came, and so the servants conveyed the friar to his chamber, and after they had made his supper, they left him to his rest. There was but a timber partition betwixt him and Mr. Welch, and after the friar had slept his first sleep, he was surprised with a silent but constant whispering noise, at which he wondered very much, and was not a little troubled with it.

The next morning he walked in the fields, where he chanced to meet a country man, who, saluting him because of his habit, asked him where he had lodged that night. The friar answered, he had lodged with the Hugonot minister. Then the country man asked him what entertainment he had? The friar answered, " Very bad; for, said he, I always held there were devils haunting these ministers houses, and I am persuaded there was one with me this night, for I heard a continual whisper all the night over, which I believe was no other thing than the minister and the devil conversing together." The country man told him, he was much mistaken, and that it was nothing else but the minister at his night prayers. " O, said the friar, does the minister pray any? Yes, more than any man in France, answered the country man; and if you will please to stay another night with him, you may be satisfied." The friar got him home to Mr. Welch's house, and pretended indisposition, intreated another night's lodging, which was granted him.

Before dinner, Mr. Welch came from his chamber and made his family exercise, according to his custom: and first he sung a psalm, then read a portion of scripture, and discoursed upon it; thereafter he prayed with great fervour as his custom was: to all which the friar was an astonished witness. After the exercise they went to dinner, where the friar was very civilly entertained, Mr. Welch forbearing all question and dispute for that time. When the evening came, Mr. Welch made his exercise as he had done in the morning, which occasioned yet more wondering in the friar: and after supper to bed they all went; but the friar longed much to know what the night whisper was, and in that he was soon satisfied; for after Mr. Welch's first sleep the noise began; and then the friar resolved to be sure what it was; so he creeped silently to Mr. Welch's chamber door, and there he heard not only the sound, but the words exactly, and communications betwixt God and man, and such as he knew not had been in the world. Upon this, the next morning, as soon as Mr. Welch was ready, the friar went to him, and told him, that he had been in ignorance, and lived in darkness all his time, but now he was resolved to adventure his soul with Mr. Welch, and thereupon declared himself Protestant: Mr. Welch welcomed him, and encouraged him, and he continued a constant Protestant to his dying day. This story I had from a godly minister, who was bred in Mr. Welch's house in France.

When Lewis XIII. of France made war upon the Protestants there, because of their religion, the city of St. Jean d'Angely was by him and his royal army besieged, and brought into extreme danger. Mr. Welch was minister in the town, and mightily encouraged the citizens to hold out, assuring them, God should deliver them. In the mean time of the siege a cannon ball pierced the bed where he was lying; upon which he got up, but would not leave the room, till he had by solemn prayer acknowledged his deliverance. During this siege the townsmen made stout defence, till once one of the king's gunners placed a great gun so conveniently upon a rising ground that therewith he could command the whole wall upon which the townsmen made their greatest defence. Upon this they were constrained to forsake the whole wall in great terror; and though they had several guns planted upon the wall, no man durst undertake to manage them. This being told Mr. Welch with great affrightment, he notwithstanding encouraged them still to hold out; and running to the wall himself, found the cannoneer, who was a Burgundian, near the wall; him he intreated to mount the wall, promising to assist him in person: so to the wall they got. The cannoneer told Mr. Welch, that either they behooved to dismount the gun upon the rising ground, or else they were surely lost. Mr. Welch desired him to aim well, and he should serve him, and God would help him; so the gunner falls a scouring his piece, and Mr. Welch ran to the powder to fetch him a charge; but as soon as he was returning, the king's gunner fires his piece, which carried both the powder and shot out of Mr. Welch's hands; which yet did not discourage him; for, having left the laddle, he filled his hat with powder, wherewith the gunner loaded his piece and dismounted the king's gun at the first shot. So the citizens returned to their post of defence.

This discouraged the king so, that he sent to the citizens to offer them fair conditions; which were, that they should enjoy the liberty of their religion, their civil privileges, but their walls should be demolished: only the king desired, for his honour, that he might enter the city with his servants in a friendly manner. This the city thought fit to grant, and the king with a few more entered the city for a short time. But while the king was in the city, Mr. Welch preached as was his ordinary, which much offended the French court: so one day, while he was at sermon, the king sent the duke d'Espernon to fetch him out of the pulpit into his presence. The duke went with his guard, and as soon as he entered the church where Mr. Welch was preaching, Mr. Welch commanded to make way, and to set a seat that the duke might hear the word of the Lord. The duke, instead of interrupting him, sat down, and gravely heard the sermon to an end; and then told Mr. Welch, he behooved to go with him to the king; which Mr. Welch willingly did. When the duke came to the king, the king asked him, why he brought not the minister with him, and why he did not interrupt him? The duke answered, Never man spake like this man, but that he had brought him with him. Whereupon Mr. Welch is called, and when he entered the king's room, he kneeled upon his knees, and silently prayed for wisdom and assistance. Thereafter the king challenged him, how he durst preach where he was, since it was against the law of France, that any man should preach within the verge of his court? Mr. Welch answered, "Sir, if you did right you would come and hear me preach; and make all France hear me likewise; for, said he, I preach not as those men you hear preach; my preaching differs from theirs in these two points. First, I preach you must be saved by the death and merits of Jesus Christ, and not your own. Next, I preach, said he, that as you are king of France, you are under the authority and command of no man on earth; those men, said he, whom you hear, subject you to the pope of Rome, which I will never do." The king replied no more, but *Et bien vous etiez mon ministre:* "Well, well, you shall be my minister:" and, some say, called him father, which is an honour the king of France bestows upon few of the greatest prelates in France. However he was favourably dismissed at that time, and the king also left the city in peace.

But within a short time thereafter the war was renewed, and then Mr. Welch told the inhabitants of the city, that now their cup was full, and they should no more escape; which accordingly came to pass; for the king took the town, and, as soon as ever it fell into his hand, he commanded Vitry, the captain of his guard, to enter the town, and preserve his minister from all danger; and then were horses and waggons provided for Mr. Welch, to transport him and his family for Rochel, whither he went and there sojourned for a time. This story, my lord Kenmure, who was bred at Mr. Welch's house, told Mr. Livingstoun, minister at Ancrum, and from him I had it.

After his flock in France was scattered, he obtained liberty to come to England: and his friends made hard suit that he might be permitted to return to Scotland, because the physicians declared there was no other way to preserve his life, but by the freedom he might have in his native air. But to this king James would never yield, protesting he should never be able to establish his beloved bishops in Scotland, if Mr. Welch were permitted to return thither: so he languished in London a considerable time. His disease was judged by some to have a tendency to a sort of leprosy: physicians said, he had been poisoned. A langour he had, together with a great weakness in his knees, caused by his continual kneeling at prayer, by which it came to pass, that though he was able to move his knees, and to walk, yet he was wholly insensible in them, and the flesh became hard like a sort of horn. But when in the time of his weakness, he was desired to remit somewhat of his excessive painfulness; his answer was, "He had his life of God, and therefore it should be spent for him."

His friends importuned king James very much, that if he might not return into Scotland, at least he might have liberty to preach at London; which king James would never grant, till he heard all hopes of life were past, and then he allowed him liberty to preach, not fearing his activity.

Then as soon as ever he heard he might preach, he greedily embraced this liberty, and having access to a lecturer's pulpit, he went and preached both long and fervently; which was the last performance of his life;

for after he had ended sermon he returned to his chamber, and within two hours, quietly and without pain, he resigned his spirit into his Maker's hands; and was buried near Mr. Derling the famous English divine, after he had been little more than fifty-two years of age.

FORTY-EIGHT
SELECT SERMONS.

SERMON I.

ON THE GENERAL JUDGMENT.

Rev. xx. 11.

And I saw a great white throne, and him that sat on it, from whose face the earth and the heaven fled away.

THE security of all flesh is wondrous great; for there is a fearful sleep fallen both upon the good and the evil. The foolish virgins are found asleep, and the wise are asleep also. And, suppose the Lord be at the door, and the hour of judgment at hand, and the seventh angel ready to blow the last trumpet, when time shall be no more, yet it is scarcely one of a thousand, yea, one of ten thousand, is to be found that is prepared, and busying themselves to meet the Lord, who is making speed to come in the clouds. And how soon that fire shall break forth, which shall kindle the heavens above your head, and the earth under your feet, and shall set all on fire; how soon the trumpet shall blow, and the shout shall cry, *Rise, dead, and come to judgment*, is only known to God, and to no mortal man. Will ye not then be awakened till this trumpet waken you? And will none of you take pains to look over the leaves of your conscience, and read what sins are written there, since ye came into the world, before that day of doom come upon you? O that ye knew that eternity, and the terrors of the day of the Lord, when the heavens above you, and the earth beneath you, shall not be able to stand before the face of him that sits on the throne! Therefore, I hope, the Lord has made choice to me of this text at this time, to give you warning before the judgment come: ye know the watchman that the Lord takes from among the people, that he sets over the city or house concredit to them,

"If ye see the sword and pestilence coming, and warn them not, the blood of them that perish under the judgment, for lack of warning, will be required, at his hand," that is the watchman's; therefore it is time for me to be making warning to you, and, in the measure of strength that God will give me, I am to make warning, not of a temporal judgment, but of an everlasting judgment that is coming on (God waken you and warn you in time!) that when ye shall see the judge sit on his throne, your hearts may not tremble at his awful countenance, having gotten your souls washen in his blood.

But, to come to the purpose, there are many visions in this book, and there are many things done here that the Son shews to his servant John. He shews him first the present state of the kirk, at that time on the world, under the name of seven stars; and he tells, " they are suffering, and had patience, and they laboured for his name's sake, and fainted not; but yet he had somewhat against them, because they had forsaken their first love." Some were in tribulation and poverty, but yet rich in God; some kept the name of Christ and denied not the faith, suppose they should have given their blood for it, as the faithful martyr Antipas did; but yet he had a few things against them, because they maintained the doctrine of the Nicolaitans, which thing he haited. Some had love, service, faith, and patience, and their work was more at the last than at the first; but yet they suffered the false prophetess Jezabel to be among them, to whom he threatens he will cast her into a bed of affliction, and them that commit fornication with her except they repent them of their works. There were some whose works were not found perfect before God : therefore he exhorts them to remember how they had heard and received, and he bids them hold fast and repent; otherwise, he tells, that he will come shortly against them. Some had a little strength, and kept his word, and denied not his name; therefore he promised to deliver them in the hour of temptation that shall come upon all the world, to try the whole earth. Some were neither cold nor hot; and therefore, because they were luke-warm, he tells them, that it would come to pass that he would spue them out of his mouth; they thought they were rich, and increased in goods, and had need of nothing; but they knew not that they were wretched, miserable, poor, blind, and naked; and then he counsels them to buy of him gold tried in the fire, that they might be rich, and white raiment that they might be clothed, and eye-salve, that they might see. So what is your case this day? Have ye not forsaken your first love? But as for tribulation is it not yet come; for our days have been days of peace, of light, liberty, and glory: but as for tribulation, it is not yet come; but as the Lord lives, the days of tribulation are not far off. As for false doctrine, God be praised, it is not among us yet, or, at least, if it be, it dare not be avowed yet; but I fear, that, who lives to see it, they shall see heresy and corruption in doctrine, and religion creep in piece and piece in this kirk; and if our works be found perfect before God or not, the Lord knows the contrary, and your own consciences bear witness to it; and if your life be answerable to your name, I leave it to your consciences to judge, if we have not a name that we are living, and yet are dead; and whether this be not the doleful state of the generation that is neither cold nor hot. It is clear, the zeal of the glory of God being so worn out of the hearts of all, plainly declares the same. But I leave this. After he had shewed him the present state of the kirk, at that time, then he tells him what shall be the state of the kirk unto the end of the world.

And, *first*, in a vision of a sealed book, containing these acts concerning the kirk, which none could open but the Lion of the tribe of Judah, for it was sealed with seven seals: Now, what was contained in these seven seals? This will take a larger time to declare, than now is meet to ware upon it.

Mark always of these things spoken, there are three consolations to the kirk of God; howsoever it be that she be in tribulation, or poverty and affliction: and albeit it come to pass, that the devil cast some of them in prison that they may be tried, and some have tribulation ten days, which is but a short time; and howsoever it be, that our adversary goes about continually "like a roaring lion, seeking whom to devour;" but yet he that rides on the white horse, with the badge at his belt, and the arrows at his side, he shall get the victory at the end of the world; and to them that are faithful to the death he shall give a crown of life.

Mark, *next*, suppose the sword, the famine, the pest, these temporal judgments be common to the godly as well as to the wicked, yet there is consolation to the "souls of them that are slain for the testimony of Jesus; they are lying under the altar, and they cry with a loud voice, Lord, how long, holy and true, dost thou not judge and avenge our blood upon them that dwell on the earth? Then it was said unto them, that they should rest for a little season, until their fellow-servants and brethren should be killed as they were, should be fulfilled."

Mark, *thirdly*, the sixth seal is opened, "And there was a great earthquake, and the sun was as black as sackcloth of hair, and the moon was like blood; and the stars of heaven fell to the earth: and heaven departed away as a scroll when it is rolled together; and every mountain and island were moved out of their places; and then the kings of the earth, and the great men and rich men, and the captains, and the mighty men, and every bond man, and every free man, hid themselves in dens and rocks of the mountains; and said to the mountains and rocks, fall on us, and hide us from the presence of him that sits on the throne, and from the face of the Lamb: for the great day of his wrath is come; and who shall be able to stand?" Then shall the kirk of God be avenged on her enemies; then she shall have power over the nations, and shall rule them with a rod of iron, as the vessels of a potter they shall be broken; then shall the saints of God be brought out of great tribulation, and have their long robes washen, and made white in the blood of the Lamb; they shall be in the presence of the throne of God, and serve him both day and night in his temple; and he that sits on the throne shall live among them, and he that is in the midst of the throne shall govern them, and shall lead them to the lively fountains of waters, and God shall wipe away all tears from their eyes. Now, I go forward. After this, he tells him, before this day the gospel shall be wonderfully restrained: "And the bottomless pit shall be opened, and the smoke of that pit shall arise as the smoke of a great furnace, and the sun and the air shall be made dark with that smoke, and out of that smoke shall come locusts upon the earth, and they shall have power as the scorpions of the earth have, and the pain of them shall be as the pain of a scorpion, when they have stung a man. And, in these days, men shall seek death, and shall not find it, and shall desire to die, and death shall fly from them." Then he tells two woes that shall come upon the earth, the one of the Antechrist, the other of the Turk, " who shall run through the world, and slay the third part of men, and shall lead their great army of twenty times ten thousand horsemen of war; and there should be two witnesses raised up, and power should be given them to prophesy so many days clothed in sackcloth; and if any man should hurt them, fire should proceed out of their mouth, and devour their enemies; and when they have fulfilled their testimonies, they should be slain by the beast that came out of the bottomless pit; but they should rise again, and the spirit of life, coming up from God, should enter into them, and they should stand upon their feet, and great fear fall upon them that seized them; and then shall they ascend up to heaven in a cloud, in the sight of their enemies."

And, at last, " the seventh angel shall blow his trumpet, and the dead shall rise, and every man shall receive according to his works." This he does till he comes to the twelfth chapter, and then he tells him, " the fights of the dragon with the woman and her seed, that keep the commands of her God, and kept the testimony of Jesus Christ: then he tells him, the two empires of the two beasts, Antichrist and the Turk, and the manner of every one of them: then he tells the noble company of the Lamb that stands on mount Zion, even the hundred and forty and four thousand, having their father's name written on their foreheads; and how he heard a voice from heaven, like the sound of many waters, and as the sound of a great thunder; and he heard the noise of harpers harping with their harps; they sung, as it were, a new song, before the throne, and no man could learn that song, but the hundred and forty and four thousand which were brought from the earth." He tells what they were, saying, these are they which were not defiled with women; for they are virgins; these follow the Lamb wherever he goes, and these were redeemed from among men, being the first fruits to God and to the Lamb; and in their mouths was found no guile; for they are without spot before the throne of God. Then he tells, that another angel flew in the midst of heaven, with an everlasting gospel to preach unto them which dwell on earth," and that is the same gospel which I preach unto you, even this, " fear God and give glory to him, for the hour of his judgment is come: and worship him that made the heavens and the earth, and the sea, and the fountains of waters. Then he tells, that another angel cried, it is fallen, it is fallen, Babylon, that great city, she made all the nations to drink of the wine of her fornication:" aye, Rome, thou shall be taken and burnt in a furnace of fire, and a milstone shall be bound about thy neck, and thou shalt be cast into the midst of the sea, and shalt be drowned; there thou shalt fall, and thy fall shall make heaven and earth, and all the angels and saints to rejoice at thy fall: Ay, God shall put it into the hearts of the kings to do it, we know not what kings they are; and then the bride shall prepare her for the Bridegroom's coming in the clouds.

Next again, of *seven vials*, he sets down again almost the same things that he prophesied before; and now here, last of all, he lets him see the last judgment. Would you know then what is here? See ye yon great throne? Ye shall see the Judge standing on the throne; ye shall all see both heaven and earth flee away from his face; ye shall all see the dead, great and small, and yourselves among the rest, standing before God; and ye shall all see the books opened, and the dead judged according to their works, and death and hell casten into the lake of fire, even these that had their hands in his heart's blood, and these that pierced his side with a spear, and these that rivetted him with nails, both hands and feet, they shall see it also. The elect shall see it, as Job says, "for I know that my redeemer liveth, and that he shall stand at the last day upon the earth. And though after my skin, worms destroy this body, yet I shall see God in my flesh: whom myself shall see, and my eyes shall behold, and not another, though my reins were consumed in me." And this was his consolation; even so these very eyes of yours, and no other, shall see with terror or with joy, either to your endless comfort, or to your endless condemnation. Now, what sees he? First, he sees a throne; ye know a throne is set for a judge to sit on; so he sees a throne whereon the Judge of the whole earth is to sit; therefore he shall come to be a judge. He came before, at his first coming, not to sit on a throne, nor to be a judge, but to be judged before thrones and tribunals of men: for John says, "that he sent not his son that he should condemn the world, but that the world through him might be saved. Christ himself says, man, who made me a judge, or a divider over you? And in another place, the son of man came not to judge, but to be judged himself." In his first coming, he comes from high majesty to baseness and humility; he came from his Father's glory to shame and ignominy; he came from a palace to a crib, from the seat of his majesty to a tree; he came like a lamb to be slain, and as a Saviour to save sinners; as the apostle says, "it was a true saying that Christ came into the world to save sinners, of whom I am the chief:

Christ himself says, I came not to call the righteous, but sinners, to repentance;" and therefore that is the name that the angel gives him, when he appears to Joseph in a dream, saying, "and thou shalt call his name Jesus, for he shall save his people from their sins, and they shall call his name Emmanuel, that is, God with us," our God made flesh, our God manifested in the flesh. So, I say, in his first testimony, he comes as a Saviour and Mediator between God and man; but in his last coming, he shall not come as a lamb but as a judge convoyed with all his angels and saints in heaven; he shall come in flaming fire, kindling the heavens before him, and melting the elements and earth beneath him; he shall come with a blast of the trumpet, with the arch-angel to gather all people from the four corners of the earth; and he shall come with a peremptor sentence, from the which there shall be no appellation, and of the which there shall be no revocation ever again, or again calling; and he shall come with his reward in his hand, to every man according to his works which he hath done in this world, be they evil, be they good. Now, ye see he has a throne, he has a throne of grace, as the apostle to the Hebrews says, " let us go boldly to the throne of grace, that we may receive mercy, and find grace in time of need. Now he is sitting on a throne of grace, that we may receive mercy, and find grace in time of need; and now he holds the door of mercy open, and lets in every penitent sinner that comes; therefore I testify unto you, if ye will flee from your sin, if you will cast away the works of darkness, if ye will hate and detest all sort of iniquity, and if thou wilt run to the throne of grace now; I will assure thee, thou shalt find mercy and grace in the time of need: so now is the throne of grace and mercy; but afterwards thou shalt see the throne of glory and justice; now is the good shepherd seeking his lost sheep, and finding them to drink of the wells of the water of life, and to eat of the fat things of his own house; but afterwards, such as would not be gathered of him, he shall bind them hand and foot, and cast them into utter darkness. Now he pities them that will not come home, as he said, to Jerusalem, "O Jerusalem! Jerusalem! how oft would I have gathered thee, as a hen doth her birds under her wings, but thou wouldst not? Behold your habitation shall be made desolate." So, wo to the souls that repine and refuse to be fetched within the sweet and loving arms of the Son of God, even these bloody arms which were stretched out upon a tree. Now, descern, I pray you, betwixt his first coming and his last coming; for now is the time of grace, and now is the spirit of grace offered, and now is the throne of grace set up, and now is the rain-bow, which is the sign of the covenant of life, round about the throne, and now the twelve ports of the new Jerusalem are standing open, that all may come in; therefore, wo to the soul that shall sit till this time of grace pass over, and will not come in time.

But I will go forward: now, ye see two things in that throne, the one is a great throne, the other is a white throne. Let kings keep silence of their thrones, and speak of this throne. O ye kings! will ye look to the heavens above you, and see that white cloud, and upon the cloud one standing like the Son of man, having upon his head a golden crown, and in his hand a sharp sickle, who shuts his sharp sickle in the earth, and cuts down the vine of the vineyards of the earth, and casts them into the great wine-press of the wrath of God: so he calls it a great throne. Solomon's throne was great, which he made of ivory, and had six steps, and twelve lions, two on every step, and the Queen of the South was astonished when she saw it; and it is said in the Canticles, "come forth, O daughter of Zion! and behold king Solomon with the crown wherewith his mother crowned him in the day of his marriage, and in the day of the gladness of his heart. But will ye come out, ye daughters of Zion, and see here another throne than Solomon's, another crown than his crown! It is a great throne, so that all the monarchs thrones under heaven, what are they in comparison with this throne? Nothing. Therefore no wonder that the twenty four elders take their own crowns, and cast them down before his throne; and it is no wonder that they fall down before him that sits on the throne; and worship him that lives for evermore, saying, "thou art worthy to receive glory, honour, and power, for thou hast created all things, and for thy will's sake they are created." O that the men of the world saw this throne! And, O that we did see the greatness of the majesty of his throne!

Now he calls it great, because of him that sits on it; great, because of them that stand about it; great, because of them that shall be judged there; and last of all, great, because of the judgment itself. Now, who sits on it? O! the Judge of the whole world! God himself, that infinite essence that men and angels have borrowed their being from; even he, whose glorious face the seraphims and cherubims do not behold for the brightness thereof; and therefore they have wings to cover their faces, because they do not bid to see him; much less so then, can any mortal man see his face and live; he that rides on his white horse, and tramples under foot all his enemies, and treads them in the wine-press of his wrath without the city: Therefore rejoice all ye whose garments are made white in the blood of the Lamb, for his throne shall not terrify you, because of the judge that sits thereon; for he is thy brother, thy advocate, and thy Saviour. O blessed for evermore is the soul of the righteous, and of such as are reconciled with the great God, before he come to sit on this throne.

Now, I said, it was great in respect of him that sits thereon; next, in respect of them that stand about it. Ye see a judge has his assizers, that sit in judgment with him, and consent to his sentence; so this great judge has his assizers, for there is not one of his angels shall be left in heaven, but all shall stand about this throne, and all the saints on earth shall be caught up in the air, and they shall all have thrones set about his throne. O the fairest parliament that ever was in the world ; O ! behold the King crowned with many crowns, standing in the midst, and all the King's servants with their crowns on their heads, and also the saints with palms in their hands, sitting on thrones about that throne.

Thirdly, great is this throne, because great is the number of persons that shall be there. All men and women in the world must be judged here ; there is never a reprobate that ever took life, but they shall be judged here, and all the elect and saints of God shall be judged here also, (so fair is this parliament) six thousand years generations shall all stand there waiting to receive an eternal and final judgment.

Last of all, great in this throne, because great shall be the judgment that shall come forth from this throne. Lords of the session think their judgments great ; but come out here, and see to whom the new city Jerusalem in heaven shall be given, and who shall be cast into the lake of fire. Now, compare all these together, and see if this throne be not great ; great is he that sits on the throne, even the Prince of life, and God of glory, and the judge of all the world ; great is his synod, even all the elect angels and saints, from the beginning of the world to the end of the world ; for ye that are in Christ shall be glorified in the clouds and the sight of your glory shall aggrege the torment of the reprobates, because they might have had it, and would not take it ; and then you shall rule them with a rod of iron, and as a potter's vessel they shall be broken ; and great is the number of them that shall be judged ; for let all flesh prepare them for it, even kings and emperors ; these that wore many crowns on the earth must appear mother-naked before the throne : Alexander, thou worest many crowns, conquered many nations, but yet thou must stand up naked as thou wast born, and thou must render a reckoning of thy conquests.

But I leave this. Again, you see this throne is white. What means this whiteness ? It is innocency or righteousness, and full of shining brightness, of an unspeakable joy. Innocent and righteous; how so? because the judge is white, innocent and righteous; all his assizers that shall sit round about him, they are white, innocent, white and righteous; all his citations, summonses and convictions, sentences and executions, are innocent and righteous, so all is white. The Judge, the unspotted, innocent and undefiled Lamb of God, sitting on his throne of justice and ordained deputy of his Father, to judge both the quick and the dead, he in whose heart was never found guile; therefore Abraham said, " shall not the Judge of the world judge righteously?" So this judge is white, innocent, and he is bright and glorious. Peter, James and John, saw him white on the mount Tabor, when he was transfigured, " and his face shined as the sun, and his raiment white as the light; and when Peter said, it is good for us to be here; if thou wilt, let us make three tabernacles, one for thee, and one for Moses, and one for Elias," Mat. xvii. 1, 2, 3. Ay, Peter, but this shall be a whiter appearing, and thou shalt think it better to be with him here. Ay, Lord, it is true, white wast thou upon mount Tabor, but whiter shalt thou be in the clouds.

He is white again, in respect of his citations. O! that our hearts were ravished with the consideration of thy righteous and just citing and summoning of all men, when thou shalt cause the earth, grave hell, and the sea, and all places, thrust out of them all their dead; just shalt thou be in glorifying the souls and bodies of them that glorify thee on earth, and just shalt thou be in glorifying thyself, by tormenting the souls and bodies of them that dishonour thee on earth.

He is white in respect of his accusations; for there shall be nothing read in thy dittay, but that which shall be found written either in one leaf of thy conscience or other; there the sins of thy conception, there the sins of thy youth, there the sins of thy ignorance, there the sins against the light of thy conscience, and there the sins against the law, and there the sins against the gospel, and all shall be presented to thy conscience.

O ! well is the soul and conscience, that dare lift up the head with rejoicing, and can say, "thou Lamb of God, that takest away the sins of the world," thou tookest away my sins when thou wast on the tree. And can any body tell how ye will compear before his throne that was never cleansed with the blood of Jesus? O! that blackness and darkness which is abiding that soul, which never yet ran to the blood of the Lamb, to make itself white in it! So the raising of all, the comparing of all, the accusation of all, the conviction of all, shall be just, and God shall be glorified in all.

There is also the absolution of the righteous, and the condemnation of the wicked; and therefore the throne is called white, because of the innocency and righteousness of the Judge. Now, brethren, I will go no further at this time than this that follows or remains to be spoken of the majesty and terror of the Judge sitting on his throne, *and him that sat on it.* Many shall sit on thrones in that day, but one shall sit above all the rest, for the saints shall be caught up in the air, and shall all sit on thrones, and give out sentence both of absolution and condemnation, and they shall say, "Hallelujah, salvation, and glory, and power be to the Lord our God, for true and righteous are his judgments." I could never yet rightly consider the majesty of this Judge. O heavens! what aileth thee to flee from the face of this Judge? O earth! what aileth thee to flee, and why art thou chased away, and never seen again? What ails thee, O heaven! that never sinned? and, O earth! that never sinned neither? for they had never understanding to be capable of a law, nor to be subject to keep a law. What means this? O! but I must leave this; for who can but wonder at this! Yet I will tell you the cause, you and I, and the generations before, that this firmament has seen, and this earth seen or born, since the first day that God made the earth, and established this heaven and earth, and since that day that Adam eat of the forbidden tree, since that day, heaven and earth have been eye-witnesses of our sins, and subject to vanity; and since that day they have been defiled with our iniquities, and since that time, they have been subject to bondage and corruption, and therefore they groan with us also, and travail with pain together until this present; and therefore, in that great day, they do not abide the face of the Judge.

Now, what is the fruit ye should make of this? I thank my God that I preach unto you so sure a gospel, even the oracles of the eternal God; the earth and the heavens shall pass away, but this word and oracle shall never pass away; therefore it is not a doubtsome message that I carry unto you, for it is surer than the heavens, and surer than the earth, and these eyes of yours, that have seen both the heavens and the earth, shall see the truth spoken here. O that the Lord would fill my heart, my belly with this verity, that I might eat it, and drink it, and feed upon it continually; and that he would fill me with the spirit of exhortation, that I might exhort you to meditate on this truth, both day and night, that the remembrance of that day might never go out of your hearts. O! that you would do it, even for his sake, that left you his heart's blood to slocken that fire which will burn both the heavens and the earth: Therefore hear, hear. What should you hear? things of the last importance. Is hell, is heaven, is the terror of that day of any importance? And this is not the blessing of mount Gerizon, but that everlasting blessing, which the Judge of all the world shall pronounce, out of his mouth, saying, "ye blessed of my Father, inherit the kingdom prepared for you, before the foundation of the world." And it is nothing to the curse of mount Ebal, but it is that everlasting curse and malediction which the Son of God shall pronounce, saying "depart from me, ye cursed, into everlasting fire prepared for the devil and his angels." And what shall I say to you? This day is coming, and the Lord is preparing himself to come down through the clouds, to sit on a great white throne, and the arch-angel is putting the trumpet to his mouth, and he is near to the blowing of it, and the rest of the angels are but waiting when they shall give the last shout, "rise, dead, and come to judgment;" the bridegroom is coming, and the heaven and the earth is waiting when the Lord shall come in in glory, in his flaming fire, to burn them up.

Now, brethren, what shall we do then? It is but this one thing that I will charge you with, hear what I am to say to you, I bear the message of God, and I preach the gospel that shall judge you; and I am here sent of God to tell you what is his will towards you; therefore I charge you all before God, and his Son Christ Jesus, every man and woman, let this be your occupation this day, turn over the leaves of your conscience, and see there what is the dittay that thou hast pinned up against thyself, since the day that thou wast born; and look on thy sins before the Lord, and come and spread them before the judge, and crave pardon of them, now in the day of grace, for he is ready to forgive thee and thy sins, were they never so great; for ay the redder that thy soul has been, the virtue of his blood shall appear the greater in cleansing thee from thy sins; therefore let none of you scar at the greatness of your sins; for here I testify unto you, that if any of you be condemned, it shall not be for your sins, but it shall be for contempt of that blood which shall condemn you. O God! full of mercy and goodness, and of fatherly care and providence, and never a greater providence found I in my lifetime, than I found this last time in my journey. I thank my God for it; and here I avow, if this blood of mine should go for it, it was acceptable service to God we did that day; I know there were many that sent up their prayers to God for the maintenance of this liberty, I am sure the Lord heard you; for I say to you, the room was never that I came to, but I found the Lord meeting me there, and confirming me that all was well and acceptable to him; so that I never found sweeter providence since I was born; I see the Lord's hand is not shortened. O Scotland! Oh that thou wouldst repent, and mourn for the contempt of this so great a light that has shined in thee ! then thou shouldst see as glorious a day on God's poor kirk within this land, as ever was seen in any kirk before from the beginning ; then the Lord should be strong, and glorious, and wonderful in all the hearts of his own: What is it to him to run sixteen or eighteen score of miles to London, and then run to the hearts of kings, princes and nobles of the land, and humble them, and subject them to the crown and kingdom of Jesus Christ ; but, let them think of it what they will, I know who has approven of us, for it is the running of the gospel through the whole land, and it is that the net of Christ may be spread over all, that if it were possible, we may fang in a world in it, that they might not perish ; it is that which we seek and when I look to the eternity of wrath that is abiding the wicked of this world, then I may say, who would not pity a world of sinners ? But I leave this, and I will give God the praise of his own glory, that he can begin and he can perfect his own work in you : Therefore this is my petition to God, that ye may all be presented blameless before him in that great day. Therefore I beseech you all, for Christ's sake, that every one of you would come in time, by speedy repentance, and that you would take up Christ in the arms of your souls, and that ye would take a fill of his flesh and blood, that ye may never hunger and thirst any more ; and in like manner, he may know you in that great day to be his own sheep, marked with his own blood. Will ye have any pleasure at his coming, when ye have eaten and drunken, and taken your pleasures here, and then shall be flung in hell hereafter ? So, I would beseech you in all lenity and meekness of mind for Christ's cause, ye would not delay at least to mint at repentance ; and if ye cannot get your hearts melted as ye would, yet run to God, and say, " Father have mercy upon me, Father, forgive me," and cause me to repent: Father send down thy Spirit to soften my heart. Now, if ye would do this ye would be welcome to him ; for I assure you, he delights to shew mercy on poor penitent sinners, that would repent and "hunger and thirst for righteousness." Now, I say no more now, but I recommend you all to him that is able to give you repentance, and remission of sins in the blood of his Son Jesus Christ: To whom, with the Father, and with the Holy Ghost, be all honour, praise and glory, for ever and ever. *Amen.*

SERMON II.

ON THE GENERAL JUDGMENT.

THE PREFACE.

HOLD your eyes upon the Son of God, who was sitting on the throne of his grace when he gave his Revelation, and who only can open your eyes to see this mystery; and ask his own Spirit, that only can make this truth powerful in your conscience; and pray that this blessed Spirit may convey this truth into your heart, and that it may be a lamp and a lantern of light to let you see within the clouds, into the glory whereunto every one of you that are his own must go.

Rev. xx. 12.

I saw the dead, small and great, stand before God: and the books were opened, &c.

THIS is the vision (as I shewed you) of that last and universal, and of that eternal judgment, which John saw after he had seen all the battles, all the warfare, all the colours, and all the victories of the saints here on earth, here beneath, and which shall be the last and greatest comfort, as the ground of all the patience of the saints; therefore for this cause the Son of God sits on his throne of grace, and lets John see all the form of that last and universal and everlasting judgment, that the saints travelling here through manifold tribulations, and are continually without fear, that they may know there is a day of harvest, and time coming when they shall rest from all their labours, and they shall be conveyed to endless glory; for, as the apostle says, "If in this life only we have hope in Christ, we are of all men the most miserable." Therefore this is the surest comfort the saints have, that they know that that day is before them; for when they look to that life, they are comforted; because they know this heaven shall pass away, and they wait for a new heaven, and for a new earth, where justice shall be for evermore; and when they look to the wicked, that is reckoned red-wood in their sins, then they think with themselves, O miserable wretch! there is an endles wrath abiding thee that thou believest not; and when they look to the rest of the saints, their fellow-brethren, and see some banished, and some persecuted, some put in prison, some slain; and when they hear the voice of God sounding again in their ears, saying, "Fear not little flock, for it is your Father's will to give you a kingdom:" And when they remember that fair crown of eternal life and everlasting glory, which shall be set on their heads, then they have great consolation in their souls; then they shall say, well am I, for the day of my refreshing is drawing near, when all the saints shall be put in their possession, looking for joy; then we will get our portion among the rest; by the contrair, the news that came to Nabal, that David was coming and his servants armed against him, and he would not leave so meikle as one to piss against the wall, this news was fearful to Nabal, for they gart the heart of him fail him, and he died ten days thereafter; but this news was not so fearful to him, as the news concerning the latter day shall be to them that are not reconciled to God. O dreadful and fearful shall these tidings be to thy heart, when it is told thee of that day! for when "there shall be signs in the sun, and in the moon, and in the stars, upon the earth trouble among the nations, with perplexity, and when the sea and waters shall roar, then mens hearts shall fail them for fear;" for they shall not know where to run; to God they dare not, because they have sinned against him; to the Saviour they dare not, for they have trampled his blood under foot; to the angels or saints they dare not, because they are assizers to the Judge: where shall they go then? I know not. But he says to his own, "Look up, and lift up your heads, for the day of your redemption draws near." So ye see this day must be full of consolation to the saints, and full of terror to all them that never found peace in that blood.

Now, in this vision, he says, he saw (may the spirit of the Son open all your eyes, that ye may see the things which he saw) *First*, The Judge. *Secondly*, The manner of the judgment. And *Thirdly*, The execution of the judgment, both upon the godly and the reprobate. He saw the Judge, and he describes him as he saw. *First*, The throne that he sat on. And *Secondly*, The awful face of him that he saw sitting on the throne; for he is coming to judgment, and that day, this shall be the proper work of the Son of God to judge ; therefore there is a throne set in the clouds, and we shall be caught up in the clouds, to meet the Lord in the air; so this throne shall be in the air and in the clouds. He saw his throne was white, for white is the Lord that sat on it; white are the saints and angels that stand round about it; innocent shall the Judge be, and innocent shall the members of that parliament be. Just shall he be in the absolution of all the believers, and just shall he be in the condemnation of the reprobate; just in thy accusation, for nothing shall be laid to thy charge, but that which thy conscience shall say is true; and just in thy conviction and condemnation; and the sentence shall be just, for suppose it be eternal, suppose it be hopeless, suppose it be remediless, and in so great severity, yet the conscience of the reprobate shall have nothing to say against it, but the Lord is just in thy condemnation; therefore ye read in Mat. xxii. 12. "That the man who wanted the wedding garment, he was speechless," and had nothing to say against it wherefore he might not be " taken, and bound hand and foot, and cast into utter darkness, where there is weeping and gnashing of teeth," so white is his throne; for there shall no wrong be done to any in that day ; the child of a year old, and of a month old, yea, the untimely birth, if it go to hell, God shall be just in their condemnation. And the throne was great, for great is the Judge that shall sit on that throne, even

God that made both heaven and earth, fills all with his presence; and great are the company that shall stand about the throne, even innumerable angels, and all the saints that ever took life shall sit round about this throne; and great is the number of them that shall be judged there, even all the devils and reprobates shall stand on the earth; then it shall be seen *many called but few chosen;* and many then shall be flung into that endless fire. And great is the sentence that shall be pronounced, the sentence of eternity shall not be called back again. This much for the throne.

The next thing whereby he is described, is by his awful countenance; and I saw one that sat on it; there was no more but one, for this Judge has no equal; and albeit there shall be many thrones and many judges, yet there shall be one above them all; so there shall be many judges, yet there shall be but one Herald that shall give out the sentence. I grant there shall not be a saint of a night old, or of a month old, but they shall all subscribe to the condemnation of the reprobate. Now he names him not, who this one was, but he may well be judged by his majesty; therefore I judge him by his power, that the heavens may fold, and the earth flee away from the sight of his countenance; judge him by his awful face, and all-seeing eye, that sees no cleanness in the heavens, nor in the earth, nor in the sea, and therefore they flee away from before him, and their place is found no more: it is true, there shall others be in their room, but this old heaven, this old earth, this sun, and this old firmament, which was compelled to look upon men and women when they sinned, because of the Lord's ordinance, that he decreed it should stand so long, and because they must be obedient to the Lord's statute, this old heaven, and this old earth, and this old sea, shall see no more; for the heavens and the earth which are now, says Peter, " are kept by the same word in store, and reserved to the fire in the day of judgment," and of the destruction of the ungodly men; so ye see this heaven and this earth, which ye see now, must be burnt in a fire; but there shall be new heavens and a new earth, a glorious world to them that get leave to see it, and to look upon the Lamb for evermore.

Men would not endanger an eternity for a present world, if they believed that this world, and all that is in it, should be burnt in a fire; but believe not, if ye will; here I testify, that both heaven and earth shall one day be set on fire; and it shall burn all the riches thereof, as silver, gold, jewels, and costly wares; and their fair palaces, and great buildings, that ye see, shall be set on fire; yea, the king himself shall not have so much as a cot-house to set his head in, more than the poorest beggar that goes from door to door. This much for the Judge.

The next thing he saw was the Judgment. (I will yet beg the Spirit of the Lord Jesus, that your eyes may be opened to see this judgment) I will wait on the Lord; and I believe none of you who are ordained to eternal life, but either at one time or another, the Spirit shall make this judgment visible to your conscience. I remember what the apostle to the Hebrews, Heb. vi. 1. says in these words, "Therefore, leaving the principles of the doctrine of Christ, let us be led forward unto perfection; not laying again the foundation of repentance from dead works, and of faith towards God, of the doctrine of baptism, and laying on of hands, and of the resurrection of the dead, and of eternal judgment." Ye see he calls this eternal judgment one of the points of religion, and one of the fundamental stones, that every christian should lay nearest their heart to hold up the building of Christ; for if thou do not this, thou shalt never build a house which shall be able to abide the trial of the storm; therefore as many of you as have not laid that ground-stone in your hearts, ye have not yet come to the grounds of christianity. He calls it an eternal judgment, because it is not a judgment that is to endure a designed time, or the the space of threescore or fourscore years, which is a man's life time, nor for a thousand or ten thousand years neither, but it shall endure for the space of an eternity. Now, there are three things that John sees in this judgment, and mark them in your books: you should mark this eternal judgment.

He sees the compearance of all before God; for ye shall all compear in that judgment. *Secondly*, He sees the process that shall be laid, and so go before the final judgment of all, which is the manifestation of all before God, when you have to compear before that tribunal; for the apostle says, "We must all appear before the judgment seat of Christ, that every man may receive the things done in the body, whether it be good or evil." So we must all compear: and therefore it is called a day of the revelation of the just judgment of God; a day wherein God shall produce the secrets of all hearts; a day wherein men and women, old and young, shall be made manifest to all; yea, there shall not be a pin in thy heart, but it shall be revealed in that day. Now the *third* thing is the judgment itself; so then, these are the things I have to speak of.

First, Of the compearance of all; and here I bear you witness before God, and Jesus Christ, that shall judge the quick and the dead, that ye shall all appear before the judgment seat of Christ. *Secondly*, I am to speak of the manifestation of all, how your consciences shall be made open in the view of all men and angels, of saints and of the devils. The *third* thing is the judgment itself. I have to speak of all this, as the Lord will furnish grace (my merciful God, lift up all your hearts, and draw them within the light of heaven, to let you see these things) O! who will not tremble to think on the last judgment? O secure world! what art thou doing? I remember Jeremiah was made to cry on the earth thrice, to hear the word of the Lord, when men would not hear it; what may we do? Will ye not hear this word of the Lord? Then, O earth, earth, earth, pillars, hills, stones, birds, hear ye this. What should we hear? We must all compear before the judgment seat of Christ. O this compearance! when the naked conscience and body of the reprobate shall stand before him that sees all things, and before all his angels and saints; and when he shall see the heavens and the earth burning about him, and an eternity of wrath abiding him underneath, wherein he must be casten, and there remain eternally. O who can tell the terrors of that doleful conscience! But I leave this, and come to the particulars. *First*, He says, "I saw the dead, both small and great standing before God." *Secondly*, "He saw the books opened, and one other book, which is the book of life." *Thirdly*, "He saw the dead judged of these things that were written in the book, according to their works." And, *fourthly*, "He saw death and hell casten into the lake of fire." O! what means all this! All this judgment shall be visible (hear ye what I say) this eternal judgment whereat ye must compear, and whereat your naked conscience shall be manifest, and whereat ye shall be judged according to your works done in this body, and whereat ye shall receive your final sentence, either of salvation or damnation; all this shall be visible and your eyes shall see it, and ye shall all see the Judge coming in the clouds: and the angels said to the disciples, "Why stand ye gazing into heaven? This Jesus, who is taken up from you into heaven, shall so come as ye have seen him go into heaven." Ye saw him go visibly from you, and ye shall see him visibly come down in the clouds; therefore John says in the Revelation, "Behold he comes in the clouds, and every eye shall see him, even these that pierced him through; and all the kindreds of the earth shall wail for him." For these eyes of thine shall see the Lord Jesus coming in the clouds; yea, every eye shall see him, even these that pierced him through, and they that put their bloody hands in his side; but then they shall wail and weep for him, and before him, when they cannot mend themselves. O! wo, wrath, vengeance, for evermore, to them that make no conscience to rive the heart of the Son of God with their sins, and will not repent, but lie sleeping in their security; for they shall have a doleful waking: they that condemned him shall see him with their eyes; for when the high-priest adjured him, saying, "I charge thee by the living God, to tell me if thou be the Christ the Son of God?" Jesus said to him, "Thou hast said it; nevertheless I say unto you, that hereafter ye shall see the Son of man sitting at the right hand of God (of his power) and coming in the clouds of heaven." He is charged here with an oath, upon the pain that he blaspheme not the living God, to tell the truth, if he be the Son of God; he may give an answer now, for he never gave an answer till he was charged, therefore he concludes with himself, "I will glorify that glorious name of my Father, by the which I am charged, and I will give an answer." Now, wo to that soul and conscience, that being charged, by that glorious name of the living God, to give a confession of the truth, and will not utter the verity. What says he? "Hereafter shall you see the Son of man sitting at the right hand of the power of God, and coming in the clouds of heaven:" when Caiaphas' eyes of his rotten carcase, and doleful soul, shall be compelled to see the Lord coming in the clouds, and sitting at the right hand of the power of God.

So this is the first, the Judge shall be visible; for he shall come in great glory, and in flaming fire; that fire shall ye see, and the heavens, and the earth trembling and shaking out the stars out of the firmament, even as a tree shakes the leaves thereof, and ye shall see the sun burnt in a low, and the earth set on fire; and ye shall see the throne, and he that sits on it; and ye shall see all the elect angels and saints round about this throne; ye shall see the dead, both small and great, stand before God; ye shall see the books opened, and the book of life also, and the dead judged according to their works, and ye shall see the reprobate casten into the lake of fire; and ye shall see the elect taken into heaven; and if ye be of that number, yourselves shall go in among the rest; so ye shall see all, for all shall be seen in that great day, and shall be visible.

Now, what saw he then? O! he saw the dead, both

small and great, standing before God. But what shall become of the living then, shall they not compear? Yes; but because there is a greater controversy of the dead, therefore he makes only mention of them that are dead; for if the dead that are rotten in their graves shall rise and compear, there is no question but the living that shall be left alive, they must compear; and if the sea and the grave dow not keep their dead, but they must thrust them out; and if hell cannot keep the tormented souls there, what then shall keep thee that art living in that day? And if the dead must be thrust out of the womb of all the creatures of God, what then can the living do? The apostle says, "We which live and remain at the coming of the Lord, shall not prevent them that are asleep." So there shall be a generation living, a fleece upon the earth, and it shall be clad with men and women, as ever it was since the beginning; for as in the days of Noah, before the flood came, they did eat, drink, marry, and give in marriage, unto the day that Noah entered into the ark, and they knew nothing till the flood came and took them all away, so also shall the coming of the Son of man be. Likewise the apostle Paul says, "Behold, I shew a secret thing; we shall not all sleep, but we shall all be changed." As if he would say, "All the souls and bodies of men and women, in that day, shall not die;" but instead of dying, there shall be changing; the changing of the reprobate shall be of the mortality of his doleful body into immortality most doleful. There shall also be a change of the elect, for their mortal and corruptible bodies shall put on immortality and incorruption, that their glorious souls may dwell in glorious bodies, and therein may glorify God eternally; and they shall never be weary nor tire; likewise the fire shall not get leave to consume altogether the incorruptible bodies and souls of the reprobate, for they shall still be dying, but never dead; so in this compearing, he saw the dead, now, much more the living; but the living shall not prevent the dead; that is, they that shall be rotten

SERMON II.

in the grave, shall be gathered out of the grave, and shall compear before them that shall be living, for the dead shall be first up.

So the rising shall be very sudden, and there will be no time of repentance; two shall be in the fields, the one shall be taken, and the other shall be refused; two grinding in the mill, the one shall be taken and the other shall be refused; and, in that day, he that is upon the house, and has his stuff in the house, let him not come down to take it out, and he that is in the field, let him not return back to that which he left behind him; for it shall be sudden, and in such short space, that they shall not get time to do any thing. The apostle says, "That we shall be changed in a moment;" a moment is soon done; and, he says again, "in the twinkling of an eye," that is set down too. And yet the dead is up before the living; "I saw the dead, both great and small," no manner of men and women excepted; there old and young; and the child that thou parted with, if ever it took life, shall be up in that day, the king and subject, the master and the servant, the rich and the poor, all shall stand up and compear before God in that day. Again, he says, *I saw them stand;* such as had thrones to sit on, shall stand and wait, either till they be caught within the air, and come into heaven with the Lord, or else they shall be waiting on the earth till they receive their final sentence of condemnation. Again, he says, *before God;* it is true, they shall be before the heaven, and before the earth burning in a fair low, they shall be before the angels and before the saints, and before the wicked and malicious spirits; but this is more, standing before God. It is true, the Son of man shall be judge, for himself hath said, "Verily, I say unto you, the hour is coming, and now is, when the dead shall hear the voice of the Son of God, and they that hear it shall live." For as the Father hath life in himself, so hath the Son, and he hath given him power to execute judgment, in that he is the Son of man: so, it is true, he is the Son of man even as he is man, he shall be sitting on a throne to judge the whole world; but he is more than the Son of man, for that same man is God, and the glory of God shall shine in his humanity, so that all shall see him, as God, and they shall all stand before God. Thus much for the compearing.

Now, I come to the process: "And the books were opened; then another book, which was the book of life." *First*, He sees many books, and the last is but one book in the singular number; what means this? *First*, There is the book of the Lord's remembrance, wherein the Lord has registrate all my thoughts enduring thy whole life time: as David says, "For in thy book were all things written, which in continuance were fashioned, when there were none of them before." Likewise Mal. iii. says, "The Lord hearkened and heard, and a book of remembrance before him was written, for them that feared the Lord and called upon his name." Ye see there is a book, wherein the Lord has written the faithful register, and ways of all men and women that ever were in the world; and it shall be first casten up; it is called, *the book of the Lord's remembrance*; not that the Lord can forget any thing, but to assure thee, that there is not an idle word that proceeds out of thy mouth, nor a wandering cogitation imagined in thy heart, but all is put up in the book of his remembrance; for the register of all men's lives shall be written in this book.

Next, there is the book of thy own conscience; so there is none of you, but ye have a book within you, wherein there are registrated all the thoughts, words, and deeds, that ever thou hadst since thou camest into the world: so every one of us has our own books, and they shall be brought forth and opened also, and these two books, the book of God's remembrance, and the book of their own conscience shall be compared together; and as there are two books or two registers, so there are two notars, that have the pen in their hand, and are continually writing the whole register of thy life, and all are recorded in these two registers: the one book is God's everlasting remembrance, the other book is thy own conscience: there are two scribes, the one is the all-seeing eye of God looking on thee continually; the other is the light of thy own conscience, that warns thee of all thy sins, and watches over thee continually; he is the notar, he shall be thy notar, he shall be thy accuser, he shall be the witness against thee, he shall be thy judge, and if it be not prevented in mercy, he shall be thy currier. It is said, these books were opened; now, were they closed before? It is true, some go with their books closed in their bodies to the grave, and their souls to hell; some, again, go as Judas did, with a leaf open and a line of it red, "I have sinned in betraying innocent blood;" and so with that red and bloody sentence, the body of him went to the grave, and the soul of him to hell: so some has had their books opened before, and some has never had them opened; but however it is, they shall be opened in that day. *First*, The book of the Lord's remembrance shall be opened and read; and *next*, The book of thy own conscience, and these two being compared together, shall agree in every thing. *Thirdly*, He sees another book, yea, indeed it is another than any of them; it is called here *the book of life;* and in the next chapter it is called *the Lamb's book of life;* this book has the names of none written in it, but of these that were ordained to eternal life, and shall " follow the Lamb wheresoever he goes, and shall reign with him for evermore;" and therefore it is called the book of life: but wherefore is it opened? There is a fair order kept here, visible things are brought out. *First*, Two visible books are brought out and read; for there it shall be seen what is written of thee concerning thy whole life: now the sentence will not yet pass upon that, but this other book must be brought out before the sentence be given out; what is in that other book? The everlasting decree of God's election shall be brought out, and looked on, and there it shall be seen whose names were put up in the book of life. So ye see there are three books brought out and opened, the book of God's remembrance, and the book of thy own conscience, and they shall agree together; but in the book of life, which if the third book, shall be found written the good-will of God to them that of purpose he hath chosen to eternal life; and thou that art the child of God shalt find these three things written in the book of thy conscience.

First, Thy calling, consisting of thy conjunction with the Son of God by faith and repentance. *Secondly,* Thou shalt find thy justification, that is, the remission of thy sins in his blood. *Thirdly,* Thou shalt find written there the image of the Son of God drawn on thy heart; so before the sentence come forth, there shall be another book opened, and it shall be seen, not only that thou art called, justified, and sanctified, but also, that thou art ordained to this kingdom before the world was made. Likewise the reprobate shall have three things written in his conscience. *First,* That if he was called, he came not, or if he came, he wanted the wedding-garment. *Secondly,* That he was never justified, nor given in the blood of the Lamb. And *Last* of all, he shall see his sins written there; and then ere the sentence given out, the other book shall be casten up, and he shall see that his name was never written in the book of life; the Lord shall say, "There is the man that I past by in my everlasting decree." Mark, I pray, the order; the book of life was not opened first, to see if thy name was put up there. So, would you know if thy name be put up in the book of life? Look first in the book of thy own conscience, and look what is written there; now, if God has written thy name in the book of life, thou shalt know by this. See the order that the Lord keeps in that day, to bring every one to the knowledge of their election or reprobation, for thou mayest not use another form of process nor the Lord uses. *First,* Thou compears, then books are brought, the Lord brings his book, and thou brings thy book, even the register of thy heart and conscience, and both these books were opened, ere ever the book of life was opened; therefore, as many of you as would have this consolation granted, and would know what is written in heaven of you, then rush not into the counsel of God at the first, but go into thy own heart, and look what is written there; for according to the things that are written in thy own heart, so it is written in heaven. How then shalt thou know if thy name be written in heaven in the book of life or not? The apostle tells you, in these words, "Whom God has predestinate them also he called, and whom he called them also he justified, and whom he justifies he glorifies." God's predestination is the book of life.

Now, in thy calling, thy justification, thy begun sanctification of life, they must be thy trial: so try if ever the Lord did come to thee with the spirit of life? And sawest thou ever darkness and light? and feltest thou ever a sweet fellowship and conjunction with Christ? And dwelt thou ever in him, and he in thee? If ever thou found these three in any true measure, then thou art called; now, if thou be called, the other two shalt thou get, if you have not gotten them already; for thou art called, thou art freely forgiven, and thou shalt be sanctified. Then again, was ever this begun glory in thee? And got thou ever a begun hunger and thirst for righteousness? If ever thou hadst had this, then thou hast had all the degrees of thy election. Now, if it be otherwise, I would have none of you to conclude reprobation, for if ever you shall find them in this life it is enough, for God has his own appointed time of calling you; but this much I will say unto you, so long as ye want these marks you cannot be sure of your election, nor you have no warrant that ever you shall enter into the kingdom of heaven.

But I leave this, and I come to the application, and so I shall conclude. Now, what shall I say unto you? See first that you must all compear before God in the great day. Again, ye see there is not one of you but must be made manifest, even all you, none accepted in that day : for there is not a sin that thou, that art the child of God, hast committed, but thou shalt see it in that great day, and yet thou shalt see it is covered with the mantle of Christ's blood ; and thou shalt see it for this end, that thou mayest magnify the more the great goodnes of God towards thee. Well, brethren, prepare you all for this day of account; may I request you to do it, I would fain have it done, and it should be well with you if you did it; may I request you all to do it, master and servant, rich and poor, old and young, great and small ; may I request you all to think upon the standing with your naked consciences before God, and to believe the necessity of the books of your conscience before the all-seeing eye of God one day : therefore, and I should never see your faces any more, for now I will say as though I was never to see your faces again, and I take the Lord to record, that I have made warnings to you in that measure of light that I have, and as he has revealed it to me : so that suppose you get no other warning nor that that God has given in his word, saying, "God now admonishes all men to repent; because he has appointed a day, in the which he will judge the world in righteousness by that man whom he hath appointed;" suppose, I say, ye got no other warning but the warning which I have made you at this hour, this should be sufficient to clear my conscience, that I am not guilty of any of your bloods, and to clear my conscience, that if you go to hell, thy condemnation is just; because thou gottest warning, that there was a day appointed when all flesh must stand before God and be judged, and every man and woman that has not had a lively faith and true repentance towards God, shall be condemned. Who then of you dare venture to compear before this Judge without these two written in your consciences ? Let me speak to you, for I would speak to you, whose faces perchance I will never see again ; I beseech you, remember on this day, and take the books of your consciences in time, and spread them out before God, and run to the throne of his grace and mercy, and cry, " Pity, pity me, Lord, for I am a vile sinner," that so ye may come away washed in his blood. And think on what I say unto you, for I hear many things of you, but I will say but this, ye should not sin against the Lord, ye should not contemn nor despise the meanest man that has a charge in kirk or commonwealth : why will ye make an evil name come upon this place? The magistrates are despised, and a good order is contemned : therefore hear, and take you warning, that he that resists the higher powers, resists the ordinance of God, and brings to himself condemnation, and it will be a fearful thing to any of you to be condemned. Therefore I beseech you, in the bowels of the Lord Jesus, that ye would bend the strength of your hearts to get the Lord Jesus honoured in your calling; and I charge you all, under the pains of disobedience to the authority of the great God, that ye submit yourselves to the ordinance of God.

Ye know what came of Korah, Dathan, and Abiram, for repining against Moses and Aaron, the one having the charge of the kirk, the other of the commonwealth; the earth opened up, and swallowed up their souls and bodies, and both were taken to hell. Remember on this judgment I pray you, and I pray God, that the like fall not upon you; but I leave this. Now, brethren, I say unto you, because we cannot tell how long our time will last together, and because the devil rages, for he envies our estate, therefore I request you here, in the bowels of the Son of God, that every one of you would repent you of your former evil ways, and that ye would labour to bring your house to repentance and reformation; and that every one of you would labour to bring your neighbours to repentance. Where are ye in the mornings and the evenings, that the house of God is so empty? And what comes of you all these times of the morning and evening sacrifice? I beseech you to spare a time from your work, and come morning and evening to the worship of God, and I promise you, it shall hinder you nothing in your calling, but the Lord shall add a blessing to your labours every day, the more that ye frequent the worship of God. Now, I say no more, but he that has the hearts of you all in his own hand, move your hearts to do so, for Christ's sake ; to whom, with the Father, and with the Spirit, be all praise, for now and ever. *Amen.*

SERMON III.

ON REPENTANCE.

Rev. ii. 2, 3.

I know thy works, and thy labour, and thy patience, and how thou canst not bear them which are evil: and thou hast tried them which say they are apostles, and are not, and hast found them liars:
And hast born, and hast patience, and for my name's sake hast laboured, and hast not fainted.

WHAT was the testimony, which the pastors and the church of Ephesus had from the mouth of the Lord in this letter sent to her from heaven by the hand of John? Ye heard that it was this: *First*, that working faith. From whence can good works come but from faith? And if any thing in the world make a man work, this faith will make him work; for it hath such a power in it that nothing can resist it; for faith draweth the Son of God down from heaven into the soul of a poor sinner, and from his blood brings life to a dead soul: faith lifts up a man from hell to heaven: faith opens the eyes of the blind, and gives ears to the deaf, looses the tongue of the dumb, and gives hands to the lame, and feet to the crooked; and a man that walks in darkness and the vale of death, faith brings to the light, and makes him walk before the Lord: the man that was deaf and dumb, faith makes him hear God's word, and to speak the language of Canan; the man that had neither feet nor hands, faith makes him work the works of God diligently, and to run the ways of the Lord swiftly: What is the thing that faith will not make a man do? The next thing he commends in them, was their labour and love; for who can work faithfully unless he hath love? For the love of Christ must constrain thee to be painful, and not to faint in the work of God, or else you or either will never do this work faithfully and diligently ; therefore he commends their patience, because they hoped for a crown of endless glory, which they knew to be laid up for them, and for all those that suffer persecution for the name of Jesus. Also he commends their zeal, lifting up their hearts with indignation, that evil cannot be suffered by them in any person, were they ever so dear to them, so long as sin did reign in their hearts, so zeal made them to try mens faults diligently : love made them to labour patiently ; and hope made them to wait at leisure, and to be content to bear the burden joyfully, because they knew there was a time of rest and peace, "when they should rest from their labours, and enjoy the fruits of them." I would have you all getting this commendation of the Lord, ye have his word, and his servants, and your own conscience must bear you witness here on earth, and that I might shew his testimony to you in that great day of his appearing.

Would you all had faith as a hand to grip Christ, and as a mouth to eat his flesh and drink his blood daily, and as a stomach to digest him, that ye may feed upon him, and live by faith. I would have all to have that love, that may make you to labour both morning and evening, and all the day long, that ye faint not. "I will rise at mid-night, saith David, and praise thee, O Lord." And I would that the love of the Lord might swallow up all your pains and labour that ye take in the work of God ; but I know, that all will not get these things always. I would ye that are his servants had it at the least ; all might see them printed in the table of your hearts, and written with great letters that all might read them.

And *Last* of all, I would that this were given you of God, that your conscience might bear you record ; that ye have that living and saving faith, which may justify you before man and angels one day ; and that ye get this testimony of the Lord that ye labour and faint not ; that ye keep patiently, waiting continually, looking daily for the coming of the Lord Jesus : and I would ye all had the zeal of God in your hearts, and that holy anger and indignation, that ye could hail sin from your very heart : this for her condemnation.

Now, I come to her challenge, when he says, " nevertheless, I have somewhat against thee :" yea, as though he would say, I know both thy good and thy evil, I will have neither of them untold ; because I desire not a spot or wrinkle in any of you ; therefore I will tell thee thy faults, that thou mayest see them, and be ashamed of them, and mayest endeavour to amend them : So dear is the love of God unto you, whom he has bought with his own blood ; for with his blood he washes you, and makes you clean ; with the garment of his righteousness he has covered you ; for he would have ye all honest and without spot ; for he has a fair palace to bring you into, where no unclean thing can enter. Why should there be a spot or a wrinkle in any of you ? The tender mother will wash the child, and make him clean, that he fouls not the sheets he lies in ; but the Son of God has given his blood to wash you with, because he hath such a love to you, that he would not have so much as one spot on you all. Now, he says, he had but somewhat, and he could not conceal it; and since that one thing was enough to be a challenge against them, what should be the challenge which he may have against many of you, that from the very womb, some of you have your tongue set upon the very fire of hell, some cursing their father and mother, and this city wherein they dwell ! Some of you has been born and brought up in ignorance, that this light of God's word never shined in your hearts ; and some of you has been doing nothing but eating and drinking, and taking your pleasure in earthly things here beneath, saying in your hearts, " we will look on heaven and hell when we get leisure :" some of you have your hands dipped in blood with oppression ; some of you never knew any thing but the world, whose belly is your god, and therefore your damnation is just : some of you are so careless and negligent, that you look but to the present time, and neglect the eternity to come.

Now, wherefore tell I these things, but to see if God will drive a nail in some of your hearts, that meat and drink, and all the pleasures and riches of the world may not pull it out again, till the blood of Christ pull it out, or else drive you to hell ; some of you have challenges of perjury ; some of you have been polluted, and your houses, with whoredom and idolatry ; some of you have the challenge of fraud, and there is untruth in your lips. Now, all these challenges I leave to your own consciences, and this day I lay them upon you all, every one according to the greatness, that each one of you this day may present yourself before the tribunal of God, with your burdens upon your backs, and with sorrowful hearts for the sin that ye have done, and that ye may never rest till ye get mercy in time.

And, suppose ye had none of all these challenges to be laid to your charge ; yet this were enough to humble you, and this day to prostrate yourself before the Lord God, and to fast and mourn in dust and sackcloth, even this is enough, that ye have all fallen from your first love, which ye had once to God and his saints, for there was a time when some of you might have said, " how beautiful are the feet of them that bring glad tidings !" And when some of you might have said, " now all my delight is in prayers, and in the promises of God ; and with David, I will rise at midnight and will call upon thy name, I will meditate upon thy law both day and night."

But mark what he says, " thou hast forsaken thy first love, as though he would say, my love has followed thee, and would never have forsaken thee ; but thou hast turned thy back upon me ; and if thy heart had been kept clean, and memory fresh, as at the first, and if thy senses had been kept open with the multiplication of my blessings, this would have renewed thy love to me continually." So learn this, there is never a blessing that proves not a new thanksgiving to God, but thou drownest it in the bottom of thy heart, and lets it plump down to the bottom thereof, and buries it with unthankfulness.

Now, I need not tell you, how the Lord has followed you with his blessings, spiritual and temporal : some of you from the very womb : I speak to you that are the children of God ; think ye this nothing that he took you not away in your sins before that he called you ? but when ye sinned against him, and justly provoked him to anger, yet he ceased not to do you good : think ye this nothing that he hath brought you out of the kingdom of darkness, and called you to a marvellous light ? and think ye this nothing, that he has given you all things ; that he hath adopted thee freely ; that he justifies and sanctifies thee freely ? think ye these things nothing ? yea, whether believe ye is justification or the kingdom of heaven greater ? whether is it a greater matter to glorify a just man, or to justify a sinner ? Or, whether is it a greater wonder to bring a sinner to heaven, or to bring the Son of God from heaven ? But I leave this.

In how many troubles have ye called upon him, and he hath heard you ? how many times has there been weeping in the evening, but joy has come in the morning ? how tenderly has God dealt with you, that he has fed you with the fat of wheat, and given you to drink the blood of grapes, and made every country and nation to serve you in the days of famine ? he has rained down the blessings upon you in such abundance that ye lacked nothing : how often has he delivered some of you from the grave, some of you from the rage of the sea, and some of you out of the hands of your enemies, and now in this time of his visitation, when other parts and congregations round about you are mourning under the judgments, and kept in for fear of the plague ? Now, he has drawn together his blessings in heaps, and made them to rain down about your habitation, both sea and land ; with what thankfulness must this be met with, or else all will be wrong with you?

Now, in all these things, mark, *First*, how God hath dealt with you freely, and not for any worthiness he saw in you more nor in others: "For mine own name's sake will I defer my anger, and put away thy iniquities, saith the Lord."

Mark, *Secondly*, how liberally God has dealt with you; how many, how great, how continual his blessings have been towards you? "Many are the good things, saith the Psalmist, which God hath laid up for all them that fear him. Thy mercies, O Lord, are above all thy other work;" the heavens are high, yet they are higher; the skies are deep, yet they are deeper; the earth is broad, yet they are broader.

Mark, *Thirdly*, he was found of you, when ye sought him not, and he came to you, when ye looked not for him, as he came to Levi when he sat at the receipt of custom, and to Peter and to John when they were mending their nets with their father in the ship.

Mark, *Fourthly*, that he hath not dealt niggardly with you, or sparingly; that when some of you hath but sought one thing, as length of days or wisdom, as Solomon did, he gives you more than ye sought for, and more nor your hearts could wish for; as it is said "the Lord gives abundantly, above all that we could seek or look for."

And *Last* of all, compare; *first*, thyself with God, and consider what a vile worm, miserable wretch thou art, and how glorious a person and majesty he is; and consider how little need he has of thee, that is all-sufficient of himself; and what would become of thee if thou wanted him. 2*d*. compare thyself with thyself, and thy present state with thy by-gone estate; what thou wast in the days of thy ignorance, and what thou art now in the days of thy light, that thou mayest so much the more wonder, how the Lord hath brought thee out of these depths wherein thou wast plunged. And *last* of all compare thy estate with others, and look round about you to other countries and towns, and see if you may not say, "no man has found so many mercies as I have found." The Lord has been wonderful in pouring out his blessing on us; Reuben got but one blessing, (let Reuben live) and ye have that; Levi got but one blessing, the Urim and the Thummim, and ye have that; Benjamin got his blessing to dwell by the Lord, that he had no further but a step out of his door, and go in to the worship of God morning and evening, ye have that also; so each of the tribes has their blessings; but let me see what blessings there are among them all, which ye have not: Now therefore, if any of you have fallen from your first love, ye cannot say but the Lord has followed constantly upon you with his blessings; wherefore, seeing he hath been so constant in loving of you, this should provoke you to love him again. This much for the challenge.

Now follows the counsel he gives here; this counsel stands in three things. *First*, He bids her "remember from whence she is fallen," and think on the case she was once in; and to remember the love she once had to him and his saints in the first of her calling, that she might see from what a glorious estate she had fallen, and what was her fall, and what danger she had fallen into; that by remembering those things, she might be brought to repentance, and by repentance she might be restored to her former estate and station; for there can be no repentance without remembrance; and the repentance of the very child of God, can never be practised but by a fresh remembrance, and recordation both of God's goodness to us, and our unthankfulness to him again.

Next He bids her, that after she had remembered, them she should repent and turn to him in time.

Thirdly, He bids her do the first works of love and zeal, of labour and patience, and all the rest; that by these means she might recover her first love, and so be restored again to her first station. Hear and mark three things.

L

First, I see the child of God is subject to falling, so long as he lives in this world: and this may very well be, because there is ever a part of his heart unrenewed, as long as he is in this life, wherefore he may fall from persuasion to doubting, from light to darkness, from joy to terrors; yea, he may be brought to this, that he may miss all grace out of his heart, through the absence of God, and the presence of wrath; therefore stumble not at this, for sometimes this comes to pass, by some particular fall into some notorious sin, as David's whoredom, and his adultery, joined with the guiltiness of innocent blood; and Peter's denial of Christ, brought on a fearful defection in them by falling from the Lord; and sometimes when God will try a man whether he will be constant or not in the profession of his faith and religion, as he did Job; and sometimes this security and defection comes on by one profaneness or other, as Noah's drunkenness, and Lot's incest; and this is the craft of Satan, whereby he steals a sin in upon a man ere ever he be aware of him. Now this defection and falling into security comes by degrees.

First, When Satan hath stolen a sin upon a man, then he sings him asleep, that he faints in prayer, and in the rest of the means of the worship of God; then comes on hardness and searedness of heart; then he loses his feeling that he neither finds comfort nor ease in the means of the outward worship of God; he hears the word, but gets no comfort by it; he prays, but he gets no comfortable answer; he uses reading and meditation, but yet he is not the better of it; then he loses his light, that there will be no more left in his conscience, but so much as may controul him only; and so the child of God may fall in these actual sins, for the which the reprobate is condemned in hell, and the Lord suffers this purposely to fall out, that thou mayest know that the meanest look thou givest from the Lord will be punished severely by falling into some notorious crime, thro' which thou shalt get much shame, or else by some visible judgment, lighting either upon body or conscience; therefore thou must take heed to thyself, and stand in awe to give so much as one look from the Lord.

The second cause wherefore the Lord permits his own to fall, is this, that thou mayest know it is by grace only that thou standest; so thy standing is from the Lord; thy falling is of thyself; and when thou standest thou shouldst give God the praise, and when thou fallest, thou should impute the blame thereof to thyself.

Thirdly, The Lord lets thee fall, that thou mayest be daily humbled with a new sight of thy sins, that thy new sins may bring thee to a new repentance.

And *Fourthly*, and *Lastly*, he permits thee to fall, that thou mayest see thy sanctification will not lead thee to heaven, for it is not perfect; but it is the blood of Christ only that must lead thee to heaven, and thou must step upon his back, or else thou wilt never get there. This for the first mark.

The next thing I mark here, is this, that notwithstanding our manifold falls, and notable defections from God; yet there is always place left for repentance, by the mediation of the blood of the Son of God: therefore cast never away your confidence and hope, how great and how many soever your sins be: and suppose you perceive the wrath of God kindled against you, yet withdraw not yourselves from him the more of it; for the Lord takes no pleasure in that soul that withdraws himself from him: and the greatest glory that Abraham gave unto God was this, that he hoped above hope: and believe when you have no matter of hope or believing; for it is the greatest glory you can give unto God, to hope above hope, when you have no matter offered to you; and when you feel nothing but terrors within, and a torment in the soul, and the wrath of God against thee: and when thou findest nothing but induration and hardness of heart, then to believe it is a great matter; and thou givest greater glory to God, to believe his promise, by ten thousand fold, than when thou hast the visible presence of God with thee, and the life of Christ sensibly felt in thy soul.

The *third* thing that I mark, is this, how sweet a thing it is to a contrite and broken heart, to know that the Lord looks upon him in all his troubles and griefs! and he puts up all his tears in a bottle, and will keep them there in a register, until the day of his appearing, that he may recompence them with the everlasting joy of endless glory: here is the comfort of the saints, and here is the patience of the saints. "I know the law is spiritual, says the apostle, but I am carnal, sold under sin; for I allow not that which I do, and the thing I would do, that do I not." Why should you that are his servants want your consolation here? I assure you that your sorrows are seen, your tears are registrate, and your labour shall be rewarded; for there is a day of harvest coming on, when you shall reap the fruit of that which ye have sown; and there is a day of rest coming at hand, wherein you shall cease from all your labours, and all tears shall be wiped from your eyes, and many joyful days are abiding thee, that hast many woful days here, morning and evening wrestling with thy corruption, and the rebellion of thy heart. Now therefore wrestle on, my hearts, for I assure you, ye shall not do it for nought; but you shall eat of the fruit of the tree of life that stands in the middle of the garden of God, and you shall drink of the pure fountain of the water of life.

But I return where I left off, he says then, that "thou hast left thy first love;" this is in great love that he writes to her; as though he would say, "thou art in the wrong to me; thou shouldst not have done this, for my love was always the greater and greater towards thee; for when I was in the world, thou hadst but my bodily presence; but now, being in heaven, I sent thee my Spirit to testify my love to thee, that it was greater now than ever it was: why should you then have forsaken your first love?" But this is a wonderful thing, that the Lord is loth to want the love of the least of his own; for what can the love of man that is but a creature, do to him that is the Creator of all, that is the heir of heaven and earth, and that is made the head of men and angels? Would the king give any thing for the love of an harlot? or would a prince count any thing for the love of a beggar? Now, you may see that God is love, and he will not want the love of the meanest of his children; herein doth he shew his love wonderfully, that when he might have taken a wife to him of the seed of angels in heaven, who are near to himself, yet he would not do it; but he will come down from heaven, and take a wife here on earth of the seed of Abraham: and now, when he has taken her to be his wife, he has no will she play the harlot. This was his love to thee, that when thou wast bathing in thy blood, and wallowing in thy corruption, then he passed by thee, and looked upon thee with pity and compassion, and spoke lovingly to thee, and spread his garment over thee, and covered thy filthy nakedness, he washed thee with his own blood, and anointed thee with oil, and gave thee his Spirit to be a love token to thee.

Now, seeing his love has been so great to thee, why shouldst thou not love him again, and he seeks no more of thee but love out of a pure and clean heart; and this is the thing that grieves him most, that ever thou shouldst have thy heart out of heaven, where he is; and it is the gift of thy heart, and the love thereof, that he requires alternately.

First thing. Now will we consider the love of God that he has had to you that are his own children, that ere ever the world was, he put up your names in the book of life, and left them standing there till the hour of your calling came, and then he tells you of it.

Secondly, Consider that ye were taken out of the damned race of mankind; for all were shut up under unbelief, yet he has passed by many thousands in the world, and would never so much as look upon them in mercy; but he has looked upon you, and has spoken friendly and kindly unto you, saying, " Come unto me, poor sinners, weary and ladned with sins, for I will refresh you; suppose I look over many others, yet I will not that you perish; hear my voice; obey my commands; believe, and ye shall be saved; abide in me, and I will abide in you; and when I come in the clouds I will take you in with me into heaven, and there give you a crown of endless glory."

Thirdly, consider, that the Father hath not a greater love-token to give thee than his own Son, whom he sent from heaven to take thy flesh and thy blood, and to be clad with the sackcloth of thy human nature, and to be subject to all thy infirmities, except sin, and to expose himself to all sorts of shame and ignominy, and to die the cursed death of the cross for thee, that thou mightest live with him eternally ; so what greater token of love could be given to thee ; he has given to thee his only begotten Son, and in his son he gives himself to thee ; and the Son by the mediation of his blood, has brought the Holy Spirit to thee : What wantest thou then that is either in heaven or earth ? thou hast the whole trinity to be thine ; thou hast the angels to be thy servants ; thou hast heaven for thy heritage ; thou shalt sit one day on a throne with himself as a crowned king, to judge the world ; and thou shalt be as a rod or sceptre of iron to break the back of the reprobate, to thrust them down to hell ; and thou shalt be the matter of aggravating his torments in hell : what more shouldst thou consider, when many hear the word as well as thou, and yet have eyes and see not, ears and hear not, and a heart that cannot understand ; for God never opens their hearts ; they are sitting in the church with thee, and perchance sitting on the same seat that thou sittest on, and hearing the same preaching thou hears, yet God touches thy heart and lets them alone ; yea, why not two lying in one bed together, yet the one left and the other received ; is not that great mercy to thee that is the child of God ? Should ye not love him again, for he is your Lord ? would ye not run over bank and brae to follow after him ? doth not your hearts warm with zeal towards his glory ? and how should not your hands clap with joy when ye hear the voice of the Lord crying into your ears, " come unto me all ye that are weary, and I will ease you." Then ye hear another voice into your hearts answering, "I would come Lord, but I cannot; gladly would I be at thee, but I have neither hands to creep, nor feet to go; therefore thou must deliver me." Again, is not this great mercy, that God calls some of you sweetly, and opens your heart at one instant, as he did to Lydia; some others he calls more violently, as he did Paul; because he knows every man's disposition, and what is best for him; some have need to be far casten down, and some others have not need; and therefore he deals with every man as he thinks expedient; some he handles gently, and some others more roughly, and all because he will not let them perish; for he will set them at his own table, and he will feed them with his own flesh, and with his own blood, and he will give them to eat the dainties of his own house, and clothe with the long white robes of his own righteousness; he will give them to drink of the water of life, that is with him in abundance; how then should ye love him? His holy saints are partakers of that holy calling; so these are the things that should move you to love him.

First, your election. 2*dly*, your redemption. 3*dly*, your calling. 4*thly*, your adoption. 5*thly*, your justification. 6*thly*, your sanctification. 7*thly*, and *lastly*, your honour and privileges, and the hope of that glory whereunto ye are called; besides all the rest of the particular benefits bestowed upon you here in this life, that when ye called, he heard you; when ye were in trouble, he delivered you; when ye were hungry, he fed you; and when ye were thirsty, he gave you drink; and when many are content to be diggers and delvers for their meat, ye get it more easily laid to your hands. Further he commands his angels to watch over you, and he guards you round about with his peace; in all thy life he is with thee, and in thy death he will not leave thee, but makes thee lay thy body with peace in the grave most sweetly, and he keeps the very mools of thy rotten carcase until the day of the resurrection, and then thou shalt cast off thy mortality, and put on immortality, and shall give thee a body like unto the glorious body of Christ, and thou shalt shine as the sun in brightness and glory; then shall he cleik thee up in his arms, and put thee in at the gates of that new Jerusalem, where thou shalt not need the light of the sun or the moon to shine upon thee, and thou shalt tramp upon the golden streets of the city of the living God, where there shall be nothing but joy, and eternity of joy to thee, when others shall endure eternity of pain, that have not sinned half so much as thou hast sinned; and thou shalt step into heaven, suppose thou wert a sinner above all sinners.

Now, whether or not should these things provoke you to love God and his saints, I leave it to your conscience. Now for the recovery of you, you hear the counsel of him that is the Father's wisdom that came out of the bosom of the Father, and was upon his secrets, and now he has revealed and told to you the whole counsel of God, here it is, and I read it unto you, the whole counsel of God, for I am but a bare witness and notary to his testament; and this is his testament which he sent fom heaven to you, whereby he will inform you, how you should behave yourselves now in the time of your pilgrimage: that notwithstanding you want his bodily presence, that you may keep his spiritual presence, which shall be more comfortable to you; will you hear his counsel then, *and mix your hearing with faith*; and will you eat up and drink in these three lines written in so sweet a letter, and sent from so loving a Lord to you that are his dear ones.

Now, I have but the bare opening of them to you, that you may the better understand his will (I can say no more) but thus says our Lord; will ye not hear him then that was in the beginning, and before the beginning, that is God, and the everlasting word of God, that came out of the bosom of God, that has revealed the whole counsel of God, that has made all things, and without him was nothing made? Will you not hear him that came down from heaven and left his gloty for a time, and suffered himself to be cloathed with the sackcloth of thy flesh and blood, and lay in a woman's belly for the space of three quarters of a year, and after he was thrust out of her womb, he was laid in a crib for thy sake ? Will ye not hear him that was tempted in the wilderness by Satan, after that he had fasted forty days and forty nights; that was weary, poor, and often hungry and thirsty for thy sake ; that did sweat blood in the garden for thee ; that was bound hand and foot, that was spitted on, that was scourged, that was mocked, and a crown of thorns put on his head ; that did bear upon his back the tree whereon he was hanged ; that was nailed hand and foot upon the tree, and did bear thereupon the curse that thou shouldst have born perpetually ? And will you not hear him that was laid full low in a grave, to sanctify the grave to you ; that wrestled with death, and overcame it, to deliver thee from that eternal and everlasting death ; that rose again, and went to heaven to take possession in thy name, and there to remain an advocate for thee until the day of his appearing, that for his sake the Father may hear you ? Will you then, my hearts, hear his voice, speaking to you in the word *hear that* ; when you shall come to his tribunal, you need not doubt but he will hear you. Now what should you hear ? I have not leisure to open the words to you ; but this is briefly the meaning of them.

First, Remember thy first love to God, to his truths and to his saints, which sometimes thou hadst, but now art fallen from it.

Secondly, Repent that ever thou fell, and made such a foul defection from the Lord ; and take never rest nor ease till thou recover it again.

Thirdly, and *lastly,* do the first works of mercy and compassion to the poor brethren, labouring with faith and hope, with patience and perseverance, without fainting ; delighting in prayer and meditation, in hearing the word, in renewing your fellowship and communion with the Lord ; by participation of the sacrament, and that by these means, you may be restored to your former estate.

Now the Lord open all your hearts, that you may drink in the gracious counsel of the Son of God, and that you may give obedience to the same, even presently, without further delay; that this day you may begin to consider of your falls, and from what you have fallen; and so you may mourn and lament that you have forsaken your first love to the Lord, and so continue your mourning and repenting till you recover your love, and till you get the love of God again shed upon your hearts, by the power of his own Spirit. This I crave to you all, and to me also, for Christ his Son's sake: To whom, with the Father, and the Holy Ghost, be all praise, glory, and honour, for now and evermore.

SERMON IV.

ON REPENTANCE.

Rev. ii. 5.

Remember therefore from whence thou art fallen, and do the first works; or else I will come to thee quickly, and will remove thy candlestick out of his place, except thou repent.

HERE is the challenge that the Bridegroom and Lord of his church, being in heaven, lays to the charge of his spouse on earth, and sends it from the throne of his majesty, written in a letter at his command, by the hand of his servant John, and directed to the minister of that church, that he might communicate the same to his flock.

In the challenge, *first*, he warns her of the leaving and forsaking of her first love that she first had to him when he first married her, and at the first hour when he shined in her heart; and therefore this wounded him to the heart, that he that was nothing but love, and to declare his love to her he laid down his life for her, and had looked on her when she was nothing, bathing in her blood; and when there was nothing in her to move him to have pity and compassion towards her, but only because he would love her; and he would come down from heaven, and he would take a spouse from among the children of men, and he would not take the seed of angels, but chused rather the seed of Abraham, and of the drowned race of mankind that was left in Adam, and being his native enemies, he would make them his friends, and reconcile them to God the Father; and that he might satisfy the Father's justice, he would lay down his life for her, whereby he would declare his unspeakable love to her: then this grieves him to the heart, that when he had such love to her, that all her sins would not hinder or stay him, but he would love her; and all these scoffings and mockings of the blaspheming Jews could not stay him, but he would lay down his life for her; and when death, and hell, and the grave and all could not keep him under, but he would arise, and abide forty days on the earth with her, and at last went up to heaven for her, and in her name to take possession; so that nothing could hinder him in his constant love towards her.

It is he that was that true Samson, who went down to the uncircumcised Philistines, and took a wife amongst them; it is he that suffered himself to be bound with strong green cords for a time, and broke them at last; it is he that carried away the gates of Gaza, and broke up the gates of hell, and led captivity captive; it was he that for love of a harlot suffered his hair to be cutted and his strength to be taken from him for a time, and to be bound by his enemies for the love of an harlot: and notwithstanding all this love he bare to her, yet she falls away from her first love to him; and therefore he tells her, that he cannot bear with so great unkindness and ingratitude. Alas! that ye knew the love of the Lord to us: a loving husband cannot want the loving looks of his loving wife that is dear to him; again, the loving wife, that is honest and will not play the harlot, she will not want the loving looks of her loving husband: even so it is here; Christ, our husband, cannot suffer his spouse, the church, to give one wrong look by him, and to cast her eyes off him upon any other; and if we be his wedded wife, we dare not wittingly suffer him to turn away his eyes and loving countenance from us. Now, he having such jealousness towards her, he writes from heaven, telling her, that "she had forsaken her first love;" and therefore he complains on her, as though he would say, "She counted me once her delight, and in whose arms she took pleasure to lie in and be refreshed; and she counted me once the precious pearl, for which she would have sold all that she had; my words were once to her as sweet as the honey, my law was once more precious to her than gold tried in a furnace; but now she is fallen from this, she has left her first love and played the harlot; and therefore this grieves me to the very heart, that I cannot endure it." Alas, then that any of us should give a wrong look from this Lord to whom we have contracted ourselves in marriage; and why should not this rather break our heart, when we hear that our Lord is grieved, than when ten thousand times a condemnation in hell is told us with the devil and his angels for evermore? Now, he has no will that she abide in this case, lest she perish therein, therefore he sends to her his counsel in write. Some husbands would have said, " Since you love not me, but have forsaken me, and taken thee to another, be doing on, I will have no more to do with thee :" but he will not say so; but suppose she was fickle and changeable, yet he will remain constant to the end.

Now, in this his counsel, he bids her do three things that she might recover her first love, and so heal the wound which she had strucken to his heart; for there is never a sin that the child of God does, after he is called, but they serve for as many spears to thrust through the side of Christ.

First, He bids her *remember from whence she is fallen*, because she had forgotten from what measure of grace she had fallen; and this is the finest plaister that he will lay to her wound, which she had put in her own heart, that she remember the estate into which she was once, and compare it with the present estate wherein she is now; that she remember the warming love that kindled her heart, and melted the fat thereof in the first time of her calling; and now consider what coldness had quenched and frozen that first love; as for the sins she had committed before he took her to be his wife, he passed over these, and he would not speak one word of them, but bids her only remember her sins which she had committed since her calling, and since the time that she first knew him: but why should you not remember the sins before your calling, as David and Paul did? Yes, ye should remember them likewise; but especially ye should remember your defections and fallings away since your first calling, when God first shined in your hearts, and wakened your consciences; for as oft as you sin, you crucify the Lord over again.

Secondly, Remember, that as many slips as thou hast made, they are as so many falls from heaven to hell, from favour to wrath, from mercy to misery, and from unspeakable joy to unspeakable torment.

Thirdly, Remember from what light to what darkness; from what persuasions to what doubtings; from what earnestness in prayer to what fainting and loathing in prayer; from what zeal and ferventness of love to what coldness; from what softness of heart to what induration and hardness; from what holiness to what profaneness; from what obedience to what disobedience; from what sweet tastes of those heavenly joys and virtues of the world to come, to what bitterness of heart and terrors of mind. So now, is there any of you reckoning with yourselves, " What was my glory? What was my happiness? What was my joy and exultation? What were my persuasions and peace? And what pleasure took I once in that blessed word? For my heart was once in heaven: my mouth delighted to talk of the words of grace, and to speak the language of Canaan: my hands were taught the works of godliness, and my feet were taught to run the ways of the Lord." What wrote I, if any of you be calling to mind the things that ye find in your first bringing home to God. " Oh, that ye knew the things that belong to your peace !" Will ye let your chambers and your tables remember you? Will ye let your meetings remember you, with what gladness and singleness of heart ye did eat your bread and drink your drink together? Compare your former days with those latter days, and consider in what case you are this day by the case that ye were in the first day that God married you; and what warming of your hearts there was one with another when ye met together; and how coldrife now ye are grown one to another. But now, whereto should ye remember all those things? Even that the remembrance of them may provoke you to repentance; for unless there be a clear knowledge and a lively remembrance of your faults ye cannot repent. Now, in thy remembrance, consider that there was never a stammer that thou madest from grace but it pierced the Son of God to the very heart.

And after thy remembrance, repent, that is, lament and mourn that thou hast not kept thy first love towards thy Lord and Husband, even as fresh in thy soul and and mind as at the first hour that he shed abroad such love first upon thine heart. 3*dly*, Detest and hate thy sin, which suffered the love of God to decay in thine heart. 4*thly*, Determine and resolve never to rest in thine heart, until thou recover thy first love again which thou hadst once to Christ and his saints. And *last* of all, when thou hast gotten that love renewed, then endeavour to keep it. This is the meaning of the Lord's counsel unto the kirk of Ephesus. The Lord lift up your hearts with reverence to him that spake it from heaven. Hear him therefore speaking from heaven to your souls and consciences, that ye may lay up these things in your hearts which are spoken here for it was not to this church only that he gave his counsel, but he spake it to his kirk which was to be upon the earth in all ages to come unto the end of the world, to learn them what they should do, being in the like case, and in the same estate that they were in, that when they have forsaken their first love, they may know the way how they should recover it; which is this, 1*st*, That they remember their falls; and 2*dly*, That they repent and mourn, because they have fallen.

Now, because I am oft-times speaking of repentance to you; and because many doubt of repentance, and they think they never had it, nor could never get it, and yet they saw it: and because many content themselves with a repentance that will do them no good, because it never brings life to them : Therefore I will now once inform you what this repentance to life is, that, if ye have gotten it, ye may be sure that your sins are forgiven you, and ye shall never perish ; and if ye have not gotten it, that ye may labour in time to get it; for if ye die without it, and go to the grave in that case, I assure you ye shall never see life, but shall die eternally.

In this information, I will keep this order by the grace of God : 1. I will tell you the names that the Holy Ghost gives to repentance in the scriptures. 2. I will tell you how many ways this word *repentance* is taken in the book of God. 3. I am minded to tell you what this true repentance to life is. 4. What are the contraries to true repentance. 5. What are the degrees of this true repentance ; for it comes not to a man all at once but it comes by degrees. 6. I am minded to tell you the sundry sorts of repentance ; for all get it not in a like measure, but some more and some less, and yet he that gets the least measure of this true repentance he may be content with it. 7. I will tell you what are the fruits of true repentance. 8. I am minded to tell you how ye shall get repentance who never yet had it ; and likewise how ye who once had it, and now are fallen from it, how ye may come by it again. 9. And last of all, I am minded to tell you what are the reasons that should move you to repentance.

As for the *first*, Repentance has four names whereby the Spirit of God styles it. 1. In Latin it is called *poenitentia*, that is, *a pain*. And indeed it is a painful pain, and a bitter sorrow, for to the child of God it is a sharp knife, and a two-edged sword, that cleaves and halves the soul in two, that sundereth the very marrow and the bones, the flesh and the skin : therefore it is called the *slaughter of sin*, for it mortifies and lays the very corruption of our flesh : it cuts the throat of sin, which would cut the throat of our souls if it got liberty. But to the reprobate it is another kind of pain ; it is a pain of pains, and the beginning of that everlasting pain and torment which they shall endure in hell for evermore. And this very beginning shall be so very painful to them, that they dow not be able to abide one look of the angry face of God, as Cain cried out, " my sin is heavier than I can bear," and so he was driven to despair. Judas docht not abide this pain, but he is forced to put hand on himself, and become his own currier : and suppose he feels an eternity of pain before sin, and an ocean of wrath prepared for him, yet he dow not abide one drop of that wrath. He knows there is a change, and therefore he will essay if change of torment will bring him any mitigation, but yet it brings him no ease nor mitigation, but from one depth he is posted to a main sea of the floods of God's wrath. Again, the pains of the elect will be painful also, and that when terrors arise on them, and seize on their consciences, they will set so sore upon them that they would give ten thousand worlds for one that would give them the meanest drop of consolation. Therefore repentance is a pain both to the elect and the reprobate : but here stands the difference, the reprobate, God forsakes him, and he is overwhelmed with the jaws of the indignation and wrath of God : therefore he has no patience to bear it, he has no hope to overcome it ; and he has not so much as an earnest desire, from the honesty of his heart, to be relieved, and to win out of it. But as for the elect, God never leaves nor forsakes them, suppose they see him not, and albeit to their judgment he has farsaken them, yet they are sustained by the sweet power of God, that they know not how : therefore he has patience to bear it, he has hope to overcome it, and he has earnest desire, from the honesty of his heart, to be reconciled to God, and so to win out of it.

The next name that repentance gets is in Hebrew called *teshshubba*, that is to say, *a returning*. What means that ? It means this much, that the sinner before he is called to repentance is out of the way wandering as a sheep that is gone astray : for he has his back upon God and upon heaven, and he has his face towards hell and condemnation, and he is in the broad way

which leads to destruction ; but repentance turns him
the flat contrary way again ; and it makes a man or
woman set their backs on hell and condemnation, and
their face toward heaven and salvation ; and so he en-
ters the strait gate and narrow way that leads to life.
Now, therefore, thou that repentest not, look what thou
art doing, for thou hast thy back upon heaven, and thy
face to hell, as long as thou remainest impenitent, suppose thou seest it not ; for thou thinkest it but an easy
matter to step to heaven, at the nearest, as long as thy
conscience is not wakened. And remember, that as
long as thou repentest not, thou art like a wandering
sheep, ay the more it wanders it is the further out of
the way, and in the greater danger of perishing : and
if thou be not brought home by repentance, thou shalt
never see heaven. And you that repent not, thou art
in the broad gate, that unless thou comest out of it by
repentance, which must take thee by the hand and
lead thee out of it, it shall lead thee to destruction ; for
if ye had not been in the high-way to condemnation,
believe ye that ever the Son of God would have bidden us so often repent and turn to him out of the wandering way, that he might set us in the way to life. So
repentance is a turning ; for the poor sinner has such a
burden on his back, mastering him, and holding him
down, that he dow neither steer hand nor foot while
God put to his hand and turn him. And thou that art
the child of God, after thou be once turned, there was
never a sweet posset that sin made to thee before thou
wert called, but it becomes a bitter drink to thee now.

The *third* name that repentance gets in scripture is
in Greek called *metameleia*, that is to say, *a grief and
anxiety of mind* after a deed done : for the sinner being awakened, has such a sting in his conscience, that
it gives him a deadly stroke, and woundeth him to the
heart. Now the reprobate, when he is stung with
these anxieties, he is persuaded that there is nothing
but eternity of wrath abiding him ; therefore he concludes, that seeing he must make to this eternity of
pain, he would fain be at it ; and therefore he will ride

post-haste while he come there, as Judas did. But if ye will say to the doleful sinner, since thou knowest an eternity of wrath abiding thee, wherefore hastest thou to that eternity? Mayest thou not suffer yet the sun to shine upon thee, and the creatures of God here upon earth yet to minister some comfort to thee? The miserable wretch will answer, I know that there is a change, and now I cannot suffer the present pain and torment wherein I am, and I know there is a place prepared for me, therefore I would haste to that place where I must abide for evermore. So repentance has a care and anxiety with it, and this repentance is common both to the elect and reprobate. But all the reprobates have not this care in a like measure in their life; for some are given over to a reprobate sense, that they commit sin with greediness, and they are never troubled in conscience, but die as a stone, as Nabal did. And some have health, and wealth, and ease enough, and nothing to trouble their minds with, therefore they are clad finely, and feed delicately, and take thought of nothing but of back and belly, and so go sleeping to hell, as the rich glutton did. Some again have sore anxieties and cares when they are wakened, that they would give any gear to be quit of them; but they go the wrong way to work, for they put them away either by pastime or company, or eating and drinking, or one unlawful exercise or other. And some have their cares and anxieties, that they can never be quit of them all the days of their life. But the child of God, when he is wakened in conscience, has his cares also, that he would give ten thousand worlds to be quit of them, and yet he wins out of them at the last. Yea, the child of God may be brought to these degrees of anxiety, 1*st*, he will say, "I have banished the Lord, and he will never come again, for he has forsaken me; and now my sins are gripping me by the throat, and presenting me before his tribunal to condemn me.' 2*dly*, he will feel the hand of God to be heavy upon him, the arrows of the Almighty to run through him, and the indignation and wrath of God to lay hold on him, that all the bones of his skin will be bruised, and all the sap and moisture thereof will be dried up. 3*dly*, he will be brought to the very brae or brink of desperation, and point of condemnation, that he would think that a little thing would put him over. And so the elect and reprobate go on both together, till they come this far that they are both brought to the edge of the brae, and there they shed ; for the reprobate steps in, and plunges himself further and further in that bottomless depth ; but the elect stands still, and waits on at leisure till God bring him back, and then he turns : The elect says, " I will bear the indignation of the Lord patiently, because I have sinned :" The reprobate says with Cain, " my sins are heavier than I can bear : The elect says, " if thou shouldst slay me, yet I will trust in thee ; I will take a grip of the sword, although it should hurt me ;" the reprobate curses and wearies God and his saints ; he casts away his confidence ; he tramples the blood of Jesus Christ under foot ; and he will not do so much as once to give a rap at the gates of God's mercy. So this careful repentance is common both to the elect and to the reprobate.

Now follows the *fourth* name that repentance gets, and it is also in the Greek, called *metanoia*, that is to say, *a change of mind*. This is when a man has been out of his wit, afterwards he comes to himself again ; for a sinner as long as he repents not, he is out of his wit, and as it were stark mad, and as a frantic man that has no feeling ; and he is as a fool, that knows not what he is doing, when he beats his head against the wall ; even so the sinner that repents not, he beats his soul upon a sharp pointed weapon, that the more he strikes on it, the deeper will the wound be ; but repentance settles a man's mind, and makes him come to himself again, after he has been out of his wit. And then he will say, O mad fool ! What is this that I have been doing ? I am dying for hunger, and there is enough at home in my Father's house amongst the very servants ; therefore, I resolve to go home to my father, and I will see if he will take me in to be his hired servant; for I shall be very humble to him, and I will desire no more but a corner of his house to abide in. By the contrary, the impenitent sinner is a mad man, that no chains can hold him, he walks amongst the graves both day and night, and he beats himself against the stones; but when the Lord comes to him, and gives him repentance, then he drives the devil out of him; and when the unclean spirits are departed, then he sits down and comes to himself; so then, thou art but a fool and a mad body that art wilfully going to hell the broad way; as Christ said to the man that threw down his old barns and built new, and said to his soul, "take thy rest now, for I have laid up plenty of food and store to thee for many years." What says Christ to him? "Fool! fool! even this night thy soul shall be taken from thee," and they shall carry thee away: "Whose then shall these goods be?" But thou art a wise man that turnest to God, and gettest repentance in time, and comest to thy right wits, after thou hast been long mad, and by thy mind.

Now this kind of repentance, that works a true change in the mind, is proper to the child of God only; for the reprobate has never this thorough change and alteration of his whole mind, but there is ever some unclean spirit or other that he entertains in his heart, neither will he suffer him to depart. Thus much for the names given to repentance.

Now the next thing that I proposed to speak unto you of repentance, it was, to wit, how many ways is repentance taken in the scripture? It is taken four manner of ways.

First, It is taken for a part of repentance, and then it signifies the pricks of the conscience, and the deadly wound that sin gives to the soul of a sinner; for sin is likened to a mad dog, that lies at the door of a man's conscience, ready not only to bark, but also to bite; therefore it was said to Cain, in Gen. iv. 7. "If thou dost well, shalt thou not be accepted? And if thou dost not well, sin lieth at the door."

Secondly, Sin is likened to a serpent, that as long as it wants the sting, a man may put it into his bosom; but when the conscience is wakened, and sin beginning to stir the tail, then it will have a deadly sting with it.

Thirdly, Sin is likened to an iron-mill, that when it lights on, it kills the soul cold dead.

Fourthly, Sin is linkened to a rod or staff, that is pointed on the end of it, and if a man shall lean to it, it runs him through the heart; Acts ii. 37. Therefore it is said, "They were pricked to the very heart when they cried out, men and brethren, what shall we do for the blood of Jesus?" which they thought should have been a staff to defend them against the Romans. That same blood became a sharp prick to them, which wounded them to the heart: So, suppose men think to make sin a staff, and an upholder to their house, whereby they think to sustain their wife and children, as by covetousness in conquering lands and goods to themselves by unlawful means, yet this will deceive them at the last. For as David says, Psal. cxxvii. 1. "Except the Lord build the house, they labour in vain that build it; except the Lord keep the city, the keepers watch in vain."

Fifthly and last of all, Sin makes a living man to become dead; for the apostle says, "before the law came, I was a living man; but when the commandment came forth, sin revived and I died:" So, suppose thou wert never so stout before, now then we may say and see, that sin has a deadly wound? sin has an iron point, or prick in the end of it; sin is a heavy mill, that kills all that ever it lights upon: sin is a serpent, that has a deadly sting; and sin will make living men become dead.

Now, to return, repentance is taken for terrors, that arise in the conscience through the sight of sin, and through the sense of the wrath of God for sin; and yet this is not repentance, but a good beginning and a fair entrance to repentance. Likewise, you see the elect and the reprobate have both their terrors; but the elect when he looks to his wounds and finds himself to be deadly stung, then he looks up to the blood of the Lord Jesus, and there he finds life: then he spreads himself hand and foot upon that crucified Lord, and draws life out of him, even as Elisha spread himself upon the Shunamite that he saw was dead; 2 Kings iv. 34. " And he put his mouth on his mouth, his hands on his hands, his eyes upon his eyes." So the poor sinner lying dead in his sins, the Lord spreads himself upon that dead soul, and by virtue of his blood, sprinkling the heart and the conscience of that sinner, he puts life in him, and his heart begins to warm with that blood. And as the Israelites in the wilderness when they were wounded with the fiery serpents, they looked up to the brazen serpent, which Moses set up at the command of God, and so they were healed; even so the child of God, when he is wounded with sin, he looks up to Jesus Christ, whom that serpent did represent, and so draws life out of him, and is healed with his blood; but the reprobate dares not, nor will not once look up to God; but he will go on forward to these depths, which the devils are so afraid of; and so he falls into the flames of that endless fire, and so he drowns in the well of God's wrath, and he never gets out of it: and these terrors are partly legal and partly evangelical; for the law has her terrors, and the gospel has her terrors too; the wounds of the law are deadly indeed, but the wounds of the gospel are more deadly: for when the law wounds a man, he looks to the gospel and a Saviour; that, therefore he has a Mediator and a blood to run to; but when the gospel wounds one, and when a man tramples under foot the blood of Jesus, then he knows not where to run to.

Now of these terrors arises a grievous sorrow, and heavy displeasure for sin that brought them into such terrors: but we must understand that there are two sorts of sorrow? the one is worldly sorrow, that bringeth nothing with it but death; and that sorrow ariseth of the sense of the wrath of God; and it is furthered by worldly crosses, or worldly fears, or the loss of worldly honour or goods; and this wordly sorrow comes partly from the guiltiness of some notable sin committed, whereby the law is broken; the which law says to a man, "The wrath and curse of God is upon thee, and thou wilt die eternally;" the conscience assumes, "I have broken the law of God;" then the law and the conscience give out the sentence and conclusion, saying, "The curse of God is on thee, and thou must die eternally;" and so thy burden and load is laid on; here comes on the dolour and sorrow: then again, sometimes this worldly sorrow ariseth of the conviction of thy conscience by the gospel, for the contempt thereof, and for the trampling the blood of Jesus under foot, and for quenching the Spirit, and for sinning against the light of his conscience, and after the knowledge of the truth, he sinned wittingly; therefore there remains no more sacrifice for his sin. Upon this, the sinner will gather, that no man that tramples under foot the blood of Jesus; that quenches and upbraids the Spirit of grace; that sins wittingly against the light of the known truth revealed to his conscience, there is no repentance for that man. The conscience assumes, "I have trampled under foot the blood of Jesus Christ; I have quenched and banished the Spirit of grace; I have sinned against the known truth;" then the woful and miserable wretch concludes, "there is no repentance for me, and so there is no remission." This sorrow then he cannot abide, but either he puts hand on himself, or else he runs to pastime, or company drinking, that he may put it away so, and it may be, it removes for a time, and he is quit of it so: but this wordly sorrow, and sudden motion goes soon away, it will never do good to a man. But there is another sorrow, which is according to God, and that is a godly sorrow, that leads a man to life; and this sorrow is wrought in a man by the Spirit of God, and in the heart of the godly; that he mourns for sin, because it hath displeased God, that is so dear and so sweet a father to him, and, suppose he had neither a heaven to lose, nor a hell to gain, yet he is sad and sorrowful in heart, because he has grieved God.

It is this godly sorrow that will lead thee to repentance indeed; and this mourning for repentance shall never leave thee till thou gettest repentance; I suppose, shouldst thou die with this mourning, it shall lead thee into heaven, suppose it were through hell, and through all the gulfs of desperation; and it shall never leave thee until the time it put thee in possession of thy inheritance in heaven. So that we may see, that both the reprobate and elect have their own terrors, and their own sorrows, arising partly from the conviction of the conscience by the law, and other times by the gospel. This conviction of the reprobate is of two sorts; for all the reprobates go not one way to hell; for some of them receive not the seed of the word, and other some of them receive the seed of the word in their stony hearts; but because it has not deep enough root, incontinent it withers when the heat of the sun arises, that is, when persecution comes on. Some receive the word gladly, and they get comfort by it; but the thorny cares of this world, covetousness of worldly riches and pleasures of this life, and voluptuous living, choaks and smothers the word: then it gets not leave to bring forth fruit. Now, it is the conviction of the conscience that makes them run to the word, and to receive and embrace it for a time, because they get some ease to their conscience by it. All these are in the first sort and rank of reprobates, having their conscience convicted of sin by the law of God: And as Herod, he heard John the Baptist gladly, and he amended many things, yet not all, for he would never grant to put away his brother's wife, which was not lawful for him to have, Mat. xiv. 8. And *Felix*, *he trembled* at the preaching of Paul, when he spake of the judgment and world to come, Acts xxvi. 28. "Agrippa was almost persuaded to be a Christian:" And yet all these were reprobates. The other sort of reprobates, are these that fall into irremissible sin, which is against the Holy Ghost, that shall never be forgiven, neither in this nor life in the world to come ; for they cast away the blood, upbraids the Spirit, and they curse and weary God that made them, and upbraids the Spirit that would have sanctified them ; but terrible is the conviction of them in the first rank and degree : but most terrible of all is the conviction of them in the last rank and degree : when a man upbraids the Spirit, throws away the promises made in the blood of Christ, and he will have nothing to do with it, when he falls out in despite and malice, against God and his Son Christ, that is to be judge of the whole earth, he cannot abide to look on the face of Christ, but he runs away from him. The Lord keep you and me both, and all his own, from casting away our confidence in the blood of Christ : To whom with the Father, be all praise, honour, and glory, for now and evermore. *Amen.*

SERMON V.

ON REPENTANCE.

Rev. ii. 5.

Remember therefore from whence thou art fallen, and repent, and do the first works; or else I will come unto thee quickly, and will remove thy candlestick.

THIS repentance, beloved of the Lord, which we have been speaking of these days by gone, I shewed you that it was taken four ways in scripture. *First,* For the terrors or pricks in a man's conscience, when it is wakened with the sight of sin, and sense of the wrath of God lying upon it for sin. Their terrors I shewed, you likewise, were partly legal, partly evangelical, and the elect as well as the reprobate will be stricken with these sort of terrors; and in these terrors the reprobate will have a light that lets him see his sins, and the wrath of God that is a consuming fire, that is kindled against him for his sin: the reprobate has a feeling of the very pains and torments that he must endure in hell for evermore; and he will feel them already begun in his soul and conscience; and the reprobate has a persuasion also, for he is persuaded, and assured in his heart, that God never loved him; God never elected him; God never called him; God never adopted him; and he is persuaded, God will never glorify him: therefore, when these terrors arise in his conscience, he has no patience to bear it, he has no hope to overcome it, and has not so much as a desire or will to get out of it; yea, he cannot do so much as give a rap at the gate of God's mercy. These terrors of the law they will terrify the child of God in the beginning of his calling, and the terrors of the gospel after a particular fall, in some particular sin, they will terrify him more after he is called ; so these terrors will often times set upon him and some are never quit of them, as Heman the Ezrahite said, *I suffer terrors*, and doubting hitherto from my very youth ; but yet for all this, he has patience to bear them, he is upholden by the secret power and mighty hand of God, which in the mean time he knows not of it ; and suppose that he believe that the Lord has departed from him, and will never come again, and that he is forsaken, yet the Lord never leaves him ; but when he thinks the Lord is far away from him, and to his judgment is clean away ; yet in the mean time the Lord is receiving him into his arms, and holding him up by the hand, that he fall not in despair : therefore, since the Lord is with him, albeit he know not of it, he may right well bear them with patience ; so then the child of God has terrors, but he has patience to bear them, he has hope to overcome them, for he longs to be reconciled with God, and hates sin from his heart, that set God and him at variance together, and he would fain have reconciliation made, and the covenant betwixt God and him renewed ; and he sorrows and mourns because he cannot find the work of God's Spirit in his heart, as he was used to do, and he cannot see the favourable countenance of God shining upon his soul as before, and the pains of the terror in his conscience is not so great a burden to him ; and he mourns not so much for the fear of the pain of hell, as because he knows he has grieved too merciful a God, and so loving a Father ; that he has contemned so precious a blood, that brought so glad news once to his heart; and that he has quenched so precious a spirit, that had once begun such a gracious work in his soul. And, mark here, the terrors of the children of God are not sent to all in a like measure, at the first beginning of their calling ; for some God calls sweetly, and he opens their heart instantly, as he did to Lydia : some again, he calls more violently, with great terrors and casting down, as he did Paul ; he sends a light from heaven, he throws him to the ground, he strikes him blind, that he is led to Damascus by them that were with him, and lets him lie there three days and three nights that he neither ate nor drank, but all that time he is occupied in prayer; so the Lord lets him be thus exercised, and so sorely handled, and violently cast down, or ever he sends any comfort to him; and some the Lord keeps long under, that they suffer terrors and doubtings, even from their very youth; as Heman the Ezrahite, which I spoke of before to you; so then, be ye not discouraged the more of your terrors, for God sends them to you purposely to hold you under, lest that you wax proud; for the Lord knows your disposition, and what is meetest for every one of you? And therefore because your sanctification cannot be perfect, nor your faith cannot be perfect in this life, ye must always have somewhat to exercise your faith, and to let you see that it is not your sanctification that will bring you to heaven. This, for the *first* manner or way that repentance is taken.

The *second* is, when it is taken for the whole conversion of the whole Christian man; that is when thou hast all the essential parts of the image of God drawn on thy soul, suppose not perfect; for thou that art truly turned to God, thou hast a true and hearty sorrow because thou hast offended him, and which sorrow is joined with a hope of remission, with a will sanctified by God, that thou art willing to keep all his commandments, and ready to do his will in every thing: and this conversion is joined with a purpose to leave every sin that may offend God, were it never so dear to thee, suppose thou mightest gain ten thousand worlds by it. This repentance, whereby is meant the thorough conversion of a sinner, stands in these five;

First, It consists either of legal, when thy conscience accuses, convicts, and condemns thee for the breach of the law of God; or else it consists of an evangelical terror, thy conscience accusing, convicting and condemning thee for the contempt of the gospel, and sinning against the light thereof.

Secondly, This repentance stands in contrition and

breaking of the heart ; for, when this repentance comes, it will break all the bones of the soul, and it will loose all the joints thereof, and it will melt and soften the heart were it never so hard : therefore it is called the contrite spirit, the pure in spirit, and mollifying and melting the heart ; for thy heart will be so broken with the sense and feeling of the wrath of God, seizing upon the conscience in such a manner, that thou art like to be swallowed up with the terrors and fears of his wrath, when thou seest God a consuming fire above thy head, when thou seest the earth trembling and shaking under thee, when thou seest hell gaping and opening itself large to swallow thee, when thou sees legions of devils waiting on ready to devour thee, then no man can tell the terrors that will be in the soul of a sinful creature, but the man that has seen them and felt them himself.

Thirdly, This repentance stands in a mollified and a softened heart ; and this is when thy heart begins, after long wrestling and debating for sins, and with the terror of the wrath of God against thee for sin ; when it begins, I say, to sober somewhat under the burden of thy terrors, and when it is somewhat softened then thou lookest pitifully, and lookest for some comfort to be sent from heaven to thy weary soul ; then thou appealest from the throne of God's justice, unto the throne of his mercy and grace ; and so thou takest thee to the blood of Christ only, renouncing thyself and all thy works and merits.

Fourthly, This repentance stands in faith, and comes in and lays hold upon Christ the mediator, and applies the blood of the Son of God as a sweet plaister to the soul that is deadly wounded, and heavily diseased and pressed down with the burden of sin ; so by faith thou grippest hard to him, and thou wilt not let him go, for thou mayest not want him, and suppose he would cast thee into hell, yet thou wilt look to him in heaven. Now, when he sees this, that thou wilt have him, and wilt not let him go, and thou concludest with thyself, " Albeit thou shouldst slay me, Lord, yet I will trust in thee, and I will grip to the sword of thy word, suppose it should hurt me ; and if thou shouldst cast me into hell, and in the bottomless deep, yet I will trust in thee, and look to thee ;" when the Lord sees this, I say, then he comes near thee, and looks on thy wounds ; and spreads himself upon thy dead soul, and so puts life in thee ; then thou beginnest to revive and take some spirit to thee ; then thou beginnest to open thy mouth and to pray for remission, and to beg pardon, and earnestly to desire reconciliation made betwixt God and thy sinful soul ; then he sends thee an answer immediately by his Spirit, or else by the ministry of the word ; and he says unto the sinner, " be of good comfort thy sins be forgiven thee." When thou hearest that thou hast got so comfortable an answer, then thy soul exults with unspeakable joy and exulting persuasion ; then thou reachest out thy hand and takest remission to thee, and so thou grippest Christ with all his benefits, his sanctification as thine, his righteousness as thine, and his perfect obedience as thine, and whatever grace is in him thou appliest it to thyself as imputed to thee ; then thou rejoicest with exulting joy, and art wondrous glad ; then thou art more than a conqueror ; then thou art a victorious captain, that hast fought a good fight, for the which there is laid up for thee a treasure of glory ; then thou proclaimed a letter of defiance to all thy enemies ; then thou criest out, " death, where is thy sting ? Hell where is thy victory ?" And when thou hast given God the glory, that thou confessest with thy mouth, and believest in thy heart, that Christ came to save sinners, of whom thou art the chief, then he gives thee this honour again, to be the Son of God, and lets thee see thy name written and put up in the book of life ; and when thou hast seen this, then thy heart leaps for joy again, and then thou hast an unspeakable joy and peace in thy conscience, the which peace passes all understanding, and it is so sweet to thee that thou wouldst not change it with ten thousand worlds : and when thou hast got to this exulting joy, and unspeakable peace, thou art at the highest, for thou canst get no further; therefore thou comest back again and lookest into thy heart, and the corruptions thereof; then thou runnest to the cape-stone of thy sins, and castest down, stone by stone, till thou come to the very ground-stone, and that original sin, which is the root of all the rest, thou labourest to pull it out also by the root; and thou beginnest to be a new-creature, and so thy new-birth begins.

And then, *Last of all*, comes in this new repentance, which we are to speak of: To you then comes that godly sorrow that I was speaking of; then thou mournest for thy sin, not so much for the fear of punishment and the fire of hell, as for the offence that is done to God, that is so loving and merciful a Father; and that godly sorrow shall lead thee to life: and yet all this is not repentance, albeit it have the promises belonging to it; so suppose thou shouldst die in that mourning, it should never leave thee till it had brought thee within the gates of heaven, and put thee into possession of that endless glory. So then, repentance is not that legal nor evangelical terror; it is not that justifying faith; it is not that new birth, or begun obedience, which is true repentance.

What is it then? I will tell you; repentance is a work of grace, turning a man or woman from all their sins unto God; which arises partly from an apprehension of the necessity of a compearing before the tribunal of God, and partly rising of sorrow breeding in the heart, because God is offended, and bringing forth fruits worthy of amendment of life. Now I call it a work of grace, because it proceeds from the free grace of God; and no man can turn to God, till he get grace first to see his sins, and then the deserved wrath of God hanging above his head for sin. 2*ly*, He must see the free grace of God in chusing him before the world was made; in calling him from darkness to light at the time appointed; in justifying him freely; in sanctifying him by his spirit; and confirming him in the hope of that glory to come, freely, without any of his merits or deservings. Again, it is a work of grace turning a man or woman from all sin; because no man can flee from sin but he that hates sin, and no man can hate sin but he that loves God, and no man can love God but he that has found the love of God shed abroad in his heart by the Spirit of God, and no man has found this but he that believes, and no man believes but he that has the Spirit, and no man has the Spirit but he that has the Son, and none has the Son but he that has the Father, and none has the Father and the Son but those that are chosen from all beginning, and none are chosen but those that are loved of God. So, canst thou flee from sin and hate it as thy mortal enemy? Then thou mayest gather, that no man can turn his back upon sin but he that hates sin, and no man hates sin but he that loves God, and none can love God but he that believes, and none can believe but they that are chosen, and none are chosen but such as are called, justified, sanctified, and shall be glorified: for this work of grace has a chain, and the first link of the chain is thy election, the last link of it is glorification, and the middle links, thy faith, thy new birth, thy new obedience, and thy sanctification.

Next, I say repentance is a work of grace that turns a man or woman to God; for sin makes a man or woman turn their back on God and on heaven; but repentance makes them turn their face to God; it makes them new creatures, and it alters and changes all the powers of the soul. Now, it changes not the substance of the body or of the soul, but it changes the quality: For art thou subject to melancholy? Repentance will turn it to a godly sorrow: Art thou subject to anger? Repentance will turn it to a holy zeal for God's glory: Art thou subject to stupidity? Repentance will turn it to meekness and softness of heart and mind: Art thou strong and couragious? Repentance will make thee strong and bold to fight the battles of the Lord, and earnest to set forward the kingdom of Christ. So, I say, repentance is a turning to God and a turning from sin, and from all sort of sin

P

without exception: for there are many false turnings, as when a man turns from professing the truth to Papistry or apostacy, and that is a turning from God to the devil: some again, when they have forsaken their corruption and the lusts of the flesh, after they have been washen and made clean in the blood of Christ, they do as foul swine, that return to the puddle after they have been washen, and as filthy dogs that lick up their vomit which they had once spued out: again, there are some that turn from one sin to another; as a man would turn from wastry to niggardness, or from niggardness to wastry; or if a man would turn from avarice and niggardness to righteousness, or from righteousness to voluptuousness. Some again will turn from some sins, suppose not from all; as Herod mended many things but not all, for he would never give to his brother Philip his wife: Acts xxvi. 28. Agrippa was almost persuaded to be a christian, but yet he was not a true christian. Indeed all these turnings are not true turnings, but false and counterfeit repentance.

But this true repentance, whoever thou be that hast it, it is a turning from all thy known sins, were they never so dear to thee; for if the true love of God be truly felt in thy heart, Christ will be sweet to thy soul, that thou wouldst cast away ten thousand worlds, and all the pleasures and glory thereof, that thou mayest entertain the presence of the Lord in thy heart, and will quit all sin that God may dwell in thy soul. This true repentance will turn thee out of the broad way that leads to destruction, and will set thee in the narrow way that leads to life eternal, and it never leaves thee till it brings thee to heaven, and set thee within the ports of that new Jerusalem.

Now this true repentance and true turning arises of two things.

First, Of the apprehension of the necessity of the compearing before the tribunal and justice seat of God.

Secondly, It arises of a godly sorrow that makes thee mourn much, because God hath given thee much, as that poor woman that sat at the feet of Christ, her heart melted with the sense of the sweetness of the love of her Lord which she felt in her soul; therefore she washes his feet with her tears, and drieth them with the hair of her head, Luke vii. 38. The man of the house marvels at this; for little knows the profane of this world how homely a penitent sinner may be with their Lord, therefore he stumbled at her doings; but Christ knowing what was in his heart, asks a question at him, and he said, "Simon, there was a creditor had two debtors, to one of them he lent five hundred pence, and to the other fifty, and he forgave them both; tell me, Simon, which of these two loved him best?" Simon answered, "I suppose he to whom he forgave most." Then the Lord applied it to himself and said to him, "Since I came into thy house, thou neither gavest me oil to my head, nor water to my feet; but this woman, since she came in, hath not ceased to wash my feet with her tears, and wipe them with the hair of her head?" As if he would say, Thou didst no such thing, because thy conscience was never wakened, nor truly touched with the multitude of thy sins; therefore I will tell thee, that many sins are forgiven her, and therefore she loves much. And so, I say, this repentance ariseth partly of sorrow, but it is a godly sorrow that leads thee to life; and that sorrow in the end bringeth exulting joy with it, that makes thee laugh at all evil that can come to thee, whether hunger, or thirst, or the pest, or the sword, thou wilt laugh at them all, and bid them all welcome; for thou art persuaded that nothing can separate thee from the love of God in Christ Jesus.

Objection 1. But it may be, some of you will say, "What will become of me that never felt that persuasion and exulting joy in my soul?" I answer thee, all come not to this exulting joy at the first, and this persuasion in an instant; for this is the highest degree of grace that the soul of man can get to in this life: therefore thou shalt know there is a meaner degree of grace given to some, that if thou hast it, thou mayest well enough rest upon it; and this is an unsatiable hunger and thirst for the flesh and blood of Christ, that the heavens cannot fill, the earth cannot, nor all the pleasures in heaven or earth cannot satisfy thee till thou gettest a fill of the flesh and blood of Christ, therefore thou longest to get the arms of thy soul folded about the Lord. Now, if thou hast this unsatiable hunger and thirst, thou mayest be glad; for I assure thee, he is coming from heaven to lead thee to the paradise of God, and to give thee to eat of the fruit of the tree of life that stands in the midst of the paradise of God, and give thee to drink of the well of life, that thou shalt never hunger nor thirst any more.

Objection 2. Yet some of you will say, that sometimes ye have felt this unsatiable hunger and thirst in your souls, when God dealt first with your conscience; but now ye are fallen into such security and hardness of heart, through the custom of sin, that now ye cannot hunger nor thirst for Christ as ye did before? *Answer*, but hear what I say to thee, a man may be in security and hardness, and yet have the spirit of Jesus within him; but I shall confirm it with examples; Isaiah, in his prophesy, Isa. lxiii. 17. complains to God in the name of the church, in his time, and in his own name also, saying, " why hast thou hardened our hearts, O God, and turned us away from thy ways?" Hear the complaint of the prophet, and shall we say that the prophet had not the Spirit of God in the mean time? God forbid.

Objection 3. But yet thou wilt say, how shalt thou know that thou hast so much within thee as shall uphold thee in the day of thy security? And how shalt thou know whether thou wilt be saved or not? For *Answer*, tell me if thou seest the hardness of thy heart, and perceivest thou thy security, and feelest thou it to be a burden to thee? and tell me, art thou displeased with it? art thou sorry thou canst not get thy heart melted and loosed as wax before the fire? and hopest thou above hope, and longest for the day of redemption, when thou shalt see thy Saviour, and the accomplishment of thy salvation? and hast thou any cries unto God for to put away the hardness of thy heart? If thou canst say, in the truth of thy heart, that thou hast this, and that thy conscience bears thee record that thou hast it; then be of good comfort; for I tell thee, north-wind and cold frost is as needful for manuring the ground, as the south-wind and warm showers are needful to loose it; and the longer the frost be, and the longer it continues, the more fruitful will the crop be that year. Even so I dare persuade thee, that the harder thy heart be, and the longer thy induration lasts, the greater shall be the 'fruit of thy joy, when the time of loosing comes, that the Lord shall loose all the joints of thy heart and soul, and shall set it at liberty; and when it begins to warm with the love of God, then it shall cast up a plentiful crop, and thou shalt bless the time that ever it pleased God to shew thee such mercy, and that ever thou foundest such favour with him.

Objection 4. Now thou wilt ask, what shall be thy warrant for this? Even this; none can sigh for the hardness of his heart, but he that has the spirit of Christ; and no man has the spirit of Christ, but he that has Christ himself; and none has Christ, but they have the Father also; and none has the Father, the Son, and the Spirit, but they shall be saved; and none shall be saved, but they that believe and repent; so this ground stands sure, and it shall never fail thee; and this is the rock whereupon thou mayest build thy salvation, for the gates of hell shall never prevail against it; for, as I said, repentance arises of a godly sorrow; but ye must understand that there are three sorts of sorrow proper to the very godly.

The *first* is a bitter sorrow, and nothing in it but bitterness; and this is when thou seest nothing but wrath and a consuming fire before thee; and this is before thou gettest a sight of mercy.

The *second* is a sorrow mixed and composed partly of bitterness, and partly of sweetness; and this is when thou lookest on thy sins on the one part, and the mercy of God on the other part : and when thou considerest thy unthankfulness to him, and his love towards thee, this will make thee to sorrow.

The *third* is only a sorrow that is sweet, and there is no bitterness in it ; and this ariseth of the sense of the love of God, that so ravishes the soul, that thou knowest not how to praise God, and how to be thankful to him, and thou mournest because thou canst not be half thankful, and because thou canst not praise God enough, and thou desirest no better than to go to the grave with that mourning ; and thou desirest no other comfort in the earth, but that sweet sorrow arising upon the sense of the love of God. Now, if thou hast the first or second sorrow, thou mayest be content, suppose thou hast not got the last, which is the highest degree of joy that any soul can get in this world.

Now, to conclude, repentance is a work of grace, that turns a man from all sins unto God, arising partly of the apprehension of a necessity of compearing before the tribunal of God, and therefore of necessity we must have a remission ; and partly of a godly sorrow, bringing forth fruit worthy of amendment of life : I say then, a penitent sinner must be fruitful ; and therefore he is compared to a tree planted by the river side, and daily watered by the grace of God ; and because he knows, the more fruitful he be, God gets the greater glory, therefore he wearies not in bringing forth fruit ; and a penitent sinner is compared to wheat because he has substance in him, and is able to abide the wind ; whereas the impenitent sinner is compared to chaff, that is easily blown away with a puff of wind, because it has no substance in it ; therefore it is gathered out and casten into an unquenchable fire, but the wheat is gathered and laid up in the barn ; and this made John to say, " the axe is laid to the root of the tree, and every branch that bringeth not forth fruit, it shall be hewn down, and branch and root and altogether, shall be casten into the fire that is unquenchable."
So ye see repentance must have fruit, and such fruit as is worthy of amendment of life ; for it is not enough

to repent thee of the evil thou hast done, and to forsake it in time coming, but thou must learn to do good, or else it is no repentance. The Lord grant that we may all try our repentance by the rule of this definition, that if ye have not gotten it ye may labour to get it in time; for now is that time, and this is the day wherein you should repent, and if ye let this time pass, it is ill to know if ever ye get the like of it again; for after this life there is no place left for repentance, and without repentance there is no remission, and except ye be forgiven ye shall never see heaven; therefore, my hearts take your time while ye may have it, and repent now, and work out your salvation with fear and trembling, that ye may be found blameless in the day of the Lord's appearing. Now, I pray God to grant it you all, and to me also; this I crave for Christ his Son's sake: To whom with the Father, and the Holy Spirit, be all honour, praise, and glory, for now and evermore. *Amen.*

SERMON VI.

ON REPENTANCE.

Rev. ii. 5.

Remember therefore from whence thou art fallen, and repent and do the first works; or else I will come unto thee quickly, and will remove thy candlestick.

IN this treatise of repentance, which hitherto we have handled, well beloved in the Lord, these are shortly the heads we have spoken of to you.

First, I told you the names repentance gets in the scripture.

Secondly, The sundry ways it was taken. As *first*, for the pricks and terrors of conscience, that is wakened with the sight of sin, after the conviction or condemnation of the law or of the gospel; therefore I shewed you these terrors are partly legal, and partly evangelical, and both the elect and reprobate are subject to both these sort of terrors; but the one sees an outgate, and therefore he waits patiently, he hopes above hope, and he would be gladly freed from them, and be reconciled to God, and in these terrors he is sustained by the secret power of God; that suppose he sees not, nor feels not the love of God in the mean time when he is under these terrors, yet he knows afterward that it was the almighty hand of God that did uphold him, and saved him, that he was not his own currier; but the reprobate sees no outgate, therefore he has no patience to bear it, he has no hope to overcome it, he has not so much as an earnest desire to get out of it; and therefore he falls into the depths, and the more he plunges in them the more he drowns.

Thirdly, I shewed you that repentance is taken for the whole conversion of a christian man, that is, when he has all the essential parts of the image of God, drawn upon his soul, suppose not perfect; this is when a man has true faith, contrition, love to God and his saints, and a begun obedience to the whole law of God; and this is that repentance that is spoken of in Luke xv. 7. "I say unto you, that likewise joy shall be in heaven over one sinner that repenteth, more than over ninety and nine just persons which need no repentance." And this is conversion and repentance, when thou mayest say, grace is not begun only, but all the essential parts of grace are formed on thy soul; and thou that hast this true conversion and repentance, thou wilt also have a true dolour and sorrow, because thou hast offended God: and this sorrow is joined with hope of remission, it is joined with a will to be sanctified, it is joined with a purpose to leave every sin, were it never so dear to thee.

This repentance is double, the one is in the first time of thy calling, the other is after thou art called, and when thou hast fallen from grace; and this is more difficult to be gotten, for the house must be swept and the ashes riddled, and the candle must be lighted, and thou must be sought out and found again after thou hast lost thyself; after thou wast once put up in the bag, as the woman did her piece of silver; and the shepherd must leave his flock, and go through moss and muir seeking thee wandering in the wilderness, till he find thee out, and when thou art found, he must lay thee on his shoulder and bring thee home, and set thee in his own sheepfold, and have a care of thee as of a lost sheep: but when thou art found and brought home again, then the Lord rejoices more of thy conversion, than of other ninety and nine that never went astray; for when thou hast been once called, and at home in thy Father's house, and thou wilt away with thy portion and lose thyself wilfully, the travel will be great in gaining thee again, and it will be long ere thou be brought home again, for it must be plain, necessity that must drive thee to it; but no matter of that thou shalt be welcome whenever thou comest: Yea, suppose thou had stayed twenty or forty years out of thy Father's family, and he shall be twice so glad, that when he had lost thee once, and found thee again, and he shall say of thee as he said of the forlorn son, "this my son was dead, and is now alive again;" as if he would say, This my son was dead, and he is my son as well as thou; he desired to go away, and I gave him leave, Luke xv. 12. he wandered far, and I thought never to have seen him again; but now he is come again, ragged and hunger-bitten, yet I will not cast him off, I will put my best robe upon him, I will slay the fatted calf, and will be merry and rejoice; because a poor lost sinner is found and brought home again.

Now, my brethren, you are all of two ranks, you that are here this day; for the one rank there are many that are yet out, and have never been in the Lord's fold nor family, nor have never received the Lord's livery, nor have born his circumscription in your hearts; here is Jesus Christ dealing: but if you will come home by repentance and will you now renounce your sins, and put on you now the Lord's livery, well it is, come your way, you shall be welcome; but if you will not come now, but you will delay your repentance till another time when you get more leisure; take heed what you do to yourselves, take heed, and behold your own misery; for as long as you repent not, you lodge in your souls the foul spirits, and make your hearts cages to the devil; you lay your souls and carcases open to the wrath of God, that is a consuming fire; ye expose yourselves to all his judgments, both temporal and eternal, bodily and spiritually: and you that repent not, neither yet are come within the compass of the blood of Jesus, there is nothing that bears up the wrath of God, off your heads, but the lenity and patience of God, that says, "I will give yet a day, or yet a year, to yon sinner to repent; and over the date appointed, my mercy has done with him, but my justice shall overtake him, for I give him over to it." Thou that repentest not, beware of thyself, for the devil has laid a snare before thee, smooring sin with some sweet pleasure, the which snare is made of three cords.

With the first, he traps thee in a sin, and so makes thee offend God.

With the second cord he driveth thee on piece and piece, that the more thou sinnest, the more thou delightest in sin.

And with the third cord he fangs and fetters thy feet hard and fast, that thou canst not get out again; then he makes thy own conscience accuse thee, convict thee, and condemn thee, and it shall be the first that shall be ready to put hand on thee, and it shall be the currier to hang and quarter thee in pieces, as thou hast not yet repented. This net is set before thee ready to fang thee, and if thou abidest so, it shall be able to bind thee hand and foot, and thou shalt be casten in that lake that burns with fire and brimstone; thou that repentest not, thou hast all thy sins at thy heels, like as many mad dogs barking and biting thee: Thou that repentest not, as many blessings as thou hast gotten from God, they shall serve for as many suburbs of hell to thee. For hell is compared to a city out of which ariseth a smoke, which blinds the eyes of them that are therein, after this smoke follows a flame, that kindleth the conscience; then last of all comes the fire and burns soul and conscience, carcase and all together; thou that repentest not, look to the thing before thee, an eternity of wrath, ready to embrace thee everlastingly, a fire of hell abiding thee, and a worm that shall never die, to knaw the eternally; and an eternity of torment to punish thee. O eternity, eternity! Who will not be astonished to think on that eternity? O soul! Why shakest thou not, and tremblest not, when thou hast mind of that eternity? Are these fables, think you, when I am telling you of these things, when I preach to you of eternity, and when I speak of a heaven and a hell to you, is it not the oracle of God? And is not this truth, which the Son himself that was from the beginning, and came out of the Father's bosom, and was upon the counsel of God, and knew all that was in the Father's heart, is it not he that hath spoken this? For he has told you that there is a fire that shall never be quenched, and there is a worm that shall never die; and he that brought the glad tidings of salvation to a sinner that repents, he has brought the same news from heaven, that one day he shall fling all impenitent sinners into a lake that burns with fire and brimstone eternally.

Now if ye will doubt whether this be true or not, and if ye will call in question the thing that God himself the Judge of the whole world has spoken out of his own mouth; be doing on, take your hazard; and if you will not believe it now to be true, persuade yourselves one day ye shall feel it. Now, if you will say, I know there is a hell, but yet I shall be saved; I shall warrant me for it I shall never go thither; for there are Jews and Pagans and Papists enow to be cast into hell, suppose I be not cast in it too. But this I say to thee thou countest light of heaven and hell, let all men, in all ages, have some excuse, for them in that great day; let Cain have some excuse, that has been suffering hitherto these five thousand years by gone; and let the old world have some excuse, for they had but one preacher, Noah, amongst them all; and let Sodom and Gomorrah have some excuse, that had but one private man, Lot, amongst them; and let the rich glutton have some excuse, that was no extortioner or oppressor of any man, but lived wealthy upon his own; and let all those have some mitigation in hell: But as for you that perish in this age for want of repentance, you can pretend no excuse; for behold I am here to summon you all before the tribunal of God, and arrest you to a day that God hath set, wherein he is to judge you all, and I proclaim repentance to you; now, if you will judge yourselves now, and condemn yourselves here, then you shall be absolved in that great day; but if ye will not repent nor judge and condemn yourselves here, I assure you, you shall be condemned one day, and when others shall say, wo is me! that I fell not in that day, when the gospel was contemned; for if remission had been offered to me in that blood, I should have embraced it; but thou shalt say, wo is me! that ever I fell in the days that the gospel shined, for I have the blood of the Son of God lying upon my back, which offered salvation to me, but I contemned and slighted it; therefore my condemnation is the greater.

Now you see in what danger you stand that delay and will not repent. I told you also that this repentance comprehends four things.

First, It has the terror of the law and of the gospel.

Second, It has contrition, for it breaks thy heart, and makes it soft and mollified. Then it brings you to this, that thou art like to be swallowed up by the wrath of God, and terror of thy conscience: now when thou seest thy conscience trailing thee before the tribunal of God, then thy heart begins to break, and thou beginnest to reason thus with thyself, " what shall I do, that I be not cast in yonder eternal fire."

Thirdly, this repentance stands in faith, that is, when thou art forsoughten and canst do no more, then thou wilt say, " Lord, I will fall down at thy feet, do with me what seems fit and right in thy sight; I believe thou art able to save me if thou wilt: I perceive there is enough in thy Son, that I desire no more nor is in him:" and then thy heart will warm, and thou wilt draw near to him, to see if thou canst get a touch of the hem of his garment; and if thou canst get to him through the press of thy sins; thou wilt do as the men that carried the sick of the palsy, who did climb up to the house top, and let him down through the roof of the house; for thou wilt climb up above all thy sins, and let down thy sick and diseased soul before him.

Fourthly, It stands in justification; that is, when the Lord speaks a word of comfort to thee, either in prayer by his Spirit immediately from heaven, to persuade thee that thy sins are forgiven thee, or else by any of his servants that will say in his name unto thee, " Son be of good comfort, thy sins be forgiven thee." Then thy soul exults in joy, and triumphs in persuasion; then thou wilt say, " Now death, I defy thee, grave, I defy thee ; hell, I defy thee ; now I have gotten enough in my Lord, that I need no more ;" then thou reachest out thy hand, and takest unto thee permission and remission, then thou puttest Christ upon thee ; then thou takest his blood to wash thee, his righteousness to cover thy unrighteousness, his obedience to justify thee, and his glory to glorify thee ; and when thou hast gotten this, then thou givest God his own glory, when thou avowest that Christ is come to save sinners, of whom thou art the chief ; and then God gives thee the honour again to be the Son of God, the brother of Christ, and fellow-heir with him of the kingdom of heaven ; from this comes an unspeakable joy and peace that passes all understanding : then thou puttest on all thy armour, thy steel-bonnet of hope, the breast-plate of righteousness, and the target of faith, the sword of the Spirit, which is the word of God ; then thou goest out as an armed man to fight against the devil, the world and the flesh, thy deadly enemies ; then thou standest waiting for the Lord's coming from heaven, and longest to see him appearing in the clouds, that thou mayest follow him in there, and sit on a throne with him to judge the whole earth.

Now, in the end thou comest back again to thyself, and thou lookest into thine own heart, and there thou runnest to the cape-stone of thy sins, and castest down stone and stone, until thou comest to the ground-stone and to original sin , then thou labourest to get it plucked up by the root, and rooted out ; then thou hast a marvellous light, that the power of the Almighty is spread over thee, and the virtue of the Most High doth over-shadow thee ; then thou becomest a new creature, and so comes in repentance, that is, when thou mournest for thy sins, not so much for fear of punishment, as that because thou hast grieved God who was so kind and so loving a Father unto thee. Then, to take it up shortly,

This repentance comprehends, *first*, a legal or evangelical terror, by considering the absence of God, and the presence of wrath, which breeds such a burning flame in thy conscience, that strikes such a dread in thy heart, that thou fearest to fall into the gulf of condemnation, but the arm of God is under thy head holding thee up.

Secondly, It comprehends a contrition and a breaking of the heart, which makes thee to have a contrite spirit, and a humble heart, that thou canst fall down at Christ's feet, thou canst lay thine ear to the word, and submit thy neck to the yoke of Christ.

Thirdly, It stands in a justifying faith, whereby thou layest hold on the Son of God, and all the promises made to them that believe in him.

Fourthly, It stands in that unspeakable joy, and exulting persuasion, that arises from the sense of the love of God in Christ, spread abroad in thy heart by the Holy Ghost; then thou art guarded with peace of conscience, when thou seest there is no condemnation for thee, because thou art in Christ, for thou hast gotten the Son, and the merits of his blood imputed to thee; then thou art more than a conqueror; then thou laughest at all the evil that can come to thee: then welcome cross, then welcome post, welcome death; for I defy you all, seeing I am persuaded of the love of my Lord, nothing " can be able to separate me from the love of God in Christ."

Object. 1. Thou wilt say, what will become of me that could never get this exulting joy and persuasion? How shall I know if ever I have gotten that repentance to life? *Answer,* All men and women that shall be saved get not this exulting joy at the first; for it is the highest degree the soul of man can win to in this life; and therefore there is a meaner degree of faith and repentance that is given to some, whereupon, if thou had it, thou mayest rest satisfied without danger; and this is either at the beginning of thy first calling, when thou hungerest and thirstest after righteousness, when thou longest to get a fill of Christ, and a new drink of his blood, and to be reconciled to God in Christ Jesus; or else it is after thy calling, when thou hast an unsatiable desire to get a new bit of the flesh of Christ, and a new drink of his blood, because thou hast quenched his Spirit by some notorious fall; and therefore thou hast a vehement hunger, and extreme thirst, that heaven itself cannot fill thee, but God himself and the flesh and blood of Jesus only: therefore thou longest to get Christ's arms folded about thee, and his blood to cover thee. Hast thou then this unsatiable desire of Christ, and this hunger and thirst for righteousness in him? Then I answer thee, one day thou shalt get a fill of him, either sooner or later; then thou mayest confidently rest upon his promises, who has said, "blessed are they that hunger and thirst for righteousness; for they shall be filled," Matth. v. 6. Then thou mayest say boldly, my Lord, that has given me this hunger and thirst with an unsatiable desire to be filled, he is now coming to fill me: for this hunger and thirst is the undoubted token of the fore-runner of Christ; wherefore I am sure he is coming from heaven to feed me with the apples of the tree of life, that stands in the midst of the paradise of God, and shall give me to drink of the water of life, that I shall never hunger nor thirst any more in the like manner.

Object. 2. Some will say again, I have found these things sometimes when God first called me, but now I am fallen in sleep and security, and hardness of heart, through the long custom of sin, that now I miss all this hunger and thirst; and some may say, I am casten in such terrors, that I see nothing but wrath, and the judgment of God following upon induration and hardness of heart. *Answer*, A man may be hardened in heart, and yet nevertheless have the spirit of Jesus; for Isaiah says, in his own person, lxiii. 17. and in the name of the church of God in his time, "Lord, why hast thou hardened our hearts? and we have turned from thy ways? This is the complaint of the prophet of God; shall we say then, that he wanted the spirit of God when he said this? God forbid; for the prophet speaks by inspiration, that is, as the Spirit of God informed him. And David, Psal. xxii. 1. also cries out, "My God, my God, why hast thou forsaken me? I cry by day, but thou hearest me not; and I cry by night, but thou takest no heed: I am a worm, and not a man, all that see me have me in derision: they make a mock of me, and they shake their heads at me: I am like water poured out, and all my bones are out of joint; my heart is like wax, and melts within my bowels;" by which words, ye may see he felt nothing but terrors within, and pain without, and yet he was a man according to the heart of God: Job also says, "fear is turned upon me, my heart passeth away as a cloud, my soul is poured out: he has casten me in the mire, and my bones are broken, and become dust and ashes; and when I cry unto thee, thou shuttest out my prayer, thou turnest thyself cruelly against me; and my sighing comes before I eat, and my roarings are poured out like water: I had no peace, no rest, and trouble came upon me:" and yet Job was the dear child of God.

Object. 3. Yet thou wilt say, how shall I know if I have that much within me, as to bear me out in that great day, or not? I answer, tell me if thou seest the hardness of thy heart, and art thou displeased with it? Art thou sorry that all the joints of thy heart are not loosed and melted with the fire of God's Spirit? And hopest thou above hope, and longest thou for the day of salvation, and hast thou any sighs and cries unto God that he would take away this hardness of heart? Then be of good comfort, for thou art in the way to heaven I assure thee: and therefore consider with thyself, that the frost is as needful for manuring the earth, as the south wind and soft showers are needful to loose the earth; and the harder the frost be, and the longer it continue in the ground, the fruitfuller and the more plentiful shall the crop be that year: even so hardness of heart

R

is as needful sometimes for a man and woman as softness of heart ; and the harder thy heart be, and the longer thou hast lain under induration, when the wind of God's Spirit shall blow upon thee, and loose thy heart, then it shall cast up a more plentiful crop, and in the greater abundance : So then, suppose thou feelest thyself bound with bonds, I dare persuade thee, that the Lord shall once loose thee and set thee free and at liberty.

Question, But yet ye will ask me, what warrant ye shall have for that ? *Answer*, I tell thee, none can sigh and pray with groans, and long for the Spirit of God, but he that has the Spirit of Jesus already, and none has the Spirit of the Son of God, but he that has the Son himself, and none has the Son but he that has the Father also, and no man or woman has either of these, but they that are chosen children of God : And this is a sure ground whereupon thou mayest build the certainty of thy salvation, and this is the " Rock that the gates of hell shall not prevail against it." Therefore, my dear hearts, be not discouraged, suppose ye find hardness of heart and the absence of the Spirit at sometimes ; for remember there was a time when thou sawest not thy own blindness and hardness of heart, even when thou wast in nature : but tell me then, who hath letten thee see thy blindness and hardness of heart ? And who makes thee discern between hardness and softness of heart ? Who but the Spirit of grace, that has pulled thee out of nature, and planted thee as a lively branch in that true olive-tree the Lord Jesus ; and seeing thou hast been ingrafted in him, thou mayest be sure always to draw life out of him, by renewing thy repentance, and by taking a new bit of his flesh and a new drink of his blood. The Lord grant that ye may wait with patience upon his time, when he shall come again to the comfort of your souls. This I crave for Christ his Son's sake ; to whom be praise, glory and honour, for now and evermore. *Amen.*

SERMON VII.

ON REPENTANCE.

Rev. ii. 5.

Remember therefore from whence thou art fallen, and repent and do the first works; or else I will come unto thee quickly, and will remove thy candlestick out of his place, except thou repent.

THIS repentance, so oft commanded by God in his word, unto which the saints of God have had their refuge in time of their need, as the only rock of their salvation, and the strong tower and fenced city to keep them from the pursuit of the enemy; and this repentance that hath so many fair promises made to it, and contained in the word of God; and this repentance that has wrought so many miracles and wonders, as is specified in scripture, for it has cloven the Red-Sea, and made a multitude to go through dry, and the enemy to drown in it; it has opened the heavens, and made the cry of the poor penitent sinners to pierce through the clouds; it has pulled down the Son of God from heaven, and brought him into the soul of a wearied sinner; it has in a manner changed and altered the very ordinance of God, and has called back his decree. This repentance I shewed you.

First, It was a work of grace.

Secondly, That it turned a man from all his known sins, were they never so dear to him, and although he might advantage himself a world by them, yet he will not do it; and that it turns a man to God, so that he sets his back upon the devil, and on hell, and his face to heaven and to Christ.

Thirdly, I shewed you, that it arises partly of a godly sorrow that works life, and partly of the apprehension of a necessity of compearing before the tribunal of God ; and therefore there must be a remission had, or else we shall not be able to stand before the judge ; for the sight of heaven and hell must be the means to drive us perforce to Christ ; and till we see our accusation, conviction and condemnation in the justice of God to be laid before us, we will never account much of Christ and his merits.

Fourthly, and lastly, I shewed you, that a penitent man must be fruitful.

This much for the description of true repentance.

Now follows, who is the author of this true repentance ? The author is God himself only ; and therefore when the saints have found the impossibility of turning of themselves, then they have looked up to God, and have prayed to him, saying, " convert me Lord, and I shall be converted ; turn us, Lord, and we shall be turned." Now, in this work of repentance, all the three persons of the Trinity have their distinct operations ; the Father looks mercifully upon thee through the infinite love which he bears to thee for his Son's sake ere ever the world was made, and to declare this his love to thee, he sends his own Son, in his own time, to take thy flesh and thy blood, and to die for thee. Again, the Son obeys the Father, and he comes willingly, and he gives himself unto thee freely, and all that he has to be thine ; he gives his blood to cleanse thee, his righteousness to cover thee, his perfection to supply thy imperfection, and his obedience to satisfy for thy disobedience ; he died to ransom thee from eternal death ; he gives his resurrection and the power thereof to be thy new birth and regeneration ; and then he sends his Spirit to thee, which he bought from the Father, by the mediation of his blood : And again the Holy Ghost being sent from the Father and the Son, he comes to thee and over-shadows thee, and so he works that gracious work in thy soul, and after such a manner that thou canst not tell how : For when Nicodemus, John iii. 4. 5. 6. 8. asked at Christ, " How can a man be born again ? Jesus answered, that which is born of the flesh, is flesh; and that which is born of the Spirit, is spiritual: The wind bloweth where it listeth, but whence it comes, or whither it goes, no man knows." Even so the Spirit of Christ works a change in thy soul, in such a manner as thou knowest not how, and yet thou feelest this work to be sensibly wrought in thy heart, but whence he comes or whither he goes, thou knowest not. So then this repentance is the work of God, and not the work of man; therefore thou that lamentest because thou canst not get repentance, and thou that mournest because thou canst not get a heart to mourn, and art sorry because thou canst not thoroughly turn to God as thou wouldst; be of good comfort, for the Lord is turning thee already, and this very morning for the thorough conversion of thy heart shall never leave thee till thou gettest the full assurance of thy salvation sealed and subscribed to thee by the Spirit of adoption. So then, it is God only that is the author of repentance; as the apostle says, Acts v. 30, 31. "The God of our fathers has raised up Jesus, whom ye slew with wicked hands, and hanged on a tree, him has God raised up again with his own hand, to give repentance and remission of sins to Israel." Mark this, where he says, to give repentance; where we may see repentance is the gift of God, and he gives it freely to whomsoever he will; and this is a part of his covenant wherewith he bound himself, even to give repentance to every believer, when they pray for it; and this is his covenant, Ezek. xxxvi. 26. "I will put a new spirit in them; and I will take from them the stony heart, and give them a heart of flesh." What is this new spirit, think ye? What is this heart of flesh? Nothing but repentance: Therefore this repentance is likened to an iron-mill, that breaks the free-stones whereof the lime is made, being burnt in the kiln; even so repentance breaks the heart, and the Spirit of God kindles the fire, that burns up the corruption of the saints, till their hearts be softened, till they moulder in pieces easily. So, as I said, God is the only giver of repentance, and he gives it to whom he will, and in what measure he will, for to some he gives it sooner, and to others later; therefore we must wait at leisure to see if God at any time will give it to any of you, when he has fanged you in his net, which daily he casts about your feet; well is the soul that is taken in this net, and so gets out of the devil's snare, wherein it was taken captive as a prisoner, and so trailed head-long to destruction; for it would have never letten thee see hell, till it had casten thee in the midst of it, nor yet the odiousness of thy sin, which he sugars over with some sweetness; and the more thou sinnest the more thou delightest in thy sin; and if thou hadst continued in this snare, he had drawn the cords at the last and so had choaked thy soul; and thereafter had casten thee into that blackness of darkness, and in that fire that burns for evermore; but repentance delivers thee out of the snare.

Now, my hearts, I know well there is none of you but have decreed a time wherein you will mend and repent, and amend your lives; now is the time, my brethren, even this is the day wherein you should repent; therefore, as the Holy Ghost says, Heb. iii. 7, 8. "To-day, if ye will hear his voice, harden not your hearts, as in the provocation;" and this sentence is twice repeated in the word of God, because it is needful, that if ye defer this day, it is hard to know if ever we get another, and so God says himself " lest I swear in my wrath, ye shall not enter into my rest." But yet I will give you some reasons, why ye should not delay your repentance.

First, Because you must all die once, and you can neither tell when, or where; and if you die impenitent, and without repentance, you will never see life, but you will be a partaker of the second death; for there is no place left for repentance after this life, now that the time of your life is uncertain; you may see young men dying daily as well as old, as the proverb is, " As soon goes the lamb-skin to the market, as the old sheep-skin;" and when many think to live twenty, thirty, forty years, perchance they will not live one year, nor half a year, yea, perhaps not a month.

Secondly, Again many think to die in their beds at home, but yet they are deceived; some die in the sea, some in the fields, and some die in a water; therefore no man can tell the place where he shall die.

Thirdly, Again, the manner of dying is uncertain, for many think to die in peace, and so get leave to put all their business to a point at the time of their dying, and perchance they will die suddenly, and so are taken away with the shot of an hagbut, or pistol, that they get not so much leave as to say, " God have mercy on me."

Now then, what if thou beest taken away sooner than thou had believest, and in a place thou had lookest not for, and after another manner than thou had believest, and so die in thy impenitency; then I answer thee, thou wilt go to hell, and you are here to-day, that perchance will not be here to-morrow; and ye cannot tell how soon the hour shall come, when death shall say to your soul, O soul, go thy way as thou art commanded! and in the same disposition as thou art presently, for thou wilt get no longer time to abide.

Second reason to move you to repentance is this, the longer thou delayest thy repentance, thou liest the longer in thy sins, and thou wilt be the loather to come from them; the further thou goest astray, the longer wilt thou be in coming home again, and thy pain the greater.

Thirdly, The more thou delayest thy repentance, thou sinnest the more, and the more thou sinnest, the more thou grievest God, and provokest his anger the more against thee; and *so treasures to thyself wrath upon wrath against the day of the revelation of God's wrath.*

Fourthly, The more sin that thou committest, thou castest the more wood in the fire of God's indignation, and so thou makest it the greater and hotter; for as many sins as thou dost commit, they serve for as much wood to kindle the fire of God's wrath, and the more wood be casten in the fire, the flame thereof will be the greater.

Fifthly, The longer thou delayest thy repentance, thou wilt find it the harder to get it; and if it shall please God at any time to give it thee, then the more thou hast sinned through delay, the greater shall be thy sorrow, and the heavier heart shalt thou have when God begins to touch thy conscience. Now last of all, let these three things move thee to repentance.

First, Because thy repentance shall make angels and glorified saints in heaven to rejoice at thy conversion; for when thou repentest, thou bringest great glory to God, and great joy both to men and angels; for it is said in the gospel of Luke xv. 7. "That the angels in heaven rejoice at the conversion of a sinner." and,

Secondly, Remember so long as thou lyest in thy sin and impenitency, thou dishonourest God and honourest the devil, thou fightest against God, and takest part with the devil, and thou displeasest God, and pleasest the devil; but on the contrary, when thou repentest, thou honourest God, and shamest the devil; thou pleasest God, and displeasest the devil.

Thirdly, and *lastly*, Remember, that thy repentance binds the eternity of thy election, and the eternity of thy glory which thou shalt have in heaven for evermore, which is begun here by repentance; and so thou makest thy election sure, when of a slave to sin and Satan, thou art made the adopted child of God: when of a fire brand for hell, and a faggot for that fire, thou art made a green olive-tree in the house of the Lord and of thy God, a lively branch planted in that tree the Lord Jesus Christ, never to be cut off again, when thou that shouldst have had thy dwelling with the dragon, the devil, and his angels, thou art made a free citizen of the kingdom of heaven and co-heir with Christ of that eternal inheritance; and when of an enemy thou art made a friend and brother of Jesus Christ.

Now, if these things will not move you to repentance, I know not what will move you to repent: this much shortly for the time when you should repent, and for the reasons that should move you to repent.

Now follow the persons that must repent, and in this point I shall be short also; I believe you all look for the kingdom of heaven, and you would all fain be there also; now if ever you look all to come there, you must all repent, or else you shall never come there; but to speak more particularly to you, you are all here of two ranks, for there are some of you that never yet got repentance, and have never been as yet truly turned to God: and there are some of you that have gotten repentance once, but now ye are fallen from it, and through security have left it off; now repentance is needful to you both, and therefore ye must both repent, thou that never yet repentest nor yet truly turned to God, hast need now to turn to God in time, and to mourn because thou wert never in the covenant of grace, and in the favour of God: and thou that once repentedst truly, and wert persuaded of the love of God in Jesus Christ to thee, thou hast need to renew thy repentance daily, and as thou sinnest thou standest in hazard of the losing the favour of God, unless thou repentest for those sins. This much shortly for the persons that must and should repent.

Now follows the means whereby God uses to draw men to repentance, and makes them to be instruments of turning souls to himself, and so to work this gracious change in their hearts. The principal mean he uses is the preaching of the word; as for example, Acts ii. 37. Peter preached to the Jews, and their hearts were pricked, and their consciences were wounded, that they would have been glad of the meanest word of consolation; and they said to Peter and John *men and brethren, what shall we do?* We would do any thing in the world that you would command us to do, if we could but be freed of this pricking of conscience, and from this heavy guilt of innocent blood which lieth upon us. They answer, and bid them *believe and repent, and ye shall be saved.* They believed

S

repented, and were baptized. So by the means of the preaching of the word to be the principal instrument for to turn mens hearts to himself; yea, it is this foolish preaching of the word, which the wise of this world count to be folly, yet it shall confound the wisdom of the wise of this world. I say, it is this foolish preaching of the gospel, that is the power of God to salvation to them that believe ; and it is the savour of life unto life to such as are saved ; and if this ordinary ministry of the world become not a mean to save thee that hearest it, it shall be the instrument of thy condemnation : for this is the condemnation of the world, John iii. 19. " that light is come unto the world, and men love darkness better nor light." Now, you must understand that both the law and the gospel have their part in the work of repentance : the law will not turn a man, but it will prepare him; for it breaks the clod of his heart, and makes it a meet ground to receive the seed of the word of the gospel. The law lets thee see, 1*st*, Thy sins, 2*dly*, The curse of God above thy head for thy sins, 3*dly*, A necessity of keeping the commandments thereof. 4*thly*, An impossibility in thyself to keep them. 5*thly* and *lastly*, It whips thee and drives thee to the gospel, there to seek a Mediator. But the gospel then is the principal mean that God uses to convert men : for it lets thee see the Son of God, and him " that thought it no robbery to be equal with God ;" and him that was the engraven person of his Father's glory, and him that made all things, to be made of nothing, and to be cloathed with the sackcloth of man's flesh, and to be made of no reputation for thy sake. The gospel lets thee see him born of a woman, and therefore he is nearer to thee than to the angels ; for he took the seed of Abraham : the gospel lets thee see him subject to all thy infirmities, but without sin, as he was tempted, weary, hungry, poor, thirsty, and all the rest of them : The gospel lets thee see him exposed to all sort of shame and ignominy : as scoffed at, buffetted, spitted, on, stript, scourged, and a crown of thorns put upon his bare head, and the sharpest pricks making the blood to trickle down his cheeks, and at last nailed hard and fast to a tree, and a spear piercing his heart's blood, and it running out of his side : The gospel lets thee see him laid in the grave, and risen again : The gospel lets thee see him risen and gone to heaven, and sitting at the right hand of the Father's majesty, and all power in heaven and earth given to him, and the angels adoring him in thy flesh : And the gospel bids thee therefore take him all to thee, take his flesh and blood to feed thee, his righteousness to cover thee, his obedience to satisfy for thy disobedience ; and take him all to thee, take his flesh and his blood to thee, for thou shalt live and not die, for the justice of the law shall not strike upon thee. Now when the gospel has done this to thee, then it sends thee back again to the law, then it says, " If thou wilt repent and believe in the Son of God, then keep his commandments :" So the law will ever wound thee, and the gospel will ever heal thee again : And this shall be the continual course of penitent sinners, to run from the law to the gospel, and from the gospel to the law again ; and betwixt these two must thy soul run, and thou must be this way exercised all the days of thy life.

Now, besides the preaching of the word, there are other four means whereby God uses to convert men.

First, He makes his lenity and meekness a mean to convert some, although other some despise the beautifulness of God's lenity, Rom. ii. 3. 4. 5. " And so treasure up to themselves wrath upon wrath, against the day of the revelation of God's wrath."

Secondly, He makes crosses and afflictions to be the means to convert some, as he did to Manasses, 2 Chron. xxxiii. 12. who ran on in all kind of impiety, that " he pulled down the altars and monuments of the worship of God, and made the streets of Jerusalem to run with the blood of the saints," 1 Chron. xxi. 16. and albeit the Lord suffered him to run on this far, till he brought him to a prison in a strange land, that, at last, he made him come to himself again, and when he was humbled with the cross, he cried to the Lord out of the prison, and the Lord heard his prayer, and he was delivered. Likewise David said, "It was good for me that I was afflicted, for before thou chastened me, I went astray, but now I keep thy word."

Thirdly, God makes the example of some honest mens conversation to be the means of converting others; as in the primitive church, Acts ix. 31, it is said, "They walked in the fear of the Lord, and they increased daily, and were multiplied." Now what made them to multiply daily? Even those that were without, seeing those that were within living so honestly, and walking so in the fear of the Lord, they were constrained to say in their hearts, surely yonder men are in the way to heaven, surely God is yonder, therefore I will go with them; and so they were brought in.

Fourthly, and *lastly*, God makes the examples of his judgments, which he executes upon the wicked, to be means to convert others, as we may see in the Book of the Martyrs. Now, my brethren, ye have all these means offered to you; ye have the word preached, the law and the gospel plainly taught unto you; ye have God's bountifulness and lenity towards you all in a wonderful manner, that I know not of any nation under heaven, or any city in the world had ever greater experience of God's lenity, nor ye have had. Hath not God been kind unto you, when that so many of the world have perished, being drowned with ignorance, and when all the world was shut up in unbelief, before Christ came in the flesh, and for the space of four thousand years before the gospel came through the world, after Christ's ascension, so that religion was not to be found before that time, but in that corner of Judea only; and likewise since the gospel spread itself, and after it had been through the world, how many millions have perished in that antichristian darkness, when the bottomless pit was opened, and when locusts were sent through the world to plague men, who had stings of scorpions in their tails, so that poor people were tormented in their consciences with their damnable doctrines, that the Lord has reserved you unto this time of that last and clearest light that ever shined since the beginning of the world? And has not God been kind unto you, that when he hath been scourging other countries and congregations round about you, some with the pest, and some with the famine, and some with the sword, but yet he hath spared you; and when many of you have been brought to your bed by sickness, and almost to the very grave, that he hath brought you back again, and restored you to your health? And as for blessings, both bodily and spiritual, temporal and eternal, hath he not been kind to you, when in a manner he hath rained down his blessings in abundance upon you? Is not all this great lenity? And should not this lenity provoke you to repentance? Yea, some of you have your crosses too, some in body, and some in mind; and for the example of honest behaviour and Christian conversation, I thank God there are some in the land whom God hath made to shine as lamps, and to go before others, both in life and doctrine. Ye have examples of visible judgments of God, that hath fallen upon some, even in this land, for their rebellion against God and his truth.

Now, therefore, let all those be preachers of repentance to you; for, as the ark of Noah was an example and preacher of repentance good enough to the Jews, even so the pest in Glasgow and Edinburgh, and in other parts of this land, is now a preacher good enough to you; for, lo, it cries unto you, Repent, repent, or else it shall be so with you, as it is with them. Now, therefore, seeing ye have so many means of repentance offered to you, and so many preachers proclaiming repentance in your ears, I beseech you my hearts, delay no longer, but with speedy repentance return unto the Lord in time, lest his wrath overtake you also, and turn unto God before the judgment overtake you; for, whenever it comes, and falls upon you, then it is no time to repent; for the cross may well humble thee, but it shall never turn thee truly to God, except it be confirmed by the word; wherefore, as ye tender your salvation and the well of your souls, I request you, brethren, and I obtest you, in the name of the Lord Jesus, that ye would run to the Lord in time, and seek him now while he may be found; for the day shall come, when men shall seek him, and shall not find him. I will say no more, but I will recommend you all to the grace of God, in Jesus Christ, our Lord and only Saviour, to whom with the Father, and the Holy Spirit, be all honour and praise, for now and evermore. *Amen.*

SERMON VIII.

ON REPENTANCE.

Rev. ii. 5.

Remember therefore from whence thou art fallen, and repent, and do the first works; or else I will come unto thee quickly, and will remove thy candlestick out of his place, except thou repent.

THESE are shortly the heads, well-beloved in the Lord, which ye have heard touching repentance:
First, Ye heard the names of it.
Secondly, The four manner of ways it is taken.
Thirdly, What was true repentance.
Fourthly, The author of it.
Fifthly, The time when ye should repent.
Sixthly, The persons which ought to repent.
Seventhly, The reasons which should move you to repentance.
Eighthly and *Lastly*, Ye heard the means whereby the Lord uses to draw his own to repentance.

Farther, this repentance that will bring life unto you, I shewed you, it was a work of grace, and not a work of nature, and this work is from God, for the preventing grace, and the preparing grace, and the working grace, the establishing grace, the persevering grace, and the crowning grace, are all from the Lord; for God must speak to thee ere ever thou speakest to him; he must knock at the door of thy heart, ere ever thou canst give a rap at the gate of his mercy; he must work faith in thee, ere ever thou canst believe in him; he must establish thee in the faith, ere ever thou canst be sure of thy salvation: he must give thee grace to persevere, or else thou canst not go forward; and, at last, he must put thy crown upon thy head, or else thou wilt never get it. And therefore repentance is the work of God, and not of any creature, nor of nature; it is evident in Paul, for as long as he was in nature, and not converted, what thought he of himself? He says, that "he was a man that walked blamelessly before God and man," according to his fathers the Pharisees: But when he was converted, and then looked into the law, he cries out, *I am a man sold under sin:* Now who made him to see this? Only the Spirit of grace, that had pulled him out of nature. So then, my hearts, if this trouble you that ye cannot get repentance, because ye cannot turn your hearts, and therefore, in yourselves, ye see an impossibility of returning upon your part, ye reason wrong, to say ye have no repentance, and that ye cannot get repentance, and that the covenant belongs not to you; that is evil said, and unjust spoken; for I say unto thee, when thou seest thy impenitency, and when thou hast a desire to repent, and when thou mournest for the want of repentance, then I assure thee thou repentest in very deed.

Object. 1. But thou wilt ask at me, how can that be? I answer, *First,* Tell me this, was there not a time when thou sawest not thy misery, and when thou feltest not thy impenitency? Is not this true? and seest thou it now? Then I pray thee to tell me, who made thee to see it? Not nature, I assure thee, but grace; therefore thou art within the covenant of grace, then cast thou not thyself out through unbelief, but believe the promise made by Christ, Mat. v. 3. saying, "Blessed are they that mourn: for they shall be comforted. Blessed are the poor in Spirit: For theirs is the kingdom of heaven." But yet thou mayest.

Object. 2. Is the sight of sin and misery an undoubted token of repentance? Cain did see his sin, and felt his misery, when he said, " My sin is heavier than I can bear, Gen. iv. 31. Judas saw his sin, and confessed that he had betrayed innocent blood, he saw that he could not mend it, he went and hanged himself; yet neither Cain nor Judas got true repentance. I answer, it is true, they saw their misery, but they had no patience to bear it, they had no hope to overcome it; yea, they had not so much as a desire to be freed from it; they had not their displeasure for the offence done to God; but take away the fear of the torment from them, they care not for any more, and they had not so much grace as to run to the throne of God's mercy, and there to beg grace and pardon; but thou that art the child of God hast all these, for thou seest thy misery, thou bearest it patiently, thou hopest although weakly, and with great infirmity, thou hast an ardent desire to be freed from it, and thou art grieved not so much for the pain of hell, as for that thou hast offended so merciful a God, and so loving a Father, who has bound himself in this covenant to give thee repentance, which thou shalt get from him, even as well as he is bound to give remission of sins to every believer.

Object. 3. But yet thou wilt say, seeing God is the only giver of repentance, and no man gets it until he give it, why then commands he us so often to do the thing which he must do himself; for he only must work repentance? I answer, distinguish me betwixt the commandment of the law, and the commandment of the gospel; the law commands thee, saying, do this and thou shalt live; but it will never promise to give strength to do it; but the gospel commands thee to believe, and repent, and thou shalt get eternal life. Now then, the conscience of the child of God answers, "Lord, I would believe, help thou my belief, for it is thy will that I believe:" wherefore be it unto me according to thy will, as Mary said; therefore, "when thou hearest the Lord in his word, commanding thee to believe, and repent," then give thou only simple obedience to his command and desire, at least to do it; and he that gives a desire and will to obey, he shall give thee also strength to perform it; say not with Zacharias, how can this be? for this saying he was struck dumb till the child was baptized; say thou with the apostle Paul, "could I be disobedient unto the heavenly vision?" Acts xvi. 19. So, brethren, I beseech you, resist not the work of grace which is wrought in thy heart by the Spirit of God, whensoever he begins to take off thy heart, and to touch thy conscience with remorse in the meanest measure, and to cast in any spunk of light or life in any of your dead souls: this much for the things I handled before.

Now follows the next point to be spoken of, which is this, What are the fruits of true repentance? Which are these shortly.

First, We must deny ourselves, and all worldly lusts also; for no man, says Christ, can be my disciple, " but he that will deny himself, and take up his cross, and follow me:" So then, this is the first fruit that repentance brings forth, viz. a denial of ourselves, and all worldly lusts; to the end we may consecrate ourselves, and all worldly lusts wholly to the service of God; and this is done, when we may say, now I am no more my own man, but I am the servant of Jesus Christ, and his disciple, ready to hear whatever he will say to me, and to do whatever he will command me out of his word: never man or woman got to this, but they in some measure repented; for the impenitent reprobate has always a foot out of the fetter, and some part of his neck out of the yoke of Christ, so that he will not be subject to all the commandments of God, for there is still one predominant sin or other that masters him; neither will he suffer Christ to reign as a crowned King over him in his heart.

The *second* and next fruit that repentance brings forth, it is this, to live godly, soberly, and righteously; for thou that repentest must live godly, that is, thou must do these four duties which God commands to be done to himself, in the four first commands. And in the first command thou must have God in thy heart, and nothing but him alternately; so that whatever thou thinkest, whatever thou speakest, or whatever thou dost, thou must always have thine eye upon God, and see if the thing thou art about to do may tend to the glory of God. Especially, in the second command, thou must do all this, the several parts of the worship of God which he requires of thee; as this, thou must watch and pray continually, thou must be thankful in all things, thou must hear his word gladly, and with faith, reverence, and fear, thou must meditate upon his law both day and night, and thou must set thy whole delight thereupon, thou must not look wildly on any of the creatures of God; and in end, thou must learn to make a right use of all the Lord's blessings, or corrections, which he sends either to thyself or to others. In the third command, thou must do all the service of God, faithfully, reverently, and fruitfully, and with preparation. In the fourth command, thou must always set every seventh day apart wholly to the service of God, from morning to evening. This for thy living godly.

Secondly, Thou must live righteously, that is, thou must do wrong to none, but give every man his own; thou must be upright in thy calling, and thou must discharge all these duties to thy neighbour, which the Lord requires in the second table.

Thirdly, Thou must live soberly, that is, thou must be content with whatsoever rank or estate that God has put thee into, and thou must desire no more of this world, nor that which God will give thee lawfully; for thy heart must be in heaven, because thy glory is there, and thy treasure is there; and what hast thou to do with the things of this world? they belong not to thee, but so far as they may further thee to the kingdom of heaven; for thy portion is not in this world, but in God himself, and in heaven; hast thou not meat to sustain thee, drink to quench thy thirst, and clothes to keep thee from the cold? what then needest thou more.

The *third* fruit of repentance, is this, a daily waiting for the Lord's coming in the clouds, and a longing in thy heart to see the Lord, thy bridegroom coming to his marriage; that then he may complete the contract which he made with thee in the earth, that he may take thee home with him to his own house, where thou mayest dwell with him perpetually; and therefore thou are preparing thyself daily for his appearing,

Now these are the fruits of repentance that God craves on thy part.

As for the fruits thereof on the Lord's part, it is this that the apostle says, " Surely godliness is a great gain if a man be content, for it has the promises of this life belonging to it, and also the promises of the life to come :" God has promised to be thy God to protect thee and defend thee from all thy enemies; he has promised to be with thee in all thy dangers and troubles; he has promised to furnish thee all thy lifetime, he shall never leave thee; he has promised to be with thee at the day of thy death, he will lay down thy body in the grave in peace, and he shall carry thy soul to heaven to Abraham's bosom, and he shall keep the mools of thy dead carcase in the earth unto the day of the resurrection, when he shall join both body and soul together, and pull thee up to himself in the clouds, and shall set thee on a throne there with himself, to judge the world; after that he shall set a crown of everlasting glory upon thy head, and shall give thee a palm in thy hand in sign of victory, and he shall put thee in peaceable possession of thy heritage in heaven, where thou shalt eat of the tree of life, which stands in the midst of the paradise of God; and thou shalt tramp on the golden streets of that new Jerusalem, where thou shalt not need the light of the sun to shine on thee, for the Lord shall give thee light, and the temple thereof, where thou shalt do nothing but proclaim and shout forth the praises of God continually. So then, it matters not how many a sore heart thou hast here that repentest, for thou shalt reap the pleasant fruits thereof hereafter; although thou hast many a woful morning and evening, yet be glad, for great is thy reward in heaven; for all the afflictions of this life are not worthy of the least portion of that glory which shall be revealed to the saints of God.

Now, I will tell you for what cause God gives repentance to some, and denies it to other some. I find these three causes hereof.

The *first* is, that he may make manifest and known to men and angels the unsearchable riches of his mercy, and the unspeakable glory of his free grace, that thou mayest wonder at it that gettest it, and magnify the Lord in that great day, saying with Mary, Luke i. 36, 48. " My soul magnifies the Lord, and my spirit rejoices, because he had regard on me his silly handmaid ;" for seeing the Jews rejoiced and were glad that repentance and salvation were offered unto the Gentiles, how much more shouldst thou rejoice and glorify God who gettest it to thyself. So the first and principal cause wherefore God gives repentance to some, and denies it to other some, it is from himself, especially, that thereby he may get great glory, in making some to be vessels of mercy, and other some to be vessels of wrath appointed to destruction.

The *second* and next cause is for thee that gettest it, that thereby thou mayest study to make thy election sure, by keeping thy course straight to heaven, and holding thee as bent upon that crown of glory that is laid up for them and for thee in heaven; and as thou runnest by the way, that then thou mayest repent, for thy repentance is not perfect here; so long as thou art in this life, thy repentance will never be ended, because thy sanctification is not perfect in this life; therefore thou must not delay to glorify God till thou gettest repentance confirmed to thee, but even as soon as thou gettest crumbs of grace in that thou findest the power of God filling thee, and the virtue of the Most High overshadowing thee, and so soon as thou findest the Lord Jesus conceived in thy womb, then thou shouldst glorify God.

Now, the *third* and last cause, why he gives repentance to some, and denies it to other some, it is, thou art converted, thou mayest convert thy brethren, and when thou repentest, thou mayest be the instrument to make others repent also; and when thou art brought to Jesus, and hast once been in his family or school, that thou mayest labour to bring another with thee in thy hand to him; as in the first beginning of Christ's church, Andrew brings Philip to Christ, and Philip brings Nathaniel: So then, wherefore does God give repentance to any of us, and denies it to others? it is that we should deny ourselves and all worldly lusts; for what hast thou to do with the world, and the lusts thereof, that hast once contracted thyself in marriage with the Son of God; " and what to do has light with darkness, and righteous with unrighteousness?" and what to do has God with Belial? " cast away the works of darkness," says the apostle, " and put on the armour of light." Thou that repentest truly, shouldst say, Sin, go thy way; world, go thy way from me; I have no more to do with you; I am not mine own man, but my Lord's, that has bought me with a precious ransom, not of gold or silver, or of precious stones but with his blood; therefore I will consecrate to him all that is within me; I will consecrate my understanding to meditate on his law both day and night; I will consecrate my memory to remember all his precepts; I will consecrate my will to be obedient to his will; I will consecrate my eyes to look graciously on all his works; I will consecrate my hands to work his work, and my feet to run his ways: so I resign myself, and all the parts of my soul and body both, to glorify God. I desire not the great things of this world; if God cast much to me, I am but a steward of it, I know he has given it to me, to try whether I will be faithful in bestowing it again to his use; and if I have little, yet I am content with that which I have, for God knows best what is my disposition; so what have I to do with the great things of this world, seeing I have gotten salvation, which is the greatest, the new heaven, and that new earth, and that new Jerusalem and eternity of joy, which shall be mine? what then should I do with these things beneath, which worldly men make much of? I care not for them, seeing I have gotten salvation, which is the most precious jewel, and the greatest and best pearl that ever was; what should I need then to take thought for any thing that is here? If God send me riches I will take them from him, I know

I am but a steward of them, and that I must render a reckoning one day of my stewardship to him, and if he has given me much I have the more to account for: so, however it be, I am content with my lot, for I have enough, that I desire no more.

Now, this is the use ye should all make of repentance.

Use First, When God gives to any of us any measure of grace, then we should not delay to give God his own glory.

Secondly, That by daily repentance we labour to make our election sure.

Thirdly, That when we get any grace, and are thoroughly converted ourselves, then we ought not to hide that grace, and dig it in the ground of our hearts, as the man that hid the talent in the earth, but let us bring it forth to the exchange, and communicate it to our brethren, that it may be put to the exchange, that we may render to God his own again with advantage.

Now it remains to speak to you of the parts of repentance. Repentance hath two parts; mortification of the old man, and vivification of the new man. I know not if ye all understand me: repentance has death in it, because it lets thee see thy Lord sweating blood in the garden; therefore thou sweatest under the burden of thy sins. Repentance has life in it, because it will raise thy soul from death to life: repentance lets thee see thy Lord bound hand and foot with cords, that thy lusts never get leave to break loose again; repentance lets thee see thy Lord scourged for thy sins; repentance lets thee see thy Lord nailed hand and foot to a tree, and laid cold dead in a grave; thou must crucify thy sins, and bury them with him. So repentance will make thee like unto thy Lord in all cases; for except thou first die with him, thou shalt never live with him. Pray therefore daily, Lord lay the savour of thy death to my soul that is poor, and wound my heart with these wounds thou hadst on the cross, that when I am wounded with thy death, thou mayest revive me with the virtue of thy resurrection. So repentance crucifies the old man, and it quickens the new; it crucifies the world to thee, and thee to the world; and repentance makes thy conversation to be in heaven. In this crucifying there are three things,

First, Thou must slay thy sin, that it never rise again.

Secondly, Thou must hate it and detest it; wherever thou seest it in thyself or in others, thou must fly from it, as from a deadly dart.

Thirdly, Thou must always be pulling down the walls of thy sin, and be casting it down, stone by stone, till thou bringest it to the ground; and the same weapons that sin would have used to slay thy soul with, thou must turn them back upon the belly of thy sin.

Likewise in thy new birth there must be three things.

First, Thou must have a constant purpose and resolution in thy heart, that thou shalt sin no more in thy whole lifetime.

Secondly, Thou must have a true love to all righteousness, and a begun obedience to all the commandments of God. And,

Thirdly, Thou must have an holy endeavor to keep a good conscience in all thy ways; and in whatsoever place or company thou comest in, thou must labour either to get grace, or else to leave some grace behind thee; or if thou canst do neither of these, yet so far as lieth in thy power, or that may stand with thy calling, see that thou slayest sin, that it break not out to the dishonour of God: try yourselves therefore if ever ye found these things, and if ye have them, ye may be sure that ye have gotten that true repentance, which shall never deceive you; but if ye have not found these things in some measure, to wit, the slaughter of your sin, the hatred and detestation of all sort of sin, and the pulling down the walls of sin, stone by stone, and of the turning of its own weapons into the belly of the same; and if thou hast not found a resolved purpose to sin no more, and a true love to all righteousness, and an holy care and endeavour to keep a good conscience; if thou hast not these things, I assure thee, thou hast not found yet that true repentance which shall bear thee out in that great day. Now I leave the trial of these things to your own consciences, and I commit you all, and the things that have been spoken, to the grace and blessing of the Lord Jesus Christ: to whom with the Father, and the Holy Ghost, be all praise, honour, and glory for ever and ever. *Amen.*

SERMON IX.

ON REPENTANCE.

Rev. ii. 5.

Remember therefore from whence thou art fallen, and repent and do the first works; or else I will come unto thee quickly, and will remove thy candlestick.

YE remember I told you the last time, beloved in the Lord, what were the fruits of true repentance; first, upon your part; and next, upon he Lord's part. I need not now rehearse them unto you. Next, I shewed you, for what cause the Lord gave repentance to some, and denies it to others. Last of all I shewed you what were parts of repentance; they are set down to you in the epistle of Paul to the Corinthians after this manner, 2 Cor. vii. 9, 10, 11.

First, There is required a godly sorrow which leads to life; and that is when the heart is opened, and when a penitent sinner is sorely grieved for the dishonour of God's name.

Secondly, An earnest endeavour and care to please God in all things, that the glory of God may be set forward, as far as his calling and power may reach to; and an earnest care that the kingdom of God be first set up in thy own heart and then in the hearts of others.

Thirdly, There must be an indignation and hatred of sin: wherever thou seest it or hearest tell of it, thou must despise it and abhor it.

Fourthly, Thou must fear to commit sin against God, lest he be offended, and so thou losest his presence.

Fifthly, Thou must have an earnest longing and daily waiting for the coming of our Lord Jesus to judge the quick and the dead.

Sixthly, Thou must have an earnest desire to get the throat of thy sin cut, that thou wouldst be as glad to be avenged upon thy sin, that brought the Lord from heaven, and that caused him to be nailed on a tree, and made him to be laid in a grave, thou wouldst be as glad to be avenged on thy sins as ever man would have been upon his greatest enemy, yea, if he had slain all his kindred.

Seventhly, and *last of all,* There must be a fervent zeal burning in thy heart with indignation, that suppose thou wert as meek as ever Moses was, who was the meekest man of the whole earth; yet, when thou seest God dishonoured, thou wilt not spare to cast out of thy hands even the very tables of the law, written by the finger of God, and thou wilt not spare to cast the most precious and dearest thing that thou hast out of thy hands, that thou mayest be avenged of the contempt of the Lord's ordinance; and then, in the end, thou wilt be very loth to communicate with other mens sins, even as a man will be loth to eat and drink with a leprous creature, or one that has the feister.

Now, then, those are the signs and tokens; whereby ye shall know whether ye have ever had repentance to life or not; I leave the trial of these things to your own conscience; therefore sit down upon the black stone, and examine yourselves, and try if you have these things in any true measure or not; search into your own hearts; if ye have and find them in it, well and good it is, ye are well; for, content yourselves, ye have gotten the repentance that shall never be repented of; for it shall lead you into the straight gate that shall bring you into eternal life; but, if you find them not, I beseech you take no rest nor ease till God send them to your souls in some measure; for, if ye get them not before ye depart this life, think on, I tell you, ye shall never see life. This much for the signs of true repentance, that the Lord hath expressed in his word.

Now, I will tell you somewhat of the sundry sorts of repentance appointed to be done by his own children, at sundry times, and after divers manners.

And, to the *first* sort, There is a repentance at the first hour God calls thee; and may be, that repentance shall be both the bitterest and the sweetest repentance that ever thou wilt get.

Secondly, There is an ordinary repentance, which thou that art the child of God must renew every day; because thou sinnest daily, thou hast need to repent daily.

Thirdly, There is an extraordinary repentance, when thou hast fallen into some notorious and extraordinary sin, whereby a whole congregation is offended, then thou hast need of an extraordinary and public repentance.

Fourthly, and *last of all*, There is an universal and extraordinary repentance, and a public humiliation of all persons, such as we should now have at this time, and all these sorts of repentance are warranted in the scriptures; as we see in the example of Paul in his first calling, Acts ix. 9, and of David and Peter, for their notable falls after their calling, they made a notable repentance; and the example of Nineveh, and of the whole land, Jonah iii. 8, and of all Israel in the time of Ahab, with many more examples, that I need not to rehearse.

Now, this for the sundry sorts of repentance.

Now, I come to the degrees of repentance; that ye may the better take them up; ye must understand, that as there are three sorts of Christians, so there are three degrees of repentance.

The *first* sort of Christians are called *babes*, and these are they that Christ is yet but forming in their souls. Now, if thou be'st a babe, thou hast all the essential parts of a reasonable man or woman, formed within thee, suppose thou canst not use them; for thou hast hands, but yet thou canst not work with them; thou hast feet, but yet thou canst not go with them; and, suppose thou hast neither a mouth to eat, nor a stomach to digest meat, yet thou hast life, and there is a secret power that upholds thee; and, suppose thou be'st a babe that knowest neither father nor mother, yet thou art fed in thy mother's womb secretly, by an unseen, unknown, unfelt power; and, if thou be'st in this case, that as yet thou knowest not God distinctly to be thy Father, and Christ to be thy Saviour; yet, nevertheless, he is thy Father, and Christ is thy Saviour. Now, when the babe is born, then he can discern betwixt light and darkness, and the sweet milk and the sour; and when he is hungry or thirsty, he can cry for meat or drink; if thou hast any light, that thou canst discern betwixt light and darkness, and if thou seest thy misery, and wouldst gladly eat of the sweet word of God, then I assure thee, thou art a babe, and thou art born over again; and, albeit thou be but a babe in Christ, yet thou mayest be content with thy present estate; for thou wast once dead in sin, but now thou art alive, and thou art born a new creature, never to die again. So this is the first and the meanest degree of repentance, the sight of thy misery, and a hunger and thirst for righteousness.

The *second* sort of Christians are compared to *young men*, who have strength to wrestle against principalities and powers; for in thy first calling thou wast a babe, thou wouldst not believe that there was such a legion of devils and unclean spirits within thee, thou must overcome ere all be done; but art thou struggling with thy corruptions, to see if thou canst get deadly wounds impressed on them? And dost thou sometimes overcome them, and gettest thou the victory at any time? Then thou art a young man that hast strength and courage to fight the battles of the Lord, and thou art a chosen and tried soldier, set in the camp of Christ: So the fighting against sin and Satan, and against thyself, and the overcoming of temptations, and the abandoning the affections of thy own heart, it is the second degree of repentance.

Now, the *third* sort of Christians are compared to *Fathers*; and these are they that are built and grounded in the faith of Christ, who have ended their battle, and have foughten a good fight, and run the race; and therefore there is laid up for them a crown of glory;

so they have confirmed their peace with God, and yet they have their own temptations left to them, to make them long for the coming of Christ, and for their dissolution, that then they may cease to sin any more; so this constant walking before God with joy and peace, it is the third degree of repentance.

And as there are three sorts of Christians so there are three degrees of repentance, now sometimes all these three will fall in one person; again, some that have been strongest become weakest; as Job, that was a just man, and upright man, and walked before God, he said, "I have terrors within, and sorrows and pains without;" and David, that was a man according to the heart of God, complains, saying, "My God, my God, why hast thou forsaken me?" Psal. xxii. 1. So these two were both strong men, and yet ye see how weak they became, and how far casten down. Sometimes again they that are weak become strong; as Moses, when he fled out of Egypt, for fear of his life, and kept sheep to the priest of Midian, and when the Lord first appeared to him in the bush, then he was but a weakly man; but afterwards being confirmed by the Lord, and sent by him with a commission to the king of Egypt, and having wrought great wonders in the land of Egypt, before the king and the Egyptians, then he was a strong man, and a valiant champion, and was made their captain; then, I say, he was a strong man and a valiant champion. Likewise the disciples, when they all forsook Christ, and left him amongst his enemies hands, then they were but weak men; but after that Christ was raised again, and after that the Holy Ghost was sent down from heaven to them, they were strong men then, and preached boldly in the name of Jesus; likewise women, who are the weaker sort, have not spared to lay down their lives for the cause of Christ. But I leave this.

So thou mayest see that the meanest degree of repentance is in thy first calling; that is, when thy conscience is convicted of an eternity of wrath, when thou neither seest nor feelest any life, nor any spark of grace in thine heart, and suppose thou hast no sense or feeling of the love of God towards thee, yet thou art sustained by the invisible power of God, until the time of thy regeneration and new birth come: so thou must be brought out of the womb, and then thou gettest light to see, and eyes to discern betwixt good and evil; and if thou hast but the meanest degree of repentance, then thou mayest be glad and rejoice, for thou shalt never perish.

The next degree of repentance is more difficult and hard to get, and this is, when thou art fallen into some notable sin, that makes all thy former sins, suppose they be remitted, to be as fresh in thy mind as the first hour thou didst them; then comes terror and fear again, that will make thee to cry, "The Lord is gone away, and he will never come again; I have grieved and quenched his Spirit, therefore he is departed: Is there a possibility that I can be renewed by repentance? I pray but, God shuts out of my prayer; I have set up a wall of hewn stone betwixt his face and me; I cannot mourn, for I want the spirit of mourning:" but yet, if thou be'st the child of God, thou wilt bow thy knees to God; if thou canst not speak, yet thou wilt sigh; and if thou canst not cry, yet thou wilt groan: now, when thou art so, God will come in an instant, and he will soften thy heart, so that it will melt within thee; he shall open thy eyes, and thou shalt look up to heaven, and there cast thine eye upon a Mediator, and lay hold on him by faith; then thou shalt see a blink of his sweet face turning to thee and shining clearly upon thy soul; and then thou wilt hear a sweet and comfortable voice sent from heaven to speak to thy soul, and to say, "Be of good comfort, poor sinner, for I have forgiven thee; now therefore I reconcile my peace with thee." Then thy hatred of sin is renewed, and thy peace with God is renewed, and thou thyself art renewed also: but yet when thou hast gotten thy peace renewed, then the devil comes in, and hearkens to thee in thine ear, "Now thou hast gotten enough, what needest thou any more? Thou art forgiven now, and thy election is made sure : therefore thou mayst take thy liberty to sin, and thou mayest do this or that, that thou pleasest," and so he will steal a sin upon thee, and this sin will banish away the Spirit from thee ; and then comes in again induration and hardness of heart, and there will be nothing left but a little light in thy conscience to controul thee : then thy sorrows begin again, and then thou renewest thy repentance : and this is the last degree of repentance, when after thou hast fallen thou risest again, and thou walkest before God, and thou goest from faith to faith, and *from strength to strength, till* thou *appearest before God in Zion:* but notwithstanding of thy security and induration of heart, yet lay for this a sure ground, thou canst not perish that once hast been born again. Now this much for the degrees of repentance, and yet there remains something to be spoken of touching repentance.

First, What are the contraries of true repentance.

Secondly, What are the means whereby thou mayst get this true repentance who has never yet had it.

Thirdly, Likewise what are the means whereby thou that hast had it, but has lost it, mayest come by it again, if thou wilt use them. And when thou hast gotten it, how thou shalt keep it.

Fourthly, and *last of all,* What are the arguments that may persuade and move you to repentance.

Now, as to the *first,* thou must know that there are many false repentances, and therefore contrary to true repentance : as *first,* And impenitent heart, that neither can nor will repent : let this man brag never so much of his repentance, yet he never had this true repentance, neither did he ever seek it, who has a hard heart and continues in sin.

Secondly, The repentance of an ethnic or civil man, who thinks it enough if he do no wrong to any body, but lives upon his own, and pays all men their debt : and suppose he can do no good, yet he does no evil : yet all this is not true repentance.

Thirdly, There is a repentance that lasts but for a time: for as there is a temporary faith, so there is a temporary repentance which is never true.

Fourthly, There is a dissimulate or counterfeit repentance, such as hypocrites have, and all the world may know that it is false.

Fifthly, That repentance which the church of Rome teaches, it is no true repentance.

Lastly, The desperate repentance which Judas had. So that all these are but false repentances, and therefore contrary to this true repentance.

As to the *first,* An impenitent sinner, that is running on in the way of ungodliness, that says in his heart, " There is not a God," and by no means will be brought back, the scripture calls him a fool, that says in his heart, " There is not a God; he blesseth himself in his heart, but he is cursed of God; he makes a bond with hell, and a covenant with death;" that is, when men will speak of hell to him, he will say, I am sure I will never go there, and in the mean time, he is posting thither as fast as he can : will a man speak of death to him, he will say, I need not be afraid, for all men know that they must die, and I know so must I die; and will a man speak of the pest to him, he will have a thousand lurking places to run to hide himself from it; and will a man speak of famine to him, he will say, he has enough laid up in store for many years; also he says in his heart, I will walk after the stubbornness of my own heart; but the Lord says, I will not be merciful to such a man.

Last of all, He is called a man that sins with a high and uplifted hand, and openly denounces war against God, and avows that he takes part with the devil; " they put the evil day far away from them; they turn judgment into gall, and righteousness into wormwood.

Now, I fear there was never an age or generation since the world began, that has brought out so many plants of impenitent sinners, as this cursed generation now living, who say in their heart, " Let us eat and drink, for to-morrow we will die ;" When need we trouble ourselves every day with preaching and praying? I know the Lord's prayer, and the belief, and the ten commandments, as well as any minister or preacher among them all; I see God has given me enough in this world, and I hope he will give me heaven in my ending day. Thus impenitent sinners make the blessings of God to serve for a rampart or bulwark to keep out the judgments of God, and when God has blessed him with the fat things of this world, he cherishes his soul with them, and so he makes his heart fat against the day of slaughter; and the more he blots out the light of his conscience, the heart of him is always the harder; even as a man's hand, the more it is rubbed and wrought, the harder is the skin of it ; and as a stithy, that the more the smith strikes on it with the hammer, it grows always the harder; and as the apostle says, "They have their minds obscured and alienate from the life of God, through ignorance that is in them, by the hardening of their hearts, who after they have repented have given themselves over to wickedness, and to commit greedily all uncleanness." Therefore seeing there are so many bastard plants in this age, I beseech you, my hearts, look that your hearts be not hardened now at this time; for of all the fearful plagues under heaven, that ever God sent upon any creature, this induration and hardness of heart is the greatest and the most fearful. This is the first sort of false repentance.

The *second* is the repentance of the ethnic and civil men, who never knew God in Christ, and yet naturally they love virtue and abhor vice; as that rich youth that thought he had kept all the commandments from his very youth, because he was no open murderer, nor adulterer, nor oppressor, nor thief, nor a liar, nor a covetous person; and yet for all that, the Lord said, " It is hard for a rich man to enter into the kingdom of heaven." So then this ethnic and civil repentance does a man no good.

The *third* sort of false repentance is that which lasts for a time, and it is compared to a morning cloud that has some appearance of rain, but when the sun rises, and the heat of the day breaks up, it vanishes away; even so a man will show some appearance of repentance, but it soon decays in him. And in another place it is compared to a cake on the gridle unturned; even so this sort of repentance lets the heart never be turned: but this true repentance will turn all the sides of thy soul upside down, first the one side, and then the other; therefore it is called the renting of the heart, "Rent your hearts, and not your garments." And this repentance, which lasts but for a time, is, when a man is wakened in his conscience, and then he resolves to flee evil and do good, but he looks over that which should make his repentance sure, and this is only the blood of Christ: so this temporary repentance is but a remorse for sin; and as long as the fear of wrath lasts, thou wilt resolve to do well, but thou wilt never seek remission esrnestly, nor the renewing of thy heart, and of thy conversion thoroughly.

The *fourth* repentance that is false, is called a dissimulate repentance: and this is, when a man lets on him to the sight of the world that he repents, when there is not so much in his heart and conscience as in Cain's, or Judas's, or Esau's; for they had a remorse for their sin in their consciences, and they wanted nothing but faith in the blood of Jesus Christ, whereas these feigned repentances have not so much as a remorse joined with them.

The *fifth* sort of false repentance is called desperate; that is when a man has neither hope to be delivered, nor faith to lay hold on the blood of Christ, nor patience to wait on the Lord's time of delivery; this made Ahitophel and Judas hang themselves: and in this desperate repentance there is not so much as a desire or longing to be reconciled with God, and nothing can waken them till their consciences leap in their throats, and so drive them to despair.

Sixthly, and *last of all*, There is the Papists repentance, that will never bring peace to the consciences; and therefore it will never do a man good when they have these terrors.

First, They say repentance is a sacrament; but a sacrament must have a seal to represent the thing signified by the sacrament; now repentance has no seal to represent any thing signified, therefore it cannot be a sacrament.

Secondly, They say there is so much free-will left in every man by nature, that may make a man to reach out his hand and grip Christ, and so get remission and repentance; but the scriptures say, "We are all dead in sin;" now, as a dead man can neither stir hand nor foot but as he is moved by another man, even so no man can by nature grip to the blood of Christ but as he is moved by the Spirit of God; for the preparing grace, the preventing grace, the turning grace, the preserving grace, and the crowning grace, must all come from God.

Thirdly, They say thou must confess all thy sins to the priest, and if thou hidest any of them there is no remission for thee; but that confession is only necessary for thee when thou hast a burden lying on thy conscience that troubles thee, and when thou hast sinned publicly, then thou shouldst make a public confession; and when thy sins are private, then thou confessest them privately to thy brother, or to any other that can give thee comfort; or when thou hast failed to thy brother, then run to him and confess thy fault, and desire him to forgive thee, and to satisfy him: and when thou hast a secret guiltiness upon thee, that thou canst get no comfort in prayer, or in hearing of the word, or in any other exercise of religion, then go to thy pastor, or to any other that can give thee comfort, and open thy mind to him, and desire him to pray for thee; but confession is not to be used any other way.

Fourthly, and *last of all*, They say it is presumption for a man to believe remission of sins to himself as long as he is in this life. Judge ye then in what a woful case they cast the consciences of the poor ignorant people. But I leave this. Now I have told you what are the contraries to true repentance, which are but false, that ye may discern betwixt the false and the true.

I come now to the means whereby thou shalt get repentance that never yet hadst it; and these means are commanded by God in his word, the which if thou usest, God shall give them a blessing.

First, Thou must put away from thee these four false rules of repentance by which many deceive themselves.

Secondly, Thou must take to thee these true rules prescribed by God in his word.

The *first* false rule thou must quit is thy natural reason and wisdom of nature; for the wisdom of the flesh is an enemy to God, and it will never be subject to God nor to the wisdom of God.

Secondly, Thou must quit thy natural sense and feeling, either in adversity or prosperity, in joy or in wrath; for thou must make none of those a rule for to lead thy life by: for thou mayest be in prosperity in this life, and yet casten into hell afterwards; as Ishmael had worldly prosperity enough, yet he was a reprobate; likewise Esau and the rich glutton, they had wealth and ease enough in this world, yet they are now in hell; for this is wrong reason for thee to say, God loves me because he hath given me enough in this world: by the contrary, thou mayest be in adversity and yet the beloved child of God; as poor Lazarus, who was full of sores, and was glad that the dogs came and licked his wounds, and was glad to beg a piece of bread at other folks gates, and could not get it, yet when he died the angels carried him to heaven. Further thou mayest be under the sense of terrors and wrath, as Job and David were, and yet be the dear child of God; yea thou mayest cry, I am forsaken, I am forgotten, and yet God may have thee in his arms; by the contrary, thou mayest be in security and joy, and cry peace, when suddenly comes destruction; and when thou thinkest thee sure of heaven thou mayest be shortly casten into hell, ere ever thou knowest of thyself; so thy sense will deceive thee.

The *third* false rule that thou must quit, is thy own lusts and affections; for some have made their honour a rule to their life, and so they will repent so far as it will stand with their honour; some have made their riches a rule to their life, and they will repent so far as they be not hurt in their goods; but they never remember that they came naked into this world, and naked must return.

Fourthly, and *last of all*, Thou must quit the false repentance of the Papists, and that temporary repentance, when men begin fairly, and give a fair show of repentance, but afterwards make a foul end. All those repentances will do thee no good, therefore thou must cast them from thee. Now, when thou hast quit thee of these false rules, take thee to these true rules.

The *first* true rule to come by repentance, it is to labour to understand the believed law, and the believed gospel, and thou must believe the naked word to be come out of the mouth of God, and thou must believe it with all thy heart and soul, and thou must believe all God's threatenings as well as his promises; and thou must believe the whole word of God constantly unto thy life's end.

The *second* rule of repentance is this, Thou must examine thyself, and take a view of thy by-gone life by the law of God; and thou must take up thy particular sins in every command; as in the first command, look to thy ignorance of God, to thy forgetfulness of his love and kindness; look to thy mistrust of God; look to thy former contempt of God, and that thou hast done worse than ever Judas did, for he sold Christ but once for thirty pieces of silver, but thou hast sold him ten thousand times, and for far less than thirty pennies. Go to the second command, and see there thy neglect and contempt of God's worship, and

SERMON IX.

look if thou be'st answerable to the commandment of Christ, saying, " Watch and pray continually; in all things be thankful ; my sheep hear my voice, and obey it; let my law be written on the tables of thy heart; let it be as a signet on thy hand, as a frontlet to thy brows, and as an honey-comb to thy mouth; let all thy delight be in the law of God, and meditate thereon both day and night." Go to the third command, and look how oft-times thou hast used the name and worship of God vainly, rashly, and irreverently, and unfruitfully, without preparation, without feeling, without reverence, and without profit, &c. Examine thyself in every command, and remember the lawgiver, who is God himself, speaking from heaven out of a terrible fire, and with a fearful voice, that all the mount shook, and the people trembled, so that they could not abide to hear that voice : and remember also the curse that is tied to every command, for it is said cursed be he that abides not in all the commandments to keep them : this was the practice of the church in the time of Jeremiah.

Next, thou must know Christ as he is humbled, and as he is glorified, and see him so in the gospel, as he is revealed there; then see if thou hast gone all these steps that Christ went before thee ; then look on his death, at his slain and crucified body, and see if it has slain and crucified thy sins, and laid them in the grave with him. Then look if his resurrection hath raised thee up from death to life ; look upon him sweating blood in the garden : look on his hands bound with cords : look on him led to Annas, and from Annas to Caiaphas, and from him to Pilate and from Pilate to Herod, and from Herod to Pilate again : look on him scourged, and a crown of thorns plated upon his bare head, and the blood trickling down his cheeks ; look upon him trailing the tree upon his back after him whereon he was crucified ; look upon him hanging upon the cross, and drinking vinegar mixed with gall, and a spear thrust through his side, and his heart's blood coming out there : then, last of all, look upon him dead, and laid in the grave, and there thou shalt have matter enough to humble thee; so judge thyself, and God shall not judge thee: but, if thou delayest the examination of thyself unto the latter day, then dreadful and terrible shall thy examination be. Therefore, if there were no more to condemn thee but the very cogitations of thy heart, suppose thou hadst never consented to do them, yet they will be enough to condemn thee; for the apostle said, "That his very thoughts, after he had known the law, they slew him."

Now, after your trial, arraign yourselves before the tribunal of God; put up your own dittay, accuse yourselves, tell out your sins, and all their circumstances, before God; last of all, give out the decree and sentence of condemnation against yourselves; and when ye have done this, then go to prayer, appeal from before the tribunal of God's justice, and run to the throne of grace and beg mercy at his hands, for Christ's sake; so take Christ with thee, and take him as the Son of God, and take him as thy brother also, and made flesh for thy sake; take him laid in the crib, tempted, weary, hungry, thirsty, poor, and subject to all thy infirmities; and, in a word, take him humbled; take him glorified: take him with all these graces; take his righteousness to cover thee, his obedience to absolve thee, and sanctification to sanctify thee; and then cry, pity, pity, pardon, pardon, cover me with thy blood: for then I know the Father cannot be angry with me; may I not get mercy where thousands have gotten mercy before? for thou hast forgiven such as have had their hands in thy heart's blood, and have cried, "Crucify him, crucify him." Thou hast said, Lord, that whosoever believes in thee, the only begotten Son of God, shall be saved: "Lord, I believe, Lord, help my unbelief." Then gladly wilt thou apply these glad news to thy own soul, when he shall say, Son, be of good comfort, I have forgiven thee: for I will not let thee perish. Then thou wilt say, what thanks shall I render to thee, my Lord, and my

God? what shall I do to please thee? then he will direct thee to the law, that thou must keep his commandments, and let them be a rule whereby to lead thy life: and if thou wouldst please God, and live godly, this is the only way to do it. These are the means whereby thou that hadst never yet repentance mayest now get it at the last, if thou wilt use them: therefore I beseech you all, in the bowels of Christ, and I charge you, before God, as ye would be saved in that great day, see ye that have not gotten this true repentance, that ye would use the means faithfully and diligently in time, that ye may get it in some measure, in this world, before ye depart this life; for, think on, I tell you, if ye will not use them, because ye think them hard to do, I tell you, ye shall think it harder to abide in hell for evermore. I will say no more, but will commend you all, and this that hath been spoken, to the grace of God in Christ Jesus, Amen. So let it be.

SERMON X.

ON REPENTANCE.

Rev. ii. 5.

Remember therefore from whence thou art fallen, and repent, and do the first works; or else I will come unto thee quickly, and will remove thy candlestick out of his place, except thou repent.

I NEED not to repeat to you the heads of repentance, my brethren, which hitherto I have handled; therefore I will put you only in remembrance of the things we have had last in hand, which were the means whereby ye might get repentance that never yet got it. Ye heard it was by examination of yourselves in the balance of the written word of God, in the believed law and the believed gospel. In this examination ye must, *First*, Put away the false rules that will deceive you. And, *next*, ye must take unto you the true rules, that will lead you to true repentance. As for the false rules:

First, Thou must renounce thy own light, and thy own natural reason, and thou must learn the wisdom of God.

Secondly, Thou must renounce thy own sense and feeling, yea, and thy own judgment according to thy sense.

Thirdly, Thou must not content thyself with a temporary repentance, no more nor with a temporary faith, because thou sinnest daily, therefore thou must repent daily.

Fourthly and *lastly*, Thou must quit the false repentance of the Papists. And, as for the true rules ye heard,

First, That ye behooved to weigh yourselves in the balance of the law and of the gospel.

Secondly, Thou must believe the whole truths of God's word, as come out of the mouth of God himself.

Thirdly, Ye must believe all his commandments to be lawful, all his promises to be true, all his threatenings and judgments to be just, and that they will come to pass, and thou must apply them to thyself as spoken unto thee.

Fourthly and *lastly,* Thou must believe all the precepts of the gospel, suppose they pass thy natural understanding.

Now, in thy believing, there must be these six things.

First, Thou must believe the naked word of God, suppose it reach beyond thy capacity.

Secondly, Thou must believe it sincerely because it comes out of the mouth of God.

Thirdly, Thou must believe not only the doctrine taught out of the word of God, to be needful and good to thy soul, but also thou must believe all the threatenings, and all the promises of God, that they will come to pass.

Fourthly, Thou must believe the whole word, with all thine heart, soul, mind, and strength.

Fifthly, Thou must believe it with an honest heart, and with a mind purposing to make it the only rule and square of thy life.

Sixthly, Thou must believe and obey it constantly unto thy life's end, and not in one place only, but in all places, wherever thou comest; and not in some companies, but in all companies, and at all occasions: but I mean not, that thou wilt get all these things at the first times, for thou wilt have many wrestlings with thy own incredulity and impenitency; and I mean not, that all these things can be perfected here, for neither thy faith nor thy repentance can be perfect in this life, but when thou hast gotten this faith and believing, thou must let it reign in thy heart as a crowned king, with a sceptre to bruise and trample down all thy doubtings and incredulity, with a sword to slay all the temptations of Satan, and with a crown as victorious conqueror over sin, and the world, and over thy own self. This faith then will draw thee to Christ, to get remission of sins, for it assures thee that suppose thy soul and thy sins be as red as scarlet, yet he shall make it as white as snow; and suppose thou beest a bruised reed, yet he will not break thee; and if thou be but a smoking flax, yet he will not quench thee. This is for thee that never hadst repentance.

Now I will speak to the way how thou shalt renew and recover thy repentance, that hast left it off, and hardly canst come by it again.

First, Thou must have a new sight and sense of thy sins by looking into the law of God, and see if this can break thy heart.

Secondly, Thou must stir up thy faith again, and renew thy grips of Jesus Christ, and so take a new bit of his flesh and a new drink of his blood, and put them all upon thee.

Thirdly, Thou must renew thy love to God, and foster it in thy heart, by remembering his kindness and his love towards thee.

Fourthly, Thou must renew thy fear, and stand in awe of God, as a son of his father, or a servant of his master.

Fifthly, Thou must shoot out thy head and wait daily for the Lord's appearing in the clouds; and thou must always be preparing, and decking, and trimming thy soul with the wedding garment.

Sixthly, Thou must watch and pray continually, and often times purge and cleanse thy heart by fasting and prayer, that the unclean spirit may be driven out that holds thee captive.

Seventhly, Acquaint thyself with God by talking familiarly with him, and by making thy heart a house for him to dwell in.

Eighthly, Thou must make a particular reckoning of God's blessings, one by one, and cast them not in a mass together, for they must not be confounded.

Ninthly, Put on the whole armour of God upon thee daily, and stand as an armed man ready to fight against principalities and powers, and not only to resist them, but also to overcome them.

Tenthly and *lastly*, Keep thy peace with God, and when thou awakest in the morning, give him the first thoughts of thy heart, and thou shalt no sooner bow thy knees to God, but the Lord shall meet thee with a blessing; and when thou hast bowed thy knees to God thyself alone, then go to thy private worship in the family; and when thou hast done this, then go to thy calling, and be faithful and diligent in the same. Again, if thou comest into good company, thou mayest be the bolder, therefore when ye meet together, sharpen one another, confess your sins one to another, and stir up and quicken one another: but if ye come into evil company, then thou shouldst labour to get some grace to thyself, or else to leave some behind thee, and when they are speaking of earthly things, then speak thou of heavenly things; as for example, when they are speaking of water, then speak thou of the water of life, and when they are speaking of bread, then speak thou of the bread of life; and in this thou followest the example of thy Saviour; and in thy calling use this world as if thou used it not, do thy office, but let thy heart be in heaven; and in all thy troubles possess thy soul with patience, for thou wilt not want thy crosses if it were but thy wife, bairns, or thy servants at home: and ere thou goest to thy bed, sit down and count every mercy that thou hast received all the day long, either in the private or public worship of God, in company or alone; and in making up thy accounts take up thy wants; so that was thy heart hardened, that thou couldst get no feeling of wants, if thou wantest the presence of God in thy calling, then confess this before God, and desire mercy and pardon of all thy sins, either in neglect, or in contempt, of thy private or public duty, or thy forgetfulness of God's mercies and blessings, or in hardening thy heart through security, and this shall confirm thy peace when thou liest down, and the same peace shall stir thee up at midnight, and it shall bid thee rise to serve God, for thou wilt think it over long to lie still till the morning. But ye will think it hard to practise these things every day, yet take the yoke of Jesus Christ upon you, and ye shall think it sweet; yea, thou shalt find it to be the sweetest burden that ever thou barest; and see that ye be not as that evil and slothful servant, which got but one talent, and because he thought it too little, therefore he would not use it, but went and hid it in the earth; so there are many that think these means impossible: No, no; try them, I pray thee, one day, and from one day to another, and from two days to a whole week, and then ye shall find the easiest and sweetest think in the world, is the yoke of Christ our Lord: but if ye will not try it, well, I can say no more, but "he that is filthy, let him be filthy still;" for I assure you, "the Lord is coming with a reward in his hand, and will reward every man according to his works;" and thou that findest mercy, shalt wonder that ever the Lord should have looked on such a vile wretch as thou art; yet this is the unspeakable riches of his mercy, that whom he hath called, them also "he hath justified;" but here is all the mystery of it, that "whom he has justified, he has also glorified," as though it were already done; this is it, thy glorious conversation: here begins thy glory, that thou wouldst not exchange thy sweet familiarity and fellowship with God for ten thousand worlds, and thou wouldst not exchange it for all the pleasures under heaven: for whose image countest thou glorious, if thou countest not the image of God glorious? Thinkest thou it nothing to be like the eternal image of the Father? But thou whose conversation is glorious, thou hast the Father's image drawn on thy soul: Shalt thou doubt then to bear his glorious image in heaven, that hast born his image on the earth.

Now, because ye will think this heavy and difficult, therefore I will tell you some reasons to move you to practise this repentance.

First, It shall free thee from thy present misery, which is this, thou hast a conscience within thee that sits as a notar, and pens up in register thereof, every the least evil thought that thou hast conceived, for to keep it into memory, and to bring it out in that great day before men and angels, the which conscience shall be the first to accuse thee, and it shall present all thy sins before thee: they shall say to thee, "I am thy child, for thou conceivedst me, and broughtest me forth; therefore thou canst not deny me:" And thy conscience shall be the first to condemn thee; yea, it shall be the first to put in execution the decree that shall pass against thee, if thou repentest not in time; but repentance will make the same conscience take another pen and subscribe thy discharge, and it shall put up, in a register, all the motions of God's Spirit that ever thou gottest, and all the faithful works that ever thou wroughtest in God's service, and shall present them before the tribunal of God, as the works of a faithful servant and penitent man. That is the first misery that repentance will free thee from.

Secondly, This is thy misery, that thou art a drudge and bond slave to the devil; but repentance makes thee a child of God. Farther it makes thy soul, that was a sty to unclean spirits, to be made the temple of God, wherein he shall dwell; and of a strumpet and harlot, it makes thee the Lamb's wife.

Thirdly, This is thy misery, that condemnation in hell is thy portion, and the wrath of God is above thy head; for "he that believes not is condemned already;" but when once thou believest and repentest, there is no condemnation to thee, then the sconce of the blood of Christ is betwixt thee and the wrath of God.

Fourthly, This is thy misery, "cursed art thou when thou goest in, and cursed art thou when thou goest out: cursed in the field, and cursed when thou art at home; cursed is thy dough in thy basket, and the meat that thou puttest in thy mouth: cursed is the fruit of thy womb, and thy cattle, and the fruit of thy land : and cursed is all that thou puttest thy hand to." But repentance turns all these curses to as many blessings.

Fifthly, This is thy misery, that as many pricks as thou gettest in thy conscience, they are as so many flashes of the fire of hell, and as many crosses and afflictions as God lays on thee, they are as so many suburbs of hell to thee ; but repentance will turn all thy terrors into joy, and all thy crosses to the best for thee.

Sixthly, This is thy misery, that there is a dungeon under thee, and thou art hanging above it, and art like to fall into it, thou hast nothing to hold thee out of it, but the small thread of thy life, which the wheels of heaven are daily winding up ; and thou canst not tell how soon that hunger-bitten worm death will knaw it in two, and so thou mayest fall into the dungeon ; but repentance will fasten thy grips, and make thee to reach up to the blood of Christ in time, and to hold him fast in the arms of thy soul, and suppose thou wouldst let him go, yet he will never let thee go ; and when the blood of Christ being reached to thee, then the arm of God shall take a grip of thee, and these two grips shall never loose asunder.

Seventhly and *last of all*, This is thy misery, that, in the time of death, when thou seest that thy glass is run, and the sun is going down on thee, and that there is a darkness before whereunto thou must pass, and that thou must go before the tribunal of God, and that thou hast no warrant nor discharge to take with thee, then thou would gladly stay, but it will be to no purpose to thee ; for when thou thinkest on heaven which thou hast lost through thy negligence and security ; and when thou seest the torment which thou must endure perpetually, then thou thinkest thy pain intolerable ; and when thou lookest into the world, and seest it but a foul mire, wherein thou hast wallowed thyself; and when thou seest thou hast been all thy days weaving a spider's web, which will not clothe thee ; and when thou considerest what a fool thou hast been, in losing an eternity of joy for a moment of pleasure ; then thou wilt shake and tremble for fear; then thy back and belly both will fall upon thee ; then thy sins shall start up against thee, and pull thee by the throat, and being armed with the wrath of God, and the condemnation of the law and gospel ; then thou wilt say, what O my conscience, art thou so severe against me? I failed never against thee; and seeing thou art so sore against me, what then will God be, whom I have offended? Can any body tell the terrors of that doleful conscience which shall be awakened, and hast not thy peace made sure before-hand? And suppose thou wouldst then repent, yet it shall flee from thee, because it is out of time, and then thou hast no knowledge how to repent.

Next, when thou wouldst call on God, then thou gettest this answer, "When I called upon thee in the day of thy peace, thou wouldst not hear me, therefore now thou shalt call upon me, but I will not hear thee now." But repentance shall free thee from all thy miseries; it shall make thy end glorious and sweet to thee, so that thou shalt lay down thy body in peace in the grave, and knowing assuredly the Lord shall keep it there until the day of thy resurrection ; and when others shall rise at the resurrection to condemnation, thou shalt rise at the resurrection to life.

Now, seeing death is said to have woolen feet, that none can hear it when it comes, and it comes speedily, were it not good then to prepare us in time to die daily, that when it comes ye need not fear it, having thy peace made sure with God ; but if thou liest not down in peace, and the assurance of mercy subscribed in thy conscience, and sealed with the Spirit of God; O! then terrible shall be thy rising in that great day ; doleful shall that meeting of thy soul and body be when they are joined together ; for the sun shall lose his light, and never shine upon thee any more ; heaven and earth shall run together, and the rocks shall cleave, and the mountains leap together ; and the seas shall roar and the elements melt ; the heavens shall roll away as a scroll of paper, and the earth shall be burnt up with fire: The Judge shall be terrible to thee, for he shall not

Y

only judge thee by the evil thou hast done, but also by the good which thou hast left undone; terrible shall thy reckoning be in that day, no excuse will be admitted there, no advocate to speak for thee, no appeal to a higher judge; and thou shalt be compelled to hear that sentence, which never shall be called back again, "Depart from me, ye workers of iniquity, into the everlasting fire of hell," where thou shalt always be dying, but never be dead, thy pain always beginning, but never shall have an end.

Therefore, my brethren, repent in time, and grip to the blood of Christ and it shall save you. The Lord work it in all your hearts, for Christ's sake; to whom, with the Father and Holy Spirit, be all honour, glory and praise for evermore. *Amen.*

SERMON XI.

OF THE CHRISTIAN WARFARE.

Ephes. vi. 10——21.

Finally, my brethren, be strong in the Lord, and in the power of his might. Put on the whole armour of God, that ye may be able to stand against the wiles of the devil. For we wrestle not against flesh and blood, but against principalities, against powers, against the rulers of the darkness of this world, against spiritual wickedness in high places. Wherefore, take unto you the whole armour of God, that ye may be able to stand in the evil day, and having done all, to stand. Stand therefore, having your loins girt about with truth, and having on the breast plate of righteousness, and your feet shod with the preparation of the gospel of peace: above all take the shield of faith, wherewith ye shall be able to quench all the fiery darts of the wicked. And take the helmet of salvation, and the sword of the Spirit, which is the word of God: praying always, with all prayer and supplication in the Spirit, and watching thereunto with all perseverance, and supplication for all saints; and for me, that utterance may be given unto me, that I may open my mouth boldly, to make known the mystery of the gospel, for which I am an ambassador in bonds, that therein I may speak boldly as I ought to speak.

BECAUSE the time either of your hearing, or my speaking unto you in the name of the Lord is uncertain, and we know not how soon the Lord will make an end of either your or my pilgrimages; therefore it is the desire of my heart, to be led by God at these times, morning and evening, to insist in those things ye have most need of; and if the Lord will give thee time, and keep the door open, for no man can shut it as long as he keeps it open, and when he shuts no man can open; I say, if the Lord will, when this exercise of your Christian warfare, whereof I mind to speak, shall be ended, then I purpose to go through every point of religion. Albeit, now I would speak of the most needful things; and what is more needful to you than your information in your Christian warfare? What is the life of a Christian but a daily battle? Suppose the profane of the world spend hours and days in trifles, and other things concerning this life; yet as many as God has called, and has given his livery to, they find that all the hours in their life are nothing but a continual falling or rising, wrestling or fighting, or one exercise or other.

Therefore, I mind, by the grace of God, to inform you, how ye shall fight your battles; how ye shall put on your armour, and take your weapons in your hands; wherewith, if ye will use them right, ye shall get the victory; and when ye have gotten the victory, how ye shall stand; and when ye are fallen, how ye shall rise again; for many never as yet have persuaded themselves to be wounded, while, in the mean time, they are most deadly wounded; and many, while they perceive themselves to be wounded and to have fallen, they know not how to rise again; many are wounded with terrors and fears, and are overcome, what with one temptation or other; but they perceive not the enemy that has wounded them, and has given them the stroke: neither can they tell how to recover.

Now, seeing no man is crowned without striving, and to him that overcomes, it is promised, that *he shall inherit all things*: but the fearful, and he that faints in the battle, and unbelievers, " shall have their portion in the lake that burns with fire and brimstone, which is the second death." Therefore as ye would have the crown set upon your head, ye must first set your feet in the field to fight; and if ye would overcome and inherit all things, ye must first make yourself fit for battle. The grounds of those things that I am to speak of are these.

First, I will tell you the necessity of this combat and warfare.

Secondly, The purpose of God in the dispensation of his grace, that he who might fully sanctify thee there, yet he will leave as much sin in thy heart as shall keep thee under a perpetual exercise of a continual warfare all the days of thy life. It is good to know the cause why the Lord doth this.

Thirdly, I am to give you such grounds as may underprop you, that ye faint not in your battle.

Fourthly, I am to tell you how ye are to prepare for your battles and combats, that ye may know your enemies, not as they set themselves down, but as Jesus Christ your captain has set them down in his word.

Fifthly, I am to tell you how ye shall furnish yourselves, and with what armour ye shall fight, and in end get the victory; the which armour, if ye will put it on, and wear it, it shall not bring a doubtsome, but a certain and true victory.

Sixthly, Then I am to come to the battle itself; and so I am a mind to tell you of all the cruel, violent, and deceitful dealings, whereby the devil uses to overcome the saints.

Seventhly, Then I am to tell you of the policy which the enemy uses, that will take the advantage of all the circumstances whereby he may overcome thee; he will look to thy disposition, whether thou beest given to this sin, or that, and he will take his advantage in that: he will look to the place thou art in, and the company thou art among, and he will take his advantage there also; he will look to thy calling, and take his advantage there also; he will look to thy present state, and see whether thou beest in prosperity or adversity, and he will take his advantage herein also.

Then I come to tell you, how each one of you shall behave yourselves in your fight, and how you shall be in readiness at all times to stand against the enemy by the power of the Lord, in the day of your temptations; and when ye are fallen, how ye shall rise again.

After these generals, I am come to the particulars, wherein I am to let you see, how that from the beginning of the first link of your salvation grounded upon the love of God, till ye come to the last link, which is your glorification, Satan has his particular assaults against every one of these links.

The *first* fountain of thy salvation is the love of God to thee in Jesus Christ, and Satan will essay to bereave thee of that, and so withhold the sense of this love from thy heart.

Secondly, From this love comes thy election; therefore he will try whether he can make thee presume or despair, and make thee believe thy name was never written and put up in the book of life.

Thirdly, He will go about to hinder thy calling, that neither the word nor the Spirit ever called thee : or, if thou beest called, he will try if he can make thee call thy calling in question, and he will make thee believe it was not effectual. And in thy calling, he will make thee call in question the truth of thy faith and repentance. Then he has his temptations against prayer, meditation, and hearing of the word, thanksgiving, and against all the parts of the worship of God, and against all the means whereby the Lord maintains his graces in the hearts of his own. Then he has temptations against thy justification, sanctification, perseverance, and hope.

And *last of all*, He has his temptations at the last hour of thy death : the which combat will be the sorest of all.

Now, I have told you the ground of these things, that, by the grace of God, I mind to speak of to you at these times.

First, That ye may not weary in coming to hear them morning and evening : that ye may know in what order and rank ye are in when ye are tempted; that knowing ye are tempted, ye may furnish to your-

selves such armour as is most meet for your estate.
Now, I hope that I am led by God in this: and therefore I beseech you to help me in your prayer to God,
and that ye would beseech God to vouchsafe his blessing and presence to this exercise.

I believe there are many of you that never yet knew
what it is to fight hand for hand with the enemy, and
many of you have never yet known his craft and policy, that sometimes can present himself to you in his
own visage and colour, and sometimes can transform
himself into an angel of light, that he may the more
subtilely prevail against you, and so bring his wicked
and cruel purposes to pass; and many, when they have
fallen, have not known it; and suppose ye know ye
have fallen, yet ye know not how ye shall rise again;
therefore what can be more needful both to you and
me, nor to know our Christian warfare, seeing every
hour of the day we have to do with the enemy? Is it
not needful then for us to know sure grounds out of
the word of God, that the Lord has set down there, to
be infallible marks, whereby we may know that he
has loved us in his Son Christ Jesus before all beginning; and that he has elected him to be our head, and
us to be his members, in that eternal decree past in the
council of God; and that he hath put up our names
in the book of life ere ever the world was made; and
that he has redeemed us by his only begotten Son?
And is it not needful to know the particular grounds
whereby we may know that we are truly called, truly
justified, and sanctified, and to know your begun glory, which one day shall be perfected in heaven?

Secondly, Let the experience of all the saints bear
witness to you of the necessity of this combat; and if
thou beest one of them, thou wilt never be so soon
brought out of the arms of the devil, and set in the
bosom of the church of God, but thou must as soon
make thee ready for legions of devils, to fight against
thee: and therefore the apostle says here, *Now finally*;
as though he would say, 'This is the last thing ye
must do, without which ye can do nothing, ye must

put on the whole armour of God. And to prove this by examples, Abel, as soon as he had offered sacrifice to God, because it was acceptable to God through faith, Cain was stirred up by Satan against him, and he slays him. The Israelites, as soon as they came out of Egypt, and passed to the wilderness to serve their God, Satan stirs up Pharaoh against them, who with a great army pursued them to the Red-sea; and yet, notwithstanding, the Lord drowned him, and all his host, and made his own people to go through safe. Paul was no sooner converted, than as soon was he persecuted. Our Lord and master, Jesus Christ, was no sooner inaugurated and authorised in his calling, but as soon Satan tempts him forty days and forty nights in the wilderness. So then you shall no sooner renounce the camp of the devil, and set thy feet in the Lord's camp, but as soon the devil will set upon thee. Now, the cause why every one sees not this, is this; as long as the strong man possesses the house, all things are at peace; but when a stronger than he comes in, then he is dispossessed; for thou mayest eat, thou mayest drink, thou mayest go, thou mayest sit, thou mayest lie, thou mayest rise peaceably, in whom the devil is, because there is not a contrariety in thee, for God is not in thee; therefore the wicked may have peace, but it is doleful peace: but the godly, because both God and the devil, light and darkness, righteousness and unrighteousness, a Jacob and an Esau are within them, therefore they cannot be without warfare; and this is casten in as an argument of comfort to thee, Rev. xii. 17. "The dragon made war with the woman and her seed, that feared God and kept his commandments;" and indeed this is a matter of great consolation, for it makes the devil war against thee when thou art at peace with God; does the devil envy thee, then God loves thee; does the devil pursue thee, then God defends thee: and, in a word, is the devil angry with thee, then God is at peace with thee; so this may bring comfort to thee that art entered into this warfare.

Now, ye feel the necessity of it; for what is your

life but a continual warfare ? And as many of you as have been brought out of the arms of that strong man, ye know this to be true ; but as to the rest, he holds them in peace, he never troubles them ; it may be ye all understand not this, therefore I will expound it to you.

Who is the strong man ? The devil. What is this house that he keeps ? The soul or the heart of man or woman. What is this peace ? It is such a rest and quietness in their mind, that the devil propines out of a golden cup to them, and they drink it sweetly ; and there is such a rest in the pleasures of this world, that such as have it, they have not so much as a desire to forsake them, and to get out of his arms : but it is otherwise with the child of God, that has renounced the pleasures of this world, and is taken out of the arms of the devil ; there is no more peace within them, but a continual warfare all the days of their life : therefore thou that art chosen, in that hour thou settest thy foot in the camp of Jesus, and fightest under the banner of his blood : and in that hour thou resolvest to go out of this world to serve the Lord in the wilderness, in that same hour the red dragon will be on thee with all his might ; as ye may see clearly by the example forecited. As long as the children of Israel were under the bondage and thraldom of Pharaoh in Egypt, and as long as they delighted in the flesh-pots of Egypt, they had peace and rest with Pharaoh ; but as soon as Moses came to Pharaoh, and desired him to let the people of God go, then Pharaoh laid heavier burdens on them, and all to keep them under, that they should not offer to desire to go out to serve the Lord their God in the wilderness ; even so, as soon as thou desirest to come out of the Egypt of this world, to serve the Lord thy God in the wilderness and quit Egypt, then cruel Pharaoh (I mean the devil) will labour to hold thee under with the grievous burdens of thy sins, that thou shalt not get leave to serve the Lord thy God with such freedom and liberty of spirit as thou wouldst do ; and if thou wilt but come out in despite

Z

of him, then he will not cease to pursue thee, and follow thee to the Red-sea.

Likewise, as long as Moses was counted Pharaoh's daughter's son, he was well esteemed of all men; but so soon as he desired rather to suffer affliction with his poor brethren, the people of God than to enjoy the pleasures of sin for a season; as soon did the devil envy him, and he is compelled to flee out of Egypt, and to serve a stranger in a strange land, and there to be a shepherd for the space of forty years. And as long as Paul was in nature, and not planted in grace, he had joy and peace enough; that he thought his life and conversation unblameable, but as soon as he begins to bear the name of Jesus, then the devil rages against him, and he bears such a malice at him, that he is persecuted from city to city, and the enemy never leave him, till he had foughten his fight, run his race, and finished his course, and was persuaded that a *Crown of glory was laid up for him*; then Satan was disappointed, God was glorified, and he was more and more confirmed.

And last of all, as soon as he that was Head and Captain of all, is no sooner inaugurate into his calling and the Holy Ghost no sooner comes down and lights on him in the likeness of a dove, thereafter he gets no longer leisure, but incontinent he is led into the wilderness, and the devil sets on him, once, twice, thrice, and he never left him during all the time of his humility, till he brought him to the grave; but in the end he overcomes sin, Satan, and the grave: he rises again, and he goes to heaven, and *leads captivity captive*. So this is true, as long as ye are sleeping in your sins, and drinking in the pleasures of this life, and as long as that armed and strong man holds the castle of your heart; then all things will be in peace, and there will be no trouble in your consciences; but as soon as the strong man is dispossest, and beaten out of you, then there will be no more peace, but a daily war within and without, at home and abroad, waking and sleeping, or whatever thou beest doing.

Now, what is the cause there is no war in thy heart, that art not in Christ? I will tell thee, there cannot be a warfare but betwixt two opposite enemies, and as for thee that art not yet renewed, God is not in thy heart, but only the devil; in the heart that is not renewed, all is but flesh: and in thee that art not renewed there is but only darkness; but in thee that are renewed there is God, and the devil both; there is flesh and spirit, there is light and darkness, and there rises a combat: so the man or woman that is not born over again, they may well have remorses and pricks in their consciences, but as for a wrestling or striving, and combat to pull up sin by the root, they never had experience of it; therefore, thou that hast no warfare, thou hast no cause to rejoice, because there is nothing within thee but the devil, darkness and the flesh; but thou hast cause to rejoice that findest a battle within thee, for if thou wert not the spouse of Christ, and fearedst not God, and endeavouredst to keep his commandments, the devil would never have made war against thee: therefore whosoever thou art, that hast this combat, it is a sure argument to thee, that thou art a child of God.

Question. But ye will ask, What is the cause that so wise, so mighty, and so gracious a Lord, filled with love and compassion, that has power to perfect thy sanctification fully in this life? why will he not renew all thy heart at an instant? and why suffers he so cruel a dog as the devil to pursue thee; that seeks nothing but his dishonour (which is a higher point than thy damnation) that because he knows thy justification, sanctification, and thy glorification will honour him, therefore he aims at these points to overthrow them?

Answer. Is this, believe ye, for want of love? No, no; it is out of love he does it; and that for two causes.

First, For his own honour and name's sake.

Secondly, For thy weal and good; therefore thou must content thyself to be under this continual warfare all the days of thy life, seeing God is honoured thereby; and also seeing it has been, is, and shall be the lot of all the children of God, from the beginning to the end of the world; God, if thou beest his, has ordained it for thee, ere ever thou wast born.

Quest. Now thou wilt ask, How turns this to the glory of God, and to thy weal?

Answ. First thy temptations bring glory to God in two respects;

First, God gets great glory, when he makes thee that art sold under sin, an impotent body, a silly, weak and feeble creature, a simple soldier overcome legions of devils, bring down the prince of the air and the god of this world, and makes thee set thy foot upon his neck, and trample him under thy feet; it is true he might do this himself, yet he will not do it, but he will have thee that art a base and wicked creature doing it, that his glory may appear the more: for ay the weaker that thou that art the instrument be, the more the power of God is seen in thy infirmity, by giving thee the victory. Therefore, as Joshua called for all Israel, and charged them to set their feet on the necks of those princes of Canaan, Josh. x. 4. so does the Lord Jesus, our true Joshua, call upon us, and charge us to set our feet upon principalities, and powers, and worldly governors, and princes of the air, and spiritual wickedness, and he commands us to set our feet upon their necks and tramp on them, that they never rise, nor get up any more to do us harm.

Secondly, God will have thee exercised with temptations, that he may bring forth his high and excellent graces that are in thee: Would ever Job's patience have been known, had it not been that he had been tried with manifold temptations, one after another? Would ever David's repentance been known, were it not for the manifold conflicts he had? or would ever Paul's strength, or Peter's zeal have been known, were it not the manifold conflicts that they had? So God will have the angels, the devil, and the world to be very onlookers on these hid mercies and graces that are in thee, that when the angels see it, they may glorify God for it, and they may say, now I see there is faith, there is repentance, there is patience, there is hope, there is grace, there is Christ; and by these means God makes known the riches of his grace in the hearts of his own, that otherwise would be hid, were it not for temptations as long as thou livest. Next, great is the good thou wilt get by temptations.

First, By temptations he will make thee confess the very sins of thy youth, as he did Job, which otherwise thou wouldst never have remembered nor repented of them; therefore by temptations he calls them to thy mind; he makes thee mourn for them, and will never let thee rest till thou gettest remission; for if thou hadst not known them, and remembered them, and repented of them, thou hadst never been forgiven; for without knowledge, no remembrance; and without remembrance, no repentance; and without repentance, no remission nor forgiveness; and except thou shouldst be forgiven in this life, thou shalt never see eternal life : so in calling to remembrance the sins of thy youth, the Lord sees to thy weal in this.

Secondly, By temptations the Lord lets thee see a world of iniquities in thee, and there is so much sin within thee as were able to condemn a world, much more than thee, that art but a creature : so by temptations the Lord brings out the secret monsters that lurk in thy heart, that if they got leave, they would soon devour thee.

Thirdly, By temptations the Lord lets thee see the bitterness of sin, that provokes the anger of God against thee ; and seeing this, thou mayest beware to rush thyself in the fire again, and to stab thy heel on a prick, and to cast thyself over in the hands of an angry God, that is a consuming fire.

Fourthly, Were it not for temptations, it were not possible to keep thy heart under ; and if thou hadst never so many graces, it would swell and puff thee up with pride, were it not for the manifold temptations that God sends purposely, to serve for as many pricks thrust in thy heart, to let out the wind of pride out of it.

Fifthly, By temptations God will make men acquainted with their own infirmities, that seeing their own weakness, they may put their trust in God alternately, and that they may see when they stand, it is of grace they stand, and when they fall, they may see their falling comes of themselves; and hereby they are taught to renounce theirselves, and put their trust in God only; and they are taught to quit nature, and to take them to grace; and this will make thee to adorn, and make much of the graces of God, and will make thee to reverence the word and sacraments; and this will make thee to watch and pray continually.

Sixthly, Were it not for temptations, we would rot in our sins, we would lay off our armour, and we would fall asleep with the rest of the world; therefore, purposely, the Lord sends temptations to hold us waking, and to make us put on and wear our armour, and to make us cleanse our hearts daily by faith in the blood of Christ.

Seventhly and *last of all*, God, by temptations multiplies his grace to thee, and as he says himself, "My power is perfected in thy weaknesses and infirmities;" and God will not suffer us to be tempted above that we are able to bear; for, as our battles are renewed, so his grace is renewed to us, and he does it for this end, that we may see that present graces will not do the turn, therefore we have need of every day's corroborating and strengthening grace, which may make us daily grow in grace, until we come unto a perfection which will not be in this life. This much for the causes why the Lord suffers his own to be tempted as long as they are in this life.

There remains yet further to be spoken in this; for I would have you thoroughly informed in the matter of your warfare, that if you give over, and be traitors to God, and your own souls, then your blood may be on your own heads; for there is no man that dies, and is overcome in this battle, but he that desires with all his heart, and is willing to be overcome.

Two things only remain to be spoken of at this time.

First, Of the grounds that may underprop you and hold you up, that ye faint not in this battle.

Secondly, I will tell you how ye shall carry yourselves to set your feet to this battle, and so to be able to fight it out.

As to the first, a combat must ye have; and therefore make you for it, and ye must put on your armour, and your weapons in your hand, and thereby not only resist, but also pursue and slay the enemy.

Now, the *first* ground to move you to do this, I take it from the author of this warfare, God has made the feud, and put enmity betwixt the seed of the woman and the serpent: so ye see God is the author of this feud, that after Satan had given a deadly stroke to the man and the woman in the garden, the Lord said, Gen. iii. 15. "I will put enmity betwixt the seed of the woman and thy seed; it shall break thy head, and thou shalt bruise his heel." Seeing therefore the Lord is the author of it, the battle is the Lord's, the victory is of the Lord, and the glory shall be the Lord's; and because it is his, he has given us a commandment to fight, joined with a promise, that he shall not overcome us, 1 Peter v. 8, 9. "He goes about as a roaring lion, seeking whom he may devour. Whom resist stedfast in the faith. And resist the devil, and he will fly from you," James iv. 7. And here, in this text, "Put on the whole armour of God, that ye may be able to stand against all the assaults of the devil." So the first ground to uphold you, that ye must sustain the battle, it is the command of God, joined with the promise, that commands all men to fight and overcome, as they would be partakers of the crown.

The *second* ground to persuade you to undergo this battle, (it is the cause of this warfare) and the thing that is foughten for, it is not for land and heritage, and worldly riches that thou fightest for here; but it is for the glory of God, and the salvation of thy own soul; the Lord concredits his glory to thee and bids thee fight for it; and the Lord concredits thy own salvation to thee, and bids thee fight for it also; now, thou that wilt not fight for that, I am sure thou wilt fight for nothing; and if thou wouldst be a traitor to God, and thy own soul, it is well bestowed thou be condemned; so ye see the drift of the enemy in this warfare, he seeks no more, but to rob and spoil God of his glory, and to betray thy soul, John viii. 44. "He is a liar and murderer from the beginning, he is a false liar and accuser of the brethren," Rev. xii. 10. See what he said, Job i. 9, 10. "Is it for nought that Job serves thee? Let me take away his goods, and see if he will not blaspheme thee to thy face;" which was a manifest lie, and a perverse slander and blasphemy, as the end declared. And, as he is a liar, so he is a murderer. The first thing he aims at, is the dishonour of God, and the next is the destruction of thy poor soul, which Christ hath bought with his own precious blood, that it may perish for evermore. Now, thou that wilt not fight, what dost thou? Thou puttest a knife in his hand, and thou givest it him to cut the throat of thy own soul; therefore at that great day thou shalt be arraigned as guilty of those two points: *First,* Thou shalt be accused, convicted, and condemned as a traitor to God's glory: And, *Secondly,* as a murderer of thy own soul; wherefore God shall say to thee, I concredited my glory to thee, but thou wouldst not fight for it; I concredited and trusted thy own soul to thee, but thou wouldst not fight for it: Therefore it is well bestowed thou be damned. I remember, Judges v. 23, what Deborah said, "Curse ye Meroz, that would not come up and help the Lord against the mighty, and let the angel of the Lord curse Meroz;" much more may it be said, let the Lord curse, and let all the angels and saints in heaven curse them that will not help the Lord against the devil; therefore, as the blessing of the Lord is upon them that fight his battles, so the curse of the Lord is upon them that will not fight his battles.

The *third* ground to persuade you to this warfare, it is this, fight these battles which last but for a time, and thou shalt have endless joy and everlasting peace hereafter; yea, if thou wilt fight against the enemy, the devil, thou shalt even have peace with God, peace with all the angels and saints in heaven, peace with thine own conscience, and peace with all the rest of the creatures of God, suppose the devil make war against thee presently. Read thou the conclusion of these seven epistles, that the Lord, sitting on the throne of his glory, sends to the seven churches of Asia, wherein he makes a promise, but to none except those that overcome, Rev. ii. 7. to 11. " He that overcomes shall eat of the fruit of the tree of life that stands in the midst of the paradise of God." Verse 17. " He that overcomes shall not be hurt with the second death. He that overcometh shall get a white stone in his hand, and upon the stone a new name written, that no man knows save he that receives it, To him that overcomes and keeps my words to the end, I will give him my power over the nations, and he shall rule them with an iron rod. He that overcomes shall be clad with a long white raiment. He that overcomes shall be made a pillar in the temple of his God." And, last of all, " He that overcometh shall sit on a throne with me, and shall sit with my Father on his throne." Now, as there is no overcoming without a battle, so there is no glory nor crown without overcoming and fighting; therefore thou that fightest not, and overcomest not, thou has no right to the promise; for is not this an equal proportion? " He that overcomes shall eat of the tree of life;" then, by the contrary, thou that overcomest not shalt never taste of the tree of life. " He that overcomes shall not be hurt of the second death ;" and so in all the rest; so there is no promise made, but to them that fight and overcome.

Fifthly, Resolve to fight, for flying will do thee no good, but fighting will free thee of the enemy's hands; for if thou fleest and failest in thy feet, and sittest down by the way, or givest place to the enemy, then thou wilt be overcome ; for he desires no more but that thou give place to him, and turn thy back, and go thy way ; therefore ye see, that, in this battle, there is armour for all the parts of the body, except the back only ; because there is nothing but death for the man or woman that flees ; there is armour for the loins ; there is armour for the breast ; there is armour for the feet ; there is armour for the head ; and there is armour for both the hands ; but there is no armour for the back : so, resolve to fight ; for it will be to no purpose to flee.

Sixthly, Fight, because ye have vowed in your baptism, where ye promised to renounce the camp of the devil, and to be faithful soldiers to the Lord Jesus ; and in sign and token thereof, ye took his badge and livery upon you ; therefore let that vow which ye have made encourage every one of you to fight, or else to be arraigned of the highest perjury that can be devised.

Seventhly, Consider your Captain, and remember under whose banner ye fight, even the Lord of lords, and King of kings, that has bound the devil, and taken his weapons from him, and has gotten the victory over death, over hell, over the grave, and over Satan himself ; and has gone to heaven with that victory, and has led captivity captive.

Eighthly and *lastly,* Let the certain hope of victory encourage you to fight ; for, if ye fight, ye shall not lose the field ; for there are none that loses, but these that lose willingly ; this battle is not like the battles of this world, wherein the victory is doubtsome and uncertain : but in this battle the victory is certain and sure : Why ? The battle is the Lord's, the armour is the Lord's, the power is the Lord's, the glory is the Lord's, and thou art the Lord's ; therefore the Lord will not let thee lose.

This much for the grounds to uphold you in the undertaking of this battle.

Now, it remains to speak of your preparation. It stands in two parts :

First, Thou must know with whom thou hast to do ; for thou must know thy enemy, his power, his craft, his malice, and his helpers ; or else thou wilt never fight rightly.

Secondly, Thou must have thy armour on thee ; for if thou comest naked, thou wilt be overcome ; therefore thou must take on thee the whole armour of God, and thou must be strong ; for a weak man, though he be armed, or a strong man, without armour, may be overcome ; and thou must not let thy armour lie beside thee, but thou must put it on thee, never to lay it off again ; and thou must stand against the whole assaults of Satan.

First, Thou must be persuaded of the strong power of the enemy.

Secondly, Thou must be persuaded of his craft and policy.

Thirdly, Thou must be persuaded of his courage, that will not spare to set upon thee, albeit thou wert a man according to the heart of God.

Fourthly, and *lastly,* Thou must be persuaded of his army and helpers, that lie ready to assist him.

Now, it is the ignorance of these things, that makes so deadly a slaughter among the souls of men and women ; for this subtile serpent, when he cannot double out his temptations by violence, he will slip in craftily, and present his poison in a golden cup to thee ; and when he cannot get in by force, he will slip in by craft and subtility ; and when he cannot prevail against thee with the pleasures of this world, he will try if he can prevail against thee with crosses and afflictions ; and if he cannot prevail with neither of these, then he will stir up thy own flesh against thee, to see if it can entice thee to sin ; such is his subtility, that it is said of him, " He is that serpent that deceives the whole world," Rev. xii. 9. And as for his courage, there was never one yet among the sons of men that were free from his assaults ; he set upon Adam in his integrity, and in the garden of paradise ; he set upon Noah, that was righteous in his generation ; he set upon Moses, that was faithful in the whole house of God; he set upon David, a man according to the heart of God; he set upon Peter, that was builded upon a rock, against which the gates of hell could not prevail. All these are great and wonderful.

But this is more than wonderful, that he set upon him; that he knew to be the seed of the woman, which should tread down his head; he set upon the man that he knew to be the son of the ever-living God: he set upon him that he knew had power to command him down to the depth; he set upon him that he knew was come to torment him; this was wonderful that he set upon him on earth; but this is the wonder of wonders, that he set upon him in heaven; as it is written, Rev. xii. 4. "There was a battle in heaven, Michael and his angels fought against the devil and his angels;" therefore, seeing he could not prevail against him on the earth, and in his infirmity, and seeing he could not overcome him while he was in the flesh, he spares not to go up to heaven, and set upon him there, even when he was exalted and reigning in glory; yet he " prevailed not; for the dragon was cast out of heaven, and there was no place found for him there." Now, seeing he is so bold, this is fearful; yet there is a number of you, ye lie down with peace, ye sleep with peace, and ye rise in peace, and ye walk all the day long in peace, and have never no combat in your souls, nor ye never offer to fight against this cruel enemy; for if this bloody murderer get the victory, look ye for any pity at his hand? No, no, as the Lord lives, ye shall find no mercy nor pity with him; for nothing will satisfy him but the blood of your souls.

Now, two things, and so I end.

First, There is a number of you that have never yet resolved to set foot to this battle, and to fight it out to the end, because ye see not the necessity of it; and it is but folly to tell you, that it is so, that thou hast a malicious, a subtile, a strong enemy: that hath a great army to fight against thee, until the Lord set thy soul at liberty, and pull thee out of the arms of the devil, and set thee within the bosom of his Son.

Secondly, There is a number whom God has delivered out of his hands, and has set them at liberty, and made them free subjects to the Lord Jesus; therefore, I beseech you, to set your feet to the battle, and make you for wars, and prepare yourselves to fight, unless ye will be traitors to God's glory, and to your own souls, unless ye will be perjured. Now, because I mind to handle these things, morning and evening, without intermixing with any other matter: therefore, I beseech you, in the bowels of Christ, that ye would all come to this morning and evening exercise, that ye may know the machinations, and crafty devices of the devil, that hath at this time drawn on a common security upon all flesh. I say no more at this time, but commit that which has been spoken to the blessing of God which is in Christ. To whom &c.

SERMON XII.

OF THE CHRISTIAN WARFARE.

Ephes. vi. 10, 11, 12.

Finally, my brethren, be strong in the Lord, and in the power of his might. Put on the whole armour of God, that ye may be able to stand against the wiles of the devil. For we wrestle not against flesh and blood, but against principalities, against powers, against the rulers of the darkness of this world, against spiritual wickedness in high places.

THE things which we have taught you in this matter which we have in hand, they are these shortly:

First, I shewed you the necessity of this warfare, and that it is proper and belongs only to the people of God; for the dragon only makes war with the woman and her seed, that endeavour to fear God and keep his commandments, therefore there is none that has this warfare that should be discouraged; for, if thou wert not of the seed of the woman, and if thou endeavouredst not to fear God, and keep all his commandments, the dragon would never make war with thee.

The *second* thing was the cause why the Lord will suffer his own to be exercised with temptations while they are in this life; which was partly for his own glory, and partly for their own weal; for by it, both he gets glory, and also thou gettest great good by it.

Thirdly, The grounds that might sustain you, and move you to fight; which were these shortly; God is the author of this warfare, and he has commanded us to fight, and with the command he has given us a promise that we shall overcome: so the battle is the Lord's, the armour is the Lord's, the victory is from the Lord, the glory is the Lord's, and thou art the Lord's, therefore he will not let thee lose. Again, it is not for gold, or silver, or land, an heritage of worldly riches, that thou fightest for, but it is for the glory of God and thy own salvation that thou fightest for, and therefore there is a blessing of God pronounced to them that fight, and there is a curse denounced against them that fight not. Again, fight here but for a short time, and thou shalt get a crown of everlasting and endless glory hereafter. Again, fight and overcome, and thou " shalt get of the fruit of the tree of life, that stands in the midst of the paradise of God, to feed thee; thou shalt get the water of the river of life to quench thy thirst. Thou shalt get a white stone, and a new name in it which no man knows but he that receives it. Thou shalt have power over the nations and rule them with an iron rod. Thou shalt be clad with a long white robe; thy name shall be written in the book of life; and thou shalt be made a pillar in the house of God; and thou shalt sit with Christ on a throne, and judge the twelve tribes of Israel." Again, resolve to fight, for flee thou must not, for fleeing will not do the turn. Again, fight unless ye will be perjured and mansworn. And last of all, let the power of your Captain, and the certain hope of victory persuade you to fight.

The *fourth* thing was concerning your preparation, and for the better preparing yourselves two things are needful.

First, Ye must know your enemy and what he is, how malicious, how powerful, how crafty; and what is the army he leads with him.

Secondly, Ye must put on your armour; for if ye come naked ye will get a sore stroke, and a deadly wound. As for your enemies, there are four things ye must know of them: it is not for nought that they are described to us in the scripture; for if it were not needful for us to know their malice, their skill, their power, and their helpers, the Lord would never put them up in his testament.

So *first*, Thou must know their malice. *Secondly*, Thou must know their power. *Thirdly*, Their skill. *Fourthly*, Ye must know their army and helpers.

First, As to their malice, it cannot be well expressed; always they are malicious enemies to God's glory, and they are malicious enemies to man's salvation; he is a liar of God unto his own, and he is a liar of God unto the wicked also; he is a murderer, and nothing can satisfy his malicious mind but the trampling of God's glory under foot, and the endless damnation of all the souls of men and women. "He is a liar and a murderer from the beginning;" so his malice is old, for it is not yesterday or the day that his malice began; but he began to be malicious as soon as ever man began to be made.

He is called Satan, that is an adversary or enemy; for he is an enemy to God and an enemy to us, for he thirsts for nothing but the dishonour of God, and the destruction of the poor souls of men and women; and nothing can quench his thirst but the pulling off Christ's crown off his head, and the pouring out of the blood of the souls of men and women, and the casting them in the everlasting fire of hell, that they may be burnt eternally: for this cause he is called that evil one that comes and plucks away the seed of God's word that is sown in the hearts of men and women, that they get no leave to understand it, and it gets no leave to take root that it may grow and bring forth fruit unto perfection, Mat. xiii. 19. And how many of you believe this, that when this word is sown amongst you it is the devil that comes and plucks it out of your hearts? Again, he is called the envious man that sows the tares amongst the good seed to hinder it that it should not grow; for it is he that sows all this evil and discord in the church of God, that thereby he may make the children of God to stumble and fall. He is called "a roaring lion, that goes about continually seeking whom he may devour." He is called *a red dragon dyed with blood*, for many millions has he slain from the first day that Adam was set in paradise unto this day: "He has seven heads and ten horns," for he has wit enough, and power enough: "He reaches out his tail, and pulls down the stars of heaven with it:" yea, there are many in Scotland this day that have been shining stars and bright lamps to go before others, and yet now he has drawn them down from heaven and made them earthly minded, and so he prevails over them. He is called a tempter, that is to say, a wily or subtile serpent, that can creep in thy bosom quietly that thou shalt not know of him till he be there, and when he is there he can lie still a while and not hurt thee; but when he begins to stir his tail, and when thy conscience begins to waken, then he will give thee a deadly sting, for he will creep in the soul of man or woman by stealing a sin upon them, because he knows that sin will make them naked to their shame amongst their enemies, and spoil them of the presence of God, that then he may take his advantage of them; as it is said of the Israelites, "And when Moses saw that the people were naked (for Aaron had made the people naked to their shame amongst their enemies,") Exod. xxxii. 25. And how made Aaron them naked? Even by causing them to commit idolatry and so to sin against God: How were they naked? They were destitute of God's favour, and spoiled of his presence; a naked prey to God's wrath, laid open to the judgment of God. He is called *the accuser of the brethren*, for he shall be the first that shall present thy sin before the tribunal of God, there to accuse thee of it, suppose he himself be the author of it; and not only is he an accuser, but also a slanderer, a false accuser, a backbiter, for that is the meaning of *diabolus*, a slanderer; he will speak evil, where there is no appearance of evil, as he said of Job, chap. i. 9, 10. "Doth Job serve the Lord for nought? Hast thou not hedged him about on every side" that I cannot get to him: "but stretch out thy hand, and touch his goods, and all that he hath," and let me take it away from him, "see then if he will not blaspheme thee to thy face." But O false liar, was not this a fearful slander, as was proved in the end? Last of all, he is called a messenger, for he is called the Lord's jailor, ready at the commandment of God, to take and bind hand and foot, whom the Lord bids, and to cast them in utter darkness; therefore it was said, that an evil spirit was sent to Saul to torment him, 1 Sam. xvi. 14. So he is the very currier sent of God to put his wrath in execution, for he never left Saul from that time forth till he made him put hand to himself.

Now, what is the fruit ye should make of all this which hath been spoken of this enemy? Should ye not beware of him? Will ye hazard your souls on him? Is he a meek lamb think ye? Will he have any pity on thee? Nay, as the Lord lives, he will not spare thee; for all the monstrous beasts on earth are not able to express his cruelty of nature; therefore he is compared to a wolf, to a lion, to a bear, to a dragon, and to that mighty leviathan. Now, we will say ye know that he is so, as you speak, but how shall we do with him, and how shall we overcome him that is so strong an enemy? I will tell you there is no way to overcome him but by resisting? "Resist the devil," says James, "and he will flee from you." Resist then, and fight and stand against him, and have never more peace with him; but take up this resolution, I will stand against thee, and by the grace of God thou shalt never prevail against me, nor get the upper hand of me with my will; thou mayest well steal a stroke upon me when I know not of thee: thou art a malicious enemy, I see thou seekest nothing but the dishonour of my God, and the destruction of my own soul; go away from me, avoid me Satan, and get thee behind me, I will have no more ado with thee, I denounce war against thee, and shall never make a truce with thee again; thou art but a liar, and deceivest all the world; and art a murderer, that hast cut the throats of all the poor souls that have gone to hell since the fall of Adam; and it is thou that hast shed the blood of all the saints of God which hath been shed since the time of righteous Abel hitherto, and shalt be the causer of the shedding of all the blood of the innocent unto the end of the world. This for malice.

Secondly, As for his power. He has power enough; he brought fire from heaven, and burnt all Job's sheep and his servants, and so devoured them; he stirred up the Sabeans and Chaldeans against him, and made them come and take away his oxen and his asses violently; he raised a great wind from beyond the wilderness, and made it to smite the four corners of the house where his children were, and the house fell upon them and killed them. He is a prince, and has more subjects at his command than any worldly prince under heaven; and he is called, "The prince of the air, that rules mightily in the children of disobedience; he is that mighty leviathan, he is that piercing serpent:" look to the description of it in Job xli. 1. &c. and compare that place with the 27th of Isaiah. He is that strong man that holds the house and castle of the heart, that none can overcome him but the power of God only; it is said of him that his name is legion, because they are many, and he has legions of devils at his command, and he has all the wicked of the world at his command and under his dominion; yea, when he cannot prevail by his own subjects, he can stir up an old prophet, to seduce a young prophet, and he can make him say, "Am not I a prophet as well as thou?" 1 Kings xiii. 15. And have not I the Spirit of God as well as thou? Even so he can stir one minister to seduce another, and all to bring his cruel enterprise and wicked purpose to pass. He is called the prince of darkness, for he may be in thy bosom at the noon-tide of the day, and yet thou not see him; he can be with thee at table when thou art eating and drinking, and yet thou not perceive him; and he can be going hard by thy side when thou art in the field, and thou not perceive that; wherefore he is called the prince of darkness, because he blinds the eyes of men and women, that they cannot see him nor perceive him when he comes to them. Again, here it is said of him, that *he is set above in the high places;* and therefore he has the advantage of thee: for except thou beest joined with thy head to Christ in heaven, thou shalt not be able to overcome him: for he is above thee, and therefore may throw down enough of temptations upon thee. Ye know a man that stands on a brae-head, he may easily cast down a stone and kill them that are below him: so Satan has the advantage of us indeed, and the only way to come about him is by true faith and sincere repentance. Last of all, he is called the god of this world, because he overcomes the most part of this world; and the most part of the world give the homage, honour, and service to him which they should give to God; and so the world makes the devil their god. And except thou hast him that is the God of gods dwelling in thy heart, it is not possible that thou canst overcome him, but wilt rather be overcome by him: therefore, Is it for nought, think ye, that he set upon David, a man according to the heart of God? Was it for nought he set upon Solomon, the wisest man on the whole earth in his time? And was it for nought he set upon Peter, that was builded upon a rock? Was it for nought that he set upon the head, Christ Jesus, while he was upon the earth, but yet he prevailed not against him? So there is nothing can overcome him, but only the strength, the power, and mighty hand of God.

Thirdly, Join with this his craft and skill, and consider it. He is that subtile serpent that deceives all the world; he is that seven-headed dragon that has such wit and wisdom as no wisdom can come about it but only the wisdom of God; his machinations and devices are strong, for he will mark thy disposition, whatever it be, and will lay assaults against it; he will mark thy estate, if thou beest in prosperity or adversity, and he will take his advantage there; he will mark thy temper, and he will mark thy custom, for he knows better what thou art than thyself does. Now, seeing ye have such a strong and malicious enemy, resolve to resist and fight against him, for if thou resist not he will slay thee; and hear what I say, he is more malicious against thee that art the child of God, and is more desirous of thy destruction than of a thousand others; and he will be busier to tempt thee to sin, because one sin in thy person brings greater dishonour to God than all the sins that are in a thousand others that have never borne the name of Jesus upon their shoulders. Therefore it is said to Peter, "Simon, Simon, Satan has desired to sift thee and winnow thee, but I prayed that thy faith fail not."

Now, in consideration of all that hath been spoken of your enemy, this is the only thing that must sustain you and hold you up, ye must know that his power is limited; he can do no more than God will give him leave to do, and there cannot a hair fall out of thy head without thy heavenly Father's permission; and he had no power over Job, his cattle, his children, his servants, his body, but as the Lord permitted him and gave him leave; nor had he power over the swine, but as the Lord gave him leave. Therefore when it is said he is powerful, it is true; but his power is limited and bounded, and there are marches and bounds set unto him, that he dare not pass over: he is but a naked enemy, for he is spoiled of his weapons; Christ has spoiled him, as the apostle says, speaking of Christ, "He has spoiled principalities and powers, and has made a shew of them openly, and has triumphed over them upon the cross, Col. ii. 15. And he is but a bound enemy, as the apostle Jude says, verse 6th, "He has reserved him in everlasting chains, under darkness, unto the judgment of the great day:" and Peter says, 2 Pet. ii. 4. "God spared not the angels for sin, but cast them down to hell, and delivered them to the chains of darkness, to be kept to condemnation." And therefore, suppose he has all this power, yet he has it against none but the children of disobedience only, in whom he works mightily, and not against any of the seed of the woman, that fear God and keep his commandments. I say no more, but the Lord give every one of you the power and wisdom of God, whereby ye may overcome this strong and crafty enemy, through the mighty power of your Lord and Captain Jesus Christ: To whom, with the Father and the Holy Ghost, be all honour and praise for now and evermore. *Amen.*

SERMON XIII.

OF THE CHRISTIAN WARFARE.

Ephes. vi. 10.

Finally, my brethren, be strong in the Lord, and in the power of his might.

YOUR life is a warfare and a continual wrestling, and now is this time of battle; but afterwards shall be the time of wearing the crown. Thou that fightest lawfully here, thou shalt get the crown hereafter; and if thou fightest not here, thou shalt never get a crown hereafter: he that fighteth and overcometh here, shall get an everlasting kingdom hereafter; none shall ever enter into that kingdom but such as may say as the apostle says, " I have foughten a good fight, I have finished my course, I have kept the faith," that oftentimes the devil essayed to bereave me of; " I have finished my course," which I have run constantly to the end: " and henceforth is laid up for me a crown of glory :" for when ye are dying (as ye will all die, for there is none of you but ye bear death about with you, and it is only known to the Lord when ye will die) I say, when ye are dying, except ye may say in some truth and sincerity of heart, and a good conscience, " I have foughten my fight, I have kept my faith, and run my race ;" except ye may say this, ye dare not say the thing that is behind, thou darest not say, " there is a crown of glory laid up for thee." But I leave this. For your preparation to the battle, I told you two things needful for you.

First, Ye must know the condition and quality of your enemies, without the which you shall never in earnest set your foot to the battle, and fight it out;

for, if ye know not with whom ye are to fight, ye will never fight in earnest. I told you what you should know of them, and I assure thee that thou art injurious to the Lord, if thou thinkest or speakest otherwise of them than the Lord thinks and speaks of them, who has so painted them out to thee in his word by his Spirit. The devil is a liar then, so that when thou art in security, he will tell thee that God is merciful; and when thou thinkest that the mercy of God belongs to thee, then he will say that thou hast nothing to do with it; and when thou hast faith, he will say thou hast none, and so make thee to doubt and call in question; and so he is a great liar, and not only a liar, but also a cruel murderer; he has the cruel paws, and devouring mouth of a strong lion, that if thou givest place to him, he will never rest till he hath sucken and drunken the blood of thy soul: and he is a liar and a murderer from the beginning; his malice, his cruelty, and his falsehood, is old: many a one he hath deceived, many a one he hath devoured, and brought to hell, since the time Adam was put out of the garden of paradise to this day; and he has prevailed mightily over the children of disobedience these five thousand six hundred years and more; and, as his malice began with the first man, so it shall end with the last man; and as he is the first to tempt thee and allure thee to sin, so he will be the first to torment thee in hell. He is a serpent, as Eve said, " The serpent deceived me, and I did eat;" for he is that subtile beast that hath deceived many a one. He is an accuser; wilt thou not believe then, that he will present thy sins before the tribunal of God, and there bring them before thee, and accuse thee before God; and say, this and this sin hast thou done, and therefore thou art worthy to die? He is a devil, that is, he is not only a liar and an accuser, but also a malicious slanderer; for he will speak of the meanest appearance of evil within thee: and therefore thou shouldst beware of him, to give him any occasion of speaking evil against thee; yea, he will not spare to accuse thee falsely. He is a rampant lion, always seeking whom he may devour. He is an old red dragon, accustomed long with the murdering of poor souls. He is called, *Principalities and powers, and worldly governors, prince of darkness that rules in the air*, spirits that cannot be seen. And, last of all, he is called *the god of this world.*

Now, what use shall we make of all this?

First, Make no truce with him; for he desires no better than that thou shouldst make peace with him.

Secondly, Set not on him with the strength that is in thyself, nor with carnal weapons; for he laughs at the sword; for it can do no harm to him; for thy strength will do no more to him than to a brazen wall; it is only the strength and power of God that will beat him down.

Thirdly, It will not be flesh and blood that will overcome him, but thou must have the wisdom of God to confute him with; Ahitophel was worldly-wise enough yet Satan overcame him; that when he saw his counsel prevailed not, he went and hanged himself; so it must be the only power and wisdom of God that can overcome him; for he is a strong party, and leads a strong army, and has many helpers; for it is no time to eat, and drink, and sleep, and take our ease, nor yet to walk unarmed, and to come naked before such an enemy, that seeks the destruction of thy soul; he leads his army, and that under two general-lieutenants, viz. the world without, and thy flesh within thee. By the world, I mean all the profane infidels and unbelievers, all the children of disobedience: for he has them all at his command. He is that angel, whose name in the Hebrew is Abaddon, and in the Greek Apollyon, that is, a destroyer; for he destroys all wherever he comes, and gets the upper hand. And he is that angel of the bottomless pit, that brought forth all these locusts spoken of in the Revelation, ixth chapter. And it is he that leads that great army of twenty times ten thousand, that ran through all the world, and destroyed the in-dwellers and inhabitants thereof; besides these wicked men, he hath the riches, the glory, and the pleasures of the world, to serve as baits to draw on his hook the simple and ignorant people; he has likewise the crosses of the world, and afflictions, to serve as pricks and thorns to hinder us in our journey to heaven; and therefore he sometimes sets on thee on the right hand, and other times on the left hand; sometimes he takes men and women up to a mountain, and lets them see the glory and riches of this world, and, as he offered them to Christ, so he can offer them to thee, if thou wilt serve him, Matth. iv. 8. He can reach poison to thee out of a golden cup, that thou mayest drink of it, and die for ever; and he can set golden apples in thy way, and make them to roll before thee, to see if thou wilt turn back on thy journey, and forsake thy course, or if thou wilt sit down on the way, to lose heaven and thy crown; and in this he hath wonderfully prevailed over many: and this hath made his tail to reach up to heaven, and bring stars down from heaven, and throw them to the earth: he presented to Demas the riches of the world, and he embraced this present world, and took it in his arms, 2 Tim. iv. 10. From whence came Judas's treason, think ye? It came from the silver that was offered him by the priests, the scribes, and the Pharisees; he took it, and put it up in his bag; so the covetousness and greed of this world, that the devil had put in the heart of Judas, caused him to betray Christ: this is one way whereby he uses to overcome men; therefore we have need to beware of this, that we set not our hearts upon any thing beneath.

The *second* way that the world helps him, is by crosses and afflictions; he lays thorns in the way to prick thy side, and casts rocks and stumbling-blocks before thee, and all to hinder thee in thy course, that thou run not with joy, and constancy unto the ring's end. And afflictions have their own temptations also, as he said of Job ii. 5. "Let me lay my hand on his body, and see if he will not blaspheme thee to thy face:" And it was afflictions that "burnt up the seed on the stony ground, and because it had not deep enough

SERMON XIII.

root, it lasted but for a season," Matth. xiii. 21. "Therefore, when tribulation or persecution comes, because of the word, by and by he is offended:" So it is not every one that can bear out these temptations of afflictions, and these temptations of worldly riches and pleasures of this life; therefore take heed to his poison that he offers to thee in a golden cup, and propines thee to drink: and take heed to the golden apples that he casts before thee; for, as long as thou countest the world thy friend, thou canst never overcome him; therefore thou must either count the world an enemy to thee, or else thou canst not overcome the temptations of the pleasures, or afflictions thereof: therefore it is said, "The friendship of the world is enmity against God, or with God;" (not but it is lawful to use the benefits of God that he casts to us in this world) for the devil by them essays, if he can draw thy heart away from God, and to get it set upon them; and when he cannot prevail by this means of honour, and riches, and worldly pleasures, then he sends crosses and afflictions, either to make thee fall clean back, or else to faint by the way.

Now, to overcome these temptations in the world, I give you some things to uphold you, that ye may remember of them; therefore think and meditate on these places of scripture, John xv. 19. "If ye were of the world, the world would love his own; but because ye are not of the world, but I have chosen you out of the world, therefore the world hateth you." Remember that in John xvii. 9. "I pray not for the world, but for them thou hast given me, for they are thine." Remember that, 1 John ii. 15. "Love not the world, neither the things that are in the world. If any man love the world, the love of the Father is not in him." Remember that again, "if any man would gain the whole world, and lose his own soul, what shall it profit him? Or what ransom shall a man give for his soul?" Not all the riches and honour of the world can redeem one lost soul. And remember that which is spoken, Psal. lxxviii. 30, 31. " When the meat was in their mouths," and when they had abundance of all things, even then " the wrath of God came upon them, and slew the strongest of them." Read Rev. xviii. 9, 10. " They that drank with the whore in her golden cup, and were drunk with her wine, they stand afar off for fear of her torments; and there was weeping and wailing, and they said, alas, alas, that so great riches are come to desolation !" So they that drink the pleasures of this world, shall also taste of the bitterness of their judgments. Read Heb. xi. 24, 25, 26. " Moses refused to be called the son of Pharaoh's daughter, and chused rather to suffer affliction with the people of God, than to enjoy the pleasures of sin for a season; esteeming the rebuke of Christ greater riches than all the treasures in Egypt; and feared not the wrath of the king; for he endured as he that saw him that was invisible." So the best way to overcome the world, and the pleasures thereof, it is to lift up your eyes, and to look to things there, which in this life are invisible. And as for the troubles and temptations of this life, he will try you with them also; and all to draw thy heart from God; for it is thy heart he craves; and it is the castle of thy heart he goeth about to gain, that he may make his residence in it; and if he cannot make thee fall down to worship him, but thou wilt worship the Lord thy God, and him only thou wilt serve; then he will send a fiery trial, great troubles, and bloody persecution, to keep thy heart under, and to make thee faint in the battle, and to see if he can make thee to give over.

Now, to sustain you in this temptation of crosses and afflictions, remember, that saying of Christ, Matth. v. 10. " Blessed are they that suffer persecution for righteousness sake: for theirs is the kingdom of heaven." Mat. vii. 13. " Enter in at the straight gate: for broad is the way that leadeth to destruction, and many enter in thereat; and straight is the gate, and narrow is the way that leadeth to life, and few there be that find it." Remember that saying of Abraham to the rich glutton, Luke xvi. 25. " Son, remember thou gottest thy comforts in this world, and Lazarus his pain; therefore is he comforted and thou art tormented." Remember that saying of Paul, 2 Thess. i. 6, 7. "It is a righteous thing with God to render tribulation to such as trouble you; and to you that are troubled, rest with us. And by many afflictions must we enter into the kingdom of God. And all that will live godly in Christ Jesus, must suffer persecution." 2 Tim. iii. 12. "And many and great are the troubles of the righteous and godly; but God delivers them out of them all," Psal. xxxiv. 19. So let these, and the like sayings, be your warrant in the day of temptations; for except ye have the word of God dwelling in your heart plenteously, it is not possible that he can overcome these temptations. (I thought with myself) surely we have not been much tried with the one of them, I mean with crosses and afflictions; but as for the other, look and see how far the world has prevailed with you, that through the love of this world, the love of God, is grown cold in you, (I doubt in some of you.) Had ye not once a conversation in heaven, when ye were eating and drinking the pleasures of heaven, and feeding upon the joys thereof? when the flesh and blood of Christ was sweeter to your souls than any meat or drink in the world was ever to your bodies; and when ye were beholding the glory of heaven, and the temple of your God? but now ye are eating the vile husks of the earth, with the swine of the world, and glutting up the filthy mire thereof. Alas! why do ye this? Would you have more than an endless crown of glory? Would ye have more than to eat of the tree of life, that stands in the midst of the paradise of God? Would ye have more than to be made pillars in the temple of your God? Would ye have more than that white stone, and that new name written on it? Would ye have more than to sit on a throne with Christ? And, would ye have more than the unsearchable riches of Christ? Will ye tell me what would ye have? Ye shall have a new heaven and a new earth; and may not this heritage serve you? Would to God your eyes were opened to see these things. Will ye look to these fair promises? Will ye look to this fair palace, where ye shall dwell for evermore? Will ye look to that fair city, and new Jerusalem, that has the glory of God in it; that has that high wall about it; that has twelve porches set upon precious stones, and has streets of pure gold, and as shining glass; and God is the temple of it, and the Lamb is the light of it? Why should these momentary things, that cannot keep your life one hour, make you lose eternal things, that never shall have an end?

Alas! why wilt thou lose that endless crown of glory for a little vain-glory here? and why wilt thou lose the everlasting joys and pleasures of heaven, for these earthly pleasures which last but for a time? So then, when crosses and afflictions come upon you, arm you with the remembrance of these things, arm you with the experience of all the saints before you, that through many tribulations have entered the kingdom of heaven. Remember that " if ye suffer with Christ here, ye shall reign with him hereafter in glory: Rev. vii. 13, 14. When John saw a great multitude with long wite robes and palms in their hands, standing before the throne, and crying, salvation comes from our God, that sits on the throne, and from the Lamb." When he asked at the angel, " What are these men?" He answered, These are they that are come out of great tribulation." And if ever God shall call any of you to suffer for Christ's sake, remember the example of many martyrs, that have endured the fire patiently for this, and for his sake, and have rejoiced in the very midst of the fire, to the admiration of the very tormentors. And remember the goodness of God to you, and how many sweet blessings he has bestowed upon you freely; and should ye not take bitter things out of his hands? " As Job said, shall we receive good from God and not receive evil also;" Even so say ye, shall I receive so many things which are good from my God, and not receive evil things also? Therefore, my brethren, prepare you for crosses; ye cannot tell how soon they will come on; for I am thinking there is something following upon the tail of this, that stars of heaven are brought down and thrown to the earth, that these golden apples are offered to ministers, and men are become earthly minded that were wont to be capable of spiritual things: as the Lord lives, I think there must be a fiery trial to follow on. But I leave this. I have told you the first help Satan uses against us, which is the world and the fruits of it.

The second help that he uses against us, is our own flesh, that inbred corruption that lurks in every man and woman by nature; ye must arm you against that also: thou must understand that there is a corruption within thee, that is spread over every part of thy soul, and there is a corruption without thee, spread over thy body, and every member of that body; and this corruption is so mixt through all, even as water and wine mixt in one cup together, where all is through other; so all the affections of thy very heart are so mixt with this corruption, that it is spread over thy soul; for thy light is mixt with darkness, even thy very renewed part; thy faith is mixt with doubting (yea the best faith of us all is so;) thy memory is mixt with forgetfulness; so there is not one part in all thy soul or body that is not mixed with corruption. That ye may know this the better, read these places, Rom. vii. 14, 18, 23. "The law is spiritual, but I am carnal, sold under sin; for I allow not that which I do; but that I would do, that I do not; but what I hate that do I. For I know that in me (that is in my flesh) dwelleth no go thing. I find no means to perform that which is good, for I do not the good that I would, but the evil which I would not, that I do. I see a law in my members, rebelling against the law of my mind, and leading me captive to the law of sin that is in my members;" this made him in the end to cry out, "O miserable man that I am, who shall deliver me from this body of death!" Read the 5th chapter to the Galatians 17th verse, "The flesh lusteth against the spirit:" and what are the desires of the spirit, he tells them in the 22d and 23d verses, which are, "Love, joy, peace, long-suffering, patience, goodness, gentleness, faith, meekness, temperance." And what are the desires of the flesh, he telleth you in the 19th, 20th, and 21st verses, which are, "Adultery, fornication, wantonness, uncleanness, idolatry, witchcraft, hatred, debate, emulations, wrath, contention, sedition, heresies, envy, murder, drunkenness, gluttony, and such like." So where he says the lusts of the flesh fight against the spirit, by lusts are meant the corrupt desires of the heart; for it hath all the parts of a man at command; it can draw away the eyes to look upon vanity, it can make thy hands to work iniquity, it can make thy feet to run the wrong way, and turn thee from the ways of the Lord. So this lust can make up a whole man. Read 1 Pet. ii. 11. "Dearly beloved, I beseech you as pilgrims and strangers, abstain from fleshly lusts, which war against the soul. Wherefore, says he, being compassed about with such a cloud of witnesses, let us put off every thing that presseth down, and the sin that hangeth fast on." As ye see that sin is likened to a mill-stone, that lieth upon the heart, and holdeth it down, and it will not let thee lift up thy eyes to heaven, for it makes thy heart heavier than all the sand of the sea were on it, and it is called, *Euperisten ten amartian;* that is, it compasses and trenches thee in, that thou canst not get out of it no way; as who would besiege a castle, and trench it round about, that the enemy might not get out till they were glad to give over; even so sin will besiege thee, and hedge thee in, and set trenches about thee, that thou mayest give place for it. Read James i. 13, 15. where he says, "Every man is tempted, when is drawn away of his own lust and enticed. Then when lust is conceived, it brings forth sin: and sin when it is finished, it brings forth death." Whereby ye see that sin draweth the heart away from God, then it lays a bait of pleasure or profit to entice thee with, and so intangle thy heart: it conceives and lets in, the father of sin. Who is the father? Satan. Who is the mother? Thy unrenewed part; and when the father and mother meet, they conceive, and of them comes the birth of sin; and sin brings forth another birth, that is, death, that except it be forgiven and slain, it shall slay thee both soul and body. So the flesh is a great help to the enemy, for it is always with thee, wherever thou art, wherever thou goest, it goes thither also, and wherever thou abidest, it abides there also; and when thou art at the table, it hath a hand at the platter with thee; and suppose it be thy familiar friend, yet kissing thee it betrays thee, and that with a kiss under pretence of friendship, delivers thee to the devil, saying to him, there the man thou was seeking. In this you have to consider how to overcome it. Now, if ye would overcome the flesh,

First, You must deny yourselves : thou must hate it, but thou must hate thyself also ; thou canst not slay it, but thou must give a deadly wound to thy heart ; so take heed to thy principal enemy, Satan, take heed to the world, his special lieutenant.

Secondly, Take heed to thyself, that art his strong captain ; if there were a town or castle besieged by the enemy, wherein there were more traitors than true citizens, is it any wonder that this town or castle should be betrayed ? Even so it is with us, the castle is our heart, the enemy is the devil that continually besieges the castle, the traitors are the rebellious cogitations that are within our hearts ; what marvel then that the devil overcome the castle of our hearts ? And except we overcome them, they will betray us.

Now, what is the way to overcome them ? No way but this, thou must take them and slay them, and put them to death ; thou must crucify the affections and lusts of thy heart, or else the devil will gain the castle of thy heart, except thou cuttest the throat of these traitors within thee ; now ye see what a fight ye have to fight, ye see the principal enemy that wars against you, that is to say, principalities, powers, worldly governors, princes of the air, cruel lions, red dragons, wily serpents, the prince of darkness, and, in one word, the god of this world. Ye see again their malice, their power and subtility ; last of all, ye see the helpers they have, *viz.* The world without you, and your own corrupt flesh within you ; now seeing ye see all these things, beware of your own flesh, that is an enemy to yourself ; therefore ye must take the unrenewed part of your heart, and lead it to the cross, and there nail it to a tree, and let it hang there till it be dead ; for as long as sin lives within thee, there will never be an hour in the day but that traitor will open all the senses of the heart, and let in seven worse spirits than ever ye had before, so thy latter end will be worse than thy first estate. So ye have need to take heed to yourselves.

First, Therefore take a daily trial, and narrow search of all that is within thee ; and first take thy wisdom, and count it the greatest enemy to the wisdom of God ; take that, I say, and subdue it first, and learn the wisdom of God ; for till thou once comest to this, that ye become a fool to learn the wisdom of God, and once come to this that ye desire nothing but Christ and him crucified, then ye shall find a virtue coming from him, and crucifying all the rest of thy affection.

Secondly, Look to the predominant evil that is in thy heart, take it and set thy foot on it, as the captain and master of all the rest, and this shall be an earnest to thee, that seeing thou hast set thy foot upon the neck of the chiefest prince and strongest king, and having trode on his neck, it shall be a token to thee, that thou shalt get easily the victory over all the rest.

Thirdly, Take heed to the pleasures of this life, and beware that they bereave thee not of the joys of heaven ; look thou make not choice of them as a staff whereon thou leanest, and when thou feelest the love of God cooling, then think with thyself thou hast gotten a deadly wound : for the love of God never so soon begins to cool, but as soon the devil begins to get possession in thy heart ; so when thou findest this love growing cold, never rest till thou recoverest thy first love again ; for if thou continuest so, it is hard to know if ever thou cease from falling, till thou fallest into the very bottomless pit of hell.

I thought to have given you arguments to have stirred you up, and provoked you to put on your armour, and to recover your first love again ; for surely there is recoiling and falling back by us all, and I find it in myself especially, and would to God ye would recover your first love, for till it be done all things be in vain.

Now, I know ye are more bound to love God than ever ye were, for he multiplies his blessings daily upon you in great abundance, both by sea and land, both spiritual and temporal, that ye lack nothing ; yet ye see there is a falling away, and surely I look for the judgment of God to fall on the carcases of these men, that are stealing in corruption in the church, for to make us fall away from the true religion of God ; therefore God shall make them examples to others, to beware to meddle again with a glorious kirk at any time hereafter. Nevertheless if we can fast and mourn, and turn unfeignedly to our God, it may be, (I say) that God may grant us peace for our days. I remember, Daniel continued in fasting and prayer, and desiring God to be merciful, and to forgive his sins, and the sins of his people, and to deliver the church in his time ; and suppose he continued long praying for the space of twenty-three days in fasting and weeping, and confessing his sins, and suppose the Lord delayed long to give him an answer, yet the Lord heard him in the very beginning of his prayer, and sent him a gracious answer at the last. So if we could fast and pray, if it were but in one family or congregation, who can tell but the Lord would send a gracious answer in the end. Think ye not that this will be a fearful time when the Lord departs from us ? *Wo unto you,* says the Lord, *when I depart from you ;* so if the Lord would grant it you, to set one day apart for your humiliation, and every one in his family, at least to mourn before the Lord, the man in the one corner of the house, and the woman in another, the servants in one part of the house, and the children in another; who can tell but the Lord would relent his hand? See ye not what the repentance of Nineveth did, Jonah iii. 4. when the prophet was sent unto them, who told them, " Yet forty days and Nineveth should be destroyed;" now when they heard these sudden news, suppose they had no assurance of delivery, yet they will trust to the goodness of God, and they will try if they can prevent his judgments by repentance, and " therefore the king, and his court, and all his nobles, and the whole city repented, and humbled themselves in sackcloth and ashes;" the Lord seeing this, he alters his purpose, calls back his own sentence, and they find mercy. See ye not what the counterfeit repentance of Ahab did, that when he rent his clothes, and humbled himself in the dust, and put on sackcloth, the Lord said to him, " He would not bring on that evil," which the Lord had pronounced against him and his house, 1 Kings xxi. 27, *in his days;* see what this repentance doth; suppose he was a reprobate. Now have you not as great cause to mourn and repent as ever Daniel or Nineveth had, or Ahab had? Is not the removing of some of the faithful servants of God out of their places, and the binding up the mouths of other some, a more fearful token of his wrath, than all the pest that hath been in this land these two years by-gone? What means the removing of these lights that were wont to shine before others? No, as the Lord lives, I think it always a forerunner of a more fearful judgment than ever came yet in this land; the Lord give us eyes to see it, and wisdom to prevent it in time, that we may not be partakers thereof; or, at least, if we fall by the temporal judgment, that we be not partakers of the spiritual judgment also.

Now, I say no more, but I commend that which hath been spoken to the grace of God in Jesus Christ, to whom with the Father, and the Holy Ghost, be all honour and praise, for now and evermore, *Amen.*

SERMON XIV.

OF THE CHRISTIAN WARFARE.

Ephes. vi. 10.

Finally, my brethren, be strong in the Lord, and in the power of his might.

THE enemies with whom we have to do and to wrestle against, I have told you out of the word of God; but nothing spoken out of the truth of God can do you good, unless ye mix your hearing with faith: therefore, I beseech you, as ye would have the crown one day, and as ye would be clad with long white robes, and have palms in your hands, and as ye would be set on the right hand of Christ one day, I would request you to believe the thing that hath been spoken concerning this enemy of your salvation. Ye have to do with Satan, an enemy to God and an enemy to your souls; ye have to do with a devil that will slander you; ye have to do with a tempter, that will steal into your hearts ere ever ye know of him; ye have to do with an accuser, that will present your sins before the tribunal of God; ye have to do with a hangman, that will be the first to put hands in you, and the readiest to cut the throat of your soul; ye have to do with a lion, ye have to do with a dragon, ye have to do with principalities and powers, and worldly governors and princes of the air; and last of all, ye have to do with the god of this world. I recommend that to your memory which hath been spoken of their malice, their power and skill: the last thing was their helpers, *viz.* the world and the baits thereof, all the riches, all the honours, and all the pleasures of it. And for the overcoming of it, ye are to set your hearts on heaven, and to hold your eye upon the glory and the everlasting pleasures that are there. The most dangerous help he hath is the inborn corruption within thee, that holds thy heart down; for thou canst not go to heaven but with a burden of sin that compasses thee about, and that traitor that opens all the windows of thy heart, and lets in legions of devils, and that monster which conceiveth such a monstrous birth, which when it is brought forth, it conceives a far more cruel birth, James i. 15. Ye heard likewise the power of inbred corruption, that it hinders a man to do good, and it is a law that rebels against the law of the mind, Rom. vii. 23. It is a false rebel, therefore it will sell thee, as the apostle said, *I am sold under sin*, verse 24. Now for the overcoming of this enemy, thou must deny thyself; therefore Christ said, "No man can be my disciple, unless he deny himself, and take up his cross and follow me," Luke xiv. 27. And ye must not only deny yourselves, but also ye must slay yourselves; and there is no way to do that, but taking the dead and crucified Lord in your arms; let the nails that pierced him, pierce you to the heart; and let the spear that wounded him, wound you to the heart; take your souls and spread them upon him, that the savour of his death may strike you to the heart, and that his wounds may give to sin a deadly wound within you; so if ye would overcome sin, and the inborn corruption within you, and that lurks in your heart, ye must first overcome yourselves; ye must run and take a new drink of the blood of Christ daily.

Now it follows how you should wrestle. That ye may be the better informed therein, I will expound this text to you: always remember that God speaks here and the Holy Ghost informs you here. Now, I know well, this doctrine will be welcome to thee that resolvest to fight; and I am sure thou wilt say, I thank my God in Jesus Christ, that has opened the way to me so clearly, and hath let me see the manner how I shall fight my battles, how I shall overcome my enemies, and how in the end I shall get the victory.

But ye that have not yet believed the necessity of fighting, and the strong party ye have to encounter with, and that ye have to do with principalities, and powers, and devils, and dragons, and wily serpents, and the prince of darkness, and the god of this world. Now to tell thee of armour, and the putting on of armour, it is all but fables, it will do thee no good; for except ye see the necessity of fighting, and the strong party ye have to encounter with, it will all be but lost labour to speak to you of a battle, and fighting of a battle, and with what armour ye shall fight; for except that a man see that he is going to the war, and that he must fight, and has a strong army and party to fight against, and that there will be no assurance taken but upon this condition, that he give over his life into his enemies hands, who, he is assured, will not spare him; I say, except a man see these things, he will think it but folly to bid him to put on his armour: even so, if I would tell you never so much, that ye must put on your armour, and ye must fight, except ye see the necessity of fighting, and the necessity of putting on armour (for no man will go naked to the wars) and except ye see the strength of the enemy, all my speaking will avail little: howbeit so many of you that see these necessities, and have resolved to fight, hear ye this, " Finally, my brethren, be strong in the Lord."

First, He says, *be strong;* for if ye be feeble, ye cannot fight; ye must first have strength, for a weak man is soon overcome.

Secondly, He says, *be strong in the Lord;* thou must not stand thyself alone; if thou beest not in Christ and Christ in thee, thou canst not prevail; so the only way to be strong is in the Lord Jesus; his side is yet open, therefore thou mayest run into it, and it is faith only that puts thee in him; and if he be within thee, thou wilt find him killing all the enemies lurking within thy heart; so ye must be in the Lord, and ye must be strong in the Lord, and that is more than to be in Christ; ye must not be feeble in Christ, but ye must take a strong grip of Christ; thou must have him as a crowned king reigning within thee; what more? *And in the power of his might;* it is no matter how feeble thou beest in thyself, if thou beest strong in him; blessed is the man that sees his own feebleness, and sees his own weakness, for this will make him run faster to the Lord, that he might get his power and his might to sustain him; and this will make him say, I quit the flesh, and all that is within me; yea, I quit all things under heaven, O Lord, that I may be strong in thee, and in the power of thy might. Now what is his might? Strong was he in descending down from heaven, strong was he in his humiliation in the flesh, strong was that blood of his, strong was his death, strong was his resurrection, when he had all the sins of the elect upon his back; and since sin was so strong, that one sin cast the angels out of heaven, without any hope of rising again, yet all these sins could not keep him under, but he rose and overcame hell, the devil, and the grave, and went up to heaven, and led captivity captive; strong was his ascension up to heaven, and strong shall be his coming from heaven again to judge the quick and the dead. What is that to "be strong in the power of his might?" That is, be strong in the power of his descension from heaven to earth, be strong in the power of his incarnation, be strong in the power of his humiliation, be strong in the power of his blood; that, and if ye were the greatest sinner that ever was, this blood can make thee clean; if thy soul was as red as scarlet, this blood can make it as white as snow; be strong in his death, that is able to slay and mortify thy sins; and be strong in his resurrection, that is able to raise thee from death to life; and be strong in his coming again, and be strong in the hope of that endless glory.

Now follows, how ye shall get this might. "Put on the whole armour of God." Mark, "Put on the whole armour," and not a part of it; for thou must have it all on: And why armour? Because you have strong devils to fight with, therefore ye must not only have his righteousness to cover you, but ye must also have armour to quench all the fiery darts of the devil; not only must ye have armour to resist, but also thou must have armour to persevere with: Then what armour is this? It is the armour of God; "Our weapons, saith the apostle, "are not carnal, but spiritual, and mighty in operation;" so there is not a bit of this armour but it is corslet-proof; and if thou put it on thee, thou shalt abide the shot of a cannon; and if thou wear it, thou shalt not be hurt; but if thou lay it off, thou wilt not miss to get a deadly stroke; thou wilt perchance think it is but weak, but indeed it is not so.

He says, "Put on the whole armour of God;" thou must take all, thou must not leave one part of thy soul naked, for he is a wily and subtile enemy that thou hast to do with; if he see any part of thee unarmed and naked, he will take his advantage, and light on thee there; then thou must put it on thee, for it will do thee no good to lay it beside thee.

What is this armour? It is a sufficient furniture of all graces needful, which the Lord gives thee in the time of thy first calling, and thou hast them with thee, but thou canst not use them. What is the putting on of it then? Look to the graces which God gave thee in thy first calling; for, as I said thou hast all this armour, suppose thou hast not worn it; thou hast verity, that in the truth of thy heart thou wouldst serve God in some measure; thou hast the righteousness of Christ imputed to thee; thou hast the promises of the gospel, which in the end shall bring peace to thee; thou hast the seed of a true and saving faith sown in thy heart; thou hast hope that makes thee look for salvation; thou hast the sword of the Spirit, which is the word of God; so thou hast all these graces in thy heart in some measure, suppose thou canst not put them on: How shall ye put them on then? Even do this, bring them forth and use them, and avow before men and angels that ye wear these graces as your livery, given of your Lord and captain to you; then he says, "That ye may be able to resist," that is, to stand against; for you may hold your head up boldly, suppose there be many stabs and pricks in thy heart at every step thou steppest, yet being shod with the preparation of the gospel of peace, thou mayest walk safely, and leap over all stumbling-blocks that are cast in thy way *in the evil day*, that is, in the day of temptation, when the evil and envious one shall set upon thee; against all the assaults of the devil, that is all his onsets, all his brangles, and all his wrestlings, whereby he thinks to overthrow you, that ye may stand as a Christian man in his calling; stand, and lie not down, and be the last man in the field, stand and fight, stand and faint not. Now he comes to the particulars of this armour, and this hath seven pieces.

First, The *girdle of verity:* Stand, and your loins girded about with verity. What is the verity? Verity has two things.

First, Thou must have this warrant in thy soul, that thy worship is according to the truth of God, and that thou worship him as he himself commanded thee; and when thou art worshipping, thou art sure then thou obeyest his commands; and therefore thy worship pleases him. What consolation mayest thou have, when thou knowest thou hast this warrant, that thou mayest say, Lord, this worship pleases thee, because it is according to thy truth, I do it at thy command, to give thee obedience! What comfort will it be to thee when thou rememberest this is truth I do, and this is pleasant to God! The Papists have never these persuasions, but are always doubting whether their service be according to the truth of God, or whether God be pleased with it or not; therefore thou shouldst count it a great mercy that God has revealed this to thee, and made it clear to thy conscience, that thy service and worship is according to God's truth, and acceptable to him through faith in Jesus Christ.

Secondly, Not only must thou have truth but likewise worship God in sincerity, and in the truth of thy heart; "for God is a spirit, therefore he will be worshipped in spirit and truth;" that is with a sincere and upright heart, that is clean and honest in his sight: for understanding of this truth, read Micah vi. 7, 8. "Will the Lord (says he) be pleased with thousands of rams, or with ten thousands of rivers of oil? Shall I give my first born for my transgression, the fruit of my body for the sin of my soul? He hath shewed thee, O man, what is good; and what doth the Lord require of thee, but to do justly, and to love mercy, and to walk humbly with thy God?" And read Isaiah lxvi. 2. " To him will I look, saith the Lord, that is poor, and of a contrite heart, and trembles at my word." What is truth then? A pure and a contrite heart that trembleth at the word of God.

Question. But ye will ask how a man shall know this truth? The church of Rome hath not another warrant for them that their religion is true, but that their clergy have said it is so. But this is a weak ground for them to lean on, for they are beguiled with it. But how shall ye know if your worship be in sincerity and truth? Answer me first, and then I shall answer to thee again; tell me if thy inner man saith to the Lord, I dare take thee to record that the thing under heaven I would gladliest do, it is to please thee in thy worship, and my conscience bears me witness, that I would serve thee in the truth and honesty of my heart. If thou hast this much, then thou hast truth. I see I will get no further at this time, or to the next piece of armour. One thing only, and so I shall come to it.

How shall ye use these graces? know ye not how deadly discouragements have befallen you when ye cannot pray with such feelings as ye would? nor yet can ye hear the word with such fruit as ye desire? nor ye cannot give God thanks so heartily as ye would wish to do? The ignorance of the manner how ye shall use the graces of God, hinders you of great consolation; but come your way, and take this truth in your hand, and say, Lord, thou art witness to me, that this is my only choice, thy glory in my salvation, and if I had strength to do thy service sincerely, I should do it gladly with all my heart, Rom. vii. 19. "But I do the thing I would not, and the thing I would, that I do not." If ye will come to the Lord, and confess your inability to serve him in that strength of thy heart which thou cravest; and if ye will resolve to use the means, as you can, suppose with little comfort, only to give God simple obedience; if ye will do this, I say ye shall find great joy and consolation afterward.

Now I come to the last thing I have to speak of at this time. The next piece of our armour is the *breastplate of righteousness;* there are two sorts of righteousness, that every chosen child of God has, the one is imputed to them, and it is Christ's, and it is called the *righteousness of God;* the other is within thee, and it is called the *righteousness of a good conscience,* or *sanctification;* this double righteousness is called a breast-plate, because it keeps all the strokes of the enemy off the heart that it be not hurt; for ye know if the heart be wounded, there is nothing but death for thee; for as long as the heart is safe, ye cannot get a deadly wound; so suppose ye get strokes, yet if ye have the breast-plate of righteousness upon you, these strokes cannot get to thy heart, and therefore they cannot be deadly. It is true ye may get great strokes, as David got a great and sore stroke, when he fell into whoredom and murder; yet because he had always this righteousness as a breast-plate, that covered the heart of him, therefore that stroke was not deadly, for he got repentance and remission; for ye may get great strokes and sore falls, but as long as thou hast this righteousness of Christ covering thee, and as long as there is place for repentance, and as long as that blood speaks for thee, and as long as thou hast recourse to that blood, and as long as thou hast this much in thy heart, that thou hast an honest endeavour to please God in all thy ways, suppose thou failest in many points, and suppose thou makest many foul falls, and gettest many sore strokes, yet as long, I say, as thou hast this honest heart, thou hast not gotten a deadly stroke, therefore thy wound is not incurable. The Lord give you and me all this sincerity and honesty of heart, for Christ's sake : to whom, &c.

SERMON XV.

OF THE CHRISTIAN WARFARE.

Ephes. vi. 14, 15, 16.

Stand therefore, having your loins girt about with truth, and having on the breast-plate of righteousness ; and your feet shod with the preparation of the gospel of peace ; above all, taking the shield of faith, wherewith ye shall be able to quench all the fiery darts of the wicked.

WHAT necessity there is of putting on the whole armour of God, I need not repeat it to you ; and if it were the Lord's mercy and his pleasure to grant me my suit, I would wish ye were all clad with this whole armour. And I will say to you, it is a great testimony of the favour of God to you, if thou wert continually under this armour, continually exercised in the Lord's wars. Now, as there are none that put on clothes, that know not the necessity and comeliness of them ; so there is no man that will put on armour, but he that sees the necessity of a battle ; there is no man that puts on clothes, but he that sees the necessity of them ; so ye will never put on this armour till ye see the necessity of it. I am as sorry as I can, that never one of us have acquainted ourselves with this armour as we should ; for it is a sore matter, that this dragon should wound men and women, and they not feel it. I leave it to the Lord to work it in every one of the hearts of his own, the necessity of standing day and night in your armour that ye be not overcome in this battle ; for there is not one hour in all thy life wherein thou hast truce with the enemy, but that is the hour wherein the devil prevails, in that hour he gives thee a deadly wound ; there is not an hour in the morning, nor an hour in the evening, but thou hast need of this armour; nay, there is not an hour in all the day, but thou hast need of it, there is not a place thou comest to, there is not a company thou comest among, but thou hast always need of this armour; beest thou at home, beest thou in the fields, beest thou alone, beest thou with good company, or beest thou with evil, thou hast, at all places, at all times, and all occasions, need of this armour, and to be clothed with it. There were two particular pieces of this armour that I handled to you.

First, The first piece was the girdle of verity; " stand with your loins girded with the truth :" (girded, says he) ye see your clothes must be first fast about you, or else they will fall off you; even so your armour must be fastened upon you, and one piece must be knit to another, or else ye will lose them; then ye must stand, and not lye down, nor sit with it; ye must be always on your feet, ready to fight with it.

What this verity was, I told you, it was the truth that the Son had brought out of the bosom of the Father, and hath revealed it to us in his word; therefore, ye know, ye call upon the living God, and ye worship him that made the heavens and the earth.

Secondly, By it is meant truth in the heart, at least in the renewed part thereof; for thou wilt get no truth in thy flesh that rebels against the law of thy mind, therefore thou needest not labour to get it there; but if thou canst get truth in the inner-man of thy heart, I say, if there be truth to God, that thou mayest truly say, in the inner man, I love the thing that God loves, and, in the inner man, I hate the thing that God hates, this is truth, and it is sufficient; but if thou beest an hypocrite, thou canst not stand against the brashes of the devil : therefore I summon all your consciences here before an all-seeing God that hath seven spirits, I charge you all in his name, that each of you be ready to try whether ye have this truth in the inner man or not. Now, thou that art the child of God, this will be the thing that pains thee most, that thou canst not get thy heart straight and upright enough before God, and because thou canst not get the mountains of thy heart beaten down, and the heights thereof beaten down, and the hollowness made plain. Shall I tell thee how to get thy heart made straight and plain, and how thou shalt get it clean? I will tell thee, by faith the heart is made clean; believe, and thou shalt see wonders; believe, and thou shalt be saved. So then ye must run to heaven and lay hands on Jesus Christ, and ye must bring him down in your hearts, and get your hearts once planted and rooted in him, and he shall make thy heart clean; for thou must not delay to lay him to thy heart, until thou gettest his assurance in thy heart that thy sins are forgiven thee; but thou must first take his blood in thy arms, and then thou mayest be sure thou shalt be forgiven.

How makes faith thy heart clean? Thou seest it is foul, thou seest it is leprous and defiled with sin; now, when thou seest this, thou runnest to the blood, thou plungest thy soul in it, thou washest thy heart in it; and thereby thou art made clean; now, after thou seest thy heart somewhat clean, if thy resolution come from this, that because God is reconciled with thee, and because thou art forgiven of Christ and made clean in his blood; therefore thou wilt leave sin, and thou wilt love the thing that God loves, and wilt hate the thing that God hates: then this honest resolution will bring truth. What is the cause so many get so little consolation in God's promises? But because they go not with faith to Christ's blood, and apply it not to their souls; and because they would always see somewhat in themselves, ere ever they dare go to Christ; this bereaves many of great consolation; therefore ye see, that in faith ye must do all things whereby ye think to please God; "Abide in me," saith Christ, "and I will abide in you," John xv. 4. So there is no way to make thy heart clean, but only by coming to Christ, for renewing the remission of thy sins, and for a new assurance of thy salvation; so if thou mayest say in the truth of thy heart, that thou knowest well that the blood of the Son hath taken away thy guiltiness, and hath made thy heart clean ; and if thou mayest avow this before men and angels, now I am sure that the blood of Jesus hath purged my heart, and cleansed it from all sin ; I have gotten remission and salvation in that blood, therefore I will beware to defile my heart with sin again, and to trample that blood under foot, and to count it an unholy thing, and to grieve the Spirit of grace by my transgressions ; if thou mayest say this, thou hast truth in thy heart.

The *second* particular of this armour, was the *breast plate of righteousness*. What is this righteousness? Even where there is so much of the fear of God in thy heart, that wittingly or willingly thou darest not sin ; and when thou hast so much love to God, that thou wouldst serve God in the inner-man, if the Lord would give thee grace ; for he that loveth righteousness doth righteous things , so, whatever ye be doing, have always the glory of God before your eyes : if thou wouldst do this, then put on the breast-plate ; and look that the devil steal not away this love of God, and hatred of sin out of thy heart ; for as long as thou hast the love of God, and the hatred of sin in thy heart, thou canst not receive a mortal or deadly wound. This righteousness shall make thy calling and election sure, because thou gettest daily a new assurance of thy honest endeavours to serve God ; and this righteousness shall make a fair entrance to thee, that thou mayest come boldly to the throne of grace, being clothed with the righteousness of Christ, and there thou mayest ask boldly in his name whatever thou hast need of, for the Father will give it thee.

Now the *third* piece of this armour, is, after thy loins are girded with verity, and after thy breast is covered with righteousness, that thou " shoe thy foot with the preparation of the gospel of peace." Your feet must be shod, for in this journey there are briars, and thorns, and iron-pikes in thy way, that thou must tread on ; thou must trample on serpents and scorpions : therefore if thou beest not shod, thou canst never run or go on in this way: But wherewith must thou shoe thy feet? "With the preparation of the gospel of peace." What is meant by the gospel? All those precious gifts and graces promised to thee in the gospel, which are so great and so precious, that they can make thee partaker of the very divine nature; they are so great and so precious, that if thou wilt shoe thy feet with them, they shall not only make thy feet beautiful, but also they shall make thee partaker of the divine nature; and what more could be said? Thou wilt ask now, what are these promises? Even these, Art thou a sinner? There is a remission offered unto thee in the Son Christ Jesus, and come and take it. Are thy clothes foul? Come with them to the blood of the Lamb, and there make them clean. Is thy hand lame or withered, that thou canst not grip? Stretch it out before him, and he shall make thee whole. Are thy feet crooked, that thou canst not walk? Look to him and he shall restore to thee thy limbs and legs, and give them strength to carry thee. Is there a law in thy members rebelling against the law of thy mind? There the promise, "there is no condemnation to them that are in Christ, that walk not after the flesh, but after the Spirit." In a word, Art thou sold under sin? There the promise, "Christ, that knew no sin, was made sin for thy sake, and hath bought thee, not with gold and silver, and precious stones, but with his own precious blood," which is able to furnish thee in all thy wants. But it is like this will trouble thee, I am weak, and cannot persevere: there the promise of the gospel, John x. 28. "My sheep are in my Father's hand, and no man is able to pluck them out of his hand; none of my sheep shall perish. Fear not, little flock, for it is your Father's will to give you a kingdom. I have given my angels charge over you, that ye shall not dash your feet against a stone;" they shall be with thee in thy life, they shall be with thee in thy death; they shall carry thy soul into my bosom; they shall raise it, and join both soul and body together, and make thee conformable to the glorious body of Christ Jesus thy head; they shall set thee on his right hand on a throne with him, where thou shalt judge the world; after that thou shalt go with him to heaven, and there thou shalt reign with him in eternal glory. These and many more are the promises of the gospel. But why calleth he it the *gospel of peace*?

First, Because by it God reconciles thee to himself, and is at peace with thee.

Secondly, The gospel brings peace to thy conscience, through the assured persuasion of the remission of thy sins: this makes thee to say, my sins have cried aloud, or high, but the blood of Christ hath cried higher; my sins have been great, but the blood of Jesus hath been greater; my sins have been wonderful, but the blood of Jesus hath been more wonderful; my sins slew me, but the blood of Jesus puts life into my soul again; my sins have brought me down to hell, but the blood of Christ hath raised me up to heaven; my sins brought upon me the wrath and malediction of God, but the blood of Christ has brought peace and the blessing of God, and have made me have a right to all his promises and graces: So I rest in that blood and it brings peace to my conscience.

Now, from this peace of conscience comes the third peace, a peace with heaven, a peace with earth, a peace with all the creatures of God; the angels in heaven are at peace with thee; "the beasts of the field are at peace with thee; the very stones of the street are at peace with thee." Job v. 23.

And from this shall come another peace, when thou hast departed this life, and when God shall bring thee into heaven, and when thou shalt rest from all thy labours, and when all tears shall be wiped away from thy eyes, and when thou shalt "rest under the altar, and after thou art come through many temptations, and tribulations, and when thou hast washen thy long white robes in the blood of the Lamb," Rev. vi. 9, 10, 11. "When thou shalt sing that new song that no man can sing, but these that are learned of God;

and when thou shalt follow the Lamb whithersoever he goes;" and when thou art made a citizen of the new Jerusalem; and when thou shalt "eat of the fruit of the tree of life, and drink of the water of the fountain of life;" and when thou shalt take pleasure in beholding God continually, and there shall be but one tabernacle; and when "God shall be the temple, and the Lamb the light thereof:" then thou shalt have unspeakable joy and peace that passes all understanding. Now, why is it called "the preparation of the gospel of peace?" What will not this gospel of peace make thee ready to do? It will make thee ready to go to the fire with the three children, Shadrah Meshach, and Abednego, Dan. iii. it will make thee go to the den of lions with Daniel; it will make thee follow Christ in all his sufferings, and make thee go all the way he went; so there is nothing can make thee go through the roughest way that ever was, but only this peace of the gospel; and if thou hast it not with thee, thou shalt soon be defeated: as Peter, because he was not shod with the preparation of the gospel of peace, therefore the voice of a silly damsel frighted him, and makes him fail by the way. What is the cause that ye lout and stoop down so oft by the way? And what is the cause ye look so oft behind you to the golden apples the devil casts so often in your way to hinder your race, but because ye are not shod with the preparation of the gospel of peace? This made Moses ready to forsake Egypt, and to "chuse rather to suffer affliction with the people of God, than to enjoy the pleasures of sin for a season;" and will make thee ready to be subject to that "King that rode upon the white horse, that is called faithful and true, and judges righteously; whose eyes are as a flame of fire, and on his head were many crowns, and had a name that no man knew but himself; that was clothed in a garment that was dipped in blood, out of whose mouth went a sharp sword, wherewith he smote all the heathen; and that treads the wine-press of the wrath of God; that hath upon his garment, and upon his thigh this name written, "*King of kings, and Lord of lords.*" What can make thee one of his soldiers, I say, and to follow him upon a white horse? What but the preparation of the gospel of peace; it will make a man to wear the name of Jesus for his livery, that all may know him to be a soldier of Jesus Christ, that is a King; this will make him to say, I will avow him before men and angels, and that Christ is a crowned King in heaven, and should also be a crowned King on earth.

Now I come to the fourth piece of armour. "Above all, take the shield of faith," not only to keep the strokes, but this buckler hath another virtue in it than any other buckler in the world; it hath a virtue to save thee from all the strokes of the devil, that they cannot wound thee: And why? Because thou wearest that blood by faith, that suppose God be a consuming fire, yet having this blood on thy heart, thou darest step up before God, and yet not fear; thou darest abide the very tribunal of his severity; for it hath nothing to say against them that are marked with his blood: and faith hath another virtue, it can " quench all the fiery darts of the devil." What is that? Satan hath darts that he throws in the heart of man and woman to wound the conscience deadly, and to kindle a fire in the conscience; that when he hath once gotten in his head, and like a wily serpent crept into thy heart, then he may kindle a fire and a flame in thy soul, that nothing in heaven or in earth can quench it but that blood allenarly. Now, to prevent these deadly strokes and fiery darts, faith will put Christ on thee, and cover thee with his own righteousness, and thou walkest with him, and thou dwellest in him, and beautiful is that soul that hath put on Christ; beautiful is that place thou dwellest in, and all the parts thou comest into; beautiful is the table thou sittest at, and beautiful is the company thou art among. O beautiful is the soul that wears that long white robe of the righteousness of Christ? And beautiful is the soul and conscience that is washed in the blood of the Lamb!

So faith can make a man or woman beautiful before God, beautiful before the sight of both men and angels; but faith will do more, when the serpent is crept in, and when the sting in stung, and the fire is kindled in thy soul, thy faith will draw down the blood of Christ to thy soul, and it quenches the fire, healeth the sting, beats out the serpent, makes thee as whole and sound as ever thou wert. O! I cannot enough express to you the virtue of faith; well is the man or woman that ever got the least grain-weight of faith. Now, seeing there is such a virtue in one piece of this armour, when it is put on you, what virtue and force then, think ye, to be in the whole armour when it is put on you? Now, God knows, it is the only thing and portion I crave, that ye may all put on this whole armour; for this armour should set you in heaven, and make you to have your conversation there with angels, glorified spirits and saints, and with Christ, and with God himself. The Lord give you it, to put it on, for his own name's sake. To him be glory and praise for now and evermore. *Amen.*

SERMON XVI.

OF THE CHRISTIAN WARFARE.

Ephes. vi. 15, 16, 17.

And your feet shod with the preparation of the gospel of peace, &c.

THE Lord work that preparation in your hearts to hear this truth as the oracle of God, and the truth of his word; for it is so indeed, and cannot return in vain. Therefore, if it were the Lord's will, I would ye had this much, that ye would receive it, not as the word of man, but as the word of the everlasting God; for it is such a pearl that all the treasures under heaven cannot buy it.

But to the purpose: Armour is not esteemed of in the day of peace, but in the day of war; therefore ye should be trying whether ye have war with the devil or not; now, if ye have war with him, ye will esteem of this armour; and if ye esteem it, ye will labour to get it put on you.

Ye have heard of four parts or pieces of this armour.

First, "Gird your loins with verity," that is, whether ye eat, or ye drink, or be employed in your calling, or whatever ye do, see that ye have the glory of God before your eyes, and see that all the day long ye have this much truth in your heart, that you can say, "Lord, in the inner-man I desire to serve thee."

Secondly, "Put on the breast-plate of righteousness;" that when Satan would object to thee that thou hast no righteousness, nor truth, nor faith, nor repentance, nor no grace, yet thou mayest answer, "I would do good, for the will is present with me, although

I cannot perform it; for the thing I would not do, that I do; and the thing that I would do, that do I not."

The *third* was, "To shoe your feet with the preparation of the gospel of peace." This gospel offers fair promises to thee: believe, and thou shalt get eternal life; thou shalt be in the covenant of grace: And what is the covenant of grace? "I will put my law in their inward parts, and write it in their hearts; and I will be their God, and they shall be my people; they shall know me from the least to the greatest of them; I will forgive their iniquities, and remember their sins no more," Jer. xxxi. 33, 34. "I will put my fear in their heart, that they shall never depart from me," Jer. xxxii. 40. or fall away from me. These are fair promises, and God will be thy God, that suppose thou wouldst alter or change on thy part, yet he shall never alter or change to thee, for he is unchangeable: And what more hath he promised? I will be with thee all thy lifetime, I will be with thee in the fire, I will be with thee in the den of lions; I shall never leave thee in the midst of trouble and persecution; when thou prayest to me, I will be with thee, and hear thee; when thou art in danger, I will deliver thee; when the course of thy life is near an end, I will come and carry thy soul to paradise, where I am; I will keep the moold of thy rotten carcase unto the day of thy resurrection, when I shall join both soul and body together, and take thee into my palace, and give thee possession of endless glory. Now, these promises being applied to thyself, they will make thee ready to do all things; those fair promises will make thee run thy race with joy and pleasure; then thou wilt not go in a slow pace, but thou wilt go on thy journey speedily, notwithstanding all the thorns, and iron-pricks, and stumbling-blocks, that shall be laid in thy way; thou wilt leap over them all to gain that crown which thou seest set at thy journey's end.

The *fourth* part of that armour was, "Take to you the shield of faith above all things." This target or shield hath two properties:

First, It can keep all the strokes of the devil off thy heart; and this virtue comes not from thy faith, but from the power of him that thy faith looks unto; for faith is but the gold-ring wherein that precious stone is, which is the blood of Christ Jesus; and it is that precious stone which healeth the wound, and not faith, which is but the gold-ring. Faith itself is as weak as any of the rest of the gifts of God; but because it hath eternal life, the essential word, and blood of Jesus, that was first humbled, and since glorified, and now is made higher than the highest heavens; because, I say, it hath this clasped within it, therefore it hath so strong and powerful a virtue. So faith can keep off all the strokes of the devil. Will Satan say thou art a sinner? Faith will answer, "Christ came to save sinners," 1 Tim. i. 15. "Christ came not to call the righteous, but sinners to repentance," Mat. ix. 13. Will the devil say thou art a great sinner, and hast a heavy burden of sin upon thy back? Faith will answer, "Come unto me, all ye that are weary and laden with sin, and I will ease you," Mat. ix. 28. Will the devil say thou art under the curse? Faith will answer, "Christ was made a curse for me, that I might be blessed." Will he say, No unclean thing can enter into heaven? Faith will say, The blood of Jesus hath made me clean, that I cannot be holden out. So faith shall object to all his strokes a contrary medicine. That is the first use of faith, to keep off all the strokes of the devil.

The *second* is, Were thy wounds never so deadly, or the fire of God's wrath never so hot kindled against thee, faith can take that blood of Jesus, and cast it into the flame, and quench the flame and fire. So, were thy sins never so deadly, whether they be sins of ignorance before thy calling, or sins against the light of thy conscience, after thy calling; yea, all sins, except the sin against the Holy Ghost, faith can quench them all, were they never so great. Was there a greater sin than David's adultery, which he did against the light of his conscience, and would gladly have smothered it, and to cover that sin he fell into a worse and committed murder? 2 Sam. xi. 4. Yet, because he believed in the Messiah to come, he repented, and found mercy. Was there a greater sinner than Manasses, 2 Kings xxi. 3. &c. that brake down the altars at Jerusalem, and corrupted the true religion and worship of God, and set up idolatry, and caused the streets of the city to run with the blood of the saints, who, for his sin, was led captive to a strange land, and there cast into prison? 2 Chron. xxxiii. 11, 12, 13. Yet, when he cried unto the Lord out of the prison, and repented him of his former sins, and because he believed in the promised Messiah, therefore the Lord heard his prayer, and granted him mercy. Was there a greater sin than Peter's threefold denial of Christ? Mat. xxvi. 71, 72, yet, because he repented, and believed in the Son of God, he was forgiven. Were there greater sinners than these men, that with their wicked hands crucified the Lord of glory? Luke xxii. 53. yet when they were pricked in their consciences, the apostle bids them repent, and be baptized with the seals of faith; they did so, and therefore found mercy. So, I say, were thy sins as red as scarlet, yet faith in that blood of Jesus is able to make them as white as snow.

Now follows the 5th part or piece of this armour, "Put on the helmet of salvation." What is that salvation? I will never go to hell, suppose I be worthy of it; I will go to heaven, in despite of the devil and all his power; I shall be saved, though many millions of reprobates be condemned. But how shall ye put salvation on as a crown upon your heads, that ye may lift up your head when the Lord is coming in the clouds, when thou seest the day of thy redemption drawing near, and when thou seest heaven and earth in a fire, when thou seest the elements to melt, and the heavens to roll away as a scroll of paper, and when the reprobates shall cry to the rocks, *Cover us*, and to the hills, *Fall on us*, how shalt thou then take salvation unto thee? I tell thee, as I said before, thou that hast ever been truly called, thou hast all this armour and all these graces lurking within thee; even so soon as ever thou art called, thou hast all this in thy heart, thou hast the righteousness of Christ imputed unto thee, and inherent righteousness begun in thee; thou hast the promises of the gospel offering peace to thee; thou hast the seed of a true and saving faith sown within thee; thou hast also the helmet of salvation, which is hope, within thee: therefore it is easy to step to thy heart, and take hope to thee, which is called *the helmet of salvation*, because thou that hast hope art already saved; so thou that hast faith, thou hast also salvation, that insomuch if the Son can be condemned, then mayest thou be condemned; and can the Lord come from heaven to die again, then mayest thou be damned; yea, I say to thee, ere thou wert damned, the Lord had rather come and die again, which is not possible. Now, what is hope? A certain persuasion arising from thy heart, grounded only upon the grace of God, that all his promises of mercy in Christ shall be accomplished in thee, and all the judgments of God shall be accomplished on thy enemies and his: so then for taking this helmet of salvation, ye have no more to do but to look into thy heart, and take it out and wear it, eat and drink, wake and sleep, hear and pray, and do all that thou dost as a man that waiteth daily for the coming of the Lord, as a man that is looking always when the heavens should rend, and when the Lord shall come in the clouds to judge the whole earth; as a man always shooting out his head, looking for the day of salvation: so put on hope, and thou shalt never fall from Jesus; put on hope, and thou shalt never want the Spirit; put on hope, and thou shalt trample Satan under thy feet; put on hope and thou shalt never be ashamed.

Now the 6th part of this armour is this, "Take the sword of the Spirit which is the word of God." This sword hath two edges, with the one it hurteth, with the other it slays; this sword is so sharp, that it can sunder the marrow from the bone; strange is the power of this sword, 2 Cor. x. 4. it can beat down principalities and powers, and every strong hold, and every thing that is exalted against the true knowledge of God; that it can bring into captivity every thought to the obedience of Christ; and it hath in readiness the vengeance of God against all disobedience; this sword of the word is able to defend thee against all thy enemies, and against all the temptations of Satan: but here is all the danger, many have a sword and hurt themselves with it, because they cannot use it; so all the policy is to use it well: and as David took the sword of Goliah, and slew him with his own sword, 1 Sam. xvii. 51. even so the devil may take the sword of the word and give thee a deadly stroke with it. How shall ye use it well? Even do as Mary did, Luke i. 19. she pondered the words of Christ and laid them up in her heart: do as David did, Psal. cxix. 92. that said, "Except thy law had been my delight, I would have perished in my affliction. Ver. 97, 98, 99, &c. Oh, how love I thy law! it is my meditation continually: by thy commandments thou hast made me wiser than mine enemies, for they are ever with me. I have more understanding than all my teachers: I understand more than the antients, because I have kept thy precepts. How sweet are thy promises to my mouth! yea sweeter than the honey or the honey-comb. Thy word is a lantern to my feet, a light to my steps. My soul is continually in my hand, yet do I not forget my law. Thy testimonies have I taken as my heritage for ever, for they are the joy of my heart." Do as the apostle speaks, 1 Thess. ii. 13. how they did, saying, "for this cause also we do thank God without ceasing, that when ye received the word of God which ye heard of us, ye received it not as the word of men, but as it is indeed the word of God, which also worketh in you that believe." Do as the apostle exhorteth the Colossians, chap. iii. 16. to do, saying, "Let the word of God dwell with you plenteously in all wisdom, teaching and admonishing one another in psalms, and hymns, and spiritual songs, singing with grace in your hearts to the Lord." Do as the Lord commands you, Deut. vi. 7, 8, 9. "These words, which I command you this day, shall be in your heart, and thou shalt rehearse them continually to thy children, and thou shalt talk of them while thou stayest in thy house, and when thou walkest by the way, and when thou liest down, and risest up, and thou shalt bind them for a signet on thy hand, and they shalt be as frontlets betwixt thy eyes; also thou shalt write them upon the posts of thy house, and upon thy gates, that thou mayest look upon them when thou comest in, and when thou goest out." Do as the Lord commanded Joshua, chap. i. 7, 8. "Only be thou strong and of a valiant courage, that thou mayest observe to do according to all the law which Moses my servant commanded thee; thou shalt not turn from it either to the right hand or the left, that thou mayest prosper whithersoever thou goest. Let not this book of the law depart out of thy mouth, but meditate thereon both day and night, that thou mayest observe and do according to all that is written therein; for then shalt thou make thy way prosperous, and thou shalt have good success."

Last of all, Do as thy Lord and master did, when Satan tempted him, he brought ay out the word and confuted him with it: even so do thou, when he would tempt thee to sin, cast always the word in his teeth: will he tempt thee with pride? bring out the word of God, 1 Pet. v. 5. "God resisteth the proud, and giveth grace to the humble." Will he tempt thee with fear and misbelief? bring out the word, "the fearful, and misbelieving, and abominable, shall have their portion in the lake that burns with fire and brimstone, which is the second death." Will he tempt thee with the cares of this world? bring out the word, "be not careful for your life, what ye shall eat, or what ye shall drink, nor yet for your body, what ye shall put on: is not the life more worthy than meat, and the body than raiment? Behold the fowls of heaven, for they neither sow nor reap, nor gather into barns, yet your heavenly Father feeds them: Are ye not much better than they? Which of you taking a care can add one cubit to his stature? and why do ye take care for raiment? Consider the lilies of the field how they grow; they toil not, nor labour not, neither do they spin; yet I say unto you, that even Solomon in all his glory was not arrayed as one of these. Wherefore if God so clothe the grass of the field, which is to-day, and to-morrow cast into the oven, shall he not much more clothe you, O ye of little faith? Therefore take no thought, saying, what shall we eat? or what shall we drink? or where-withal shall we be clothed? (for after all these things do the Gentiles seek) for your heavenly Father knoweth that ye have need of these things: but seek ye first the kingdom of heaven, and the righteousness thereof, and all these things shall be ministered unto you: care not then for to-morrow, for to-morrow shall care for itself: the day hath enough for its own grief," Matt. vi. from the 25 ver. to the end. Bring out the word, "Fear not, little flock, for it is your Father's will to give you a kingdom." Bring out the word, "Labour not for the meat that perisheth, but labour for the meat that endureth to life everlasting," John vi. 28. Bring out the word, "When we have food and raiment let us be content; for they that are rich fall into temptations, and snares, and many foolish lusts, which drown men into perdition and destruction: for the desire of money is the root of all evil; which when some lusted for, they erred from the faith, and pierced themselves through with many sorrows. But thou, O man of God, flee these things; and follow after righteousness, godliness, faith, patience, and meekness. Fight the good fight of faith, and lay hold on eternal life, whereunto thou art also called," 1 Tim. vi. 8, 9, 10, 11, 12. "Cast all your care upon him, for he careth for you, 1 Pet. v. 7. Cast thou thy burden on the Lord, and he shall nourish thee; he will not suffer the righteous to fall for ever," Psal. lv. 22. Will he tempt thee with the love of this world, and the friendship thereof? Bring out the word, Matt. x. 37, 38. "He that loveth father or mother better than me, is not worthy of me; and he that loveth son or daughter better than me, is not worthy of me," saith Christ, " he that taketh not up his cross, and followeth me, is not worthy of me; and whosoever shall be ashamed of me and my words, amongst this adulterous and sinful generation, of him shall the Son of man be ashamed also, when he comes in the glory of his Father with the angels:" Bring out the words, 1 John ii. 15, 16, 17. " Love not this world, neither the things that are in this world. If any man love this world, the love of the Father is not in him; for all that is in this world, as the lusts of the flesh, the lusts of the eye, and the pride of life, is not of the Father, but is of this world; and this world passeth away, and the lusts thereof; but he that doth the will of God, abideth for evermore." Will Satan tempt thee to anger? bring forth the word, Mark x. 24. " Let not the sun go down upon thy wrath." Bring forth this word, " Be angry and sin not." Will he say, thou believest not, and therefore belongest not to the promise? bring forth the word, " Lord, I believe, Lord, help my unbelief." Will he tempt thee with desperation, because of the greatness of thy sins? bring forth the word, Matt. xi. 28. " Come unto me all that are wearied and ladened, and I will ease you." Will he tempt thee with unthankfulness? bring forth the word, " Watch and pray continually; in all things be thankful." Will he tempt thee with forgetfulness? bring forth the word, " When thou enterest into the land that floweth with milk and honey, which the Lord thy God hath promised to thee, beware then to forget the Lord thy God." Will he tempt thee with the breach of the sabbath? bring forth the word, " The sabbath was made for the man, and not the man for the sabbath; wherefore the Son of man is Lord over the sabbath."

Now this is your misery, that ye cannot use the word of God; for had ye as much light and integrity as Adam had, and had ye as great wisdom as Solomon had, except ye have this written word ready to produce and bring forth, ye will be deceived; but measure this with flesh and blood, ye will but think this a weak weapon; but will ye judge rightly, and ye shall find this word mightier than all your meditation, all your prayers, and all your thanksgivings, or whatever ye can do to further the service of God, and to overcome the temptations of the devil.

The *seventh* and *last* part of this armour is prayer, and it is put in the last room, because without prayer all the rest will do no good; prayer teacheth thee how to wear all the rest of thy armour; prayer teacheth thee how to put it on, and how to keep it on when thou hast it: so prayer is the most effectual grace of them all: Moses's prayer did more than Joshua and all the chosen men of Israel could do against the Amalekites; for, " when Moses held up his hands, Israel prevailed; but when he let his hands down, Amalek prevailed," Exod. xvii. 9, 10, 11. Even so in the hour that thou faintest in prayer, then the devil prevails; but as thou growest in prayer, so grace groweth for thee and increaseth in thee; the very sparks of fire of the zeal and love of God, which the Holy Ghost puts in thy heart, he puts them in especially when thou art praying, so great is the force of prayer: ye would think the sun swift, but prayer is swifter; Josh. x. 12. " Joshua prayed and the sun stood in the midst of heaven, and hastened not to go down for one whole day, till Joshua had overcome all his enemies." Ye would think the sea deep, Jonah prayed out of the midst of the whale's belly, in the midst of the sea, and the Lord heard him, and made the whale come to land, and brought him out safe and sound, Jonah ii. 2. " Elias prayed that it might not rain for the space of three years; and he prayed again that it might rain and it rained. Paul and Silas prayed in the prison, and there was a great earthquake, so that the foundations of the prison were shaken, and by and bye the prison doors were opened, and every man's bands were loosed," Acts x. 25, 26. The church made earnest prayer for Peter, when Herod had cast him into prison, and the Lord sent an angel to him, and bid him " rise quick, and come away, so that the chains fell off his hands;" so the angel brought him "to the iron-gate of the city, and it opened of its own accord to him," and so Peter was delivered, Acts xii. 7, 8, 9, 10. So great are the wonders that prayer wrought since the beginning; but I will tell you the heads shortly, that I mind to speak of concerning prayer:

First, I will tell you what prayer is.

Secondly, I will tell you the causes of moving you to pray.

Thirdly, I will tell you some circumstances of prayer.

Fourthly, I will tell you the manner how ye should pray.

Fifthly, I am minded to tell you of the joys that ye shall get by prayer; in the mean time I request you to put on this armour. Will ye essay it for a day, or if ye cannot bear it a whole day, yet try it for half a day; and if ye cannot bear it half a day, yet will ye but try it for an hour or two; and from that time ye shall find more joy and consolation, and more strength, than ever ye had all the time of your life heretofore, that ye wanted it; and will ye wear it for this time of your pilgrimage and warfare which is but short? and one day ye shall bless the Lord that he ever thought you worthy to put you in this battle, and to fight under his standard, and to make war under the banner of his Son Christ Jesus: to whom with the Father, and the Holy Spirit, be all praise and glory, for now and evermore. *Amen.*

SERMON XVII.

OF THE CHRISTIAN WARFARE.

Ephes. vi. 18.

Praying always with all prayer and supplication in the Spirit, and watching thereunto with all perseverance, and supplication for all saints.

THE last point left unto us of this armour, that ye must have on you, if ye would fight the Lord's battles constantly, and in end to get the crown, it is prayer; but I would ye remembered the former parts of this armour also, and I would ye put it on you all, even this same day; but till the Lord let you see the necessity of this armour, ye will never take pains to wear it; for this is one of the drifts of Satan, that he would hinder you to put on your armour. But, my hearts, be no longer deceived with him; and if ye have not yet put it on, or if ye have laid it off again, after ye had once put it on, notwithstanding these things, yet, even now, put on all the armour of God this day: put on *verity*, and gird your loins with it; put on *righteousness*, and cover thy breast with it; then remember the great *promises* that God hath made to you in the gospel, and *shoe your feet* with them, that the pleasures of this life make you not sit down, or hinder you in your race, and that ye may leap over all the rocks and stumbling-blocks that may be laid in your way; then, above all things, take on you *the shield of faith*, and unto all the temptations of the devil object always Christ; for as he was not able to overcome him in the wilderness, neither shall he be able to overcome them that are in Christ; and if there be any of you wounded through imprudence, and no watching and take heed to yourselves, take that blood and apply to your wounds, for it can cure them, and can "quench all the fiery darts of the devil;" yea, if thou canst not get to it as thou thinkest, and if thou darest not lay thy foul hands upon it, yet look up to that blood with the eye of faith, and it shall heal the sting of thy conscience, as they that but looked to the brazen serpent that was a figure of Christ, they were preserved from the sting of the fiery serpents in the wilderness, Numb. xxi. 8, 9. Then take the helmet of salvation, take hope that thou shalt never perish; hope that thou shalt persevere to the end; hope to die in the Lord; hope that thy soul shall be carried into the bosom of Christ, and that thy body shall be kept in the grave to the last judgment; hope that thou shalt rise again, and soul and body shall be joined again together, and that thy body shall be made conformable, and like to the glorious body of Christ; hope that thou shalt sit on a throne with Christ, to judge the twelve tribes of Israel; and hope that thou shalt get a crown of endless glory. Then the last point was, *take the word of God*, that naked sword of the Spirit, into your hand, and always when the enemy sets on, have always the word in readiness, that therewith thou mayest give him a backward stroke. Now, would to God ye could delight to read, to speak, and to meditate, day and night on that word, and then doubtless ye shall be blessed as David says, Psal. i. 1, 2. "Blessed is the man that walketh not in the counsel of the wicked, nor stands in the way of sinners, nor sits in the seat of the scornful; what doth he then? it follows in the second verse, "but he delights in the law of the Lord, and in his law doth he meditate both day and night." Now, what is this to meditate both day and night? It may be ye all understand it not; I will tell you therefore the meaning of it; he meditates day and night upon the law of God, that eating or drinking, sleeping or waking, lying down or rising up, at home or abroad, he hath always the word of God to be his guide, and to be a lanthorn to his feet, and the thought of that word never goes out of his heart; it is so sweet to his mouth that he would not change it with the honey or the honey-comb ; therefore he delights to read it, he delights to speak of it, and he delights to think and meditate on it.

Now, ye have the express command of God to do so as in the vi. of Deuteronomy, and in the xvii. of Deuteronomy, and in Joshua i. 8. Ye see what is spoken of the virtuous woman in the Proverbs xxxi. 26. " She openeth her mouth with wisdom, and the law of grace is in her tongue." That is, she delights to talk of the word of God. Now, my hearts, do as this woman did, this would not hinder your calling, but rather further you ; will ye be talking of the word of God, when ye are carding or spinning at the wheel, or whatever ye be doing within the house, or without it, in barn or byre, at home or abroad, let always the word of grace be in your lips ; ye that can read, will ye take the book of God and read two or three lines of it to the rest, and talk of it to them ; and ye that are learned, teach them that are unlearned ; and ye that are ignorant, ask at them that are learned, and desire them to resolve your doubts ; and this ye should do, and the law of God binds you to do it ; and if ye could come in acquaintance with this, then should ye say with David, Psal. cxix. 97. " O Lord, how love I thy law ! It is my meditation continually." And if David, had such pleasure in the law, that was but a shadow and a dead letter ; what pleasure should you have in the gospel, that is the substance, and brings spirit and life indeed ? I know the reading and talking of the word, and hearing of it, will be loathsome and tedious to thee that hast thy heart filled with this world, that thou canst not hold any more ; for a man that is sick, and hath his stomach filled and gorged with foul humours, the very savour of meat will fill him ; even so, as long as your hearts are filled with the cares and voluptuous pleasures of this life, there is no room in your hearts for the word of God ; so you must cleanse your hearts and empty your stomachs, or ever this word of God can do you any good; so except ye have verity and truth in the inner-man ; except ye have righteousness covering your heart ; except your feet be shod with the promises of the gospel ; except ye have faith in the blood of Jesus ; and except ye have the hope of that endless glory, ye will never give yourselves much to the hearing, reading, meditating or conferring upon the word : and suppose ye come and hear for a time ; yet except your heart be clean, your hearing will do no good : so, my hearts, above all things keep your hearts clean.

Now, ye will ask, how ye shall keep your hearts clean ? By these means ye shall keep them clean :

First, Keep always the love of God in your hearts, and let the sense of that love be always fresh in your souls ; and keep sure this persuasion in your hearts, he is my God, and I am his child ; he is my Saviour, and I am one that he has bought with his blood ; he is my Shepherd, and I am one of his flock : Now, the sense of this persuasion will always hold thy heart open to receive the graces of God offered in his word.

Secondly, Be always in readiness to do every good work ; and when thou failest in any good work, and when thou failest in any point of thy duty, either through neglect or contempt of the means ; then run to the Mediator, and desire him to cover thee with his own righteousness, and to purchase a pardon for thy offences, and to cleanse thy polluted soul by virtue of his blood.

Thirdly, Keep always the promises of God made to you in Christ, keep them ay in your heart, set them always before your eyes, and think always with yourselves that they belong to you.

Fourthly, By faith the heart is made clean ; take this as the principal means to cleanse your hearts, grip to the blood of Jesus ; that if your hearts were never so foul and leprous ; yea, suppose they were but dens of incarnate devils, and filled with unclean spirits, yet that blood is able to drive them all out, and make the heart clean, that it may be a temple to his Spirit to dwell in.

Fifthly and *last of all*, "Put on the helmet of salvation," which may encourage thee to take pains and labour upon thy heart; and then take the word itself, and it shall help to cleanse thy heart; "Sanctify them by thy truth," says our Saviour, John xvii. 7. "for thy word is truth." Now, my hearts, I beseech you, for all the love and mercies of God bestowed upon you, and for the glory that ye hope shall be revealed to you one day, remember this is the time of your pilgrimage, and the days of your warfare; and remember also that there is a crown before you, which ye will not get till ye get unto your rink's end; and ye have not yet ended your race; and ye must always be running whilst that ye are here; for ye shall think all your labour and travel well bestowed, when ye shall see that crown set upon your head, and when ye shall be put in possession of that glory that is now hid from you, and which ye hope shall be revealed one day.

Now remains the last part of this armour to be spoken of, which is prayer: Do this, and thou shalt do all the rest; therefore he puts this last, as the most needful, and without the which the rest can do no good; because it is not thy former graces, that is, it is not thy truth, it is not thy righteousness, it is not thy promises, it is not thy faith, it is not thy hope, nor is it thy word, that will sustain thee in the day of temptation, if thou wantest prayer. Why? Because new temptations must have new graces, and by prayer only the graces of God are renewed: "Call upon me," saith the Lord, "in the day of trouble, and I will hear thee." Then, by the contrary, if thou callest not upon me in the day of trouble, I will not hear. "Watch and pray," saith Christ, "that ye fall not into temptation. Then, by the contrary, if ye watch not, and pray not continually, ye shall fall into temptation. So, without prayer, I say, all the rest will do thee no good: so that, suppose thou hast truth in the innerman, yet there is always "a law in thy members rebelling against the law of thy mind." Suppose thou hast righteousness in one part of thy heart, yet there is unrighteousness in another part of it. Suppose thou hast faith, yet it is always mixed with doubtings; and suppose ye have hope, yet it is always mixed with mistrust; so thou hast always need of prayer, to uphold thee that thou despair not; and suppose the word to be in thy mouth, and suppose thou hearest and speakest of it, yet how often wantest thou the right use of it, that neither thou gettest comfort to thyself by it, nor yet givest comfort to others; now, when all this cannot comfort thee, and when thou hast almost given over all, then thou runnest to prayer, and it brings comfort to thee; and prayer will learn thee to put on all the rest of thy armour; prayer will make thee to say, now I will gird my loins with verity; now I will put on the breast plate of righteousness; now I will shoe my feet with the preparation of the gospel; now I will take to me the shield of faith; now I will put on the helmet of salvation; now I will take the word to be my guide, for I am going in the presence of my God, that searcheth the secrets of all hearts: so prayer runs to heaven, and brings him whom the heavens cannot hold; it brings Christ to thy soul; and as long as thy hands are holden up to God, thou shalt prevail against the enemy; but whenever thou beginnest to faint in prayer, and thy hands begin to fall down, then the enemy prevails; even as Moses, "so long as his hands were holden up to God, the Israelites prevailed; but when his hands fell down, then Amalek prevailed;" therefore Aaron and Hur set a stone under his arms, and held up his hands: so, when thou canst not pray thyself, desire others to help thee in their prayers, and to pray for thee. But, to come to the particular heads I intended to handle about prayer:

First, Ye must know what prayer is.

Secondly, Ye must know how ye shall get prayer.

Thirdly, Ye must know how ye must persevere in prayer, and not faint therein.

Fourthly, Ye must know to whom ye must pray.

Fifthly, Ye must know after what manner ye should pray.

Sixthly, For whom ye should pray.
Seventhly, What ye shall get by prayer.
Eighthly and *last of all,* What are the things that may further you in prayer.

As for the *first,* Remember when thou prayest, the heavens are opened, and thou gettest the chamber of his presence open to thee, (I speak to believers only) and thou comest in and gettest God's eyes ready to look favourably on thee, thou gettest his ears open ready to hear thee, and thou gettest his hands ready to help thee, and thou gettest his feet swift to come unto thee; thou seest him coming over the hills and mountains of thy transgressions, swiftly as a hind, or a chased roe. Then comes prayer. What is prayer then? It is a sweet conference betwixt God and thy soul, when the soul talks homely with God, by laying before him, as a merciful father, its own wants and necessities as God revealed them to him: so there is no need of a master of requests there, for to receive thy bill, and to present it to the king, and see if he will accept of it or not; but thou mayest step to the King thyself, or to the King's Son, that shall take thee by the hand and lead thee unto his Father, and by his blood he hath made a way into heaven, that a sinner may step in boldly upon that blood, not to the holy of holies, but into the highest heavens; he hath made us priests, that we may step into the Father all the hours of the day, not with the blood of bullocks, or of goats, or other beasts, but with the blood of his own Son the Lord Jesus; not once in the year, but every hour in the day; not into the holy of holies, but into the highest heavens: for prayer makes thee very homely and familiar with God, and prayer is nothing else but an homely and familiar talking with God.

The *second* was, How ye shall get prayer. For the getting of prayer ye must know, that prayer is the gift of God, and therefore it must be gotten from God himself, and he must give it, or else ye will never get it. Now to give you scripture for this, that prayer is the gift of God, read Joel ii. 28. "And it shall come to pass afterward, saith God, I will pour out my spirit (meaning the spirit of prayer) upon all flesh; and your young men shall see visions, and your old men shall dream dreams; and on my servants and handmaids will I pour out my spirit, and they shall prophesy; and whosoever shall call upon the name of the Lord shall be saved."

The apostle Peter brings in the same prophecy, Acts ii. 17. proving, that this prophecy was fulfilled in those days, immediately after Christs ascension, when the disciples had received the Holy Ghost; read Zeph. iii. 9. " Surely then will I turn to the people a pure language, that they may all call upon the name of the Lord to serve him with one consent." Read Zech. xii. 10. "And I will pour upon the house of David the spirit of grace and supplication," that is, the spirit of prayer, " and they shall look on me whom they have pierced, and they shall lament for him as one doth for his only Son, and be sorry for him, as one that is sorry for his first born." Read Rom. viii. 15. "For we have not received the spirit of bondage to fear again, but the Spirit of adoption, whereby we cry Abba, Father, ver. 26. likewise also the Spirit helpeth our infirmities; for we know not what to pray for as we ought; but the Spirit itself makes request for us with sighs that cannot be expressed." Read 1 Cor. xii. 3. " I tell you no man speaking by the Spirit calleth Jesus execrable; also no man can say Jesus is the Lord, but by the Holy Ghost." Read Gal. iv. 6. "Because ye are sons, God hath sent forth the Spirit of his Son into your hearts, which cryeth Abba, Father." So by these places, ye may see that God must needs send the spirit of prayer to us before that we can pray as we ought; and this may be great consolation to thee, when thou knowest it was not flesh and blood, but it was the Holy Ghost that led thee to prayer, and whenever thou hadst a heart to cry Father, father, as oft hast thou had the Spirit of adoption, sealing up to thee that thou wast the son or daughter of the living God: for never one could yet rightly pray, but the child of God only ; they may well, with Balaam, desire to "die the death of the righteous," Numb. xxiii. 10. but they never desire the grace and glory of God to be set forth in their life and conversation : they desire not to live the life of the righteous, and with Esau, seek with tears a worldly blessing, but they never seek the kingdom of God in the first place, and they never esteem salvation the chief pearl of their souls ; this is only proper to the child of God.

Now, when ye want prayer, run to the Lord, and beg the spirit of prayer, for he is bound to give it thee, and hath promised, that whosoever calls upon the name of the Lord shall be saved," Rom. x. 13. So if thou wilt call for the Spirit, he will send it unto thee ; for the Son hath bought him with his own blood, and when thou hast need, he will beg him of the Father, and send him unto thy soul; therefore Christ said, "It is expedient for you that I go away, for if I go not away the Comforter will not come unto you ; but if I depart I will send him unto you," John xvi. 7. "And he will lead you into all truth, and he will teach you how ye should pray, and what ye should pray." So ye see the Son bought him of the Father, and giveth him in a gift to his elect. Now this gift was given to you in the time of your first calling : I know well the spirit of prayer was poured upon you then, when your conscience was first awakened ; but it may be that now ye are sleeping in security, and cannot always remember that ye had the Spirit once : remember that ye are called to the supper of the Lamb, and blessed are they that are called to the Lamb's supper ; remember that thou art pulled out of nature and planted in Christ ; remember that all the promises of the gospel, made in Christ only belongs to thee ; he hath promised to send the Comforter, therefore thou must pray him to send the Comforter ; yea, I will say more to thee, if thou canst look pitifully to him, he will be ravished with one of thy eye-looks, for he cannot abide them ; if thou canst but touch the hem of his garment, and lay hold upon the blood of Jesus, thou mayest step boldly to heaven when thou wilt, for thou wilt get in; for he is that porter that holds the gates continually to thee that art renewed, and he is the Advocate that speaks to thee, and for thee, when thou darest not, nor canst not speak for thyself: so when thou canst not get a heart to pray, "Stir up the gift of God that is within thee," as Paul said, 2 Tim. i. 6. "For he hath not given to us the spirit of fear, but of power, of love, and of a sound mind." So when thou desirest to pray, thou hast the spirit of prayer within thee; stir him up then, and blow at the coal, and kindle the little spark that lurks in thy heart, and it shall break out in a great fire at the last, which shall melt thy heart, that thou mayest pour it out before the Lord thy God: as David said, "I will pour out my heart unto the Lord." Again, when thou canst not pray, ask the gift of prayer, ask the Holy Ghost to teach thee, Mat. vii. 11. "For if their fathers, that are evil, give good gifts unto their children, how much more shall our heavenly Father give good things to them that ask of him." Ye have a command to ask, and ye have a promise, that if ye will ask, it shall be given unto you, your asking shall be granted. Let this now encourage and stir you up to pray: I say no more, but the Lord give you all a spirit of prayer.

SERMON XVIII.

OF THE CHRISTIAN WARFARE.

Ephes. vi. 18.

Praying always with all prayer and supplication in the Spirit, and watching thereunto with all perseverance, and supplication for all saints.

THE last thing was that last piece of armour which ye must have for your warfare, which is prayer, without the which there is no deliverance out of temptations, nor no new grace to be had to sustain thee in the day of thy temptations; and without prayer ye cannot have use of all the rest of the graces of God, unless ye join prayer with them; for when your hands weary and fall down, then Amalek must prevail; but when your hands are holden up, and are constant, then ye shall prevail; and all the rest of the graces that are within thee take all their strength and vigour from prayer, for it is the common instrument appointed by God for the obtaining of good, and deliverance from evil. Your truth will not abide long without prayer; ye cannot wear the breast-plate of righteousness long without prayer; the promises of the gospel will not abide long with you without prayer; ye cannot keep your faith long without prayer; salvation cannot abide long upon your head without prayer; the word will do you no good without prayer: therefore prayer is both the mean whereby thou mayest get grace, and it is the mean to confirm and maintain grace, when thou hast gotten it.

There were two things spoken of; *first*, That it was a very conference and second talking of the soul with God, for we have all this privilege in Christ; he hath made us all priests that we may step in before God, not with the blood of bullocks, or goats, but with the blood of Jesus, not once in the year, but at all times; not into the holy of holies, but into the highest heavens; ye may come in before the mercy-seat of God, and there thou mayest pour out all that is in thy heart, be what it will that is in thy heart; thou mayest say with David, Psalm lxii. 8. "I will go and pour out my heart before God." It is true, that blood hath opened the way, and rent the vail, and gone into heaven before thee to hold the gates open to thee, till the very hour he comes in the clouds to sit on his throne, and to judge the quick and the dead, when thou shalt go in with him, and never come out again.

It may be that the child of God thinks that the gates of heaven are shut, and cannot be opened; but it is not so; the Lord desires thee to knock, and he has promised to open to thee; he knows thy voice; he is that porter that opens to thee, thou art the sheep, hearing his voice; he calls on thee by name, and leads thee out, and goeth before thee, and thou followest him, for thou knowest his voice; so he may well let thee knock for a time, but he cannot hold thee out, for he must let thee in at the last; especially, when thou appealest to the throne of his mercy, and seekest remission in the blood of Jesus: he cannot abide the cry of a poor penitent sinner that cometh to him with the consciousness of his own guiltiness, desiring him to be merciful for his Son Christ Jesus's sake.

The next thing ye should know concerning prayer is this, that ye understand whose daughter prayer is, for we cannot pray of ourselves because the apostle says, "We know not what to pray, or how to pray as we should," Rom. viii. 26. And who was this, think ye, that knew not what to pray or how to pray? It was the apostle Paul, that was ravished to the third heavens, and knew all the counsel of God, and had revealed it; a man in whom the prophecy of Zacharias was fulfilled, saying, "I will pour the Spirit of prayer and supplication upon them." The lesson here is twofold, the one is when thou wantest prayer, thou

SERMON XVIII.

knowest how to get it, even from your heavenly Father, that cannot deny you good things when you ask them, and from the Holy Ghost, that is the Spirit of prayer. Remember that saying of Christ, Matth. vii. 11. " If ye then that are evil can give good gifts unto your children, how much more shall your heavenly Father give his holy Spirit to them that ask him ?" So thou never knewest how to pray till this Spirit was sent unto thee, and thou never gottest the holy Spirit until the Father sent him. And in what measure the Spirit is given to you, in that same measure is the gift and grace of prayer given you : now, would ye know in what measure the Spirit is given to the Son, it is given without measure ; but unto you it is given in the same measure that prayer is given : " He was annointed with the oil of gladness above his fellows," Psal. xiv. 7. But thy measure is limited and measured to thee ; and thou wilt get no more than God thinks fit to vouchsafe upon thee. Now thou shalt know the measure of the Spirit, by the effects wrought by the Spirit ; as the sun riseth and goeth to the height, so it casteth forth its beams, and makes the flowers to smell with the heat of it ; even so the Holy Ghost, so soon as he shines in thy heart, it kindles a fire, and the fire draws out the incense and sweet savour of thy requests unto God ; and this smell runs up to heaven, and draweth down first fire to burn thee, and set thy heart in flame ; next it draweth down water to quench that fire, and to water thy heart with the dew of God's grace ; and as prayer groweth and increaseth, so the holy Spirit groweth ; and as prayer decays, so all the rest of the graces of the Spirit may decrease also. This for the things spoken of before.

Now followeth the *third* point, to know what will make thee to persevere in prayer, and what will stir thee up that thou faint not therein ; for prayer is the thing that the devil envies most, and he labours most to suppress prayer of all the graces that is in a man : therefore oft-times thou wilt find greatest temptations, oft-times even in the time of prayer ; for then the devil throws in strange cogitations in the heart, either to make us leave off to pray, or to hinder the fervency of the spirit in our prayer; he can bring in the world, and the cares and pleasures thereof, that our hearts be not in heaven, and that " drawing near to God with our lips, our hearts may be far from him ;" he can breathe in a false spirit in the old prophet to deceive the young prophet; and he will bring motions that ye would think to proceed from the Spirit of God for to distract thee from the worship of God; but whenever ye shall try them, they shall be found but to be the motions of the spirit of error; he can cast in crafty means whereby thou mayest bring a purpose to pass; but try them when thou wilt, thou shalt never find the blessing of God joined with them; so ye should beware of his cogitations, that he casts into you in the time of prayer, and learn to discern them from your own thoughts, and from the motions of the Spirit of God.

Now, I come to the grounds that should uphold you in time of prayer that ye faint not therein. The *first* is this, think that it is the commandment of God, and therefore it is not an indifferent thing to you to do or not to do, at your own pleasure, but it is a commanded worship instituted and ordained by God himself, " call upon me in the day of trouble and I will hear you, and thou shalt glorify me, Psal. l. 16. Ask, and it shall be given you, saith Christ, seek, and ye shall find, knock, and it shall be opened to you, Matth. vii. 7. Watch and pray that ye fall not into temptation, Luke xxii. 40. Pray continually," says the Apostle, " in all things be thankful." Now obedience to the command of God is better than sacrifice, and of all the special commandments of God, prayer requires a special obedience; for of all the parts of honour and glory that a creature can give to God, his Creator, in this life, prayer is the foremost; for by prayer thou givest God,

First, This glory, that all obedience to his commands brings glory to him; he hath commanded us to pray, therefore obedience to prayer brings glory to God.

Secondly, Thou givest glory to God, when thou professest God to be the searcher and the tryer of thy heart, and in prayer thou professest and confessest God to search and try the reins of thy heart.

Thirdly, By prayer thou confessest in the singleness of thy heart, that God is all sufficient, as the Centurion said to Christ, " Speak the word only, and my servant shall be healed," Matth. viii. 8. And as a leprous man said, Lord, I believe thou canst make me clean, if thou wilt.

Fourthly, By prayer thou professest that God is good, gracious and merciful, and therefore thou wilt wait upon his grace and mercy ; suppose thou beest a sinner, yet he is very ready to forgive ; as he said himself, " my thoughts are not your thoughts, neither your ways my ways, saith the Lord ; for as the heavens are higher than the earth, so are my ways higher than your ways, and my thoughts than your thoughts," Isa. vi. 8. So, suppose thou wouldst not pray for thyself, yet the glory of God would not let thee alone, but it will constrain thee to pray, because thy prayer bringeth glory to God.

Now for the places of scripture that I thought to be sufficient to stir you up. Read Psal. li. lxi. lxxvii. lxxxi. lxxxii. civ. Isaiah lv. John xv. and xvii. Luke xv. 11.

Secondly, Let the promises of God stir you up because fair promises are made you ; " Ask, and it shall be given you ; seek, and ye shall find ; knock and it shall be opened to you. If ye that are evil can give good things to your children, how much more shall your heavenly Father give the Holy Ghost to them that ask him ?" And Luke xviii. 7. " Shall not God avenge his elect, that cry unto him day and night ; yea, though he seem to delay for a time ? John xv. 16. Whatsoever ye shall ask in my name from the Father, he shall give it to you." And who speaks this ? even the Son himself that came out of the Father's bosom, and was upon the counsel of God, and is now himself in heaven, at the right hand of his Father, making intercession for you. When he was on the earth he prayed for you, John xvii. 9. "Saying, I pray for them; I pray not for the world, but for them that thou hast given me, that they may be one as we are one. When I was with them in the world, I kept them in thy name; those that thou gavest me I have kept, and none of them are lost, but the child of perdition; that the scripture may be fulfilled." I remember the Persians made a law, that whoever came to the king in the inner court, that was not called upon, that he should die, except he to whom the king should hold out the golden sceptre; but it is not so here for ye may step in boldly to the king, for he hath already reached out the golden rod to you; and therefore ye need not to fear. Remember also that saying of the prophet David, Psal. xxvii. 8, 9. "Lord, thou saidst, seek my face; my heart answered to thee, Lord, I will seek thy face; hide not therefore thy face from me, nor cast away thy servant in displeasure; thou hast been my help, leave me not, nor forsake me, O God of my salvation."

Now, I know the devil will alledge many things to hinder you to pray. 1*st*, He will say, What needest thou to pray, thy Father knoweth well enough what thou needest, therefore thou needest not to tell him? Now, for answer to this, it is true, the Lord knoweth thy necessities well enough; but yet the Lord will have us telling him ourselves what we want, that we may be homely with him; for if the Son himself behoved to ask, and therefore this made him so earnest in prayer, that sometimes he would spend whole nights in praying; if he, I say, who was the Son, and in whom the fulness of the Godhead dwelt bodily, and upon whom the Spirit was poured out above measure, if he spent whole nights in prayer, how much more have we need to be earnest in prayer? And what made him so earnest, think ye? but because it was his Father's command. "Ask of me," saith the Father to the Son, "and I will give thee the heathen for thy inheritance, and the ends of the earth for thy possession," Psal. ii. 8. Now, because it was the Father's command, therefore Christ gives obedience to his Father in this, as he did in all the rest; for he was obedient to the very death of the cross.

Object. 2. The devil will cast into thee, and make thee say, what need is there for me to pray, for it hath been decreed of God from the beginning, what measure of grace shall be given me? therefore that same measure of grace shall I get, and no less, suppose I never open my lips to seek it. For answer hereto, this is the machination of Satan to say, God hath decreed to give me as much grace as I get, therefore I need not to seek it, for I will get it: no, if God hath decreed to give grace to thee, he hath also decreed to give thee a heart and mouth to seek it; and in that measure thou seekest it, in that measure thou shalt find it granted unto thee: *Open thy mouth wide,* saith the Lord, *and I shall fill it,* Psal. lxxxi. 10. So let always the promises allure thee to pray; let them make you bold, and give you confidence and trust in God; then shall ye call, and the Lord shall answer; then shalt thou cry, and he shall answer, Here am I: "Before they will call, I will answer; and whilst they are yet speaking, I will hear, Isa. lxv. 24. So thou canst not but be heard that prayest, for the Spirit prayeth for thee, and helps thy infirmities? "the Spirit itself maketh request for us, with sighs that cannot be expressed:" and will not the Father hear the mediation of the Son by his own Spirit? so if thou gettest the heart to pray, thou must be heard. Indeed it may be, thou thinkest that the Lord tarries long, as sometimes he will do; as he did to Daniel, that prayed and mourned for the space of twenty-three days ere ever he got an answer: And David said, Psal. xl. 1. *I waited patiently on the Lord.* The meaning of the word is, by waiting on, " I waited on the Lord, and he inclined unto me, and heard my cry." Yet, I say, suppose he seems to tarry long, wait ye on, for he will come at the last: "I will stand on my watch, and set me upon the tower, and I will look and see what he will say unto me, and what I shall answer him that rebuketh me. And the Lord answered me, write the vision, and make it plain upon tables, that he may run that readeth it: for the vision is yet for an appointed time, but at last it shall speak and not tarry." Hab. ii. 1, 2, 3. Though it tarry, wait; for it shall come, and shall not stay.

Now, if the prophet was commanded to tarry, and wait till the judgment was accomplished, and the vision come to pass, how much more should we wait till the promises of the Lord be fulfilled to us.

Again, remember God will be angry if you pray not; for he says, "I will pour out my wrath upon the families that call not upon my name; and Dan. ix. 13. All this plague is come upon us, as it is written in the law of Moses, yet made we not our prayer before the Lord our God, to turn from our iniquities and to learn thy truth; therefore hath the Lord made ready the plague, and brought it upon us; for the Lord our God is righteous in all the works that he doth, for we would not hear his voice." Ye see the prophet Daniel, amongst the rest of their sins, he reckons out this as one of the chiefest, that they made not their prayer before the Lord, which was one of the greatest causes that brought the plague of God upon them; so ye see, if we pray not, God will be angry with us; for prayer is a part of his worship, and when we neglect prayer, we neglect the worship and service of God; and what master will not be angry at his servants, if they do not the service he commanded them to do? Even so, if we do not the service of God, which he himself commanded, is it any marvel that he be angry with us?

Last of all, pray, because ye have a Mediator and Advocate in heaven, even Jesus, the just; he makes continual intercession for you, and he is spreading out his arms ever in his word, and saying to every one of you, come in here, sinners within the compass of my blood, wash your souls in this fountain; come in unto me, and I shall present you and your prayers both to the Father, I will perfume them with the incense of my righteousness, and the Father will accept of them for my sake. Besides this, ye have the example of all the saints that have gone before you, and of all them that are now living; they offered their prayers to God; they cried in the time of trouble and were heard; they besought the Lord in time of peril and he delivered them. Now, besides all this, ye have this to encourage you to pray, remember what prayer hath done; prayer clave the Red sea, that the people of Israel might go through safely, and it caused the same sea to drown Pharaoh and all his host, Exod. xiv. 16. Prayer made the rocks to cleave, and the water to come out in abundance for the people and their cattle, Numb. xx. 11. Prayer made the sun stand still in the firmament, that it never moved for the space of one whole day, Josh. x. 11. Prayer closed the heavens, that it rained not for the space of three years; and again it opened the windows of heaven, and caused rain to come down and water the earth, 1 Kings xxii. 7. Prayer caused the sun to go backward ten degrees, 2 Kings xx. 11. Prayer in a manner altered the very sentence of God given out against Nineveh. Prayer hath overcome fires, stopped the mouth of lions, and made the earth to tremble and quake, and hath opened the prison doors, broken the fetters, and delivered the saints of God. And, last of all, prayer has opened the eyes of the blind, and hath given hands to the lame, and feet to the crooked, Isa. xxxviii. 5. And prayer hath healed the sick, raised the dead; so, what is the thing prayer cannot do? Now then, should not this encourage you to pray? Suppose ye find not the fruit of your prayers at the first, in case he deny a temporal blessing, yet he will give a spiritual grace instead of it, and that is far better; and though he delay to hear thee for a time, yet he will give thee patience to wait on, and assurance that thou wilt be heard at last. Therefore, my hearts, let these be sufficient arguments to stir you up to prayer; and when ye address yourselves to God in prayer, remember ye go as forlorn sons and daughters to a merciful Father, in the name of a Mediator, believing his promises, "that whatsoever ye shall ask in his name, it shall be granted to you;" as James said, i. 6, 7. "Ask in faith, without wavering; for he that wavereth is as the waves of the sea, tost to and fro; neither let that man think to receive any thing of the Lord."

Now, unto the Lord be all honour and praise for now and evermore. *Amen.*

SERMON XIX.

OF THE CHRISTIAN WARFARE.

Ephes. vi. 18.

Praying always with all prayer and supplication in the Spirit, and watching thereunto with all perseverance, and supplication for all saints.

THE Lord open your hearts and ears, that that truth and verity, which it shall please his Majesty to put into my mouth, may pierce your ears, and enter your hearts: I am but a bare witness of the truth, and a simple ambassador sent from God, to offer life and salvation unto you, if ye will take it; and, if ye refuse to take it, I am sent to seal up death and destruction to your souls, and to ratify both by his truth and word; therefore the Lord stir you all up by his holy Spirit, that ye may give ear to the voice of the truth, and give your hearts to embrace and receive it, as the truth of God, and not as the word of man.

The sum of all that hath been spoken is even this, There is a crown of endless life and glory in the hands of the Son of God, keeping it in heaven for to give to every one that fighteth the Lord's battles, and overcomes the enemy here in this life; and there is none of you that shall get this crown of glory set upon your head, but such of you as in this your pilgrimage here fight and overcome him here; for if ye be foiled and killed here, ye shall die for evermore hereafter; and if ye fight not here, ye shall never get in at the ports of heaven, to see that glory that shall be hereafter. Now, ye have to wrestle not only with flesh and blood, but ye have them also to fight withal; for never one that is called, but they have a law in their members rebelling against the law of their mind, and ye have the old man fighting against the new man, and ye have the lust of the flesh fighting against the soul and spirit; not only, I say, have ye to fight against yourselves, but also ye have a world to fight against; ye have principalities and powers, and worldly governors, princes of the air, malicious spirits, red dragons, subtile serpents, princes of darkness, and the god of this world; ye have all these to fight with; as many of you as are the children of God, and truly called, ye know this to be true. But I know there are many of you that are not brought in yet, nevertheless, I will wait upon the Lord's good pleasure and time, when it shall please him to bring you in. I know there are a number of you that have not God nor his Spirit dwelling in your hearts; and therefore ye have no warfare, and therefore ye lie dead and slain; ye are led blindfolded by the prince of darkness; he holds you fast bound with chains of darkness, that ye can neither stir foot nor hand; for he is the strong man that keeps his possession peaceably, till another that is stronger than he come and beat him out. But I leave you, and speak to the chosen and called children of God; ye have the riches and pleasures of this world set in your way, to hinder you to get that unsearchable riches of Christ, of everlasting glory; ye have also a strait gate to go through: But it is not this only, and indeed this were strong enough for us, but ye have to fight with strong powers, and cruel enemies, and incarnate devils that cannot be satified with less than the dishonour of God, and the endless damnation of your souls: sleep not, he is even now here among you, looking if he can rock you asleep, and make your ears heavy, that ye hear not this truth; for he thinks when he hath got that, he hath gotten a fair advantage, when by seeing ye see not, and by hearing ye hear not, and when your hearts are hardened that ye cannot understand; he desires no more then, but to make your ears heavy, that your souls get no good by this word, which is the power of God to salvation. The Lord give you grace to believe this, for it is over sore to thee when he hath prevailed ; for then he will say, thy damnation is well bestowed, for thou hadst salvation offered to thee, but thou wouldst not take it : it was never offered to me, therefore I could not get it ; thou heardst me, but thou wouldst not hear the voice of Christ, therefore he will not hear thee now. It will be over sore for thee to be led within the gates of hell, and never to get out again ; it will be over sore to have that currier and the bloody dog to stab you through the heart with the flames of that endless fire, that shall burn up soul, and conscience, and carcase perpetually ; this will be over sore when ye feel it, suppose ye will not believe it now ; therefore blessed is the man or woman that believeth these things in time ; and well is the soul that knoweth it hath to do with those enemies that I have spoken of, and yet am to speak of to you. I tell you, ye have to do with a malicious enemy ; ye have to do with a subtile serpent ; ye have to do with a bloody dragon, that will not spare to set on you, that hath not spared to set on the dearest of God's children before you ; he will not spare to set on thee a weak member, that spared not to set upon the Head, whom he knew to be the seed of the woman, that should tread down his head ; whom he knew to be the Son of the everlasting God ; whom he knew as sent to torment him : whom he knew had power to command him to go down to the depths ; notwithstanding he knew all these things of him, yet he spared not to set upon him once, twice, thrice, in the wilderness ; yea, he never left him all the time that he was here on earth ; and not only so, but also he followed him up to heaven, and sets upon him there ; yet he prevailed not, but was cast out of heaven for evermore, Rev. xii. 7. 8. 9. Therefore I would ye understood with whom ye have to do ; for it is not for nought that the Spirit of God hath painted him out so clearly in his word : mark ye, gin ye hear, ye shall reign in heaven for evermore hereafter ; gin ye hear the fairest crown that ever was shall be set on your head hereafter : mark again, fight and ye shall gain ; for none shall lose but he that desires to lose ; none shall be slain, but he that desires wilfully to be slain ; therefore fight, and ye shall gain ; and if ye fight, and get the victory, ye shall get long white robes put on you ; ye shall eat of the tree of life ; ye shall get a white stone in your hand, and a new name written on it, that no man knoweth but he that gets it ; thou shalt be made a pillar in the temple of thy God ; thou shalt be set on a throne, and a crown put on thy head, and thou shalt follow the Lamb wherever he goeth. But if ye lose, ye shall never come to heaven ; ye shall never get the crown ; ye shall be debarred from that glory ; ye shall be bound hand and foot, and casten into utter darkness, and in that fire that shall never be quenched or put out, and in that place where there shall be nothing but weeping and gnashing of teeth for evermore. So I beseech you fight, and ye shall get the victory.

Now, for obtaining the victory, what must ye do ? Your own strength, your own wisdom, your own wit, your own will, cannot do the turn. Adam had strength enough while he was in the garden, in his integrity, yet he was overcome, because he followed not the counsel of God, but disobeyed his command, and gave place to the devil, and he crept into his heart ; therefore ye must renounce your own wisdom, ye must renounce your own strength, your own will, and your own wit, and learn the wisdom of God, and be strong in him ; and for this cause the Holy Ghost gives you comfort in this scripture, bidding you " be strong in the Lord, and in the power of his might ;" so, if ye overcome, ye must overcome by the blood of the Lord ; for strong is that Lord, strong is that blood, strong is his descending down from heaven, strong is his incarnation, strong is his humiliation, strong is his ascension, and strong is he in all his works ; he overcame the devil, he ashamed him upon the cross, and spoiled him of all his weapons ; therefore he is a shamed and naked enemy, and he cannot stand before you, if ye be strong in the Lord, and if ye have his armour upon you.

Now therefore, if ye would overcome, ye must put on the whole armour of God; and when ye have put it on, ye must stand in the field clothed with this armour, that ye may be the last in the field, and that ye may resist in the evil day. What this armour was, some of you heard, but not all: sleep not, the Lord waken you. Am I speaking of fables to you? Alas! ye know not what ye are doing: now when ye sleep, ye let the mouth of the dragon be opened to receive you, ye give place to the devil when he rocks you asleep; but " he that will be filthy, let him be filthy still; and he that will be holy, let him be holy still :" And whosoever will be holy, let him put on this armour.

First, Gird your loins with verity, that is the first part of this armour; see that ye have a sure persuasion that ye serve and worship the true God. 2*dly*, See that ye have a sincere heart in the worship of God, and beware of hypocrisy; that is the first part of this armour.

The *second* part is, " to put on the breast-plate of righteousness;" that is, see that ye be in readiness to do every good work, and see that ye hate every evil work.

Thirdly, " Shoe your feet with the promises of the gospel;" that if ye were to run through a fire, ye may run your race with joy and peace, and always hold the moon under your feet; that ye may count all things in this world dirt and dung in comparison of the excellent knowledge of Christ; and that ye may count all things but loss that would hinder you from your Lord, and not let you have your conversation in heaven.

Fourthly, " Take the shield of faith;" that is, put on the Lord Jesus upon you, take that blood in your hand for a buckler; then when you find a fire kindled in your conscience, then ye may take it and quench therewith all the fiery darts of the devil, wherewith he thinks to burn up your souls and consciences perpetually.

Fifthy, "Put on the helmet of salvation:" for if thou hast the former, thou mayest take to thee salvation boldly; hast thou that verity, salvation is thine; and hast thou that peace that passes all understanding, salvation is thine; and hast thou faith, salvation is thine; for he that believeth is already saved, as he that believeth not is already condemned; therefore if thou hast this in any true measure thou hast salvation; also therefore thou mayest take it to thee. Then put on that salvation, and wear it on thy forehead, that all the world may see it, and may say, there is a man that hopes for glory; there is one that is saved; there is one that is washed in the blood of Jesus; there is one that walks with God; there is one that looks to reign with God eternally.

Sixthly, "Take to thee the sword of the Spirit, which is the word of God:" take it to you and fight with it, exercise yourself day and night in it, read, meditate, and confer thereupon continually; for oftentimes by vain words and idle talk the devil gets entrance. What made Joshua, think ye, overcome so many strong kings, but that he had the book of the law continually with him wherever he went, and looked on it both day and night? And by the contrary, what made David fall so foully, but that he forgot to look upon the book of the law? For if he had remembered and looked on the book that said, "Thou shalt not murder; and he that slayeth, shall be slain with the sword:" again murderers and adulterers shall never inherit the kingdom of God;" if he had remembered such and such sayings in the word, he would not have fallen so foully. What made Sampson fall, that was the strongest man that ever was in the world? What made him suffer his hair to be cut, and his strength to be taken from him, but that he looked not to the law of the Nazarites, which said, "A rasor shall not come on his head," Judg. xiii. 5. What made Solomon fall in idolatry, that was the wisest in the world, but that he looked not to the law of God, which said, "Thou shalt worship the Lord thy God, and him only shalt thou serve," 1 Kings xi. 4, 5.

Deut. vi, 13. What made Peter, Mat. xxvi. 69. for all his zeal, fall at the voice of a silly maid, but that he remembered not the word of the Lord that said to him, "Ere the cock crow, thou shalt deny me thrice?" So then, had ye the strength of Sampson, had ye the heart of David, that was a man according to the heart of God, had ye the wisdom of Solomon, had ye the zeal of Peter; yea, had ye Adam's integrity, they would not all bear ye up, if thou holdest not this word before thee; therefore thou must take this word unto thee, thou must fight against him with this word, or else thou wilt never be able to overcome him : and therefore this made our Saviour to confute him with this word, and suppose he might have otherwise stopped his mouth, and by his authority commanded him to keep silence, yet he would not do it; but in this he will go before us in his example, that we may likewise take the word and fight against him. Now, I know well this word will not return in vain; I am sure God will give a blessing to it in some of you; and I know well some of you will make this use of it, that this word shall be a rule to you to live by for all the days of your life; and this word shall be dearer to you than ever it was, and ye will use this word oftner than ever ye have done, and this word shall dwell in you more abundantly than ever it did. I am persuaded some of you will resolve this with yourselves.

Seventhly and *lastly*, Without the which all the rest will not avail. It is prayer; for suppose ye have all the rest of the armour, yet if ye want prayer, ye cannot use them; therefore they will do no good. Alas! how many of you are naked this day, that ye have neither truth nor righteousness in your heart, nor ye have not put on the shoes of the promises of the gospel. Alas! how many of you have not reached out your hand, as it were, out of hell, and have drawn down the blood of Christ to your dead souls and wounded consciences; and, being in those depths, have lifted your souls defiled with sin, and have sprinkled them with his blood, and thereby gotten unspeakable joy and peace to your consciences that passes all understanding, by laying hold on that blood? And how many of you, when your hearts were sore wounded, and when an intolerable fire was kindled in your souls, ye took it and cast it into that fire to quench it? And how many have put salvation on your heads, and shewed to the world, that ye hope for that glory, and for the coming of the Lord in the clouds? And how many of you have taken the word of God for your defence against all the temptations of Satan? Alas! there be very few of you, I think, that have experience of these things; but yet in all these ye will get no profit, except ye join prayer with them; thy faith will soon fail if thou prayest not. Thy peace will soon depart if thou prayest not; thy heart will soon fail if thou prayest not; thy righteousness will soon be undone if thou prayest not: therefore above all the rest thou must have prayer.

Now, as for prayer it opens the heavens to thee, and comes to the door of God's mercy, and knocks thereat, and cries at the gates, then the porter that hath bought thee with his blood, he knows thy voice; for thou that knowest the voice of the Lord crying to thee here in his word; therefore so soon as thou by prayer shalt come to heaven, he shall hear thy voice, and he shall say, this is my sheep, he hears my voice; therefore it is good reason that I hear his voice again; he heard me when I called upon him, therefore I will hear him when he calleth upon me: he followed on me when I cried to him, therefore I will come to him crying upon me; he opened the door of his heart, and let me in when I knocked at it; therefore I will open the door of my mercy, and let him in, seeing he is knocking at it.

Now, would ye know how prayer comes, and after what manner it is wrought in the heart of man or woman? I will tell you.

First, The Lord comes and stands knocking at the door of your heart, saying, Cant. v. 2. "Open, my dove, my love, my undefiled, the locks of my hair are wet with the dew of the night," for I have bought thee dear, open thou to me, and let me in, and I shall tarry all the night; then thou risest and openest the door of thy heart, and he comes in and tarries with thee.

Thou again by prayer goest to the gate of heaven, and to the door of his mercy, and thou knockest thereat; then thou sayest, Lord, here am I, that heard thy voice speaking in thy word; here am I, that opened the door of my heart, and let thee in, and by thy presence I found peace. Now, Lord, I am come to thee with a heavy burden on my back, and so heavy, that it was much for me to get up the hill: many a sigh and groan I gave before I came hither; many a wrestling and battle I had ere I got here; and, Lord, were it not by the power of thy might I had never come hither; now, seeing by thy strength and mighty arm, I am come at the last; therefore open the door of thy mercy, and the bowels of thy pity, and let me find rest there to my weary and faint soul, that is forfoughten and weary with the load of sin and wrath that I have borne so long. So this is prayer, and this kind of prayer gets a gracious answer from the Lord, saying, come thy way, ask what thou wilt and it shall be granted to thee. Is it remission of sins that thou wouldst have? Be of good comfort, thy sins are forgiven thee. Is it righteousness to cover thee? Behold my righteousness, take it to thee and put it on thee. Is it a clean heart thou wantest? Lo, there my blood, believe in it, and it shall make thee clean; so whatever thou wantest I will furnish it to thee.

Now, if ye would have your prayers heard, and your requests granted to you, then you must join these two together.

First, Ye must hear the Lord speaking to you in his word; for he is in the still voice of the preaching of the gospel, and he kythes himself in it before all other means, as when he appeared to Elijah, (1 Kings xix. 11, 12.) he saw him not in the fire, he saw him not in the wind, he saw him not in the earthquake, but only he sees him in the still and soft voice; and Elijah knew that the Lord was in that voice, therefore he covered his face with his mantle, when he heard his voice, in sign and token of reverence thereto. So I say, if ye will hear his voice speaking to you here in this ministry of ours, and if ye will open your hearts to embrace him, I bear you witness that the Lord will hear you praying, that hears him now speaking in his word, and he shall open the chamber-door of his presence and mercy to let thee in, that opens thy heart to him, and lets him in that stood knocking at the door of thy heart; and he shall be found of thee when thou seekest him, that was found of him that sought thee in this ministry.

Now followeth how ye should pray; well is them that can get the right manner of prayer. Now, for the better understanding of this, mark two circumstances set down here.

First, Pray always; that is, at all times. The Apostle, in another place, expounds it himself, 1 Thessal. v. 17. saying, *pray continually*; and in another, *persevere in prayer*; and he had not this of himself, but his Master and Saviour taught him; the same in Luke xviii. 7. by putting forth a parable of a widow and an unrighteous judge, to whom this widow came day and night seeking justice of him, and although he neither feared God, nor regarded man, yet, because she was so earnest and importunate upon him, he is forced to hear her at the last; and all this parable tends to this, that thereby we may learn to be instant in prayer: Now, I know it will be much grace that will hold you up, that ye faint not in prayer; for, as I told you, Moses behooved to have two to uphold his hands, that they fell not down, and that he fainted not in prayer; for they knew, as long as his hands were holden up to God, they would prevail. Therefore, if thou wilt continue in prayer without fainting, ye must resolve to say, with David, *Thou saidst, Lord, seek ye my face, and my heart answered, Lord, thy face will I seek continually.* And if ye would not faint in prayer, set up these two props under your hands.

First, Remember the command of God.

Secondly, Remember his promise, the command, " call upon me in the day of thy trouble;" the promise, " and I will hear you, and deliver you." The command is, " ask, seek, and knock :" the promise is, " it shall be given to you, ye shall find, it shall be opened." So these are the props that must underprop you, and hold up your hands that ye faint not in prayer; look always to the commandment of God, that hath bidden you always watch and pray continually. Remember therefore that thou must pray, unless thou wilt be disobedient to the Lord, and so provoke him to be angry against thee. Next, look to the promise that he hath made, that he will hear thee, he will grant thy requests, and open the door of his mercy, and he will come to thee at the last ; that suppose he tarry a while from thee, and suppose he seem to be absent himself very long, yet, in end, he will come, and give thee a sweet and gracious answer, as he did to Daniel ; that, suppose he continued praying and fasting, for the space of twenty-three days, and all that time the Lord delayed to give him an answer ; yet his prayer was heard in the very first moment when he opened his mouth to pray.

Now, if these two props will not serve thee, put other two to them : *First,* Remember, that thou hast an Advocate and Mediator in heaven to request for thee ; for he hath gone before and paved the way with his blood, and has made a new and living way to thee, that by it thou mayest come to heaven ; he hath opened the gates of heaven that he may let thee in ; who then can bar thee out? And because thy prayers are foul and corrupt with sin ; therefore he is that angel that stands with that golden censer in his hand before the altar, " to whom was given much incense, that he should offer it with the prayers of all the saints upon the golden altar, which was before the throne ; and a great smoke of the perfume came up with the prayers of the saints, before the face of God, out of the hand of that angel," Rev. viii. 3, 4. He is that Aaron, that puts in that sweet odour of his blood, and perfumes thy prayers with the sweet smelling savour of his righteousness, and then presents them to the Father; for thou mayest not step to the Father at the nearest, but thou must go first to the Mediator, and desire him first to perfume, and then present thy prayers to the Father; and that he would request the Father to accept of them, and to be merciful unto thee for his sake. He is an Aaron to hold up one hand: But where will ye get an Hur to hold up the other hand? Ye are bidden bear one another's burdens. I tell you, ye have the saints to pray for you, ye are bidden pray one for another: Abraham prayed for Lot, and he was heard; Moses prayed for the children of Israel, and by his prayer turned away the wrath of God that was kindled against them; Daniel prayed for deliverance to his people that were in captivity, and he was heard, Dan. iv. the saints prayed for Peter, being in prison, and they were heard, for God delivered him, Acts xii. 5. Paul says to Timothy, "I thank God, whom I serve from my forefathers with a pure conscience, that, without ceasing, I have remembrance of thee in my prayers day and night." What should more? The scripture is full of examples as these. Now, this for the first circumstance, that we should pray.

Follows the next, which is, pray with all manner of prayer and supplication; that is, pray for all manner of grace, and all sort of blessings needful both to soul and body; pray for all sort of grace, both spiritual and temporal; pray for the glory of God to shine in your hearts; pray for the kingdom of God to come down in your souls; pray for the remission of your sins in the blood of Jesus; pray for faith; pray for repentance; pray for the love of God; and pray for the gifts of the Holy Ghost; thou mayest pray for all these graces absolutely, without exception, because God has commended and has annexed a promise without a condition; for the Lord is bound to give them to thee absolutely without exception. Next, thou mayest pray for all manner of blessings belonging to this life; but in another manner, and upon a condition; thou mayest pray for meat and drink when thou art hungry, but upon this condition, thou must remember " man lives not by bread only, but by every word that proceeds out of the mouth of God," Deut. viii. 3. and Matth. iv. 4. And upon this condition, that thou carest not so much for the meat that perishes, as for that meat that endures to life everlasting: but thou mayest pray for the glory of God, and the remission of thy sins, and for true and saving faith, and for repentance to life, and for a clean heart, and for all the rest of the graces of the Holy Ghost absolutely, without any condition, and this shall be a sure token to thee that thou shalt be heard, and thy request granted; for if ever the Lord hath put in thy heart sighs and groans to pray for the Spirit, and the graces of the Spirit, then thou mayest be sure it is the absolute decree of God to give them to thee; thy warrant is this,

First, Call upon me in the day of trouble, and I will hear thee.

Secondly, Pour out thy wrath, O Lord, upon the families that call not upon thy name.

Thirdly, All that call upon the name of the Lord shall be saved.

Fourthly, Let the mediation of the Son be a warrant to thee; he is requesting in heaven for thee; he hath sent thee his Spirit to help thy infirmities, with unspeakable sighs and groans that cannot be expressed; so when thou canst not pray, the Spirit within thee shall help thee to pray.

Fifthly, and last of all, Let the price of his blood confirm thee, because it hath brought all these graces to thee. Let these be sufficient warrants for thee, and to thee, that the Lord will give thee these graces freely, without price, or any condition required on thy part; but as for these outward things pertaining to this life, the Lord hath promised to give them to thee, but upon this condition, in so far as they tend to his glory, and so far as they will serve for thy weal, to further thee to run thy race; for what hast thou to do with the things of this world, that hast forsaken and renounced the things of this world? It is true, that prayer hath brought down from heaven earthly blessings: for prayer did bring bread from heaven, that fed the people of Israel in the wilderness for the space of forty years; prayer made water run out of the rocks, that gave drink to the people and their cattle in abundance; prayer made their shoes and their clothes to last these forty years, that they neither rent nor waxed old; and suppose they had neither wool to card, nor lint to spin, yet they lacked not raiment.

Then he says, *pray in the spirit.* Prayer in the spirit comprehends four things.

First, Pray in the spirit, that is, pray in humility. 2*dly,* In fervency. 3*dly,* In faith. 4*thly,* In sincerity.

First, To *pray in the spirit,* that is, to pray with an humble heart; for St. Peter says, 1 Pet. v. 6. "God resisteth the proud, but he gives grace to the humble:" Likewise God himself says, "I dwell in the high and lofty place, with him also that has a contrite heart, and a humble spirit, to revive the spirit of the humble, and to give life to them that are of a contrite heart." Isa. lvii. 15. Abraham prayed in humility, Gen. xviii. 27. saying, I have begun to speak unto my Lord, and I am but dust and ashes;" Jacob prayed in humility, Gen. xxxii. 10. saying, "I am not worthy of the least of all the mercies and truth that thou hast shewed unto me, thy servant;" The Publican prayed in humility," Luke xviii. 13. when he "stood afar off, and would not do so much as lift up his eyes to heaven, but smote upon his breast, saying, O God, be merciful to me a sinner;" The Centurion prayed in humility, when he said, "Lord I am not worthy that thou shouldst come under my roof:" The Canaanitish woman prayed in humility, when she said, "have mercy on me, O Lord, thou son of David, my daughter is miserably vexed with a devil;" again she says, "Lord, help me;" and the third time she says, "truth, Lord, I am but a dog, yet indeed the dogs eat of the crumbs that fall from their master's table," Mat. viii. 8. All these persons prayed in humility; therefore when thou prayest, come with a humble heart unto God.

Secondly, *Pray in the spirit*, that is, pray in fervency, or with a fervent spirit; for prayer in the spirit brings a fire from heaven, that kindles the heart in a flame, and melts the heart of a man or woman that hath the spirit; as the sun in a hot summer day casts hot beams that melteth the wax set against it; even so the hot beams of the Holy Ghost draweth down fire from heaven into thy heart, that setteth it on a flame, and then thy heart melts with the sense of that happy and sweet conjunction betwixt Christ and thy soul; then thou wilt cry out, with the spouse in Cant. viii. 6, 7. "Love is strong as death; jealousy is cruel as the grave; the coals thereof are fiery coals, and has a vehement flame. Much water cannot quench love, neither can the floods drown it: If a man would give all the substance of his house for love, it would utterly be contemned." So prayer may well be called fervent, for it burns up the heart with the fire of the love of God, spread abroad upon thy heart by the Holy Ghost: It is true thou wilt not always be so when thou prayest, for some of the saints have cried like "wolves in the desert, chattered like cranes, mourned like doves on the house-top, and like a pelican in the wilderness," Psal. cii. 6, 7. Some of them have cried with strong cries and many tears; indeed prayer hath made men to sweat on the forehead: when I remember of that bloody sweat of our Lord in the garden, when he prayed so fervently once, twice, thrice, saying, "Father, if it be possible, let this cup pass from me;" and when he did sweat drops of blood trickling down to the ground; when he, I say, who was the heir of all, was so fervent in prayer, what should we be, that are miserable beggars, and have nothing but as we receive from him.

Thirdly, *Pray in the spirit*, that is *pray in faith*; therefore it is said, Mat. xxi. 22. "Whatsoever ye shall ask in prayer believingly, ye shall receive it. As Jonas ii. 2. He prayed when he was in the whale's belly, in faith, and the Lord heard him, and he was delivered. Prayer in faith hath done many great things, it hath run up to heaven and brought down the judgment of God upon their enemies; and again, prayer in faith hath taken away the judgment of the enemies; and opened the womb of the barren, 1 Sam. i. 27. 1 Sam. ii. 5. and made them bear children; it hath opened the windows of heaven and brought down rain; it hath made the rocks to cleave, and waters to gush out; it hath opened the eyes of the blind; it hath cleansed the leper; it hath raised the dead; it hath made the earth to tremble; it hath loosed the fetters, opened the prison doors; and, to be short, it hath laid hold on that glorious Spirit, and brought him down from heaven to the souls of believers; therefore "pray in faith, and wave not, says James i. 6. for he that wavereth let him not think to receive any thing of the Lord."

Fourthly and *last of all, Pray in the spirit;* that is, pray in the truth and sincerity of thy heart, without hypocrisy, and not for a fashion.

Question, Thou wilt ask, what thou shouldst pray for?

Answer, Pray first for the glory of God, and the kingdom of heaven to be let down into thy soul, pray for true faith, pray for repentance, pray for sanctification, and all the rest of the spiritual blessings belonging to thee in Christ.

Secondly, Pray that thou mayest get new strength, and new grace every day, to uphold thee in the day of temptation.

Thirdly, Pray for all things necessary in this life, so far as thou mayest be furthered in the service of God.

Question 2d. For whom shalt thou pray.

Answer. Pray for all men and women that pertain to the election, called, or uncalled; then thou mayest pray for special persons, with whom thou hast a special bond; there is a special bond betwixt the husband and the wife, the parents and children. Jacob prayed for his wife and children, Gen. xxxii. 11. The husband is obliged to pray for the wife, and the wife for her husband; the parents are bound to pray for their children, and the children for their parents: there is a special bond betwixt the master and the servant; therefore Abraham's servant prayed for good success to his master's business, Gen. xxvi. 12. There is a special bond betwixt the king and his subjects, therefore Solomon prayed for his people, and they prayed for him, 1 Kings viii. 22—66. There is a special bond between the pastor and his flock, and betwixt the master and his scholars; therefore Paul prayed for Timothy, and he desired Timothy to *remember him in his prayers*: Samuel prayed for his people, 1 Sam. xii. 18. at their desire, and the Lord sent thunder and fire with rain from heaven, and the people feared the Lord: So we should pray one for another, for praying one for another hath done great things: for John says, 1 John v. 16. "If any man see his brother sin a sin that is not unto death, let him ask of God, and he shall give him life;" that is a great thing. When the wrath of God was kindled against Israel, Moses prayed, and God was pacified: Job prayed for his sons and daughters, Job i. 5. while they were feasting, and they were kept; the saints prayed for Peter when he was in prison, and the Lord delivered him by an angel, Acts xii. 5.

Now then, pray, and ye have gained the plea: Now is the time of prayer since ever the world was; for there is a great necessity of prayer. I put it to yourselves, if ye have need to pray or not. Where from comes all this blindness, this incredulity, but from the want of prayer. Therefore pray that ye enter not into temptation, for be ye sure, how soon soever ye leave off prayer, the devil shall be as soon ready to tempt you. Besides ourselves, we have to pray for all the saints of God on earth. Will ye look to the earth, will ye look to the world, and them that are under the Turk's dominion; look to his cruelty, that sends his men of war to the Christians, and takes their male children from their mother's breast, and trains them up in his religion, that they never get leave to know Christ; and when they come to age, he trains them up in his wars, and makes the most deadly tyrants to the Christians, so that the son will be the first ready to slip a sword in his father. What if this judgment come to Scotland! Then we may say, alas! we never took pains to train up our children in the fear of God, therefore this is justly come upon us: then pray for them that are under antichrist and his slavery; and remember also our poor church in our neighbouring country, that is kept under bondage, and hath not the freedom to serve God as we have; we have need to pray that God would not take away this light of the gospel that we have, and that we be not consumed with the plague that is in this land. I would have you all thinking on these things that ye should pray for; therefore, I beseech you, pray that the glory of the Lord shining in the gospel, which is the spirit and life, that it depart not from us; I mean not the outward glory, let it go to Babel and to antichrist, for it is he that hath the gold and riches of the world, but the glory of the gospel makes our hearts to shake and tremble; that was the glory of the Lord, when the rocks of men and womens hearts did rend at the voice of the gospel; and that was his glory, when men and women, that were lying dead and rotten in the grave of their corruption, rose from death to life, at the hearing of his voice in this ministry of the gospel.

There are two judgments hanging over our heads; that is, the pest in the midst of the land, and the appearance of the departure of the Lord's glory out of the land; for he is removing and taking away his visible presence out of the midst of the cherubims, he is taking away his power from the ministry in this land, for it is not possible that his presence and our sins can abide together; so long as we retain our sins and repent not for them, the Lord cannot abide with us; and go he away, I denounce then judgment to come afterwards, and not only I denounce it, but the Lord says, "wo be to you when I go away and leave you," read Psal. lxxviii. Ye there shall see diversities of plagues poured out upon the children of Israel for their sins, when the Lord left them to themselves. I remember when Eli heard that the ark of the Lord was taken, which was a figure of the visible presence of God, he fell backward and brake his neck and died; and when his daughter-in-law heard that the ark of God was taken, she bowed herself and travailed (for her pains came upon her) and she died also. What should we do then, when not only we hear, but with our eyes we may see the visible presence of God taken out of the hearts of men and women, and it is like to be taken out of the whole land? But, go thou away, Lord, well is the man that gets a cottage in another country! for there are fearful tidings to come after that; there is a sword to come that shall be drunk with the blood of babes and sucklings, that neither old nor young, man nor woman, rich nor poor, shall be spared; the Lord knoweth wherefrom it shall come, but I think I cannot be quit of it, but this land defiled with blood, it must be cleansed with blood again; but if we could be humbled and run to God by prayer, if we could seek the Lord with fasting and mourning, if we could assay it in our families and persons, doubtless there should a blessing follow on it, and it may be, peace should be sent by God in our days; therefore I remember what the prophet Zephaniah says, "gather yourselves, even gather you, O nation, not worthy to be beloved, before the decree come forth, and ye be as chaff before the fierce wrath of the Lord come upon you: seek ye the Lord, all the meek of the earth, that have wrought his judgments, seek righteousness and lowliness, if so be that ye be hid in the day of the Lord's wrath," Zeph. ii. 1, 2, 3. So, brethren, gather ye yourselves together, ere the decree come forth; for if it come forth, it cannot be called back again, and nothing can stay it but only repentance; therefore I beseech you, mourn, and renew your mourning as though ye had never mourned, and who can tell but the Lord will have mercy upon us? However, if it be that his judgments overtake us, and it may be that some measure of light be left to our posterity, that they may say, God be thanked that our fathers have left so much behind them to us.

I say no more, but I recommend this that hath been spoken to the grace of God in Christ Jesus. To whom, with the Father and the holy Spirit, be honour and glory, for now and evermore. *Amen.*

SERMON XX.

UPON DIVERS POINTS OF RELIGION.

1 John iv. 7, 8.

Beloved, let us love one another; for love comes of God, and every one that loveth, is born of God, and knoweth God.

SOME being deluded and beguiled by the devil, think that they know God, and love him well enough, when yet they never saw him nor loved him, and therefore they were never sure that God loved them: for there is none that have been persuaded of the love of God to themselves, but their persuasion hath raised a love upon their heart to God, and his saints for his sake. So then, thou never hadst a persuasion of the love of God to thy own soul, nor thou was never yet within the compass of that love, that hadst never a love to God, nor his saints for his sake; therefore deceive not yourselves. But as for you that are the children of God, the devil would deceive you, when he would have you to presume of that love to you, and would make you fall asleep, that when ye have once gotten a taste of the sense of that love in your own hearts, and have been filled with the joys of the Holy Ghost, and now have lost the persuasion of that love, he labours to make you believe that your persuasion was not true, nor your joy was not true, and so to drive thee to despair. But what should ye do in this case? Never rest till thou gettest thy persuasion renewed, and desire yet to confirm it over again, and dream not to yourselves of a love whereof ye have no warrant out of the word of God; then when God and his word says that he hath loved thee, then I am sure they will all draw this out of thy soul.

First, A love to God the Father, as the fountain and well-spring of thy salvation.

Secondly, A love to God the Son, as the perfecter and accomplisher of thy redemption.

Thirdly, A love to the Holy Ghost, as the instrument of thy comfort and sanctification.

Fourthly, and *lastly*, A love to every one of the saints of God. I know well, many of you have experience of this, that oftentimes when ye have gotten a persuasion of this love spread abroad in your hearts by the Holy Spirit, then ye have had great joy and consolation; but when ye had lost this and your feeling, because your love to God and his saints hath been weakened, therefore ye were bereft of all comfort to your souls. Now therefore, my hearts, whenever ye get this persuasion, let it learn you this lesson given by the apostle Paul, that seeing " the grace of God that brings salvation to all men, hath shined in your hearts, and teacheth you to live soberly, righteously, and godly in this present world, looking for that blessed hope, and the glorious appearance of the great God, and our Saviour Jesus Christ, who gave himself for us from all eternity, to purify unto himself a peculiar people zealous of good works," Titus ii. 11, 12, 13, 14. So I beseech you for the Lord's sake, as ye would have that sweet consolation of the Spirit abiding in you, beware of worldly lusts, beware of the deceits of the devil, that would bereave you of the sense of this love, to the end that he may weaken your love to God and his saints; therefore the more that he would weaken the sense of this love in you, be ye always the stronger to hold a grip of it, and let him not prevail, but grow in faith and love, and, in the sweet love of God, feed your souls. So the first temptation of Satan cast against the child of God, is this, to make thee doubt, whether God ever loved thee or not : and why? To weaken thy love to him, to waken thy conscience, to kindle a flame therein, that it may burn thee, and so to keep thee under doubtings and terrors; for as long as thou doubtest of the love of God to thee in Christ, thou canst never set thy heart fully to love God, nor his saints for his sake; thou canst never have love and readiness to do every good work, and thou canst never be faithful either to God or man in thy calling; thou canst do nothing in faith or love, as long as thou doubtest of the love of God towards thyself; therefore, my hearts, beware of doubtings, be stedfast in the faith, resist the devil, and stand fast in the day of temptation; hold fast your feet that he make thee not to stumble; let never the devil bereave you of the persuasion of this love of God; and when he makes thee call the love of God in question, he hath his own grounds and arguments; therefore,

First, He will say, men and women have gone as far on in religion as thou hast done, and they thought themselves sure enough of the love of God, and yet in the end, have been found reprobates; and the event hath shewed, that their persuasion hath been presumption; and to confirm this he will cast in the example of Cain, that confessed his sin to God, and said, *It was heavier than he could bear*; he mourned for his sin, and said, " Behold thou hast cast me out this day from before thee, and whosoever finds me shall slay me;" and he got this answer from the Lord, " Doubtless, whosoever slayeth Cain shall be punished seven-fold; and the Lord set a mark on him, lest any finding him should slay him, Gen. iv. 14, 15. yet he was a reprobate." He will cast in Judas, that confessed, saying " I have sinned in betraying innocent blood," and in sign of repentance, he threw back the silver again; yet he was a reprobate. He will cast in the example of Esau, *that sought the blessing with tears*, yet he was a reprobate. He will cast in four sundry sorts of ground that received seed, and how fair shews of fruit some of them brought forth; yet there was but one of them that brought forth good fruit. He will cast in that of the vi. of the Hebrews, how the reprobates will get " lightnings, and tastings of the heavenly gifts, and be partakers of the Spirit, and taste of the good word of God, and of the powers and virtues of the world to come ; yet they have fallen away, and there was no place left for their repentance ;" therefore they were reprobates ; but thou couldst never come so far as these : what warrant hast thou then of the love of God? Now, to take these away, thou shalt answer, it is true, the reprobates have had their lightnings and glances from heaven thrown per force into their hearts, and letting them see a glory they never got to, nor durst never put out their hand to reach to it, and take it to themselves ; it is true, he hath been partaker of the gifts of the Spirit ; but he never had the spirit of adoption, that he should cry Abba, Father ; nor he durst never claim to the mercy of God, nor to the promises of salvation, nor apply them to his own heart ; it is true he hath had his tastes and prievings of the sweet goodness of God, and of the virtue of that blood ; but he never fed upon the blood of Jesus ; his flesh and his blood was never meat and drink to his soul, nor the soul of him never delighted nor took pleasure in the word of God, that he could meditate thereon both day and night ; nor he never resolved to make it the square of his life, or the rule to live by, or a lanthorn to his feet, and the only guide to lead him to the kingdom of heaven ; it is true they have had shews of faith and fair blossoms, and mended many things, as Herod did, Mark vi. 20. they have trembled at the preaching of the word, as Felix did, Acts xxiv. 25. but they had never a constant purpose in their hearts to mend all things, nor they never resolved to drink in the sincere milk of the word of God to their poor soul's food ; it is true, they have blessed themselves when God cursed them, and they have cried, peace, when there was nothing but sudden destruction to come upon them and so they have dreamed of the love of God ; but they never felt sensibly the love of God in their souls, and spread abroad in their heart by the Holy Ghost ; the wicked man had never the spirit of adoption, he had never a love to the saints, nor he could never say with David, Psal. xvi. 2, 3. " Lord, my well doing extends not to thee, but to the saints that are on the earth, and to the excellent in whom all my desire is." He had never the hatred of sin, nor true desire of righteousness; it was never the purpose of his heart to leave off all sorts of iniquities, but there is always one sort of sin or other that bears mastery over him, or rules or reigns in his heart; but the child of God has all these marks in his heart in some measure.

To try yourselves therefore by these marks, look if ever ye had a lively sense of the love of God spread in your hearts, and look if this hath bred a true love to God, and a love to your brother for Christ's sake; look if ever ye had the spirit of adoption bearing witness to your consciences, that God hath loved you, that God hath chosen you, his Son hath redeemed you, persuading you that ye are called from darkness to light, that ye have gotten remission in the blood of Jesus, that ye have had the righteousness of Christ covering you, and ye have felt the virtue of this blood washing you from sin and sanctifying you to newness of life; then remember that there was never a reprobate who had a love to God from the bottom of his heart; that had a true love to Christ, or his saints for his sake; there was never a reprobate persuaded of the love of God to himself; there was never a reprobate sure of his election; there was never a reprobate sure of his redemption; there was never a reprobate sure of his calling; there was never a reprobate sure of his justification, nor sure of his sanctification; nor he had never a sure hope of that endless glory.

What then should ye gather of this? Ye should gather, I am sure of these marks and tokens, and my conscience bears me witness, that sometimes I have had these things; therefore I will rest upon the former experience of God's love and kindness; and therefore the devil shall never be able to bereave me of that thing, that I know well I had once; for, suppose my sense fail me, yet my faith will never fail me; therefore I will say with Job, Lord, "though thou shouldst slay me, yet will I trust in thee;" so when ye lose your feeling, and your persuasion begins to weaken, then remember upon the bygone experience ye have had of the love of God towards you, and this shall uphold you. This for the first temptation whereby Satan essays to bereave us of the love of God.

The *second* is another temptation, when he will say to thee, it is true the Lord beareth a love to his church, and this love is general, all his promises are general; but, as for thee, thou art but a particular person, what to do then hast thou with these general promises, thy name is not here? For answer to this, the love of God is free, his grace is free, his promises are free, and all his gifts are freely given to the believer, and he hath given a particular command to every one to believe; therefore the general promise, and particular command, is a sufficient warrant to me that believes, that the promises belong to me.

Again, he will make thee call in question, whether thou beest a member of the church, or not? and whether thou wast ever ingrafted in Christ's body or not? He will say, it is true, if ye knew well ye were in Christ, and that ye were a member of his body, and in the bosom of the church, I know then ye might boldly put to your hand, and apply the promises to thyself; for they are made to all in general, but to the church in special; but tell me whether thou art a member of the church or not?

Now, you shall answer to this, Christ is the Saviour of sinners, yea, of the chiefest and most notorious sinners, I Tim. i. 15. John ix. 5. Christ is the light and life of the world; for he looses the bands of death, and lets the prisoners go free; he shines in the midst of darkness, and gives light to them that walk in the valley and shadow of death; and as the Father's love is free, even so is the blood of the Son free to all that will come and take it; "for there is no respect of persons with God," Rom. ix. 15. "He shews mercy on whom he will, and he hardens whom he will?" What should let him, then, but he should shew mercy to me, if I will come and seek it, and apply it to

SERMON XX.

myself? The which thing I do. Therefore, when the apostle says, God loved the world, he subjoins, *and me also*, whereby he applies the general love of God to himself in particular, as if he would say, " God loved the world, and he loved me too :" Likewise, in another place, when he had said, " It is a worthy saying, Christ came to save sinners," he subjoins, " of whom I am the chief," 1 Tim. i. 15. Therefore he counts himself the chief of all sinners, whom Christ saves. Now, he saves none but his own members; and how knowest thou that thou art a member of Christ ? For answer to this, if thou wouldst know whether thou beest a true member of Christ, or not, thou must not try thyself by thy present state, for thou mayest be sometimes whole, and sometimes sick ; and when thou art sick, thou art not in the same state that thou wert in when thou wast whole ; for sickness may bereave thee of thy senses, and so make thee think that thou art another man than thou art, and thou mayest be so sick, that there is little difference betwixt thee and death ; only this, thy veins stir, thy pulse moves, thy breath goes, as long as thou hast this, thou art living ; for, tell me, stuckest thou ever to the body of Christ ? And suppose thou beest sick, and hast not the right use of thy senses, and thou mayest be sick for a time, but thou shalt not die or perish in that sickness ; for he that is the Head will not forget the members of his own body. Now, seeing thou knewest well that once thou wert a member of his own body, thou mayest be assured that he will not let thee perish ; for once in that body, and never to be pulled therefrom again ; once coupled to the Head, and never to sunder again ; once brought into the bosom of the church, and never to be shut out again ; once drawing life out of Christ, never to die again ; so thou mayest be sick, and long sick, but yet not sick unto death.

The third temptation that is more dangerous than the former, it is this ; he will say, How canst thou that art a vile sinner persuade thyself of the love of God towards thee ? For God is holy, and thou art unholy, God is light, and thou art darkness; God is righteous, and thou art unrighteous; what fellowship can be betwixt thee and him? God abhors sin wherever it is, and he hates sin in every person, and thou knowest that there is sin enough in thee; how can he love thee then? or how can love and hatred stand together in God? Since God is righteous, he must do justice, and he must punish sin without respect of persons; now, the punishment of sin is death, both of soul and body, in the everlasting fire of hell for evermore; thou hast sinned, therefore he must punish thee with hell-fire eternally; how can he love thee then? What presumption then, or what blasphemy is this to thee that art so vile a sinner, to persuade thyself of the love of God, that will punish sin with most rigorous severity? Thou that dreamest of a love that thou wilt never be the better of, God is pure and clean, and loves purity; thou art unclean, therefore beware of presumption.

What canst thou answer to this? I will tell thee, thou mayest boldly say, God can love sinners, and can look upon them with the eye of mercy, even when they are lying in their sins; for he looked on the sinful woman that "sat at his feet, and washed them with her tears, and dried them with the hair of her head," Luke vii. 37. that was such a sinner, that there was seven devils cast out of her, Luke viii. 2. that was such a sinner, that the good man of the house said, If he knew what a woman this were, he would not let her come near him, nor admit her in his company; yet the Lord says to him, in effect, She is more righteous than thou, for many causes he reckoned out, which I need not to rehearse: But what says he to the woman? "Woman, be of good comfort, thy sins are forgiven thee;" and therefore thou lovest me much, because much was forgiven thee.

And who was such a great sinner as that bloody man Paul? Acts ix. 1. that "breathed out threatenings and slaughter against the saints of God;" yet he was beloved of God, and so loved, that he is made a "chosen vessel to bear the name of Jesus ," and he is made such a vessel of mercy, that " where sin abounded, there grace superabounded ;" and suppose he was " one born out of due time, yet he laboured more than all the rest of the apostles."

Who was so great a sinner as Manasses? that "made the streets of Jerusalem run with the blood of the saints, and filled the city with idolatry, and overthrew the altars, and the true religion ; that exceeded in wickedness all the kings that were before him ;" yet he was loved of God ; for when he was brought into captivity into another country, and there laid in prison, and out of prison confessed his sins unto God, and cried for mercy, then it pleased the Lord to shew him mercy ; so he let not the devil deceive him, 2 Kings xxi. 3, 4. And so let not the devil deceive you, in making you believe God cannot love thee, because thou art a sinner : No, God can love a sinner; but such sinners that have known God hath loved them in Christ, then they begin to mourn for their sins, because their sins brought Christ down from heaven into the grave ; then they begin to love God again ; and because their love cannot get to God in heaven, therefore they will pour out their love on the saints on earth for his sake : so, take heed to this ; for it is not every sinner God loves, it is only penitent and believing sinners.

Now, to persuade you that God can love sinners, ye shall lay this ground, " Herein hath God manifested his love, that when we were enemies, he sent his Son to die for us ;" when we were bond-slaves to sin and Satan, it pleased him to set us at liberty, and make us his own free subjects, to serve him without fear ; when we were dead in sin, and had not a word to speak to him, nor could not so much as cry for mercy, it pleased him to put life in our dead souls, and words in our mouths ; and when we were deaf, and dumb, and blind also, it pleased him to open our ears, to loose our tongues, and make us cry for mercy : was not this great love he bore to us, even when we were his enemies? how much more shall he love us now, being reconciled to him through Christ?" Rom. v. 9, 10. And since he loved us, when we could neither seek his favour, nor love him again, how much more shall he love us now, when we desire to be loved of him, and endeavour to love him again?

Again, remember that the love of God is free; for he loves us not for our worthiness and righteousness, but his love goeth beyond all our sins; he loved thee of grace, he chused thee of grace, he redeemed thee of grace, he called thee of grace, he justified thee of grace, he sanctifies thee of grace, and he shall glorify thee of grace; so all that he doth to thee is of grace, and not for any respect he hath to the fewness or multitude of thy sins; for he knew before he loved thee, or chused thee, what sins thou wouldst fall into, and he would have mercy on such as he knew to be the greatest sinners, that so much the more his free grace might shine clearly in thy salvation: So now, to quit thee of this temptation, there is the answer. It is in Christ the Father loves thee, and the righteousness of the Son is imputed to thee, that thou mayest be made the righteousness of God through his righteousness; therefore, being covered with the righteousness of the Son, the Father sees no sin in thee.

Now in the last temptation, there are two things, 1*st*, Satan wilt say to thy conscience, If thou wilt not believe me, nor the example of them that are gone before thee, nor thy own heart, yet believe the Lord: And this is a strong temptation, that the thief will bring in the Lord against us. Look, says he, to the strokes and rods the Lord lays upon thee; if he loved thee, he would not deal so roughly with thee; if he loved thee, his hand would not be so heavy upon thee; if he loved thee, he would not have shown manifest signs and tokens of his anger and wrath against thee. This is a sore temptation.

But thou shalt answer him on this manner, Thou art a liar, Satan; "For whom God loves, he chastises, and the way to heaven is straight and narrow; for through many tribulations we must come to the kingdom of heaven," Mat. vii. 14. "All that would reign with Christ, they must suffer with him," 2 Tim. ii. 12. "It is good for me that the Lord corrected me," Psal. cxix. 71. Well, we must be partakers of the cross of Christ, if we would be partakers of his crown of glory: "Many are the troubles of the righteous, but God delivers him out of them all," Psal. xxxiv. 19. Therefore we must be content with our crosses, and bear them patiently for a short time; "For our light afflictions, which are but for a moment, cause unto us a far more exceeding and eternal weight of glory.

The other part of this last temptation is this, What matters of the common crosses that other men have? But thou hast the very beginning of hell in thy conscience, and thou feelest the wrath of God seizing on thy soul, and thou hast the arrows of the Almighty's indignation running through thee, and piercing thy heart. Psal. lxxxviii. 7. Job vi. 4. So that thou hast nothing but fightings without, and terrors within, and all thy bowels are consumed with grief, thy bones are dried up and withered for want of sap, there is no moistness in them, Psal. xxxii. 3, 4. Thy conscience is burned up with the very flames of the torments of hell; how then can God love thee, being in this case?

Indeed I grant, this is the heaviest temptation of all; but, to clear you in this point, there are four things I mind to speak of:

First, There are many that feel wrath, and yet are not under wrath, but under love.

Secondly, There are some that feel no wrath, nor yet are under wrath, but in love to God.

Thirdly, There are some that are under wrath, and yet feel no wrath.

Fourthly and *last of all*, There are some that feel wrath, and they are under wrath, and they have the very flames of the fire of hell begun in them, that shall never have an end. Afterward, I am to tell you, how ye shall discern the stings of the reprobates that feel wrath, and are under wrath, from the stings that are competent to the child of God that feels wrath, and yet is not under wrath. These things I mind by the grace of God, to tell you at more length; and until that time, I commend you, and this that hath been spoken, unto the grace of God in Christ Jesus. *Amen.* To whom, &c.

SERMON XXI.

UPON DIVERS POINTS OF RELIGION.

2 Corinth. vii. 5.

But we were troubled on every side: without were fightings, within were fears.

Psalm lxxxviii. 1.

O Lord God of my salvation, I have cried day and night before thee.

I KNOW there are but few of you that need this consolation which I am to speak of; and yet I cannot tell how soon the Lord will waken your consciences, that ye should be glad of the meanest consolation of the least of the saints; and ye would be glad of the meanest persuasion of the love of God, that any of his children ever had before you; and ye would be content of the least grain weight of grace, and of that smallest measure of the Spirit to sustain you in your conflicts. Therefore I will wait on while the Lord send this gracious wakening to some of you. And I beseech God, for his own Son's sake, that he would send his own Spirit to convey this truth into every one of your hearts and souls, that this word may be the savour of life unto life to you: the sore temptations I speak of, are very perilous and heavy.

First, The children of God, when they have seen the light, the zeal, and the grace of some reprobates, and yet they were not saved; and when they consider, that they could not get farther, then they begin to reason, How shall they be persuaded of the love of God?

For answer to this, Howsoever it be that they have had their own graces, yet they never got the love of God, or the love of Christ, nor the love of the saints for Christ's sake; they never got to a true hatred of sin; they never got the true love of righteousness; they never got saving faith, or to the repentance of life. But the other, viz. the child of God, gets all these in some measure. Now, what consolation would ye have gotten, if ye had applied all the promises of grace to yourselves, and if ye had said, They are mine, and I will take them to me; for they belong to me in special; therefore I will apply them to my own soul? What comfort ye might have had of this, I leave it to your own consideration.

As for the second temptation, If ye doubt whether ye be a lively member of Christ's body or not, ye shall know by this, if ever there was a conjunction betwixt Christ and your souls, and if ever there was a communion betwixt thee and every member of his body, and if ever thou hast been pulled out of nature, and planted in grace; then thou mayest be sure, that thou art a member of Christ's body, never to be plucked from him again.

Now, as for the third temptation, Whereas ye have oft-times measured his love with your own unworthiness, and the power of God with your weakness; and whereas the sense of your indignity hath brought great grief to your souls, this hath bereft you of many and great comforts; let this be your consolation now, that suppose thou beest a great sinner, yet thy sins are finite and the love of God is infinite; suppose thou beest changeable and unconstant; yet the love of God is constant and unchangeable; "for whom he loves, he loves to the end;" suppose thou beest weak, and easily overcome, yet the love of God is strong and invincible; and, remember, the love of God is free; and his grace is free; therefore my unworthiness, were it never so great, it cannot hinder the grace of God to shine when and where it lists, nor it cannot stay him to "have mercy on whom he will have mercy;" therefore shall I not accept of his mercy, seeing he will have mercy?

Last of all, Whereas these outward afflictions and bodily crosses will make thee often-times to think, that if there were no anger with God against thee, he would not deal thus with thee. Think ye not that this was a sore temptation to Lazarus, that he had not so much as one to bind up his wounds, and to comfort him, and to give him a bit of bread to refresh him, but was compelled to lie at the glutton's gate begging, and was glad that the dogs came and licked his wounds? Luke xvi. 20. 21. Was it not a sore temptation to the cripple man that lay so long at the pool of Bethesda, and when the angel came to stir the water, he had not one to let him down? And was not this a sore temptation to David when all his kinsfolk had forsaken him, and his familiar friends had left him, and when they that sat at his table had lifted up their heels against him; was not that a sore temptation, think ye? Yet, I assure you, these outward afflictions may stand very well with the love of God; for ye dare not say but the Lord loved Lazarus, notwithstanding of all his sores and outward miseries; because after his death his soul was carried into Abraham's bosom, that is, into the kingdom of heaven. Ye dare not say, but the Lord loved that cripple man, notwithstanding he lay so long at the pool and had none to let him down into it; because he sent his own Son to heal him. Ye dare not say but the Lord loved David, notwithstanding all his troubles, crosses and afflictions that he sustained before he came to the kingdom; because the Lord delivered him out of them all, and confounded all his enemies with shame, and put him in peaceable possession of his kingdom.

Now, as for the last temptation, which is the most dangerous of all; for our bodily infirmities and diseases may very well be borne with, as long as the spirit is whole; but when the spirit is troubled, and the heart broken, what can comfort thee then? And when the soul is burnt up with a consuming fire, and with a burning flame, and when the heart is pressed down with the terror of wrath, and when the soul is like to cleave asunder with the fierceness of God's anger, and when the arrows of the indignation of the Almighty run through thee, and when thou art brought to such a strait, that thou seest not an outgate, who can abide that comfortless estate? What consolation can be had to them that are in such a case? Now, to clear you in this point, I was telling you, that there are four sorts of men and women in the world: 1*st*, There are some that feel the wrath of God seizing upon their consciences, yet are not under wrath. 2*dly*, There are some that feel not the wrath of God, neither are they under wrath. 3*dly*, There are some that feel not the wrath of God, and yet they are under it. 4*thly* and last of all, There are some that feel wrath, and are under it indeed.

As for the first sort, that feel the wrath of God on their souls and consciences, and yet are not under wrath, these are the saints of God: Examples ye have here, Paul, the chosen vessel of God, that bears the name of Jesus, he had fightings without and terrors within." Heman the Ezrahite said, "The waves of the Lord's indignation are gone over my head, so that they are like to drown me; I suffer terrors and doubtings from my very youth, so that I can never be quit of them," Psal. lxxxviii. 7. and both these were the dear children of God. Now, if thou wilt say, that thou art of this sort, that feelest nothing but wrath, and thou wilt ask how thou shalt take it up, either if thou hast been in this estate, or if thou beest in it, that when thou art bearing such a wrath, that, put all the sand of the sea in balance with it, it would not overweigh it; and when thou hast such a fire in thy conscience, that, put iron and brass in that fire, it would melt them; for they were not able to bear it, or how shalt thou know in this case, that thou art loved of God, and that he hath chosen thee to eternal life?

I tell thee, if thou beest the chosen child of God, and a vessel of mercy, under the sense of wrath in this estate, this will be thy disposition:

First, Thou wilt hate and detest thy sin, which is the cause of thy misery, and hath brought thee to this pain.

Secondly, Thou must have some dolour and sorrow for thy sin, and thou lamentest because thou hast provoked God to anger against thee.

Thirdly, Thou wilt have a desire to be reconciled to God, and thou wouldest gladly be at peace with him, that thy sins may be taken away out of his sight.

Fourthly, There will be a hunger and thirst for the blood of Christ to quench that wrath, and for his righteousness to cover thy soul.

Fifthly, There will be a patient waiting upon the Lord's deliverance, and when thou canst not get to this persuasion, that there will be a hope above hope, and thou wilt say with Job, Job. xiii. 15. "Lord, I will trust in thee, though thou shouldest slay me." Thou wilt say, It is an easy thing for me to cast away my confidence, I know a little thing will put me over the brae; yet I will not despair of the Lord's mercy, but if I perish, I shall perish praying; and if I go to hell, I shall go with hope in the blood of Jesus: Thou wilt say with David, "Though all men forsake me, yet, Lord, thou wilt gather me up; though I walk under the shadow of darkness, and in the valley of death, yet thou wilt restore my soul to life."

But thou wilt ask, What shall be thy exercise when thou art in this case, and under the sense of wrath? I will tell thee thou must do four things:

First, Do as thy Head and Saviour did in the time of his fear, and under the sense of the wrath of his Father; he, with strong cries and many tears, and with earnest prayer and supplication, ran to the throne of God's mercy, and besought him, that that cup (if it were possible) might be taken from him, and if it might stand with his Father's will; this was his exercise, and *he was heard in that he feared.* How was he heard? Was that cup taken from him then? No: but suppose he tasted of the bitterness of that cup, yet he got patience to bear it, and in the end he got victory, and so overcame it; even so do thou; run to God by prayer, and desire him to remove that fierce wrath and indignation, if it be his pleasure; and he shall give thee patience to bear it, and strength to overcome it. What more shouldst thou do? Grip to the promises as thou canst; look off wrath, and hold thy eye on mercy; look through the fire unto the blood of Christ; wait on the Lord's deliverance as thou canst; wrestle against the temptations as thou canst; look through the consuming fire of the wrath of an angry God, unto a Saviour and Mediator, and desire him to quench that fire with his blood; look into the bottomless depth of the love of the Father, first unto his own Son, and next unto thee for his sake, and there thy soul shall find rest and peace. This should be thy exercise when thou art in this case, that thou feelest nothing but wrath. This much for the first sort of men and women that feel wrath, and are not under wrath.

Now, follows the *second* sort that feel no wrath, neither yet are under wrath; and there are four sorts of these folk, and they all belong to the kingdom of God.

First, There are some of the children of God, whose calling hath been sweet, and with joy, and softness of heart when God hath opened their hearts at one instant, as he did the heart of Lydia, that with one preaching was converted, for the word ran to her heart, and she believed, and was baptized, Acts xvi. 14. So there are some that God calls softly and sweetly, and there are some that he calls more violently. *Secondly,* So there is another sort that have had their terrors and wrestlings with the wrath of God, but, by the grace of God, they are brought through them, and now have gotten the joy and consolation of the Holy Ghost; and have witnessed to their consciences that they are loved of God in Christ; they are chosen to eternal life; they are redeemed by the blood of Jesus; they are called from darkness to light; they are justified with the righteousness of the Son of God; they are cleansed by faith in him; and they hope for everlasting glory; and this has brought unspeakable joy and peace to their consciences which passeth all understanding. These feel no wrath, neither are under wrath, for they have past all danger, and peril of danger, or perishing.

Thirdly, There are some that feel no wrath, and are not under wrath, neither indeed need they to fear wrath; and these are they that have felt the love of God shed abroad in their souls and hearts by the Holy Ghost, and they have gotten joy and consolation by the word, and by the Spirit, and they rest upon this joy; therefore they are not so much troubled with the terrors of conscience, for they have found mercy in the blood of Jesus, and the sense of that mercy hath softened their hearts; for as the induration of the heart of the reprobate comes by wrath, so softening of the heart of God's elect comes of love and mercy; so when God opens the heart sweetly, and when God makes men and women to *drink in the sincere milk of the word of God gladly*, as their souls food, and when with no great difficulty they claim to the promises of mercy, what needs them to doubt of the love of God, which by faith they have apprehended; and therefore they feel no wrath, neither are they under wrath.

Fourth Sort of those that feel no wrath, neither are under wrath, are these, that are not much moved either with the sweet sense of God's mercy, but apply the promises to themselves; neither are they yet touched with the want of God's wrath, and bitterness thereof, and yet they believe all God's curses and threatenings to fall on the reprobate. And indeed this is the hardest state of all, and when thou neither feelest the angry face of God striking a fear in thy soul for thy sin wherewith he is offended, nor yet thou findest the sweet mercies of God alluring or provoking thee to love him again, nor softening nor breaking thy heart with sorrow for the offence done to him, he being so loving a Father to thee, and thou so wicked a son, and so merciful a God to thee, so wicked a sinner;

that is a hard case; and when thou art so, thou wilt say, can the Holy Ghost be where induration and hardness of heart is? My heart is hardened like a very stone, how can I then be persuaded that I have the Spirit of Christ? And how can I be sure of the love of God to me? And how shall I have a warrant that I am not under wrath? I know well, if I had the true sense of that love, it would make my heart warm and melt with love to him again; I know well, if this threatenings and curses ran to my heart, it would break with sorrow for the sins that I have committed against him, and for fear of the curse which I have justly deserved: How can I be persuaded then, that I am the child of God, seeing I have such hardness of heart, and seeing I lie over in such security? Indeed it is hard to persuade thee of the love of God, so long as thou art in this case; and yet this is the estate of the most part of the children of God; they fall asleep they lie over in security, and they oftest complain of the induration of their heart, and of the absence of God's Spirit. Now, to let you see that they have been so, that thou who complainest of the hardness of thy heart, and mournest for the absence of the Spirit, may take comfort to thyself, because it is not thy case alone, but it hath been the lot of the children of God before thee; ye see the wise virgins fell asleep and could not be wakened till *the cry rose, the Bridegroom is coming:* Yet when they were awakened, there was oil in their lamps, which they had provided afore-hand, and they lighted their lamps, and followed in with the Bridegroom to his chamber.

David fell sound asleep in security under the guiltiness of whoredom and blood, and never wakened till the prophet Nathan came to him and wakened him; but when he was wakened, he felt both the sense of God's wrath lying on his conscience for his sins, and it was so heavy to him, that unless the prophet Nathan had ministered comfort to him immediately, he had not been able to bear it; and he felt likewise the sense of God's mercy offering remission to him of his sins;

in the blood of a Saviour that he believed was to come forth out of his loins. Peter fell sound asleep, that for all the warnings he got, first by the Lord himself, saying, "this night ere the cock crow thou shalt deny me thrice ;" next, by them that opened the door ; thirdly, by a maid ; and last of all, by them all that stood about the fire with him : Yet, notwithstanding of all these warnings, nothing could waken him, till the Lord himself turned him about, and looked on him; but being wakened he *went out and wept bitterly*. And farther, the very bride that gets so fair a commendation in the fourth of the Canticles, yet she falls asleep, *but her heart waked ;* and suppose the Lord himself stood knocking at the door, and crying without, " open to me, my love, my dove, my fair and undefiled one ;" yet she would not rise out of her bed of security, until the time he was gone his way ; then she missed him ; and, missing him, she rises and goes and seeks him, and never rests till she finds him : So ye see there is a sleep that may befal the very children of God ; and as long as they are sleeping in security, they can neither be moved with wrath nor mercy. But thou mayest ask, how shalt thou, that art the child of God, discern thy security from the security of the reprobate ? I will tell thee, thou shalt know it by this, seest thou, and feelest thou thy senselessness and incredulity ? Missest thou the Holy Ghost away ? Lamentest thou for the absence of God out of thy heart ? Mournest thou for thy sin, that hath brought on this security upon thee ? Wrestlest thou against this hardness of thine heart ? Longest thou for the Lord's returning to thy soul ? And labourest thou to get thy heart cloven and drawn asunder, that the love of God may yet be shed abroad in thy heart by the Spirit ? And usest thou the means diligently ? If this be thy case under thy induration and security, it is an undoubted token that thou art the child of God ; for where there is a minting and endeavouring to do well, God accepts of the will, and in his own time he will give thee the strength and grace to perform it : So falling into security may very well stand with grace. Shalt thou then cast away thy hope in the time of thy security? No, God forbid! for in the time of thy security, thou canst not discern thyself, for thou knowest not what thou art; thou must not look then into thy own heart, and think to get thy happiness placed there; no, no, but thou must look into the purpose of God in that unchangeable decree wherein he decreed to love thee eternally: So that however so great thy security be, yet the door of his mercy stands open to thee, and therefore all thy sins that thou hast done, were they never so many, or never so great, they cannot all shut the door of God's mercy, so long as he will hold it open; nor they cannot all hinder him to love thee, and to shew mercy unto thee, seeing he hath decreed to shew mercy.

Now, as for the third sort of men and women in the world, they are such as feel no wrath, and yet are under wrath; and the most part of reprobates are in this case, as David said, " the wicked have no bands in their death;" they hate to be reformed; "because they feel no changes, therefore they have no fear;" they say in their hearts, that God can neither do good nor evil; "they make a covenant with death and with the grave;" therefore they think they are sure enough. Now, of all the cases under heaven, thy case is the woefullest, that hast thy heart fatted and frozen with the blessings of God, " and yet despisest the bountifulness of his rich mercy, patience, and long-suffering; not knowing that the bountifulness and long-suffering of God should lead thee to repentance: But thou, after thy hardness of heart, that cannot repent, heapest unto thyself wrath upon wrath against the day of wrath, and of the declaration of the judgment of God:" And thou that hast no care in the world, but of thy back and belly, as the rich glutton that fed delicately every day, and was clad with purple and fine linen; and with the rich man, that did cast down his old barns that were old, and builded up new ones in their stead, and said to his soul, " now soul, take thee rest, for thou

SERMON XXI.

hast laid up store to thyself for many years:" But take heed what the Lord said to him, " fool, this night shall they come and take thy soul from thee:" So what art thou but a fool that carest only for the things of this life, and lookest not to eternity, and to the life to come? So look that ye be not in this case, and that ye go not sleeping to hell, and never think that there is a hell till you fall in the midst of it.

As for the last sort, that both feel wrath, and are under wrath, these are reprobates: But I leave you till the next time; and I recommend that which hath been spoken to the grace of God in Christ Jesus. *Amen.*

To whom with the Father, Son, and Holy Ghost, &c.

SERMON XXII.

UPON DIVERS POINTS OF RELIGION.

Psalm lxxvii. 1, 2, 3.

O Lord God of my salvation, I have cried day and night before thee; let my prayer come before thee, incline thine ear unto my cry. For my soul is full of troubles, and my life draws near to the grave.

HERE is a complaint of a man according to the heart of God; of a man endued with the gifts of the Holy Ghost; here is the complaint of a distressed soul cast down with heaviness and anguish of heart: here he confesses that the Lord heard him when he cried; suppose he knew not that in the mean time. After his confession, he falls out in a description of his trouble, where he says, "My sore ran in the night, and ceased not;" as if he would say I got no rest by day nor night; "my soul refused comfort," that is, comfort was offered to me, and I would not have it; I was so sore handled, that when they were cast to me, I would not drink of the rivers of consolation; then he says, "I did think on God and was troubled;" as if he would say, he that should have been the greatest matter of consolation to me, he was the greatest matter of my grief, when I did think upon him. Then he says, "I prayed, and my spirit was full of anguish;" that is, there was not a corner in my soul, but it was replenished with dolour and grief; then he puts to the word Selah, whereby he would have all men to consider the greatness of his grief. Then he tells you piece and piece, how he rises out of trouble, and by degrees how he comes to consolation.

First, He "considered the days of old and the years of ancient time;" and he advises with himself, and says, what is this I am doing? I know well there was a time when I had consolation, suppose I have none now.

Again, he says, "I called to remembrance my song in the night;" I remember there was a time when I would rise about midnight to praise thee; then he says, "I communed with my own heart, and my spirit searched diligently;" as if he would say, he would not let it go so; but I ripped up the whole truth of the matter; then upon this he begins to reason this way with himself, saying, "Will the Lord absent himself forever?" He was once present, I know well I had him once, but now he is away; yet will he abide away forever? "Is his mercy clean gone? doth his promise fail for evermore?" this was a sore perplexity he was in; then he concludes, *this is my death*, that is, I am but a dead man: and yet it was not so. Now, upon this he gathers comfort, and he tells you, he gathers comfort in his heart; and he says, "I remember the years of the right hand of the Most High, I remember the works of the Lord, certainly I remember thy wonders, O Lord, of old, I did also meditate on all thy works:" then he tells, that upon remembrance and meditation on these things, he found comfort. This shortly is the mind of the prophet in this psalm.

Let the Lord lead me, and let the Spirit of the Lord open every one of your hearts, that the blessing he will vouchsafe to his own words may be poured on every one of your souls, that ye may find consolation this day; and I look for so much mercy from God, that if this gospel shall be hid from any of you, that it shall be hid from none but such as perish.

Now, I come to the purpose we have had in hand these days bygone, which was this, to let you know out of the word of God, which of you may justly lay claim to the love of God in Christ; the certainty whereof may provoke you to love him and his saints. Again, what are the temptations that the devil casts in to bereave you of the certainty of this love: ye have heard them, and I will not repeat them. The last thing, was the four sorts of men and women in the world, that I spoke of.

The first sort are they that feel an intolerable pain and anguish of spirit, but yet they are in the favor, love, and covenant of God. And, if ye would know if ye be of this sort, this shall be thy exercise, that suppose thy anguish and pain be intolerable, and suppose thou bringest in strange reasons, as the prophet doth here, saying, *this is my death;* yet thou art not as thou thinkest thyself to be; for in this case if thou hast a lamentation for sin; if thou hast a thirst to be reconciled to God; and if thou longest for the day of thy salvation; and if thou hast a hope above hope; and if thou hast a rest upon the promises; suppose thou hast no feeling of God's mercy, yet thou art in the covenant of grace.

The second sort, are these that feel no wrath, nor yet are under wrath; and these are the children of God, and in the covenant of grace also; and of these there are also four sorts.

First, There are some whose calling is sweet, when the sweet hand of God hath opened their hearts in an instant, as he did the heart of Lydia, who was converted at one preaching.

Secondly, There are some in whom the love of God hath been shed abroad in their hearts by the Holy Ghost, and these are easily persuaded of the love of God towards them; therefore they feel no wrath, neither are under wrath.

Thirdly, There are some that have wrestled through the perplexity of their souls, and have waded the depths of the terror of God's wrath, and have come through safely, and have overcome them; therefore instead of dolour, they have gotten joy; instead of terror, they have gotten peace; instead of doubting, they have gotten persuasion, that "nothing shall separate them from the love of God in Christ;" and therefore they feel no wrath, neither yet are under wrath; but without difficulty they are easily persuaded of the love of God towards them.

But as for the *last* sort, that neither feel the terrors of wrath, nor the sweetness of mercy, it is hardest to persuade them of the love of God; and yet, indeed the saints of God will be oft-times in this case; for they will fall sound asleep, and lie over in security for a while; as David, Peter, and the spouse herself, and the wise virgins, they fell sound asleep: but when thou art in this case, how shalt thou know that thou art not under wrath, but in the compass of love, and in the covenant of grace? Thou shalt know it by this, the security of thee that art the child of God, it is a seen and felt security; thy hardness is a seen and felt hardness of heart; thy death is a seen and felt death; so thou seest it, thou feelest it, thou mournest for it as thou canst, and thou wrestlest with it as thou canst: but the security of the reprobate is unseen and unfelt; he is blind, and sees it not; he is dead, and feels it not; he is in the arms of the devil, but wrestles not to get out of them, for he counts it no bondage; he is in great misery, but he laments it not; and take away the fear of hell, and a felt terror of conscience from him, he desires no other heaven; and as long as he has no pain in his security, he desires not to be wakened out of it: therefore, if thou hast no more but this, that thou feelest thy incredulity, thy blindness, thy security, thy hardness of heart, thy deadness, and thy bondage; and as long as thou art compelled to do the things thou wouldst not do, because they are evil, and thou art compelled to leave undone the things thou wouldst do; this is a sure enough token that thou art in the covenant of grace, and within the compass of the love of God. This for the first two sorts of men and women in the world, and these belong to eternal life.

Now, the other two, that is, the third and fourth sort, they belong not to grace, neither yet are they under the convenant thereof: And for the third sort that feel no torment nor wrath, and yet are under wrath, they are the most part of the reprobates: and indeed, this sort goes beyond all the rest in number; for there are numbers in the world that never felt a torment or perplexity in their spirits; because they never felt a law, accusing, convicting, and condemning them for sin, yet they are under torment and wrath, and they are going the straight way to hell. Now, there are two sorts of these:

First, There are some without the church, that were never partakers of the visible covenant; as Jews and Turks, Heathens and Papists, these were never called, nor their consciences never wakened.

Secondly, There are some within the church, and are partakers of the visible covenant, in hearing the word, and receiving the sacraments; and these are of three sorts:

First, There are some that profess the truth, but they want knowledge; therefore they never have a felt joy, nor a felt pain in their consciences, because their conscience depends on their knowledge; for as thy knowledge is, so will thy conscience be.

A *second* sort of these that have knowledge, but only of the letter, for they want the spirit; and of these the prophet speaks, saying, "Ye shall hear indeed, but shall not understand; ye shall see, but shall not perceive: make the heart of this people fat, make their eyes heavy, and their ears dull; lest they see with their eyes, hear with their ears, and understand with their hearts, and lest they be converted, and I heal them," Isa. vi. 9, 10. These folk have a certain sight and knowledge given them, but because they abuse them, therefore they perish in the just judgment of God.

A *third* sort, are those whose consciences are seared as with a hot iron, and the spirit of slumber is poured upon them, and they have hearts past feeling; therefore they are given over to commit sin with greediness, and they delight to drink in iniquity, as the beast doth water. All these three are not feared for judgment, because they feel no wrath, therefore they are careless, and look not for it.

Now I come to the *fourth* sort, which are such of the reprobates, whose consciences are wakened, and feel wrath kindled in their bowels, and their consciences stound with the very stings of reprobation, that come from the severe justice and immutable decree of God; and they have not the Spirit of Christ to comfort them, nor to stir them up to get to a Saviour or to his blood, therefore they go the wrong way to work; for either they smother the torment and fire in their consciences, by unlawful means and uncomfortable helps; or else they plunge themselves in the bottomless depths of desperation, and so continue unto the end of their life; or else they post from the temporal torment unto the everlasting and eternal pains of hell. All those are under wrath; and all those stings are but beginnings of the endless stings they shall endure in hell for evermore; and this begun flame in their conscience, is but a spark come from the unquenchable fire, wherein both conscience and carcase shall burn eternally. Now, I grant that sometimes God wakens the conscience of the reprobate, sometimes sooner, and sometimes later; as Cain, his conscience was soon wakened; for immediately after the slaughter of his brother Abel, the Lord comes to him, and tells him, that the blood of his brother cried unto him from the earth," and therefore he cursed him, and the earth for his sake: then his conscience was wakened, and he cried out, " my sins are heavier than I can bear; there is never a body shall meet me but, they shall slay me:" and he abode under this sense and terror all the days of his life; so he was soon wakened, and he abode long under it: but Judas was later in wakening, that for all the warnings he got of the Lord, saying, " the Son of man must be betrayed; but wo be to that man by whom he shall be betrayed;" yet he never wakens, till news come to him, that Christ Jesus, whom he had betrayed, was condemned to die. Then he wakens, then he feels the flames of hell begun in his conscience for betraying of innocent blood. It is true also, some bear this torment longer, even in this life, as Saul and Cain; and other some bear it shorter while, as Ahitophel and Judas. But I leave this and come to another point :

First, To tell you of the estate of the reprobate under this torment.

Secondly, The degrees how he comes to it.

Thirdly, The difference betwixt his exercise and the exercise of the elect under their torments.

Fourthly, How far the elect and the reprobate may come to agree together in their torment.

Fifthly and *lastly*, To tell you how the Lord raises the one, and lets the other fall : how he turns the elect and lets the reprobate go forward to their own place.

As for the first, concerning the state of the reprobate under torment; he hath light and he hath feeling, he hath persuasion ; he hath light that lets him see his sins in the law accusing, convicting, and condemning him before the tribunal of God ; he hath light letting him see God a consuming fire standing above his head, and letting him see an eternity of torment, both ceaseless and remediless, prepared for him, which he cannot eschew ; he hath feeling, for he feels a wrath that is unsupportable, he feels a devouring flame and burning low seizing upon his conscience, and he feels the very stounds of reprobation cleaving his soul asunder ; and this he feels without longing for mercy, without a thirst for peace, and without a desire to run to a Saviour ; for he sees the door of mercy shut on him for evermore ; and hath a persuasion, for he is persuaded God never loved him, nor choosed him ; he is persuaded that Christ never redeemed him ; he is persuaded that the Spirit never sanctified him ; he is persuaded that he is utterly cast off ; and he is persuaded that all the creatures in the earth are armed with wrath and vengeance against him, and are ready to execute the decreed judgment of God upon him : this is for his estate. Now for the degrees how he comes to this torment.

The first is profaneness. "Look, (says the apostle, Heb. xii. 19:) "that there be not a profane person among you, as Esau was, that for a mess of pottage, for a wombful of meat, sold his birth-right," because he counted nothing of it ; so profaneness, or the light estimation of the graces of God, is the first step to reprobation.

Now, as Esau left one step behind him, so Ishmael left another. ... .at ... He mocked his brother Isaac: so that is the ... nd step to reprobation, the mocking or scorning of religion, or of the promises of God made to the saints. Cain, he brought another step, he murdered his brother Abel, and after he had done it, he denied it.

So this denied iniquity is the third step to reprobation: Saul he leaves another step behind him: What was that? he left undone the things he should have done, and he did the thing God never bade him do, under pretext of religion.

So this hypocrisy, or counterfeit dealing with God, is the fourth step. Judas, he left another step behind him: What was that? The heart of him was never renewed; for he had always the devil in it, and covetousness reigned within him: He thought to himself, I will take the silver offered to me; he can deliver himself I know he loves his life as I do mine; I know I will get his favour again, so I shall keep the silver, and nobody shall know of it. So ye see the reprobate piece and piece comes on, and goes forward by degrees while they come to the highest and last degree. Now, as ye would escape the middle degrees; therefore look " that there be not in any of you an evil heart of unbelief, to depart away from the living God." Eschew the way of Cain, and be not malicious as he was; eschew the way Esau, and be not profane as he was; eschew the way of Ishmael, and be not scornful as he was; eschew the way of Saul, and be not a hypocrite as he was; and eschew the way of Judas, and foster not a devil in thy heart as he did; eschew the way of all these men, as ye would eschew the torments of conscience here, and as ye would be kept out of the endless torment of hell hereafter. This much for the degrees whereby the reprobate come to their torment.

Now, I come to the difference between the exercise of the reprobate under their torment, and the exercise of the elect under their terrors ; ye cannot tell how soon your conscience will be awakened, and that torment may arise to you ; for an unrepented cogitation may kindle that flame, and may stir up the very furies of hell in your souls ; and whether ye be now stopping the light of your conscience or not, I know not, therefore I leave you to the Lord ; always it stands you all in need to know, what should be your exercise when your conscience is awakened, and is touched with this torment ; how then shall ye know either what to say to yourselves, or yet to another, when ye are awakened ? I will tell you what should be your exercise that are the children of God, and what is the exercise of the reprobate in this case, that ye may know the difference betwixt the two exercises.

The *first* difference is this, As for the reprobate under torment, it is only the avenging hand of God tormenting him for his sin, that pains him ; so take away the torment, and he shall be well enough. But, as to the child of God, it is not so much the torment that pains him, as his sin, which is the thing that brought the torment, and provoked God to anger against him ; therefore he hates his sin, he laments for his sin, and he repents him of his sin, and he would gladly be reconciled to God. So if thou hast these things then thou art well, suppose thou hast terrors and fears in thy conscience ; for the reprobate had never a true hatred of his sin, that he would gladly have been avenged upon it, because it displeased God ; he had never a true repentance unto life ; he had never a saving faith laying hold upon the promises of God, applying them to himself ; nor a hunger and thirst for the blood of Jesus, to make the reconciliation betwixt God and his soul : these things the reprobate never had ; therefore if ye have them in any true measure, it is an undoubted token to you that ye are the children of God.

The *second* difference is this. The pain of the reprobate is intolerable, and therefore he hath no patience to bear it, he hath no true desire to get out of it, nor hath he hope that he shall be delivered out of it ; he either labours to smother it, or he hastens to that endless torment, thinking that change of torments shall bring ease to him ; but it is not as he thinks : for now is but the flame, but hereafter is the fire ; now is but one drop, but hereafter shall be the ocean-sea of the wrath of God thrown upon his soul and body, conscience and carcase. Now, by the contrary, the elect's torment is tolerable, for he is upholden by the secret hand of the Almighty God ; therefore he hath patience to bear it, he hath a desire to be reconciled to God, and so to be freed from it ; and he hath a hope to be delivered ; therefore he groans as he can, and he prays as he is able ; he runs to the Lord as he can ; he claims the promises as he is able ; and so he hopes above hope ; therefore says, as Job xiii. 15. " Suppose thou should slay me, Lord, yet 1 will trust in thee." Then he languishes and faints under his burden, therefore he says, " Will the Lord absent himself for ever ?" hath the Lord forgotten to be merciful ?" And if he be called, and hath had experience of the Lord's mercies before, then "he would gladly remember the days of old, and call to remembrance his song in the night."

Thirdly, The reprobates, in their torment, they do either as Judas did, that hasted from the temporal torment unto the eternal ; or else they do as Saul did, that called for instruments of music to comfort him, and put away the present torment ; so they seek vain comforts and comforters, as pastime and company, or eating and drinking ; but all this will do them no good ; or else they do as Cain, that desired God to spare his life for a while, and let come after what will come ; so they desired not to be posted to that endless torment, but rather to take their pleasures here a while, and hereafter let come what will come ; or else they do as Esau, that regarded not the blessing which Jacob got, for he sought not a portion of it, but he desired another blessing ; so they seek the blessing of this life, and they will take their hazard of the life to come ; so give them wealth of riches, of honour, of pleasure, of ease, here in this life, they regard no more. But the child of God, his disposition is far otherwise; for nothing can content him but a fill of the flesh and blood of Christ; for he knows nothing can satisfy his hungry and thirsty soul but that only; nor nothing can quench the wrath of God lying on his conscience, but only the blood of Christ; therefore he will have no rest nor ease, nor comfort, nor consolation, but that which his blood brings to him; therefore all things in heaven and earth cannot content or satisfy him till he get a fill of this flesh and blood of Jesus in eating and drinking him by faith.

Now the *fourth* thing I proposed to you to speak of, was this, To let you see how far the reprobate comes together with the elect. I mark four degrees especially, that both the elect and reprobate steps on together.

First, The elect have seen the top of their sins gone up to heaven, and run in before the tribunal of God, and sees them standing there accusing, convicting, and condemning them; they see also a wall standing between God and their souls, that they can see no access to mercy, and when they pray, they see their prayers shut out, and God will not let them come in before him; this the elect will see as well as the reprobate.

Secondly, They have been destitute of all consolation under heaven, that they have had no sense of love, nor certainty of election, and almost they have been past all hope ever to come to heaven; therefore they have said, Is the Lord gone away for ever? hath the Lord forgotten his tender mercies and compassions?" Therefore they have cried out, " The waves of the Lord's indignation are gone over my head, so that I am overwhelmed with them," Psal. lxxxviii. 16.

Thirdly, The Lord will appear to be a very great enemy to them, and to bend his bow, and shoot his arrows at them; therefore they have cried, " The arrows of the indignation of the Almighty are run through me." And the Lord will seem to take a mell and break all the bones of their body, that they have neither moisture nor rest by day or night for them; "therefore they have howled like owls in the desert, they have cried like a pelican in the wilderness," and they have roared like a lion in the forest, "they have chattered like a crane, or as a sparrow on the house-top," they have mourned like a dove wanting her mate.

Fourthly and *lastly*, The child of God will be brought to this point, that he will curse the day wherein he was born; they will curse all that ever helped them in their young age; and they will be brought to this extremity, that they will long for the day when God shall put an end to their life; now the elect and the reprobate will both come on this far together.

Now remains the *last* thing to be spoken to, To tell you, where they sunder and disagree, and what makes the sundering; there is the difference, thou that art the child of God, in the mean time, when thou art under thy torment, there is a secret work within thee which thou seest not, till thou beest brought out of thy temptations: what is that? There is a persuading and exulting light that lurks in thy conscience, which, when it breaks out, shall bring an unspeakable joy with it, and a peace that passes all understanding, the which will take away all thy terrors and doubtings and shall bring joyful news to thee that wast mourning, and the spirit of gladness to thee that wast troubled with the spirit of heaviness; so the Lord sustains thee, that thou fallest not into the bottomless pit of that endless torment; and, suppose thou perceivest it not, yet there is a desire of mercy in thy heart; and suppose thy terrors be predominant, that thou canst not see the blood speaking for thee, yet thou wouldst gladly look through the wrath to mercy. But, as for the reprobate, God leaves him, he falls in it, and the more he plunges in these depths, he is the more overcome with them; so he never gets out again. Now, seeing ye are all in some of these four sorts of men and women which I have spoken of, I am persuaded that there are most of the third sort, who have never felt wrath, and yet are under wrath. I cannot tell you how soon ye may be freed from it, (and I beseech God to hold you waking) for I assure you the Lord is coming, and ye cannot tell how soon the door of mercy shall be closed; therefore look to yourselves, that ye may get in in time, that when the door shall be shut, ye shall be found to be therein; for this I protest to you, there is an unquenchable fire, and everlasting torment prepared for all them to lie over sleeping in their security, and will not be awakened nor repent in time: therefore since now this is the time, I beseech you take your time, for if ye let this time slip, and if ye die in your impenitency, ye shall never get the like of it again, nor ye shall never see life, nor get mercy once offered unto you, do with it as ye will, I say no more.

SERMON XXIII.

UPON DIVERS POINTS OF RELIGION.

Psalm xlii. 1, 2, 3.

As the hart panteth after the water brooks, so panteth my soul after thee, O God. My soul thirsteth for God, for the living God: when shall I come and appear before God? My tears have been my meat day and night, while they continually say unto me, Where is thy God?

THERE is here the very anatomy or picture of a distressed soul, wrestling with anguish and great perplexity and grief of mind; and it is written for the consolation of all such, whose souls are exercised with the like temptations of anguish or grief for the want of God's presence.

This doctrine cannot be pleasant and profitable to any, but to those that have a distressed and a cast down soul; the soul that is filled with consolation hath no need of it, and the soul that is lying in security, and not wakened, cannot apply it, therefore as yet it hath no need of it; but the soul that is wakened, and sees that God is absent, and therefore pants for the living God, and the soul that is disquieted, and can get no rest, and these that have the waves of God's wrath going over them, and have one deep calling upon another deep, and standing between wind and wave, they, I say, being plunged in the depth of God's wrath, would gladly look into the depths of God's mercy; such, I say, as are this way cast down, will bear with the doctrine, and they will be glad of it; such of you as have your souls filled with consolation will bear with it also; and such of you as are in security, and would be glad to be wakened, ye will bear with it too; for they that are securest now, it may be there come times that the remembrance of those things may bring consolation to them. But to come to the purpose.

The thing that I left at was this, how far the child of God may come on with the reprobate; how far he may be cast down, and what are the degrees of his casting down. Now, I know well, that the consideration of this will bring some comfort to the soul that is cast down, that when they hear the saints of God before them have been brought to this, that they will see their sin accusing them, convicting and condemning them before the tribunal of God's justice, and they see when they pray, their prayer was shut out, they have been deprived of all consolation, deprived of the sense of love, deprived of the certainty of election, deprived of the gift of faith and repentance, and, to their own judgment, deprived of all grace and mercy; and, last of all, they have almost cast away their hope, and cursed the day, the night, the time and the hour wherein they were born; and cursing all creatures that ever did them good, and shewed them any consolation. I remember Job said, Job vi. 2. " Oh! that my grief were well weighed; as if he would say, It is so heavy, that none can bear it; and, in another place, he says, "Am I iron or brass?" As if he would say, Ye wonder at my perturbation; but if iron or brass were in my stead, and if they were cast in the flame that is in my soul, I am sure that flame would melt them. Was not this a strange torment he was under? And think ye this a little thing, that made the Son of God himself fear, that he was glad to ask comfort of his disciples, who could not comfort him, and was glad to make his moan and pour out the complaint of his soul to them, saying, " My soul is sorrowful and heavy, even unto death;" and desired them to watch and pray with him, and he prayed, that " the cup might be taken from him," Matth. xxvi. 28. What made him do this, think ye, but the very torment and pangs of the fire of hell, which he endured in his soul for our sins, that he had lying on his back. Now there are none of you can tell how soon ye have to do with this, nor yet how soon God will awaken your consciences for your sins, and your soul then would be glad of the meanest drop of consolation that ever was given to any of the people of God. For your exercise then, if ye would desire a word of consolation in this time of need, ye must understand that God hath a double work in the souls of such of his own as are cast down; the one work is secret, and so secret that it only bears them up that they cast not away their hope; but they stand waiting with patience till God bring consolation; and this work is so secret that thou canst not look within thine own heart, to see if there be any grace there to comfort thee; yet there will be a displeasure for sin that hath brought on so great a judgment upon thee, there will be a hatred and detestation of it; there will be a hunger and a thirst after righteousness; there will be a longing for the Lord's deliverance; there will be a patient waiting on, and hope above hope: thou wilt have all these things in thy heart, suppose thou knowest not of them.

But thou wilt say, I can have no comfort here: but take heed to this, when thou art in this case, thou must not judge thyself by thy own sense or feeling, thou must not rest on it; but the more thou art hindered to believe, labour the more to grip to the promises, and see this necessity lying upon thee, I must believe under the pain of endless condemnation; I must hope above hope, or else I will never get that blessed seed Christ Jesus: and if this necessity will not move thee to believe, then beware to add this blasphemy to all the rest of thy sins, as to make Christ a liar; for he hath said, "Blessed are they that hunger and thirst for righteousness sake;" thou hungerest and thirsteth, therefore thou must be blessed; so the more thy sense fails thee, believe thou the more, for this brings greater glory to God.

Last of all, Rest upon the promises of God, saying, "Come unto me all ye that are wearied and ladened, and I will ease you; he that believes shall never be condemned;" believe and thou shalt see wonders.

But if thou wilt say, the promises belong not to me: beware of that, exclude not thyself, for God hath not excluded thee; so beest thou Jew or Gentile, or of whatsoever nation thou beest, thou art not excluded; were thy sins never so great, and thy soul as red as scarlet, yet thou art bidden come to that Lord, and he shall make it as white as snow; wert thou never so blind, so deaf, so crooked or lame, yea, never so leprous, yet thou art bidden come to the marriage of the King's Son: So this is not the bidding of God, to cast away the promises of God; but this is the command of God to grip to the promises, and to claim a right and a title to Christ.

Another work hath the Lord with his own, when he hath come and given thee consolation, then goes away again; when he is gone away then thou beginnest to call in question all the former work of God, and thou beginnest to doubt, whether it was the Lord that came or not. But to know that it was the Lord (take heed to what I am to speak) when the Lord comes, he brings light with him, and this light shines in thy soul so clearly, that thou seest both heaven and hell; and this light never leaves thee till it persuade thee that the Father hath loved thee in the Son, the Son hath redeemed thee with his blood, and thou art freely forgiven all thy sins; then this persuasion brings unspeakable joy with it, and peace to thy conscience that passes all understanding.

Now, it is the Spirit that works these things, suppose thou canst not tell how. Therefore to try if this be the true work of the Holy Ghost in thee, thou shalt mark these three things.

First, Mark what was thy estate before that this light came to thee; look if there was a felt blindness, a felt hardness of heart, and a felt absence of the Spirit; then this light lets thee see thy blindness, thy hardness of heart through security, and lets thee see the absence of the Spirit, that thou canst discern when he is present, and when he is absent; thou feelest this, and thou wonderest at the change when it comes.

Secondly, Mark the power of this light; if it renew thy heart, and if thou findest a new change or alteration in thy mind, and if it lets thee see these things, that when it comes it lets thee see the love of the Father clearly, thou seest the blood of Christ speaking for thee clearly, thou seest thy remission clearly, and thou seest thy name put up in the book of life clearly.

Thirdly and *last of all*, Mark the stamps or the prints that this light leaves behind it in thee; look if this light doth let thee see the love of God to thee; if it ravishes thee with love to him again; that all thy delight is in his presence; and if thou mayest say, the Lord, whom that light doth represent unto me, is dearer unto me than any thing else in heaven or in earth; this presence of my God is sweeter to my soul than all the pleasures under heaven; I desire no other joy than the fruition of his presence, and that joy that comes from this light. Again, look if this light lets thee see thy sins forgiven thee in the blood of Christ? if it brings a hatred and detestation of all sort of sin, and when thou mayest say, well is my soul, when I know my God is honoured; but wo is my soul, when I know he is dishonoured: And look if this light lets thee see thy infirmities, and makes thee to long for the day of thy dissolution, and for the day of the Lord's appearing in the clouds, that thou mayest see the day of thy salvation accomplished; if this light hath left these stamps behind it, then it comes from the Lord, and it shall never leave thee altogether; for the gifts and calling of God are without repentance:" Therefore if thou hast gotten this true light of the Spirit, and if it were but once in thy lifetime, thou mayest be glad; for in all thy temptations God shall be with thee, and his infinite mercy will not let thee be overcome with wrath.

I say no more now; but try your light by these marks which I have told you. And I commend that which hath been spoken to the grace of God in Christ Jesus: To whom with the Father and the holy Spirit, be everlasting praise, honour, and glory, for now and ever. *Amen.*

SERMON XXIV.

UPON DIVERS POINTS OF RELIGION.

Isaiah xlii. 1.

Behold, my servant, whom I uphold, mine elect, in whom my soul delighteth.

Matth. xi. 4.

Jesus answered and said unto them, Go and shew John again those things which ye do hear and see: The blind receive their sight, and the lame walk, &c.

THE Father here speaking of the Son, that he was to send into the world, he pointed him out after this manner: He calls him his servant, because he came to serve him; as he testifies himself, saying, "the Son of man came not to be served, but to serve:" Then he calls him his elect servant, because he had chosen him to be the head over all his own church, and the Saviour of his own body: then he says, he will rest on him: for he says in Matth. iii. 17. "This is my beloved Son, in whom I am well pleased:" Then he tells them, they shall know him by these and these marks, "he shall bring forth judgment to the Gentiles; he shall not cry, nor lift up, nor cause his voice to be heard in the streets:" And among the rest, he says, "a bruised shall he not break, and the smoaking flax shall he not quench." This is the point I would be at, and that, by the grace of God, am minded to touch somewhat at this time. Now in the xi. chapter of Matthew, 2, 3 verses, John the Baptist, in prison, sends two of his disciples to Christ, for to be informed by him in the mystery of their salvation; Christ begins at this, and tells the work he had with every man that came to him, verse 5, saying, "the blind receive their sight, the halt go, the lepers are cleansed, the deaf hear, the dead are raised, and the poor receive the gospel; and blessed is he that shall not be offended in me." Now, what comfort these two places of scripture will offer to you, ye shall hear afterward. The thing that ye heard last, was, how deeply oftentimes the children of God will be plunged in temptations, and what fearful unease will be in their souls, and how the Lord will make them to possess the very sins of their youth; and how he will write bitter things against them. I told you again, how wonderfully they are holden up, that, albeit with the one hand he casts them down, yet with the other he holds them up; therefore, these are the signs whereby the child of God, in his temptations, may be discerned from the reprobate; in this torment the children of God have a secret dolour for sin, a secret desire to be at one with God, a secret desire to be avenged of their corruption, a secret hope that they will not give over, that if they cannot pray, yet they will sigh and sob; and if they be not able to speak, yet they will look up; and when the Lord hath tried them, and melted their hearts in the furnace of temptation, then contented would they be to get one to tell them glad news: Then, at last, the Lord sends them light instead of darkness, peace instead of fear, and joy instead of terror; then this light persuades them of the love of God in Christ to them; that light points out the man Christ Jesus on whom the soul of the Father rests, for in him he is well pleased; so that his anger is pacified: this light makes thee to look to him, and he is ravished with one of thy eye-looks, for ne cannot abide it. Therefore, to try this light, whether it comes from God or not, the which, when we have tried, and when, had ye got it, ye might have had great consolation through it in the time of your trouble; always, if ye have never tried it, be wise in the Lord, and try it yet, that ye may say, Surely the Lord hath been here, and I was not aware of it. There are three things to try it by:

First, Look to the estate thou wast in before it came.
Secondly, Look to thy disposition when it came.
Thirdly, Look to the stamps which it leaves behind it.
 As for thy estate before it came, look if thou wast blind, and thou seest thou wast blind; look if thou wast lost and gone in thy own sight, and thou seest that; look if thou wast deaf, and dumb, and lame, and crooked, and a leper, and thou seest it was so; and hast thou a light now that thou hadst not before? Findest thou a change in thy soul, that thou hadst not before? Then the Father tells thee here, that it is the Spirit of Christ sent to thee which hath wrought this change; as John sent two disciples to ask him, "Art thou he that should come, or shall we look for another Saviour?" Christ answers, "Go tell John, The blind receive their sight, and they that halt receive their feet; the dead are raised, and the lepers are cleansed, and the poor receive the gospel." So wouldst thou know if thy Saviour be come to thy soul? And wouldst thou know if thou hast gotten earnest of thy salvation, that shall never be taken from thee again? Thou shalt know by this, thou wast blind, but now thou seest; thou wast dead, but now thou art alive, for that blood did revive thee; thou wast a leper, but that blood did cleanse thee; thou wast poor and needy but now thou art made rich in Christ: Hast thou these things? then I assure thee thou hast the earnest of thy salvation, and the kingdom of heaven let down to thy soul; therefore it belongs to thee, and this earnest shall never be taken from thee, till thou beest put in possession of that eternal life, and heavenly inheritance whereof thou hast gotten the earnest.

 Secondly, The next thing to try thy light by, is to mark the disposition of thy present time, when it came to thee, look if this light lets thee see clearly the love of God to thyself by name, and if it lets thee see thy own name put up in the book of life; and therefore thou wilt now put the helmet of salvation upon thy head; therefore thou wilt now make thyself worthy of the calling of God, and as a man or woman bought with the blood of Jesus Christ, and made heir of eternal life; therefore thou wilt long for the day of thy dissolution, that thou mayest be with the Lord, and thou wilt look daily for him coming in the clouds; if this be thy disposition, then thy light is true.

The 3d thing to try this light by, is, the stamps that this light leaves behind it; and the stamps are these, that light that hath presented to thee a loving Father in a loving Son, by a loving Spirit; this will make thy soul glad to be acquainted with that blessed Trinity: this would make thee say, Surely I would love the sweet Father, he hath loved me, and chosen me before the world was made; surely I would love my dear Lord and Saviour Jesus Christ that hath redeemed me with his precious blood; surely I would love the blessed Spirit that hath comforted me, being in great anguish and grief; and as long as this lasts, it will make thee homelier with God than ever thou wast with thy wife that lieth in thy bosom, than ever thou wast with thy own child, and homelier than ever thou wast with thy dearest friend thou hadst in the world; and this light will leave this stamp, that the remembrance of it will bring consolation to thee afterward, and it will leave that stamp, that, at that time, at the least, thou hatedst sin wherever thou sawest it, or heardst tell of it, and thou wast wae when thou knewest God was dishonoured, and thou wast glad when thou sawest God was honoured, and got his own glory. Now, it is like, some will say, The man or woman will be glad forsooth that has felt these things in their soul, and if it were but once in their life-time; and I know well these are chosen to eternal life; and I know well they shall be crowned with endless glory: but what will ye do with them that have never felt these things? Is there no word of consolation to be given or spoken to the soul that never felt that persuading light, that renewing light, that comforting light, and that exulting light? Have ye nothing to say to them that never had this light? My soul never felt that exulting joy which comes through the light; what will become of me then? and what warrant can I have then of the love of God? Now, for the easing you of this point, here are two things I have to speak of to you:

The one is, to tell you of the greatest measure of light of that triumphant joy which the soul can get in this life, that there is not another beyond that light: the other thing is, to tell you the meanest measure that God gives to his own in this life, that if thou hast but the meanest, thou mayest be sure that thou shalt never perish.

As to the first thing, the greatest measure of light and joy that ye can get to, and no further in this life, it is this, when the love of God, by the holy Ghost, is shed out as a flood on thy soul, that the streams of that love carries with it all the desires and affections of thy heart; and when thy heart exults with exceeding joy, that all the corners thereof are filled from bank to brae, and is running over, that thou canst not keep it in; and when thou mayest cry out, death, I defy thee now; hell, I defy thee now; grave, I defy thee now; sin and Satan, I defy you all now: " for I am persuaded, that neither death, nor life, nor angels, nor principalities, nor powers, nor things present, nor things to come, nor height, nor depth, nor any other creature, shall be able to separate me from the love of God in Christ Jesus my Lord." Rom. viii. 38, 39. This is the highest degree of joy that any man or woman can get to in this life, and the saints will get it sometimes, but it will not tarry long; and they get it either in prayer, when they have such strong and unsatiable desires to be filled with that love that they cannot take a nay-say; and suppose thou seest him not with thy bodily eyes, yet thy soul is filled with exulting joy, through the beams of his loving countenance that shines in thy soul; sometimes they will get it by hearing the word, when the word and spirit concurs together in making thy persuasion sure: sometimes they will get it by meditation, when their hearts and hauntings are in heaven beholding the glory of the Lord which is with the blood of Jesus Christ, and made heir of eternal life ; therefore thou wilt long for the day of thy dissolution, that thou mayest be with the Lord, and thou wilt look daily for him coming in the clouds ; if this be thy disposition, then thy light is true.

The 3d thing to try this light by, is, the stamps that this light leaves behind it ; and the stamps are these, that light that hath presented to thee a loving Father in a loving Son, by a loving Spirit ; this will make thy soul glad to be acquainted with that blessed Trinity : this would make thee say, Surely I would love the sweet Father, he hath loved me, and chosen me before the world was made ; surely I would love my dear Lord and Saviour Jesus Christ that hath redeemed me with his precious blood ; surely I would love the blessed Spirit that hath comforted me, being in great anguish and grief; and as long as this lasts, it will make thee homelier with God than ever thou wast with thy wife that lieth in thy bosom; than ever thou wast with thy own child, and homelier than ever thou wast with thy dearest friend thou hadst in the world ; and this light will leave this stamp, that the remembrance of it will bring consolation to thee afterward, and it will leave that stamp, that, at that time, at the least, thou hatedst sin wherever thou sawest it, or heardst tell of it, and thou wast wae when thou knewest God was dishonoured, and thou wast glad when thou sawest God was honoured, and got his own glory. Now, it is like, some will say, The man or woman will be glad forsooth that has felt these things in their soul, and if it were but once in their life-time ; and I know well these are chosen to eternal life ; and I know well they shall be crowned with endless glory : but what will ye do with them that have never felt these things ? Is there no word of consolation to be given or spoken to the soul that never felt that persuading light, that renewing light, that comforting light, and that exulting light ? Have ye nothing to say to them that never had this light ? My soul never felt that exulting joy which comes through the light ; what will become of me

curity wherein they have lain long, as the bride did.
Now, if it arise off a long security, and if thou beest
in this case, that thou missest thy Lord, thou seest he
is gone away, then thou wouldst gladly rise and seek
him, and thou wilt never be content till thou gettest
him, nor thou wilt admit no comfort in his room, till
the true comforter of thy soul come again; and if thou
thinkest his absence the death of thy soul ; this is
enough to bear thee up, for he will come again, and
thou shalt find him at the last, suppose it will cost thee
much pains and labour ere thou gettest him. But thou
wilt say, what shall the man or woman do that lieth in
security, and cannot rise up to seek the Lord, nor cannot pray, nor use the means gladly to find him ? I answer, take you this comfort to uphold you here, Isa.
xlii. 3. " A bruised reed he will not break, nor a
smoking flax he will not quench :" so, if thou hast
but a will to be at him, I assure thee he shall come
to thee, suppose thou canst not come to him ; if thou
hadst never so mean a light left in thy soul, if it were
but of the security controuling thy conscience, I assure thee, he will not put out that light ; for I assure
thee, the Spirit of Jesus may be in a secure, yea in an
obdured heart. Isaiah, lxiii. 17. said, " Why hast
thou hardened our hearts, and made us to err from thy
ways ?" And I am sure the prophet had the Spirit of
God when he said this ; yea, if thou hast a felt and
seen blindness, always thou hast this comfort, here is
a Saviour to give light to the blind ; here is a Saviour
to give ears to the deaf, to give hands to the lame, feet
to the crooked, and a tongue to the dumb ; here is a
Saviour to cleanse the leper's heart were it never so defiled with leprosy ; and thou hast this comfort that is
said of Lazarus, " Lord, the man that thou lovest is
sick ;" yea the man that the Lord loves may be dead
for a time, and may lie a long space sick, and in the
grave of his corruption ; yet this is thy comfort, if
ever thou wast loved, and if ever thou hadst life in
Christ, this sickness shall not be deadly, nor thou shalt

not lie long in the grave of security, but the Comforter shall come at the last, and raise thee to life again. I say no more, but so many of you as have need, apply these to your own souls. I recommend you all to the grace of God in Christ Jesus. *Amen.*

SERMON XXV.

UPON DIVERS POINTS OF RELIGION.

John xi. 3, 4, 11, 12, 13, 14.

Therefore his sisters sent unto him, saying, Lord, behold, he whom thou lovest is sick. When Jesus heard that, he said, this sickness is not unto death, but for the glory of God, that the Son of God might be glorified thereby. These things said he: and after that, he saith unto them, our friend Lazarus sleepeth, but I go that I may awake him out of his sleep. Then said his disciples, Lord, if he sleep, he shall do well, Howbeit, Jesus spake of his death; but they thought that he had spoken of taking of rest in sleep. Then said Jesus unto them plainly, Lazarus is dead.

THERE remained one thing to be spoken of further on this point, and if the Lord would permit, I would conclude it at this time, and go to the next. I am to tell you what temptations Satan casts into the heart, to bereave the weak child of God of the love of the Father in Christ to a poor sinner, the which love is the fountain of our salvation. The last thing ye heard was, the threefold state of the called child of God; either he is sleeping, and yet the heart is waking; or else he is walking under terror, yet free from wrath; or else he is triumphing in peace and joy through the sense of his love and favour; and there is never one of you called from darkness to light, if ye belong to God, but ye are in some of these cases: either thou art under terror, and doubting of the love of God; or else he, that is the true shepherd of thy soul, hath brought thee home again, as a wandering sheep after long going astray, and so thou wonderest at the unchangeable love of God that never alters; or else thou art sleeping, and thine eyes are closed, that thou canst not see; thy ears are stopped, that thou canst not hear; thy heart is senseless, that thou canst neither pray to, nor praise God; and thy soul loathes comfort, because thy stomach is filled, and cannot receive it: And from this comes it, that thou art almost ready to cast away thy hope, if it were not for the bygone experience ye have had of the love of God, and of his kindness; else ye would cast away all grace from you. Now, of these three states, there is only one comfortable, that is, the state of a lively believer, when thou seest and tastest, in a manner, the very joys that the saints have in heaven; then thy heart exults with joy; then thou hast peace in thy conscience; then thou art ready to do every good work; and then there is a willingness of mind to please God in every thing. Indeed the other two are full of discouragements, and I know well there are many that mourn, because they are not in that state of triumphing joy, seeing it is only the state that can glorify God most; and many mourn because their state is so changeable, and because their souls are oftest in one of these two extremities, that they are always in security or terror.

Now, to prove the child of God may be in both these extremities, even after they are called to the hope of that glory, ye heard it already, I need not to repeat it. I would that ye remember the exercise of the child of God in that estate; he desires to be at one with God; he loves not his security and incredulity; he runs to prayer as he is able; he groans when he cannot pray; he pants for the living God; and when he cannot cry, he lets his tears cry for him; and he will never consent to cast away his confidence in that blood; and he will never admit another consolation, till he get the Comforter himself; and he will get no ease till he get the arms of his Lord about his soul. This for the first estate of the children of God, when they are under terrors, the which is very dangerous, that when a man hath been brought out of the depths, then to be plunged in them again; this is a thing intolerable.

Now the other state of security is as dangerous; for in thy security thou sleepest, but thy heart wakes: yet thou hast no feeling of thy wants, and suppose thou beest careless of thy right to eternal life, yet thou wilt not sell nor give over thy right to the blessing, as Esau did; and suppose thou canst not get to sit at the table with the children; yet thou wilt say, let me get the crumbs that fall from their table; and if thou canst not get so far as to be a son; yet thou wilt say, Lord, let me be a servant. But thou wilt say, what is the cause that thou art shortest and seldomest in that estate that brings most glory to God? I answer, this is done for two causes: The first is in ourselves, that seeing in us there is such a weakness in the soul, that it is not able to bear long the infinite weight of that joy, no not for one moment of an hour, unless it were upheld by the extraordinary power of God; and therefore of necessity the Lord permits this vicissitude or change to be in the soul, that now thou art in exulting joy, and within a while, thou art lying in security, and afterward in terrors, fearful terrors; that when thou art in security, and afterward in terrors, then thou mayest see the necessity thou hast of the grace of God to uphold thee, and to keep thee in thy best estate. Now ye will ask, how ye shall keep your best estate? I answer, for keeping your happy estate, when ye get your earnest given you, in token that God loves you in Christ, then lay it up in your heart, and keep it well, not so much for the earnest itself, nor yet for its own use only, but for to keep thee in the assurance of the love of that faithful Lord, that now and then is reaching down grace from heaven to thy soul here, and that he hath laid up for thee an unchangeable estate of glory everlasting in heaven: Therefore it were good for you to mark the particular places, and times, and companies, when and where, amongst whom ye have got such a blessing, that when ye have to do with it, ye may bring it out, and produce it before the Lord, and that thou mayest say, Lord, this and this grace thou gavest me here, in sign and token of thy favor and love, therefore thou wilt not leave off to love me still unto the end. Now, if ye will do this, ye shall find great consolation in the day of trouble; and when ye have fallen, ye shall find it easy to rise again.

Now, for a scripture-proof, here it is, Lazarus sends his two sisters to the Lord, who said to him, "Lord, he whom thou lovest is sick;" where I see sickness may very well stand with the love of God; for whom he loves, them he corrects; then the text says, *he tarried two days* before he went to see him; so wonder not that the Lord tarry from you long, and that he come not in an instant; for he will let thee cry, and cry again, and wait at leisure, and this he doth to try thy patience: then he tells what manner of sickness he had, saying, *This sickness shall not be unto death:* where I see, that the sick soul of the chosen child of God, suppose it be heavily tormented with security and terrors, yet it shall not perish under them: then he tells what was the end of his sickness, viz. "The glory of God, that the Son of Man might be glorified;" so this is the end wherefore God sends troubles to his own, that he himself may get glory through their mighty deliverance.

Now, when Jesus is coming to see Lazarus, Martha comes out to meet him, and she says, "Lord, if thou hadst been here, he had not died;" where we may see what is the cause of the deadness in the hearts of God's children, even the Lord's absence; whereas, by the contrary, his presence is the life of the Lord's saints. Then he said, "He should rise again;" she answered, "I know he shall rise again in the resurrection at the last day;" whereby it is evident, that she believed in one part, and doubted in another. The thing I mark here is this, I see the faith of the dearest children of God is mixed with doubtings, neither can it be perfect so long as they are in this life. Now, he says to her again, "I am the resurrection and the life;" as if he would say, None can rise from the dead, but by me; none can live the life of the righteous, but by me; further, he says,

"He that believes in me, though he be dead, yet he shall live; and whosoever liveth and believeth in me, shall never die." How is that? He may well taste of the first death, which shall be but an entry to eternal life, but he shall never taste of the second death, which is the tormenting of soul and body in hell-fire eternally. The thing I mark is this, I see faith can work wonders; it can make a dead soul, suppose it be stinking in the grave of corruption, rise and live again by the power of him who is the fountain of our faith; so ye should make much of faith, ye that have it; and such as want it, they should sell all that they have, and buy it; for it is the only jewel of the soul.

Now, when Jesus was come to the grave and saw where they had laid him, *he wept* sore; where we may see the tender love of God, his pity and compassion towards his own that suppose he layeth crosses and afflictions upon them, yet he hath pity on them; and as a loving father correcteth his child, by the time he hath laid on the rod, he repents that he did it; therefore, when he hath done, he takes the rod, and casts it into the fire; even so the Lord dealeth with his children.

Now, the last thing here, is this, verse 39, he bids "roll away the stone; and they did so:" Whereupon I mark, That we should remove every impediment that may hinder us to rise out of our security; we should cast away sin that compasses us about, and hangeth fast on us, or else we can never rise to newness of life: Therefore, as ye would have the new man reviving in your soul, ye must daily more and more crucify the old man, and so roll away the stone of sin and hardness of induration that lies upon your heart. Now, I say no more, but the Lord grant us grace to do these things, through the assistance of the Spirit of Grace in Christ. *Amen.*

SERMON XXVI.

UPON THE SAINTS FAITH.

Hebrews xi. 1.

Now faith is the substance of things hoped for, the evidence of things not seen.

THE end of this ministry of mine among you, is to root you and ground you in the Lord Jesus, that ye may find grace in him, and through him, and that ye may be filled with his peace, and joy in the Holy Ghost, and that your mouths may be filled with his praise. Now, there is nothing can plant you in Christ but faith; and there is nothing can make Christ dwell in your heart but faith; and there is nothing can fill and ground you in the Son, but faith in the Lord Jesus.

The sum of all that the Lord craves of you in his gospel is faith; and that he craves of you whom he has bought and purchased with his blood, is faith; and whom he has minded to glorify with everlasting life and eternal glory, the sum of all is faith in the Lord Jesus, and repentance towards God; these two are joined together, and cannot well be sundered, as it is in Mark i. 15. "Repent and believe the gospel;" and in Acts ii. 38. "Repent, and be baptized every one of you in the name of Jesus Christ:" for baptism is the seal of faith, and, in the Acts, witnessing both to the Jews and Gentiles, repentance towards God, and faith towards our Lord Jesus.

So there are two things that every Christian should labour to have, viz. faith and repentance; for without faith it is impossible that thou canst please God, and without faith all that thou dost is but sin, Rom. xiv. 23. before God; "Whatsoever is not of faith, it is sin;" thy eating and thy drinking, thy sleeping and thy waking, thy praying and thy thanksgiving, yea, the best work thou dost, if thou dost it not of faith, it is but an abomination in the sight of the Lord; and always the greater that the work be, if thou wantest faith, the greater is thy sin; for aye the more pure and precious the liquor is, the greater is the loss when it comes through the unclean vessel; so, as ye have here in the 6th verse, "without faith it is impossible to please God." There is not a way left to the lost generation, and the corrupt seed of Adam, there is not a way left to either man or woman whereby they can please God, but only by faith in the Lord Jesus; for thy praying without faith is but an abomination, before the Lord; thy hearing is but sin, if it be not mixed with faith; "For unto us was the gospel preached, as also it was to them; but the word that they heard profited them not, because it was not mixed with faith in them that heard it;" so the preaching of the law or gospel will never do good, except thou hearest it with faith: and, in a word, without faith thou shalt never be converted in this life, nor yet be transported to life eternal hereafter; therefore the Son of God himself testifies, John iii. 16. "God so loved the world, that he gave his only begotten Son, that whosoever believes in him should not perish but have everlasting life;" and, in the 18th verse, "He that believes in me shall not be condemned; but he that believeth not is condemned already; because he believes not in the name of the only begotten Son of God." And, in the last verse of the same chapter, "He that believes in the Son hath everlasting life, and he that believeth not the Son, he shall not see life, but the wrath of God abides on him." Therefore there is nothing but condemnation sealed in thy conscience, except thou believest in the Son; and without faith there is nothing abiding thee but an absolute condemnation.

For this cause I am minded (if the Lord will, and in the measure that he will give me) to let you see wherein stands the practise of a living and saving faith, and how ye shall use it, and handle it as it is set down here, by the examples of the saints of God; for faith is the ground that must be first laid, or else a gracious conversation can ye never have to glorify God by it; for without faith, yea, even the best actions ye do, as I was telling you, they are abomination in his sight; and the best works that thou dost are but as so many beautiful sins in the presence of God; and therefore they shall bring thee no consolation in that great day. So, first, I will lay the ground unto you, whereupon ye may build all the rest of your Christian conversation; and then I am minded to let you see the particular way, that every one of you that mints to that kingdom, should walk in before the Lord your God.

As for the first, I have chosen this place of scripture to inform you in it. Now for the chapter that ye may understand it the better, the scope of all this chapter is set down by the apostle, it is to exhort such as he writes unto, that they would forsake sin, and follow faith; as ye have it in the beginning of the next chapter, where he says, "Wherefore, seeing we have such a great cloud of witnesses, let us cast away every thing that presseth down, and the sin that hangeth so fast on; and let us run our race with patience that is set before us, looking to Jesus Christ the author and finisher of our faith; who for the joy that was set before him, endured the cross, and despised the shame thereof, and is set down at the right hand of the throne of God." Now, the argument that he uses to move them to this, is only this, even faith: Faith is the excellentest gift that ever God gave to man or woman, or the lost sons of Adam; it is the most excellent gift that ever God bestowed upon a sinner; for, of all the gifts God gives, there is none comparable to this gift of faith.

Therefore the excellentest gift would be most followed; and to prove the excellency of faith, 1*st*, He points out three properties of faith, and which faith has, that no gift of God has the like. The first property of it is "the ground of things hoped for, and the evidence of things not seen; that is, it can make things to be, which are not yet come to pass, and it can make invisible things to be seen to the mind of man, that the eye never saw, nor the ear ever heard, nor the heart of man could never understand; so thou art but a dead blind body, that wantest faith; "Therefore, they could not believe," because, as Isaiah says, he hath blinded their eyes, and hardened their hearts, that they could not see with their eyes, nor understand with their hearts, and should be converted, and I should heal them." The next property of faith is this, it can make a sinner be well reported of, both with God and man, as Enoch. *Thirdly*, It can make all the mysteries of God, that are incredible, and contrary to the sense and reason of man, to become credible and known by them all: These three properties ye have set down in the first three verses. The next thing he brings in to prove the excellency of faith, is this, all the good that all the saints have ever gotten, they got it only by faith; all the good that ever the saints did, they did it only by faith.

SERMON XXVII.

UPON THE SAINTS FAITH.

Romans i. 17.

The just shall live by faith.

THAT ye may understand this sentence the better, he tells before, that he was ready to preach the gospel to every one, and he tells the cause wherefore, viz. "That he was not ashamed of the gospel of Christ his Lord, for it is the power of God to salvation to all that believe it:" And therefore, as if he would say, should I be ashamed of that gospel, which is the arm of God to them that believe; for none that believe, but they feel the very arm of God drawing them out of hell. Again, it is *the righteousness of God*, and this is another than that of the law; for the gospel tells thee, that the righteousness of the Son shall save thee, and all them that believe in him; and now, he tells that *the just live by faith.* There are three things here,

First, The just man, that is, he who is covered with the righteousness of Christ, he lives by faith, that is, he is blessed. And David, Psal. xxxii. 1. and the apostle says, "blessed are they whose iniquities are forgiven, and whose sins are covered; blessed is the man to whom the Lord imputeth not sin:" So thou shalt never live well nor godly, unless thou knowest and believest that thy sins are forgiven thee, and except thou beest persuaded that all thy iniquities be fully and freely pardoned in the blood of Jesus, thou wilt never live godly here, nor yet get life eternal hereafter.

Secondly, Then the just man lives, that is, the just man makes the law of God his delight, these ten words proclaimed out of that terrible fire upon Mount Sinai, which the people could not abide to hear them, these ten commands of the Almighty God, he makes them the delight of his soul. First, he will have God in his heart, and he will have no other thing beside him, or above him. Next, he will have all the means of his worship set up in truth in his heart. Thirdly, He will have a regard to the glory of God above all things, and this will be his only care, that the glorious name of his God be not dishonoured. Fourthly, He will turn away his feet from the sabbath, from doing his own will, or speaking a vain word on that day.

Thirdly, The just man lives, but how ? By faith. Now, who knows what ye have been doing since the morning that ye were here ? What know I if any of you have been chiding yourself, and turning it over in your hearts, and thinking with yourself, what have I been doing ? Should I come into the world and be but a wanderer all my days ? I never set my heart yet to serve God in the strength of my soul : has God sanctified me, and died for me, and has the Lord loved me, that he has given his life for me ? Well, Lord, hast thou done so ? Is it not my part to love thee again ? Is it not my part to ask at my soul, what shall I do to glorify God in all the course of my life ? How shall I honour God in this world ? Again, have ye been thinking that, that ye may have a respect to all the commands of God ?

First, Ye must say, thou, O God, art my Lord, and thou hast bought me with thy precious blood, and redeemed me from hell and condemnation ; and seeing thou art the only Lord, therefore I will make choice of thee alone to be my Lord, and my God. Have ye resolved upon this ? It is well, but yet it is not enough, for ye will not get a fill of God, nor of his presence easily, so as to have him your whole delight, your love, your fear, your reverence, your estimation, and to make him all in all to you ; and Christ says, " if any man love me, he will keep my word, and my Father will love him, and we will come unto him, and we will dwell with him." O to have God dwelling in your soul ! were not that a sweet dwelling to you ? God to come to thee, he that fills the heaven and the earth; the Almighty and all-sufficient God, to dwell in the soul of a sinner, that is a strange thing; then might ye say with David, Psal. xxvi. 1. "The Lord is my light and salvation, whom shall I fear? The Lord is the strength of my life, of whom shall I be afraid? Then may ye say, the Lord is my shepherd, I cannot want; God, he is on my side, who can be against me? God justifies me, who shall condemn me?" Rom. viii. 33. "Or who shall separate me from the love of God?" So would not this be glad tidings to thee, to know that God is thy God? But when thou hast another Lord, another delight, another treasure, another reverence, another estimation, another for the Lord thy God; then thou hast another God, and he is not dwelling in thy heart, therefore thou canst not live godly. It is said, that God delights to dwell with a man of a humble and contrite spirit: What pleasure, and what honour brings this to God, thinkest thou, when he sees thy heart cleansed by faith, which before was a stinking sty, a cage for the devil, and all unclean birds to dwell in? What delight takes he to see the enemy cast out of thy heart, and his good Spirit dwelling in thy heart? Will ye ask then, how ye will honour God in this life? I will tell you, it has ten parts according to the ten commands.

First, Take not another God to thee but him, and make him the whole delight of thy soul, and love him with the whole strength of thy heart.

Secondly, If thou lovest him, use all the parts of his worship; pray continually; in all things be thankful to God; hear his word, and receive his sacraments; let thy talking be of the word of God, and works of God; mark all the blessings of God; mark all his corrections and judgments, and tremble thereat; look with the eye of faith upon all the creatures of God, that ye may behold in them the majesty of God, and that ye may say, "how excellent is the Lord in all his works? And how excellent is thy name, O Lord, in all the world! who has set thy glory above the heavens: For the heavens declare the glory of the Lord, and the firmament declares the works of his hands." Will ye do this, and always endeavour to worship God, when thou art at the table, or when thou art in the fields, or when thou art in company, or in thy chamber, or in thy family? thou must ever remember the worship of God. Will ye remember that he is a strong and jealous God, that punishes the sins of the fathers upon the children to the third and fourth generation; and therefore thou must keep his commands, or else he will be avenged upon thee? Will ye keep his commands, and then all that thou puttest thy hand to shall prosper, and thou shalt have all the blessings spoken of in Deut. xxviii. But on the contrary, if thou wilt not serve the Lord thy God, nor keep all his commands, then thou shalt have all these curses, and all these plagues spoken of in the same chapter, or in the whole book of God, to be poured upon thy soul, conscience and carcase: If thou escapest them in this life, yet thou shalt feel them eternally in the life to come: therefore it is good for you to worship God.

Now the *third* part of this honour is this, besides the private and public worship which thou must use, I call that both your private and public worship, which is, when ye serve God in the congregation, or in the family, or in your private prayers and meditation, when ye are alone; besides this, I say, there is a third part of this honour and worship, and it is set down in the third command; that is, to sanctify the name of the Lord thy God; mark thy thoughts, words, and deeds, this should bring great joy to thee, if thou wert but sweeping the house, and riddling the ashes, or making ready thy meat; if thou thinkest this with thyself, Lord, I do this to honour thee, my God; that is great glory to God, when with the strength of thy heart, either in thy own person, or in thy calling, or in the hearts of thy family, or in the hearts of others, thou labourest to set up the glorious name of the Lord thy God; and therefore thou must resolve with Joshua xxiv. " Choose ye this day whom ye will serve; but

I and my family will serve the Lord." Do this, for if thou dost it not, the Lord will not hold thee innocent, notwithstanding of thy outward and inward worship, except thou endeavourest to hallow the name of the Lord in all thy ways. These first three commands ye must have them in mind all the days of the week, ye must have God in your heart every day, ye must have the worship of God set up in your hearts every day, and ye must set the glory of God before your eyes every day, ye must not keep these to the sabbath-day, but ye must have them all the days of the week also, but so, as thou mayest use thy calling also; but as to the sabbath-day, thou must put it wholly apart for the service of God, and thou must spend all that day in the worship of God, without intermeddling with thy calling. Now, what joy might ye have had in this godly and christian conversation, if ye practised the same? Will ye do it, and know what it is to do it? I tell you, it is the only way to keep life in the soul. Some of you have had sometimes good motions, and sometimes ye have had great comfort; but when these motions went away, then ye lost all your comfort, and your sorrow began again, because ye looked not to the godly life which should have followed thereupon; that is, that ye should have God in your soul, and ye should have delighted in the worship of God continually; and thou shouldst always have the glory of God before thy eyes, and that ye should have consecrate one whole day every week to the service of God. How many of you have thought that ye have done well enough if ye have not absented your bodies from the kirk, suppose ye left your hearts at home, or in some other place? But that was not enough, seeing that ye knew that there was more required of you, " for to whom much was given, much will be required of them again;" and many think they do very well, if they envy not their neighbour; and if they seek not a revenge of their enemy, if they bear no malice in their heart, but can find a heart to agree with them, and if they hate them not, they think they do very well; and they think it enough, if they live a quiet life on their own, and humble towards all men ; if they bear no evil will to any man, nor no man bears evil will to them ; they do no wrong to any man, nor no man does wrong to them. But will ye come to this point, I pray you, have you loved your neighbour as yourself, and that for Christ's sake, because he has commanded you to love one another ? I know not any man of you that has set his heart to do this : The Lord open your eyes to see it, that ye may say, Lord, I have been too long doing my own will, now, I will begin and do thy will ; and seeing it is thy will that I love my neighbour as myself, for thy sake, therefore I will do it, because thou hast commanded it so to be done. Now, that love that ye should bear to your neighbour, it will break out in these six duties contained in the other commands.

First, Thou wilt break out in shewing that dignity and honour which thou oughtest to shew to several persons to whom thou art bound, either by age, or by calling, in kirk or commonwealth, to superiors or inferiors. Is this little honour to God, trow ye, when thou sayest, Lord, I will not only honour thee, and reverence thy glory, but also I will reverence thy very image, and the footsteps of thy glory ; I will maintain the dignity of them that God has set over me, for Christ's sake : But perhaps ye will say, who can do this ? O ! but this is not impossible, for *the just shall live by faith*. So then if ye will reach up your hand to the blood of Christ, and apply it to thy soul, then ye shall find the Spirit writing every one of these laws in thy heart.

Next, in the *sixth command*, the life of thy neighbour will be so dear to thee, that thou must pity thy neighbour's life when he is in misery ; and because God breathed in life, thou wilt be loath to think any of thy neighbour's lives, or of thy family's to be grievous to thee ; but rather thou wilt say, I have a pleasure in such a family, in such a kirk, or commonwealth as this, where I see the worship of God set up. Now, well is the soul that will resolve to live in such a manner that thou canst say glory be to God in the highest heavens, for I will never tire to glorify my God, if it were in the midst of the congregation among my brethren, "I will teach thy ways unto the wicked, Psal. li. 13. and sinners shall be converted unto thee." For thou mayest murder the soul of thy neighbour, as well as thou canst murder his body: but well is the soul of him that can save the soul of his neighbour. What glory to God and what joy and peace would you bring to your consciences, if ye would endeavour to live such a life, as might bring glory to God, peace to your own souls, and salvation to your neighbours.

Then, thirdly, in the *seventh command*, ye must eschew all uncleanness of the body, thou must keep thy body clean and holy; for wo to you that defile that body that Christ bought so dear; thou must eschew all filthy speeches and unclean communications, that it proceed not out of thy mouth; and thou must beware of all unclean thoughts and filthy cogitations, for they will banish the good Spirit of Jesus.

Then *fourthly*, in the *eighth command*, thou mayest not use unlawful means to win thy living: for art thou a beggar? yet thou mayest not steal for that, because God hath forbidden it; but rather thou wilt say, God hath made me poor, because he knows that estate of life is best for me; what is the matter! I am content, I shall get the kingdom of heaven, and the unsearchable riches thereof, Christ, to make me rich; God has given me that riches wherewith I ought to be content. And ye that God has given riches to, say, God has given me riches that I may use them lawfully to his glory, and to the supply of the necessities of the poor; therefore I am but a steward of these things that God has given me; therefore I will bestow them upon the poor again, for his sake that gave them to me; and I believe, " he that gives to the poor, lends to the Lord;" and God will take it in oker, and God will pay a large annual rent for it. Christ says, " make you friends with the riches of iniquity, that when ye shall want, they may receive you into their everlasting habitations. He that is faithful in the least, he is also faithful in meikle ; and he that is unfaithful in the least, he is also unfaithful in meikle ; if then ye have not been faithful in the wicked riches, who shall trust you with the true treasure ? And if ye have not been faithful in another man's goods, who shall give you that which is your own ?" Now, I pray you be faithful, and take not away from your neighbour wrongfully, and thou shalt find the blessing of God for doing of it : and suppose ye might gain ten thousand pounds with a lie, yet do it not, because all that is conquest after that manner, is but stolen gear. Now, if there were this faithfulness, ye would not destroy one another as ye do ; and if there were that love amongst you, ye would not suffer any of your neighbours to want.

Fifthly, in the *ninth commandment*, if ye remembered it, ye would not swear so oft as ye do at your bargains making, but singly say, this I gave for it, and this I will have again, or else let it be to myself; for suppose men have gained great riches with their lies, and by their swearing, and by fraud, yet what pleasure shall they have in them when they are on their deathbed ? They shall neither bring comfort to themselves, nor commodity to their wives and children. Again, ye should not lie against your neighbours to bring them to shame or skaith ; yea, suppose he were your mortal enemy : and, again, when any body comes and tells an evil tale of your neighbour, ye should say, I would not hear you, ye are in the wrong, ye should have told himself.

Now, if ye were thus occupied, would ye have your tongues so railing out, and backbiting your neighbour as you do ? No, no, but ye would say with David, " I will take heed to my ways, that I sin not with my tongue ; I will keep my mouth with a bridle while the wicked is before me."

Then, *last of all*, in the *tenth command*, take such account of thy thoughts, that if there arises an evil cogitation, or an evil wish to thy neighbour, then thou mayest say, God has set a law in my heart, that I think not so meikle as an evil thought against my neighbour; therefore avoid, Satan, and tempt me not; for these are thy thougths, and not my thoughts.

But if ye will ask, how ye shall get this done? I answer, ye shall get it by faith; for all things are possible to him that believes; and thou shalt not fail to get it, when thou art persuaded of these six things.

First, When thou canst not say, I am persuaded of my salvation in Christ Jesus, because he has saved whomsoever believes in him, and they never shall be condemned.

Secondly, I am persuaded, that God will write all his law in my heart, and he will put his fear in my inward parts, that I shall never depart from him.

Thirdly, I am persuaded that there is never a blessing given of God to me, but it is given out of his love; and there is never a correction sent to me of God, but he sends it out of love, to humble me and keep my heart under, that it swell not with pride, nor sleep not in security.

Fourthly, I will follow this mean, and this in my calling; because I am persuaded, that God has set it before me; I will not cast in this and this doubt, but I will use the means, and commit the success thereof to God; for this is the cause why you are discouraged in your calling, when ye see that things go not with you as ye would, even because ye leave not the event and success of it to God; but if thou wouldst cast thy care upon the Lord, doubtless he would care for thee: so however it be, thou mayest say I have been serving God in my calling, and therefore he has prospered me; and if he send thee a curse in thy calling, yet thou mayest say, I know the Lord has set me this lot to try my patience, and to put me in remembrance of him, who disposes of all things as pleaseth him.

Fifthly, Faith will make thee say, now, I will get to my calling joyfully, I have warrant for it out of God's word; because I know the Lord allows it, and I have a promise of a blessing to be joined with it, and

I know God shall get glory by it, and so I shall find comfort in it.

Last of all, Faith will say to thee, " all things tend to the best of them that love God ;" however matters shall go with me in my calling or otherwise, I know that all shall tend to my well ; for I love God, and God loves me. What, can any man tell what sweet life this should be to you ? I beseech God to give you the sweet taste of it, that afterward ye may endeavour to live that holy and heavenly life ; that, after this life, ye may be partakers of eternal life with Jesus Christ our Lord. To whom, with the Father, and with the Spirit, be all praise for ever.

SERMON XXVIII.

UPON THE SAINTS FAITH.

Galatians ii. 2.

Thus I live, yet not I, but Christ lives in me.

THERE is the example here and practice of that which ye heard yesternight, viz. That *the just man lives by faith*. The apostle testifies here, that he has the experience of this in his own heart and person. What the life of godliness was I told you, (I pray God to give you hearts to put it in practice) that out of a pure and honest heart, cleansed by faith in the Lord Jesus, ye may endeavour to walk in all the commands of God, and ye may study to please him in all things; and that ye may be fruitful in his vineyard, and given continually to every good work; that ye bearing much fruit, God may be honoured thereby, who has called you to the hope of that glory; and that ye may have joy and peace in your consciences, that passes all natural understanding; for great is the joy and great is the peace that comes to a Christian, who has given his heart to serve the Lord continually; he thinks it is his happiness when he knows that his Father is well pleased with him in Christ.

First, Because of the justice of Christ, that he has put on him.

Secondly, Because of that begun grace, which is wrought in the heart of him who has the Lord dwelling in him; and this begun grace, suppose it be not perfect, yet it brings glory to God, and the Father accepts of it in his Son as if it were perfect, and this brings joy to the conscience that has it, and he is sure, that as he glorifies God in this world, so God shall glorify him in the world to come; but, alas! all the joy, and all the consolation that the most part has had, they had it in this, that God is merciful to sinners: but as for their joy, which comes through this holy conversation, it is but small with many, and therefore this makes so few Christians to shine through their good works before men; and as for this walking with God, as Enoch did, it is a thing that not only the most of the world never knew, but the most part of Christians; because their life is so full of troubles and discouragements, therefore they think that of all lives in the world, the life of a Christian is the most miserable; but I assure you, brethren, it is not so; for who can tell what glorious and unspeakable joy there is in the soul of man or woman who have their conversation in heaven? indeed, if ye could get it, ye would say, yon is the pearl that I was seeking, I would sell all I have in the world to buy it with, and I would sell all the joy and pleasure I have in the world, and all carnal liberties, to have it continually, and walking as in the presence of God. I told you the way how this should be gotten, *the just man lives by faith;* it is only by faith ye must get this, ye must reach out the hand of your faith, and lay hold on that salvation by Jesus Christ's blood; and let this be the ground of your joyful conversation, that salvation is offered to you freely in Christ; for where is there joy and consolation to be had, if it be not in them who have their conversation in heaven with that glorious Trinity? That joy is unspeakable and most glorious. Then reach out thy hand to all the promises in the word, and thou shalt find abundant consolation therein; believe that God will not only forgive, but that also he will slay thy sins; for there is another virtue in the death of Christ than the paying of thy ransom, even a virtue to crucify all thy sins, and to bury them all in the grave, that they shall never rise again; for the promise is not only the remission of thy sins, but also of the renewing of thy heart, and of writing all his laws in thy inward parts, and of setting thy heart in the heavenly places where Christ is.

That promise also belongs to thee that believes, and the Lord is bound, by his promise and oath, to perform the one as well as the other : So, I say, there is a virtue in the death of Christ, to cause thee daily to die unto sin ; and there is a virtue in the resurrection of Christ, to raise thee daily from death to life, and make thee a new creature ; there is a virtue in the ascension of Christ, to lift thee up to heaven, and set thy heart above, where Christ is. Therefore, I say, it is only faith that can do this ; it can shut in the hand of thy soul within thee, in the very fulness of the Godhead dwelling in Christ bodily, and there it can draw down to thee grace upon grace, out of that well of salvation ; it can bring to thee light and life, from him that is light and life itself ; it can bring every thing that can make a man to live well here, that he may live well for evermore hereafter. Again, whereas many faint in the worship of God, yet faith will make the worship of God easy to thee, that when thou canst not pray, faith will get words enow ; when thou canst not get a heart to give God thanks, faith can get it to thee ; and when thou canst not get the Spirit, faith will get it to thee ; and there is no grace requisite in the law or in the gospel, but faith will get it to thee ; if thou canst believe and say, Lord, thou art my Saviour, I believe that as thou hast forgiven me all my sins, so I believe also that thou wilt renew me ; for thou hast promised the one as well as the other. Now, if ye would bring faith with you, it would make all the parts of the worship of God easy to you : How walked Enoch with God ? Was it not by faith ? Where got Abraham grace to leave his own country, and to apply the promise, " In thy seed shall all the nations of the earth be blessed ?" Was it not by faith ? Where got Moses grace to " refuse to be called the son of Pharaoh's daughter, and chuse rather to suffer adversity with the people of God, than to enjoy the pleasures of sin for a season ; and esteem the reproach of Christ greater riches than the treasures of Egypt ?" Was is not by faith ? Where got Moses grace " to forsake Egypt, that he feared not the wrath of the king? Was it not by faith? How ordained he the Passover, but through faith? How past the Israelites through the Red Sea, as by dry land, but by faith? How fell the walls of Jericho down, but by faith? How was Rahab's receiving of the spies peaceably, but by faith? How got Gideon victory, but by faith? And, to be short, wherefrae gets all the holy men of God their commendation in the scripture, but frae faith? So if thou wantest faith, thou art but a dead lump, and thou wilt never do good in the worship of God; but faith will keep the life of the Son of God fresh in thy heart, and out of him it will draw life: therefore, the apostle says here, "thus I live, yet not I, but Christ that lives within me;" for faith draws him down, and makes him to have residence in the soul.

What is faith then? Keep the promises of God in Christ, and apply them to thy soul, and there is faith; for thy feeling is not faith, but the application of the promises is faith. But ye will say, how can faith do this? I answer, it is not thy faith does it, but it is Christ, who is the object of thy faith; it is not the hand that puts the meat in thy mouth that feeds thee, but it is the meat itself; and it is not the hands that puts on thy clothes that clothes thee, but it is the clothes: nor it is not the hand that applies the salve to the wound that heals the wound, but it is the salve itself: so it is not thy faith that feeds thy soul, or clothes it, or makes thy sick soul whole, but it is Jesus Christ the object of thy faith who makes thee whole, and feeds and cleids thee; therefore, says he, "I live not, but Christ lives in me." But how lives Christ in thee? O! by faith; and therefore, he says, "I live by the faith of the Son of God;" that is, I believe the Son of God loved me before all beginning; I believe the Son of God choosed me to be one of his members, before the world was made; I believe the Son of God died for me, and therein stands my life: for ye must not let the grip of faith go, "I live by faith in the Son of God;" for thou must apprehend that love of God in Christ, and thou must believe, suppose thou feelest it not; and thou must believe that Christ was crucified, and that he died for thee; thou must lay hold on that, and comfort thyself with it; and apply it to thyself, Christ loved me and died for me, or else thou shalt never feel the power of Christ's life dwelling in thy soul: there is the thing then that I told, ye have been put in mind of this, that for the love that Christ has borne to thee, and for all the mercies of God towards you, ye would offer up "your bodies a living sacrifice, holy, acceptable, and without blame, to God, which is your reasonable serving of him." The pattern of his service is the law, ye must have respect to all the commands of God; this would always hold you going on in your journey, and not let you sit down; this would always keep you in the fear and reverence of God. When ye look in the glass of the law, ye would say, is God yet all in all to my soul? O! is all my delight in the presence of God? Is my heart given to see clearly the infinite majesty of God? Is my love, and all my delight, and my joy, and all my life, in beholding that glorious Lord? Again, have I such love and reverence to his worship, that I believe his all-seeing eye is always looking upon me, that his law should be your meditation day and night? For it can never be sufficiently repeated by you; therefore David said of the blessed man, that his delight is in the law of the Lord, and in that law doth he meditate both day and night." Is not the meditation of the law in the day enough, suppose it be not in the night? No, it is more that God craves of you; for he craves the love of your soul with all your strength, for he is worthy of it all. Again, ye have to look to the second command, what is your estimation of the means of his worship? Again, ye have to look to the third command, what care and endeavour ye have to glorify God in your conversation: Again, in the fourth command, ye have to look to the setting apart every seventh day of the week for the service of God: Again, in the fifth command, what reverence, and honor, and obedience, ye have given to your superiors, and what care and love have ye had of your inferiors: and, in the rest of the commands, ye are to look what respect ye have had to the life, honesty, goods, and the persons of your neighbours. This will let thee see, that thou art not at thy race end: Yet I have not aimed at the mark, I have not yet so foughten the good fight; therefore I must have a new virtue and a new grace from Christ, that I may begin again where I left off; I must have my conjunction renewed with him again; for there is not enough in my soul yet to transform me to his glorious image. This is the first.

Secondly, Ye must aim by faith: that is, ye must take a strong grip of him; ye must look better to his incarnation, his birth, better to his life and conversation, better to his choice, better to his death, and better to his resurrection and ascension; and not only to that, but faith must make thee grip to all the promises in the word, and this will make thee joy in the doing of thy calling; so that, if thou findest a blessing in it, faith will make thee to say, this calling has the warrant of the Lord, therefore he has blessed me; and if thou findest a curse in it, faith will make thee say, my sins have deserved this; therefore the Lord corrects me; because he loves me and has care of me, therefore he chastises me, and all to try my patience.

So this is the *second* point, to meditate on the incarnation, on the birth, on the life, on the death, on the resurrection, and on the ascension of Christ, and to apply all the promises of God in his word to thyself. Now, because some of you find so little power of grace in your hearts to perform this, and therefore ye are loath to begin; but ye must not do so, but ye must believe that God will send his Spirit to write all his laws in thy heart, that then thou mayest say, "Christ lives in me, and I in him:" Now there are other two things that I would say,

First, Because many are discouraged in this life, and think it impossible to serve God in such a manner; therefore they never begin.

Secondly, Some think it enough if they get good notions now and then; and some think it enough if they leave some evil and do some good; and some think if they have done so as I have said, they need never do another turn: But they are all beguiled; for this is not impossible, for the saints before us have win to it; Enoch walked with God continually, and Abraham lived in faith and died in faith: Moses was faithful in all the house of God; what was Job? He was a just and upright man, and one that feared God and eschewed evil; when he was in prosperity he looked for a change, and when the cross came he bore it patiently: What said David? " I have set the Lord always before mine eyes; he is at my right hand, I shall never be moved. I will keep thy statutes. I have hid thy promises in my heart, that I might not sin against thee. I have had great delight in the ways of thy testimonies, as in all riches. I will meditate on thy precepts, and consider thy ways. I will delight in thy statutes, and I will not forget thy word," &c. Now if these men had such a love to God, and such a delight in his command, much more now may ye have it, seeing your Lord has gotten the victory, and is now reigning in heaven; and ye may have now experience that this is a time of grace, and there is enough to be had, if ye will come and get it; " He that comes to me, says Christ, shall have life in abundance;" for he is exceeding rich and abundant in grace, that ye have to do with, and ye may go boldly to him, for he will cast none away that come to him.

And *first*, if thou livest a Christian life, then God shall be exceedingly glorified, and I suppose that is no little thing to thee that lovest that glory; I am sure it will be a weighty argument to thee that art the child of God; yea, weightier than who would give thee ten thousand worlds of thy own. Now, if thou couldst believe that this continual walking with God brings greater glory to God than the work of the creation of the world, wouldst thou not strive to do it? What glory brings this to God, when ye may say, yon man was blind, but now he sees; he was deaf, but now he hears; he was dumb, but now he speaks; he was lame and crooked, but now he is restored to his hands and feet again; he was dead, but now he is alive? What glory was it to God to see the change of Zaccheus, who was a publican, and yet made the Son of Abraham, and of an oppressor was made to give the half of his goods to the poor, and was made to restore four-fold to such as he had taken any thing from? Luke xix. 5. What glory to God was it to see the change of Paul, who of a bloody persecuter, became a notable preacher? What glory was it to see such a sinful woman, of whom they said, "if he knew what this woman were, he would not suffer her to come near him;" to see such a change in her, that "she sits at his feet and washes them with tears, and dries them with her hair?" Luke vii. 37. So what glory, what joy, and what pleasure should this be to God, when he sees you walking before him in this Christian life and conversation?

Secondly, What honour should it be to thyself: what should be spoken of thee in Zion? It was Solomon's glory, that he builded a house for the Lord's name to be called on there; what glory then would it be to thee to build a house to the Lord in thy own heart? The Father is glorified, when of thy stony heart he makes it a golden heart, and melts it with the fire of the Spirit; the Son is glorified, when he sees such a virtue in his blood, and he rejoices to see such a change made by that same blood; and not only he rejoices, but also the angels and the saints rejoice in heaven at the conversion of a sinner: the Father infinite in himself, he rejoices in his Son, that he sent to work the work of our redemption: the Son rejoices in the Father, that ever he employed him in such a work; the Holy Ghost rejoices in the Father and in the Son, that ever he sanctified, first the head, and then the members. Now, if thou believest these things, this would make thee to say, " My beloved is all fair, my well-beloved is white and ruddy, the chiefest among ten thousand. His head is as the most fine gold, his locks curled and black as a raven. His eyes are like doves eyes upon the rivers of water, washed with milk, and fitly set. His cheeks are as a bed of spices, and as sweet flowers; his lips like lilies, dropping down pure myrrh. His hands are as the rings of gold, set with crystal; his belly is like white ivory, set with sapphires. His legs are as pillars of marble, set upon sockets of fine gold: his countenance is as Lebanon, excellent as the cedars. His mouth is most sweet, and he is all delightable." Cant. v. 10, 11, 12, 13, 14, 15, 16. And this should make Christ again to give thee his commendation, " My well beloved, behold thou art fair, thy eyes are like doves eyes; my well beloved, thou art fair and pleasant; yea, also our bed is green; arise my love, my fair one, and come away; my dove, that art in the hold of the rocks, and in the secret place of the stairs; shew me thy face and let me hear thy voice; for thy voice is sweet, and thy face comely."

Now, the *third* and *last* reason is this, " your light should so shine before men, that they seeing your good works, may glorify your Father which is in heaven." And what glory shall this bring to God? And what joy shall it bring to your souls, when not only yourselves glorify God in your life and conversation, but also other men glorify God for your good works?

Now, I leave the rest, and I beseech God to give a blessing to that which has been spoken to you in the name of the Lord Jesus; to whom, with the Father, and with the Spirit, be all praise, honour, and glory for ever and ever. *Amen.*

SERMON XXIX.

UPON DIVERS POINTS OF RELIGION.

Matt. xxvi. 40.

After he came to his disciples, he found them asleep.

THE Lord is in the garden here, and he is sweating blood under the heavy burden of the wrath of God for our sins; and therefore he runs to prayer to get ease thereby; but when he comes to his disciples he finds them sleeping; this was a great discouragement to him; therefore he rebukes Peter by name, and then he gives a particular command to every one of them, that they " watch and pray, lest they enter into temptation;" and then he gives reason wherefore, saying, " the spirit is ready, but the flesh is weak." Now, to remember you what are the things which have been shortly taught you heretofore? They are these, the main thing that you should shoot at, is salvation and eternal life: the ways to attain to this are two; the one is faith, making you to lay hold on the Son of God, to eat his flesh and drink his blood, and to apply his death to slay sin in thee, and his resurrection to revive and quicken thee; the other is but your Christian conversation, and your holy life, " for without holiness none shall see God:" so every one that believes must fling sin from them; ye must cast away the works of darkness, and ye must put on the whole armour of light; ye must flee evil, and do good: and then ye must know what is evil, and what is good. Then your heart must be set in right order, and there must be obedience to all the commands of God, at all times, and in all companies; there must be integrity and uprightness of heart in the worship of God; there must be diligence in the work of God; for the sloathful servant will get nothing ; there must be perseverance unto the end, or else ye will lose your reward ; there must be meekness of heart, and humility of mind, or else ye cannot take on the yoke of Christ, nor it will never be sweet and easy to you ; then ye must have a respect to all the commands of God in the law.

The *first command* will teach you to have God only in your heart, and none besides him.

The *second command* will teach you to have respect to all the parts of his worship.

The *third command* will teach you how to glorify God in all your ways, and to reverence his name above all other things under heaven.

The *fourth command* will teach you to keep holy the sabbath-day, and to consecrate it as glorious to the Lord, and to spend that whole day from morning to evening in the service of God.

The *fifth command* will teach you your duty to your superiors and inferiors, what reverence and obedience ye owe to the one, and what love and care ye owe to the other.

The *sixth command* will teach you to abstain from all malice and envy, all strife and debate, and from hurting or murdering your neighbour.

The *seventh command* will teach you to flee from all filthy cogitations, all unchaste and unreverent speeches and from all sort of filthy lusts of the flesh.

The *eighth command* will teach you to beware of covetousness, and unlawful means to get your riches, or win your living by.

The *ninth command* will forbid you to make lies, or to bear false witness against your neighbour.

And the *tenth command* will teach you to beware to think an evil thought against thy neighbour.

Now the last two truths that ye have heard were these :

First, Ye must live by faith ; for repentance, amendment of life, living justly, soberly, and righteously, and living by faith are all one : for he that lives by faith, lives godly, soberly, and righteously ; he that lives by faith, he repents and amends his life, because none could do these things but he that lives by faith? it is Christ that must rent your heart and take away your stony heart, and give you a heart of flesh; it is Christ that must make your heart clean, and it is Christ that must make you bring forth fruits worthy of amendment of life; and ye cannot keep Christ but by faith; therefore hold a grip of him by faith, for there is no satisfaction to you but by faith.

The *last of all*, was your Christian conversation, which brings great glory to God; for he is honoured when your light shines before men, and when they glorify God for your good works, because they see Jesus written on your hearts, and the image of God is imprinted on your souls, and so the name of God is well spoken of: but on the contrary, thou that livest ungodly and unrighteously, ye make the name of God to be evil spoken of, and thou crucifiest over again the Lord Jesus, if once thou professest Christianity, and thou countest that blood, that was able to purge thee from thy sins, to be profane, and an unholy thing: therefore ye should take good heed to yourselves, how ye spend all the days of your Christian conversation; for a reckoning must be made, and an account given in of the whole time of your life, how it has been spent in the service and worship of God. Now, these are the things which ye have heard.

Now, what remains, God has given thee in his word, that may strengthen and encourage thee to lead such a holy and Christian life; so that, if thou usest them, thou mayest live godly and happily here, and thou mayest make thy end glorious, and therefore get eternal life.

Secondly, I am to tell you how ye shall drive every day in particular, that when thou hast done, thou mayest say, Lord, I care not suppose thou comest in the clouds ere the morning; and when thou risest, thou mayest say, Lord I care not suppose thou comest in the clouds ere evening, for I am ready; for this is needful for you to know how to walk before God, and how to please him in all things ; it is needful, I say, to thee that has tasted of the sweetness and goodness of God, and of the joys of heaven, and of the virtue of the world to come, and to thee that lookest for the crown of eternal glory.

The *third* thing I am to tell you, is to let you see what are the particular drifts that the devil has to entice you, either to do evil, or else leave good undone.

Last of all, I am amind to let you see and know who has faith, suppose never so weak, and what are these glorious prerogatives and privileges which God has given to thee that believest, wherein thou mayest rejoice ; seeing thou knowest they belong to thee, I will tell you them over again.

First, I am to tell you the means, that if ye use them, ye shall have a fair gate, and an open door unto you to step into heaven, where ye shall get a fair heritage and a pleasant portion.

Secondly, I am to tell you how ye shall drive over all the whole day, and all the night until the morning ; then, when either morning or evening comes, it may be joyful and welcome to thee.

Thirdly, I am to tell you what are the drifts of the devil, whereby he uses to entice you to evil, or to hinder you of good.

And *last of all*, I am to speak of these glorious prerogatives, and rare privileges of the sons of God, as they are set down in the word.

Now, as to the first, what are the means that God has ordained every one of his own to use, that thereby they may come to his kingdom : For he has hedged a way, and opened a gate and made an entry, which shall lead thee blameless to that kingdom, if thou insist in it. Many resolve to please God, and to walk in his ways ; but because they know not the means how to perform this, therefore they are cast into such doubts, they wot not what to do : But what are these means which God has ordained you to use in this world, so long as you are strangers here, and absent from the

Lord? For when ye come to himself, ye shall not need them. I will tell you, some of them are used ordinarily, and at ordinary times; and there are other some that are extraordinary, and are used at extraordinary times. Again, these ordinary means, some of them are used at the public worship of God, as the hearing of the word, and receiving of the sacraments, as baptism and the Lord's supper: I fear many of you as yet have not had great comfort in your baptism; because ye have not considered, that it is ordained of God, to be a mean to strengthen and confirm you in the promises of salvation made to you in Christ, and sealed up to you by his blood, signified by the water in the sacrament of baptism. Again, I fear the use of the Lord's supper has not been profitable to you, because of the want of holy preparation before the action, and of that holy disposition in the doing of the action, and that holy resolution after the receiving of the same: Even so, I say, in hearing of the word, many of you have rashly and unpreparedly heard it, not taking head to your feet when ye are entering into the house of the Lord; many are evil disposed in the time of hearing, and few resolve to do that which the word commands: But if these means were used with reverence at the ordinance of God, ye should find a blessing in them; and if ye would come and hear the word of God with reverence, thinking that ye are in the presence of God, this would do ye meikle good. Now, besides this public means, ye must use private means also, or else the worship of God cannot be kept in integrity. These private means ye should both know them and use them diligently.

The first is watchfulness, and it is here commanded, "watch and pray that ye enter not into temptation." Ye must watch continually, and have an eye to all thy works, that they be conformable to the law of God, and that in them thou neither declinest to the right hand or to the left.

Secondly, Ye must pray and pray continually, as the apostle commands.

Thirdly, Ye must have that heavenly meditation of the saints of God upon his whole law, his whole word, and upon all his works, so far as thou canst remember them.

Fourthly, Ye must put on the whole armour of God, and wear it. "Gird your loins with verity, put on the breast plate of righteousness, shoe your feet with the preparation of the gospel, cover your head with the helmet of salvation; and above all things take unto you the shield of faith, that ye may quench all the fiery darts of the devil; and the sword of the Spirit, which is the word of God."

Fifthly, Mark the experience of the wonderful love of God, wrought both on yourselves and others, concerning your infirmity, and concerning the grace of God sustaining you. Now, besides this, there are privy confessions, privy thanksgivings, privy conferences, and privy communions with the saints. Now, if all these were used, ye shall find the use of these means make up a fair Christian. But I leave these things; only this I beseech you, "watch and pray, that ye enter not into temptation;" for there is nothing to keep you from temptation, but diligent watching, joined with prayer, and taking heed to all thy ways, both in thought, word and deed, that they debored not from the law of God; together with a sweet conference and communion with the Lord thy God, in sending up thy requests to the Father, and to the Son, by the Spirit: To whom be all praise, and honour, and glory, for now and ever. *Amen.*

SERMON XXX.

UPON DIVERS POINTS OF RELIGION.

2 Corinthians v. 14, 15.

For the love of Christ constraineth us, because we thus judge, that if one died for all, then all were dead: And that he died for all, that they which live, should not henceforth live unto themselves, but unto him which died for them, and rose again.

THAT ye may the better understand this, he is telling before, that his life is a daily dying, and that he was under many crosses and afflictions for Christ's cause, and he is telling the comforts that bare him up under these burdens of affliction, in this life, which is but for a moment, "and they cause unto us a far more exceeding weight of glory; and therefore he looked not to the things that are seen, seeing they are temporal, but he looked to the things that are unseen, and seen only with the eye of faith, seeing they are eternal: Then he tells what he knows, when this body of his, which he calls an earthly house of his tabernacle, shall be destroyed, he has a better to get for it, even a building given of God, that is, an house not made with hands, eternal in the heavens:" And to confirm this, he brings in the certainty of his time from the Author of life, which is God, " who also had given him the earnest of the Spirit," and therefore he rests: Then he tells that here he was but a stranger, and *absent from the Lord*, therefore he would fain remove out of the body and dwell with the Lord; and he tells, there is but one thing he shoots at, which was this, *whether he died or lived*, or whether he was dwelling at home, or removing from home, *he might be acceptable to the Lord*, and might study to please him in every thing. Then he tells the reason why he shot at this only, "for," says he, "we must all appear before the judgment seat of Christ," where all shall be made manifest, be it good, be it evil, "that every man may receive the things which he has done in his body, according to that which he hath done, whether it be good or evil: Then he says, knowing therefore the terror of the Lord, we persuade men:" For must not that be a terrible day when heaven and earth shall all be set on fire, and when mountains shall shake, and the earth tremble, and the rocks shall rive. "Knowing, says he, the terror of the Lord, we persuade men;" that is we assure them of the terrible day, and we exhort them to do things that may be acceptable to God now, in the days of their pilgrimage; and he takes God and their own consciences to witness, that he was faithful in the doing of it; and lest some should think that he past the bounds of his calling, and were out of his wit; therefore he meets this, in these words, and he says, " whether we be out of our wit, we are it unto God; or whether we be in our right mind, we are it unto you;" and then he comes to this that I have read, and I will expound it to you, *the love of Christ constrains us;* that is, it binds me with such bonds, that I dare not but endeavour to be acceptable to God, and to persuade all men in the world (so far as my calling may reach) to prepare them for the day of judgment; for it will be a terrible day to such as are not prepared in some measure for it: Then he tells them what was this love that so constrained him, because says he, "we judge that if one died for all, then all were dead;" as if he would say, this was the love of Christ to us, that he died for us; and I am persuaded, that this death of his is as sufficient for my redemption before the tribunal of God, as if I had died and borne the curse myself, as if my own head had been chopt off; and so mayest thou be that believest in the Son; thou mayest be sure that malediction was borne for thee, and thou shalt never perish, but have eternal life; thou mayest be as sure as if thyself had been the man that bore it, and had been obedient to the

Father to the very death of the cross; therefore ye have need to pray for faith, because it is the only jewel in the world; for it shall make thee live well here, and get eternal glory hereafter. And he died for all. Why died he for all? Why died he for thee? What brought him from heaven? What nailed him to the tree? What brought out his heart's blood? What but thy sins, and the sins of the elect?

Now, what looks he for from thee? What craves he at thy hand for that thirty-three years banishment from heaven for thy sake? there the thing that he craves; that seeing thy sins are forgiven thee, and seeing that there is no condemnation to thee, and seeing thou shalt live for evermore, for it is so with thee that believest the promises; seeing then it is so, that the end of all this is even that ye live not to yourselves, that the rest of thy life thou mayest not spend it for thy back and belly, but for Jesus Christ, who first died for thee, and now is risen again; there is the end, that ye be no more your own, but the life that ye have to live, ye may live to glorify him that died for you, and rose again, and has taken in with him a part of you, and the best part of you, to heaven with himself. Then he says, "henceforth we know no man after the flesh," &c. As if he would say, this is my judgment, now I shall esteem no more of myself, nor of no man after the flesh, no, not for Christ himself, according to the carnal prerogatives which he had, as he came of the stock of David, and succeeded to his kingdom, and sat on his throne; but I know him as he is the Son of God, and a crowned king in heaven. And then he says, " therefore if any man be in Christ, let him be a new creature: Why? Because all old things are past away, and behold all things are become new." How is that? Since the day that blood was shed, heaven and earth, and all things therein, are become new, and they are all waiting for the day of their final redemption: Now, seeing all creatures are growing new, it becomes thee that art in Christ to be a new creature. This for the exposition of the words. Now, there are two things that ye have to take notice to: The first is, the manner how ye should live: The next is, the reason to move you to live so; and ye have both these set down here, the manner how ye should live, not to yourselves, to serve your own appetites, but to live to Christ and serve him: The reason to move us to this manner of living, is first, "Because ye must all appear before the judgment seat of Christ; and therefore ye should all be doing good, for according as your travail will be, even so shall your reward be, as Daniel saith, xii. 6. "They that be wise shall shine as the brightness of the firmament, and they that turn many to righteousness, as the stars for ever and ever. Again, every man shall receive according to that which he hath done in the body, whether it be good or whether it be evil:" Therefore we should study to be acceptable to God, and so to regard that day, for he that regardeth not that day, will never be prepared for it.

The next reason is, the love of Christ which he has poured out upon thee, and shed abroad upon thy heart by the Holy Ghost; but thou wilt not feel this love, unless thou judgest, and beest persuaded in thy heart that the death of the Son is as effectual for thee as if thou hadst died that death thyself; and that the obedience of Christ to the Father unto the death of the cross, it is as well thine, as if thou hadst done it thyself, to have a true and undoubted right to all the promises of salvation made in Christ, and to all his merits; and thou must believe that there is no condemnation to thee, because thou art in Christ.

But to return, how should ye live? Now, would ye know this? Ye had all need to know it, for ye shall all be made manifest before God, and all your consciences shall be harled out bare and naked before his tribunal; then ye that have lived well shall not be ashamed, for ye shall rise to the resurrection of life, but the wicked shall rise to the resurrection of condemnation. Would ye know, then, how ye should live well, and honour God in this life, that hereafter ye may get eternal life? I told you them already, and yet I would ye remember them.

First, Ye must be "filled with the knowledge of his will, in all wisdom and spiritual understanding," and therefore ye had need to pray for the Spirit, who will teach you all things. That is the first.

The *second*, Ye must keep ay the love of God in your heart, and this shall make you ready to do every good work, and to please God in all things.

Thirdly, Ye must obey God in eschewing the evil that he forbids, and in doing the good that he command you. Now, to help thee, thou must have an honest and upright heart; for thou art a perfect Christian, if thy heart be upright; there is no other perfection that God requires of thee in this life.

Fourthly, Ye must be diligent in the service of God, ye must set yourself apart for the work of God, and thou must think, that for no other thing thou wast sent into the world, but for to serve him. Ye heard of the diligent man, he is made rich, but the sluggard lusts, and his soul has nought:" Therefore ye must not sit down here; ye must ay be running, suppose thou wert ravished to the third heavens, and suppose thou sawest things that were impossible for to utter, as Paul did; yet thou must not sit down there, but thou must go on forward, and run thy race with patience till thou winest to the mark.

Fifthly, Ye must have perseverance; and therefore ye must take the yoke of Christ upon your shoulders, and ye must say, let others think what they will, I shall think thy yoke sweet to my soul, and far be it from me, that I should think it a burden to me to study to please thee in all things; but although I may well tell you out of his word, how you should please God, without faith and practice, my telling you of it will do you no good.

Last of all, Ye must have meekness of heart, and lowliness of mind, that God's word may be a law to you to meditate on both day and night: There are many of you when ye lie down and when ye rise, I wot not if ye have so much as a cogitation to think with yourself, what is this that I am doing? Is it agreeable to the will of God? Have I a warrant for it out of the word? Well, I had need to look to the word, that I may make it the only rule of my life all the day long: therefore ye must take good heed, lest there be an evil heart in any of you to depart away from the living God; and being delivered out of the hands of our enemies, we should serve him without fear." Now, for the rule of this, we must understand the commands; for that is the only way to serve him, even to keep his commands. Some of you, ye think, serve God well enough, if ye pray morning and evening to him; some of you think it enough, if ye get some sorrow for sin all your days; some think it enough if they get any tears at any time: but all this is not that Christianity that will make you shine as stars for ever and ever; but ye must have respect to all the commands, as David had, from the first to the last. And then, in the

First command, let this be your meditation, thou, O Lord, art my God who broughtest me from hell, and from the bondage of sin, and from the slavery of Satan; therefore I will not have another God besides thee; this is the service that he craves, this is glory to say, thou art my God, and thou broughtest me from hell, and thou hast an eternity of joy prepared in heaven for me; therefore, for my part, I will choose no other God but thee only, and I will have no other besides thee; and I will delight only to know thee, to reverence thee, to fear thee, to love thee, to fill my soul with thee, to set my heart on thee, to walk before thee, and thou shalt be all in all to me; away with all joy and delight, but that which I have in the Lord my God; he is the Lord my God, and therefore I will have none but him: so look when you will, ye shall not start another in my heart. Now, when thou hast gotten this, thou must not rest there; but thou must go forward to the

Second command, and there thou wilt say, Lord, I know that thou art a strong, and a mighty, and a jealous God, and thou wilt have me to give obedience to thy commands; therefore I will love thee, and keep thy commands, that I may find mercy to the thousand generation. I know that I should hear thy voice diligently, I know I should pray continually, I know that I should be thankful in all things, and I should fill my mouth with thy praises, and I know that I should talk of thee to others, and I know I should confess my way to thee, and I should confess thy truth to all that calls it in question, and I know this is the worship thou cravest to be done to thee in spirit and truth; therefore, next unto thyself, thy worship shall have place. Now, ye may not rest there either; but ye must go through the whole points of the law, until ye may say with David, Psal. cxix. 97. " O Lord, how love I thy law! Psal. cxix. 10. It is sweeter to me than honey, and the honey-comb;" and this will not be impossible to thee, for thou wilt get all this by faith; therefore reach up your hand to that blood, and ye shall get that sweet Spirit sent down to you, who shall open all these laws, and write them all in your hearts.

Then go to the *third* command, and say, Lord, thy name is precious, and dear to me, thy name is glorious in my sight; therefore in my calling and conversation, this shall be the only thing that I shall aim at, to set forth thy blessed name; so that whether I eat or drink, I shall labour to shoot at the glory of my God, that his blessed name be not dishonoured, neither by myself nor by others, so far as I can stay them; and I shall help so far as in me lies, that the name of God may be feared and reverenced by all.

I will go no further at this time than these three commands, and they should guide you daily, and in them ye should see God continually, and set him before your eyes, that daily his worship may be thy only delight, and that his name and glory be the only aim that thou shoots at in thy life and conversation.

Now, would ye do this, this should make you shine as bright buring lamps to the world; and men seeing your good works, should glorify God. O what glory should this bring to God, and what unspeakable joy and peace to thy own soul! Thy conversation should be in heaven: then the blessing of God should be multiplied on thee, and thy seed after thee; then, the worship, of God should be easy to you, and the yoke of Christ should be the sweetest yoke that ever ye bare, and your labour in the service of God should not be grievous to you. Now, will ye do this, my hearts, and I assure you, ye shall find by experience, that it is not in vain to serve God. The Lord grant that ye may do it, for Christ's sake; to whom with the Father and Holy Spirit, be all praise, for ever and ever.

SERMON XXXI.

UPON DIVERS POINTS OF RELIGION.

Exodus xx. 4, 5, 6.

Thou shalt not make unto thee any graven image, or any likeness of any thing that is in heaven above, or that is in the earth beneath, or that is in the water under the earth. Thou shalt not bow down thyself to them, nor serve them: for I the Lord thy God, am a jealous God, visiting the iniquity of the fathers upon the children, unto the third and fourth generation of them that hate me: and shewing mercy unto thousands of them that love me and keep my commandments.

THE thing that we left off at, was, the pointing out of the means and exercise which God has, out of his word, commanded you to be occupied in, while ye are in your pilgrimage, and during your absence from the Lord and your head; to the which means God has promised a blessing, if ye use them; and also he has denounced a curse upon them that neglect them: and because there is no place in scripture points out these means so well as the second command, therefore I have chosen this place to the same purpose; and this is the difference betwixt the first and second command; the first craves the presence of God to be in thy soul; the second points out the means how thou mayest entertain his presence in thy soul, and without the which it is not possible for thee to keep the presence of God with thee. As for your obedience to the first command, your light, your life, your liberty, stands in it; that is, in your blessed conjunction and sweet fellowship with one God in three person, Father, Son, and Holy Ghost; your understanding to be filled with the knowledge of God, in all wisdom and spiritual understanding; your

memories to be filled with the remembrance of his
love, and favour, and kindness, and presence, above all
things; your will to be subject and obedient to his
will in all things; your heart and all the affections
thereof to be filled with fear and love, and with reverence and estimation, with delight in him, and humility. This command has never been obeyed by any
on the earth, but by Jesus allenarly; and this command shall be then perfect, when God shall be all in
all to you; that is, when God shall be all thy light, all
thy life, all thy joy and rejoicing, all thy freedom and
liberty; and because this is the thing that ye are all to
aim at, even that blessed communion with your God,
(for wo is to the soul that wants this communion and
conjunction with God, for where wilt thou get light,
and joy, and liberty, but from him who is light and life
itself?) Therefore thou wilt never get a fill of the presence of God until thou seest him face to face. This
made David to say, Psal. xvii. 15. " when I shall rise
out of the grave then shall I be filled with thy pleasure
for evermore." And this is the goodness of our God,
that not only has he given us a command, that we
should have the presence of himself, but also he has
prescribed such and such means whereby thou mayest
get his presence; and when thou hast gotten it thou
mayest entertain and keep it with thee. Therefore in
the second command he forbids to make any graven
image; under which is understood all the devices of
man, that he would thereby pretend to cause thee to
seek the presence of God; for no invention of men
and angels can further us in this spiritual conjunction
and communion with our God, but only the means
which he has appointed in his word; therefore he forbids to make or devise any such thing. Then,
next, he forbids to bow down or worship it, after it is
made.

Thirdly, He sets down the reasons of these words,
" for I am the Lord thy God, I am a jealous God;"
therefore thou must do all I bid thee do, and thou
must be subject to my command, and to no other's,

for I am married unto thee, therefore if thou dost otherwise than I command thee, thou wilt commit a double idolatry ; the one against the first command, in setting up any thing in thy heart, but me, and any thing that thou lovest more, reverencest more, fearest more, obeyest more than me, thou settest that up in thy heart as a god to thee : And when thou wouldst go about to serve or pleasure me, the Lord thy God, after another way than I have commanded, then thou breakest the bond of marriage which was knit up betwixt me and thee ; for this cause he says, *I am a jealous God :* that is, I cannot bear with it that thou shouldst serve me another way than I have commanded thee in my word.

And, *last* of all, he threatens a judgment against them that will not use the right means, or will but devise means of their own ; and he pronounces a blessing upon them that use the lawful means, for he takes it as a token of love to him ; therefore he says, " visiting the sins of the fathers upon the children," (take heed) there is never one of you but ye will think this a sin, to have another god in your heart ; but ye see not all that this is a sin, to use the means which either men of their own hearts bid you do to serve God by them, whereof ye have no warrant out of the word of God, and yet ye see that sundry have been punished, because they did the thing which was not lawful for them to do in their persons, and yet lawful for others having the calling ; as ye may see in Aaron's sons, who thought it no sin to bring in a strange fire in the tabernacle to burn incense therewith, yet the judgment of God fell on them in their very service, Levit. x. 1. likewise Uzzah put his hand to the ark, when it was like to fall, suppose he did it for the zeal he had to the glory of God ; yet because he wanted a calling of God, the judgment of God came upon him, and he fell down dead : so in all your doings when ye are reproved for that which is wrong, this is a common word in your mouths, our minds are good : but your minds are not good without understanding ; for if thou servest God without the understanding of his commands, that is a breach of the covenant betwixt thee and him, and he will punish it, "visiting the iniquities of the fathers upon the children," and this sin amongst the rest: many will not think that God will visit such an iniquity, as when men are serving God after their own phantasy; but ye may see the contrary here, and may see that God, who has contracted such a large law within so short bounds, nevertheless he is so large in setting down the second command, what in forbidding; what in informing, what in threatening, what in promising; and all because he knew well that a word would not persuade to obey that his command; therefore he says, "thou shalt not make to thyself any graven image;" that is, thou shalt not invent a mean of thy own to serve the Lord thy God. Again he says, "thou shalt not bow down to it;" that is, thou shalt not use the means invented by thyself, or by any others after their phantasy, when it is invented. What more? "for I am the Lord thy God, I am a jealous God;" therefore I will know when thou committest idolatry, and fallest away from me, following thy own phantasy, and doing after the manner of other nations; and now, seeing, I know it, I will not bear with it, but I will punish it: What more? "visiting the iniquities;" it is an iniquity to serve God otherwise than he hath himself commanded: What more? "of the fathers upon the children unto the third and fourth generation;" I will visit the iniquity not only upon thyself, but upon the third and fourth generation that comes out of thy bowels, and the fourth generation shall pay for it. And lest they should have said, Lord, thou wilt not punish us who have a heart to serve thee, not as thou commandest us, for we love thee; therefore he says, "of them that hate me;" as if he would say, no, no, I count that no love, however your intent be, thou hatest me that servest me not according to my own commanded ordinances. Nadab and Abihu, Saul and Uzzah, thought that they loved the Lord, but they hated him, because they did not according to his ordinances: What more? "shewing mercy unto thousands of them that love me and keep my commands;" here he tells what recompence of reward the use of the means of the worship of God shall have joined with it; *shewing mercy*, that is, thou shall get thy miseries pitied, thou shalt get thy sins pardoned, and thou shall get the blindness and hardness of thy heart removed, thou shall have free mercy, not only to thyself, but also to the thousand generation that comes of thee; he says, "of them that love me and keep my commands;" the keeping of the second command is a token of thy love towards God, as the breaking of it is a sign of thy hatred of God: why? *first*, Because it is the command of God: *next*, Because there is set down the duties that thy husband requires of thee his married wife; and, 3*dly*, Because it is a trial of thy love toward him, for as thou lovest him, so wilt thou be careful to use all the means whereby thou mayest entertain him. Now, for this cause I have expounded the second command, to see if this mean, and by it ye may be in readiness to hear the means of God's worship which I am to speak of to you. Are ye ready then? And may ye say, speak, Lord, for lo thy servant hears? And are ye ready to hear the means how ye may get a fill of the presence of God in this life, and how ye may be persuaded that ye shall get mercy in that day and for evermore? Hear them now, that ye may live well, and when thou diest thou mayest say, Lord, I was ready to use all the means of thy service with the strength of my heart and integrity, while I had my health, suppose not in perfection, yet in the honesty of my heart; the same shall be imputed to thee as a perfect obedience to all the commands. Would ye know, then, what are these means that ye should use, and there are more than one or two of them?

First, There is the public worship of God, in hearing of the law and gospel preached and proclaimed to you in this ministry, and in joining thyself by consent to the public worship of God, in the public congregation, by saying *Amen* to the public prayers of the saints of God, and in reaching out thy hands and taking to thyself the seals and sacraments of the visible covenant of God, and in consenting to the censures of the kirk, and giving place to the keys of the kingdom of heaven; these are the public means of the worship of God, as also public fasts and thanksgiving: therefore this is one of the means we are commanded to use, even to come out, as it were in the open fields, and to avow before the world, that thou wilt join thyself with the members of Christ, and " thou wilt take the cup of salvation, and pay thy vows among the rest," Psal. cxxvi. 18. for there are many of them to be put together in one cup, and this is one of the means whereby thou mayest fill thy understanding, thy memory, thy will, and all the corners of thy heart, with the presence of God; therefore if ye love him by hearing his word, and as long as ye live be partakers of the fellowship of his saints; that ye may say with David, " one thing have I desired of the Lord, and that I will require, that I may dwell in the house of the Lord, all the days of my life, to behold the beauty of the Lord, and to visit his temple, Psal. xxvii. 4. How amiable are thy tabernacles, O Lord of hosts! my soul longeth and fainteth for the courts of the Lord, for my heart and flesh rejoices in the living God. For a day in thy courts is better than a thousand elsewhere: I had rather be a door-keeper in the house of my God, than dwell in the tabernacles of wickedness," Psal. lxxxiv. 1, 2, 10. And when thou diest, then thou mayest say to thy bairns, I loved the Lord, and delighted in all the means of his worship, morning and evening: I will be filled with his presence, and I was blessed in my calling, and I drank of the rivers of the waters of life; and I was filled with the fat things of the Lord's own house; therefore I beseech you to do the same, and ye shall find a blessing as I did.

Now this *second command* has more yet than these public means which you may use with the rest of the saints in the midst of the congregation with thy brethren; it has these privy means, which must be done every day with thy calling, in the day thou wilt be either in thy family with thy wife, and bairns, and servants, or else thou wilt be alone, or else ye will be with other company when ye are in your families and how ye ought to behave yourselves in your families. I beseech as many of you as make conscience of the worship of God, that ye use the private means in your house, at the least morning and evening every day; I wot well some of you has found the blessing of God there in your families. And how you ought to behave yourselves in your families all the rest of the day, even do as Solomon did when others see that comely order in your house, they may say, "happy are thy men, and happy are thy servants that stand here before thee, and hear thy wisdom, blessed be the Lord thy God that loved thee," and gave thee a house, and set thee over a family, and that your own servants may say, well were we, if I could get leave to stand at my master's table, that I might hear the wisdom and gracious words that come out of his mouth. And ye that are women and mistresses, let the words of grace be in your mouth, and in your lips, like threads of scarlet, " that ye may open your mouths with wisdom, and the law of grace may be in your hearts and tongues." Let this be your exercise when ye are in your family. Next, again, when ye are in company, confess your sins one to another; exhort one another, rebuke, instruct, comfort one another, and ay be doing some good in whatsoever company thou beest or comest in. And, *last of all*, when thou art alone, read the word of God; for blessed is he that reads the words of this book and does them. What more? *Pray continually*, and pray in the Spirit with fervency, pray for all men. What more? Confess your sins before God, see them, and detest them, and hate them. What more? Be thankful in all things. What more? Watch continually, that in all things ye do, ye take heed to your heart, take heed to your mouth, take heed to your feet, that they slip not in any point of your duty. What more? Meditate upon the word and works of God; muse upon your own misery, and muse upon the Lord's mercy: meditate upon the law, and meditate upon the gospel; think upon your fall in Adam, and think upon your rising again in Christ. What more? "Put on the whole armour of God; gird your loins with verity, put on the breast-plate of righteousness, shoe your feet with the preparation of the gospel of Christ, cover your head with the helmet of salvation; and, above all things, take to you the shield of faith, that is able to quench all the fiery darts of the devil; and take the sword of the Spirit, which is the word of God." Put on all this armour, and stand armed all the day long, and lie down with it at even, and sleep with it all night. What more? *Last of all*, Mark with yourself every night before ye come to your bed, the experiences of God's mercy that ye find every day, who, as a husband, sends love tokens to you every day; even as a natural man, being a-field from his wife, he sends now and then love tokens to her, to put her in remembrance of him; she will take them and put them up in her chest; suppose they be not meikle worth, she will keep them there, because she loveth him that sent them; so should ye do, for the Lord your loving husband sends love tokens to you every day, to put you in remembrance of him, and to see what estimation ye have of them for his sake. Should ye not receive them with thankfulness, and put them up in your hearts, and keep them there for his sake that sent them? Now, these are the means that every one of you must use, if ye would have the presence of God filling your hearts, and as ye would find mercy to your souls, and as ye would leave a blessing to your children behind you, for thereby ye may make a fair testament; and if ye must leave a fair legacy to your children, thou mayest proclaim to them the whole promises of God made in the blood of Jesus Christ. I say no more, but unto this Lord Jesus, with the Father, and with the Holy Ghost, be all praise for now and ever. *Amen.*

SERMON XXXII.

UPON DIVERS POINTS OF RELIGION.

Exodus xx. 4, 5, 6.

Thou shalt not make unto thee any graven image, &c.

Deut. xii. 18.

But thou must eat them before the Lord thy God in the place which the Lord thy God shall choose, thou, thy son, and thy daughter, and thy man-servant, and thy maid-servant, and the Levite which is within thy gates: And thou shalt rejoice before the Lord thy God, in all that thou puttest thy hands unto.

WE remember whereat we left in the morning; the thing that we should principally esteem of, it is, the continual presence of God in our hearts, the keeping of his love, his joy, his peace, his fear, and his light; for therein stands our happiness and our life; for where the Lord is, there is life and liberty, and comfort; and therefore the Lord has provided all the means that we may use in his worship, and set them down in his word, that may lead us to this happy communion, and keep us in the fruition and possession of the presence of God; yea, he has given thee the free use of them all, that in his life we may find life, and by them we may be daily growing up in that life.

The first is set down in the first command, the rest in the second command; wherein ye heard, that not only it is a sin to have another God, and so to grieve him, but also it is a sin if ye grieve him, because ye will not serve him as he commanded you; and therefore the very contempt of the means whereby we should come to a communion with God, is a token that thou hatest him; and the best trial of thy love is the diligent use of the means of his worship; and therefore the Lord has promised a blessing, not only to them that use these means, but also to the third generation, and thousands that shall come after them. What know I, if ye have been using the means since ye heard them; it is a fearful thing, that the devil should get such a mastery over men and womens souls, that there are not many of you that heard this in the morning, that ever have done so much as once thought upon it sinsyne. Shall not that account of you one day be sought? O! shall not this your beginning in religion fail, if ye be but hearers only, and not doers of the word? There needed not so oft repeating of them if ye were delighted in them, or the love of God in your heart: And where is the practice and the doing of the will of God? All the preaching in the world will do no good, for it is only the doing the word that can do it, and keep it only in thy heart.

What these means were I told you in the morning, and now I tell you them over again: there is first, the public worship in the hearing of the word of God, and receiving the sacraments, fasting, and solemn thanksgiving, and exercise of discipline: Some of you make conscience of this, but I fear ye do it, not with preparation and with a holy disposition; for when ye present your bodies here, your hearts are away, and when ye enter into the house of God, ye take not heed to your feet. But I leave the public, and come to the private, without the which the public will do no good to you; therefore as many as would have the blessing of God multiplied upon you in the word and sacraments, I request you, that ye would make conscience of the use of the private worship of God. The first of these private means is watching, and standing continually over your heart, taking heed that the devil creep not in, and bereave thee of this, that thou canst not say, God is my delight, my joy, my love, my fear, my reverence and my crown. This watching is so needful, and therefore is so oft commanded in the gospel, ye have it in Matth. xxvi. 42. "Watch ye therefore, for ye know not at what hour the master cometh." Ye have it again in Matth. xxiv. 41. "Watch and pray, that ye enter not into temptation." Ye have it in Mark xiii. 35. "Watch therefore, for ye know not at what hour the master of the house cometh, at midnight, or at cock-crowing, or in the dawning, lest if he come suddenly he find you sleeping; and these things that I say to you, I say unto all, watch." Ye have it in Acts xx. 31. "Therefore watch, and remember." Ye have it in 1 Thess. v. 6. "Therefore let us not sleep as others do, but let us watch and be sober. For they sleep, sleep in the night; and they that are drunken, are drunken in the night." Ye have it in 1 Pet. iv. 7. "Be ye therefore sober and watch unto prayer." Ye have it in Rev. xvi. 15. "Behold I come as a thief in the night. Blessed is he that watcheth and keeps his garments clean, lest he walk naked, and men see his filthiness." What means this, that the Lord in his scripture so oft commands and commends this point of religion, watching? Because without watching it is impossible to keep thee out of the hands of the devil, it is not possible that thou canst pray continually, and be thankful in all things, and use the rest of the means, without watching. But how many of you have come to this point of religion, of a continual watching over your hearts? But rather ye cast up the door of your heart open to the devil to come in at every occasion, and so ye give place to every temptation that he casts in your way; therefore that is the cause that ye have so great difficulty in the worship of God, and his service is such a burden on you, even because ye have let your heart loose all the day long, and ye have not watched over all your ways. So then, if ye would make progress in religion, ye must watch and take heed to your hearts; for the devil watches continually about you, and there is no way to keep you out of the paws of that devouring lion, but by continual watching over thyself; therefore the Lord says, *watch and pray that ye enter not into temptation.* Now, because ye have not had the glory of God, and your own salvation as the principal care of your souls; therefore ye have not watched over your hearts so carefully as ye ought to have done; therefore except the love of the glory of God, and of your own salvation in Jesus Christ, be laid in the ground of thy soul, thou wouldst never make count to watch and pray continually; so if nothing will move thee to watch, let this love of the glory of God move thee to watch, and constrain thee to watch earnestly, in all places, and at all times, and in all companies. For the want of this watching causes great evil; and this watching is so uncouth to you, that, except in the set hours in morning and evening, I true ye fling your hearts loose to the devil all the day long; and therefore ye have acquainted your heart with such a ranging and following the world, and the pleasures thereof; and now, when ye would gather it up again, and bring it up before the Lord, it is so hard a thing for you to do it: Therefore, there is a trial of your love to God in watching over your hearts continually, that neither the love of God be taken from you by violence, nor yet that the serpent get leave to creep in. I leave it to your own consciences, to try how far every one of you is behind in this point; I would think ye had learned a great lesson in religion, if ye could watch over your hearts all the day long, and all the night also. Remember what Christ says in Luke xxi. 36. " Watch therefore, and pray continually, that ye may be counted worthy to escape all these things that shall come to pass, and that ye may stand before the Son of man. Blessed is he that watcheth and keepeth his garments clean." And there is no way to keep Christ as a garment on thee, but only by watching. So, I say, if there were no more learned at this time, but this one lesson of watching and praying continually, it were well; if there were not one hour in all the day, but thou mayest be saying, Lord, art thou in this action? If this were learned, I would think all my day's work well spent. And this is the cause that men and women make so little progress in Christianity, even because there is so little required of watching.

Now, with this watching join meditation; set your heart apart, and muse upon your own misery, and meditate upon the blood of Christ who has redeemed thee; meditate upon thy manifold sins, and upon the infinite mercy of God; meditate upon his works, and upon his words, and upon his promises, and meditate upon his threatenings, meditate upon his corrections, and meditate upon his judgments: this must be thy exercise when thou art alone, and when thou art among company; be ay doing good, or receiving good, or staying evil; therefore if ye would do this, your heart must ay be in heaven; then your spiritual armour must be put on, and ye must stand armed with it both to fight and resist: then mark your experiences of the mercies of God shown to you daily; and when thou hast found the blessing of God, either in meditation and prayer, or in thanksgiving, or in hearing the word, let this be the mean to cause you to return to the means; that is, the reading of the scripture to your families when ye have leisure, then your praying continually, your thanksgiving in all things; for there should never be a benefit received of God, but it should constrain thy love towards him to grow, and it should stir up thy desire in thee to proclaim the goodness and loving kindness of God in all places that thou comest in; then endeavour to please him in every thing, and a zeal to every good work; then the confession of your sins daily, with accusing, convicting, and condemning of yourselves, worthy of this death; and the sins whereof thou convictest thyself, and condemnest thyself, see that thou abhor, detest, and eschew them, and think of them no otherwise, than of those sins that brought down the Son of God from heaven, and made him die for thee. But some of you will say, when I go to meditate, I want matter whereupon. But I answer thee, wilt thou look to thy own heart, and how then canst thou want matter enough? But yet thou wilt say, my heart is full of reveries, that I cannot wait upon it. I answer, there is no marvel, seeing thou lettest thy heart to loose, and wouldst open it to the devil and his temptations, that they may enter in; but if thou wouldst watch thy heart, and give no place to reveries, which are nothing else but temptations of Satan, and the suggestions of the devil cast in thy heart, to hinder thy exercise of the worship of God: Therefore in that case, "resist the devil, and he will flee from you; and draw near to God, and he will draw near to thee." Now, I will say no more at this time; and I beseech God, of his infinite mercy, to grant you this grace, that ye may use the means of the worship of God, both public and private to the honour of Jesus Christ, and the comfort of your souls: To whom, with the Father and the Spirit, be all praise. *Amen.*

SERMON XXXIII.

UPON THE FREEDOM OF THE SAINTS.

Luke i. 74, 75.

That he would grant unto us, that we being delivered out of the hands of our enemies, might serve him without fear, in holiness and righteousness before him, all the days of our life.

WE ask the blessing of God, and the multiplication of his Spirit to be conveyed with his word, in every one of your hearts, to the use of these means appointed by himself, for the entertaining of his presence in our souls. Now, for the understanding of this, ye shall wit, that this is Zacharias's prophecy, which he prophesied after that he was strucken dumb for the space of three quarters of a year, because of his incredulity. Now, when as the child is born, and he is to be circumcised, his tongue is loosed, and, being filled with the Holy Ghost, he utters this prophecy; wherein, first he breaks forth into a thanksgiving to God for keeping of his promise, and sending his Son to redeem his lost people; and next, he tells you to what end this was done, to wit, " that we being delivered out of the hands of our enemies, might serve him without fear all the days of our life, in righteousness and holiness before him." Now, to come to the purpose, I will first let you see how this depends upon the former things spoken.

Secondly, How far we are come, and what we are to handle; and then I will speak a word or two of this shortly.

There have been four things taught you for leading of a godly and Christian conversation, the understanding and practice of them all is so needful, that ye must do them, if ye would glorify God here, and have your part of eternal life hereafter; ye must both know them and do them, or else all the labour ye take in religion will be in vain.

First, Ye must have that saving faith laying hold on salvation, which was sealed, promised, and shown, and ratified, conquest and purchased by that blood of Jesus Christ; and this is the foundation and rock that ye must build your house upon, if ye would have it standing, both in this world and in the world to come; and this is the rock whereupon not only ye must build your repentance, but also your salvation, and without the which all religion is in vain; for if thou buildest not upon this ground, all that thou buildest will fall down, "and another foundation can no man lay than that which is laid," which is Jesus Christ apprehended by faith: this must be the ground whereupon thou must build thy salvation; for all is but lost labour that thou hast spent in religion, if thou beest yet halting between two, and if thou hast not gotten thyself fast rooted and grounded in Christ, that thou mayest cry a defiance to hell, to death, to the grave, and all the rest of thy enemies, that thou mayest say, I have gotten salvation in the blood of Jesus, and subscribed to my conscience by his own Spirit: this must be the first thing that ye must have, before ye can serve God in your Christian life and conversation, and should serve him without fear; and therefore ye have here, " that we being delivered from the hands of our enemies, should serve him without fear:" There will be no service to God, till first thou believest that God hath delivered thee out of the hands of the devil, of sin, of the justice of God, and of all thy enemies; there will be no service to God, except that first thou knowest that thou art made a freeman and burgess of that new Jerusalem; therefore this is the first ground that ye must first lay, the believing of your redemption, and deliverance out of the hands of all your enemies: I trow there is none of you that have laid this ground yet, therefore I beseech you begin and lay it now, for

Jesus Christ's sake. Why should ye be thrust back from him, when he comes in his great glory? And will he know any, think ye, but his own members of his own body, who have gripped unto him by faith? Will any win in into that new city, but such as come, having their garments washed in the blood of Jesus? Will there be peace in heaven as there is on earth, or in thy conscience, to any but to them to whom his blood has bought it, and they that have believed in it? Therefore, I say, begin and lay this, as the load-stone in thy heart, faith in the Lord Jesus.

Another ground, I told you, which was this, faith, not only to reach to the promises of salvation, and remission of thy sins, but also ye must believe all that is written in the word of God, in the law, and in the prophets, and in the New Testament; ye must believe all the commands of God; ye must believe all his threatenings, all his promises, both of this life and of that life to come; for the distrustful cares of the world, will soon cut thy heart, and cast thee into such uncertainties, that, unless thou believest the promises of God, it is not possible that ever thou canst keep thy peace with God: So, I say, thou must reach to all the promises of God, belonging to thee in this life. Art thou in trouble? Remember his promise, "call upon me in the day of trouble, and I will hear thee." Art thou in anxiety and perturbation, because thou canst not get the law of God written in thy heart? Remember his promise, "I will write my law in thy heart, and put my fear in thy inward parts, that thou mayest never depart from me." Art thou feared for want of perseverance, and that thou mayest not run thy race to the end? Remember his promise, "none of his sheep shall perish. I will be with you to the end of the world. I will send the Comforter, who, when he shall come, shall lead you into all truth." Thou must believe all the threatenings, and all the curses in the law, and this will make thee to account more of the blood of Jesus, who has freed thee from the curse, and has taken the hand-writing away, and nailed it upon the cross. Thou must believe, that if thou goest out of the way, thou shalt meet with briers and thorns in thy side, and with divers plagues and diseases, and manifold crosses and temptations; and this shall ay keep thy heart in fear; and thou art bound to believe all his threatenings, and all his curses, under no less pain than of an endless condemnation. It is no wonder that there is such looseness in religion, because these grounds are not laid surely in the hearts of men and women.

And *first*, Believe salvation; that thou mayest say, Lord, I am thine, and thou art mine, we are knit together with the bond of the Spirit, and nothing can separate us; and therefore whatever thou biddest me do, I will do it. Faith in these things would make you continually in God's house and family, that ye durst never look out at the door, except the blood of Christ were covering you. This is the *first ground* of religion.

The *second* thing I told you, was, the change of the heart, your renovation, or regeneration, or conversion, or new birth, or whatever ye will call it; it is all one. There must be a thorough alteration or change made in thy life and conversation; and this is the next ground ye must lay, repentance towards God; for to that end are ye clean, and washed by faith in that blood of Christ, who, " through the eternal Spirit of God, offered up himself without spot to God, even to purge your conscience from dead works, that ye may serve the living God :" for as long as there are monsters, and dragons, and devils dwelling in thy heart, and keeping the castle thereof peaceably, all thy religion will be in vain, until the strong man be dung out by a stranger; and therefore thou must have a purge put in thy heart, that may purge and make it clean for the Holy Ghost to dwell in it: ye must cast away the works of darkness, and put on the armour of light; ye must do as the prophet Isaiah says (Isa. i, 16, 17.) Wash you and make you clean, put away the evil of your works from before my eyes; cease to do evil, and learn to do good ; seek judgment, and relieve the oppressed ; and so judge the fatherless, and defend the widow ;" and so thy heart is made clean by faith.

Now *Thirdly*, Not only must ye make it clean, but also keep it clean ; now, therefore, ye must oft draw it out before the light of God's word, that ye may see what foul things are within thee, and that thou mayest be quit of them ; for it is not one purgation that will cleanse thee, but thou must have many purgations by that blood ; nor, it is not one drink that will do thy turn, but thou must be oft drinking of that blood ; because thou sinnest daily, and consequently thou defilest thy heart daily.

And *Fourthly*, and *last of all*, Ye must look into the law of God, and meditate thereon both day and night, and let it never depart from before your eyes. Upon these grounds thou must build thy house in God, and it shall not fall, and thou mayest lay stone upon stone, for God will dwell there ; and it is good building upon such a foundation : Now, on what must ye build a Christian conversation, a manner of living that may please God ; it stands thee hard in eschewing of evil and in doing of good ? I answer, thou that hast gotten eternal life begun in thee ; thou that believest all that is written in the law, and in the gospel ; thou that hast gotten a sweet drink of the blood of Jesus Christ, and thou that hast gotten that sweet Spirit, and that Holy Ghost comforting and entertaining thee, I am sure thou wilt not entertain an open enemy in thy heart to banish him out, and I am sure thou wilt do what in thee lies to entertain that good Spirit; and the only way to do it, is by eschewing evil and doing good. I shewed the good that ye should do, and the evil that ye should not do, and this is set down in the commands. Blyth may thy soul be to have thy hands filled with these good things, that the Lord in his word commands thee to have done.

The *last* thing I told you, was, the means that ye should use, the manner of living that God would have you to live, and the manner of life ye may get if ye will seek it, and it brings glory to God and joy to thy own soul ; forget not God's great glory, when thou, that wast before the servant of the devil, art now serving God ; thou that wast in the way to hell, art now in the way to heaven ; thou that wast lost in Adam, art now saved in Christ ; and will not that also bring great joy and peace to your soul ? Therefore I told you the variety of means God has given you, the which if ye will use, ye may serve him godlily.

And *first*, That glorious presence of God, in the public congregation, by the ministry of the word and sacraments, which he himself has reckoned out to you ; *there* the blood of the New Testament, or covenant, which he shed for the sins of many, *there* peace, *there* righteousness in that blood ; and *there* is all that thou wouldst have.

Next, He has ordained these private means of watching and praying continually ; a diligent and careful taking heed to thy heart, that it pass not the limits or bounds of God's law ; that meditation or musing upon spiritual or heavenly things, that thereby thou mayest set thy heart where Christ thy Lord is.

Thirdly, The whole armour of God, that ye should put on, and wear daily, " stand therefore and your loins girded about with verity, and having on the breast-plate of righteousness, and your feet shod with the preparation of the gospel ; above all things taking the shield of faith, wherewith ye may be able to quench all the fiery darts of the devil ; and take the helmit of salvation, and the sword of the spirit, which is the word of God ; and pray always with all manner of prayer and supplication, and watching thereunto with all perseverance, and supplication for all the saints." Ye must put on this armour, and never put it off again, and it shall make your heart like the heart of a lion, and thou shalt be a cup of poison, and as coals of fire, and as a brazen wall to all thy enemies ; for, as the apostle says, " the weapons of our warfare are not carnal but spiritual, and mighty, through God, to cast

down strong holds, casting down every imagination,
and every high thing that is exalted against God, or
his knowledge, and bringing into captivity every
thought to the obedience of Christ : and having ready
the vengeance against all disobedience, when your obedience is fulfilled." So there is no contrary point
dare resist, when thou art clad with the armour of
God. Then what experience of your own, that ye
may say, here I fell, here I rose again ; here I was
cast down, and here I was lifted up ; here I was troubled, and here I was comforted ; and when I could
do nothing myself alone, then I spoke to others, and
the word came no sooner out of my mouth, but as
soon the Lord came in the midst of us, and our hearts
warmed with the sense, that thou mayest say with
Jacob, " the Lord is here, and I was not aware of it."
Now, thy own experience will comfort thee much,
and especially thy former experience will stir thee up
and encourage thee, that if thou missest him in one
street, thou wilt seek him in another, and so find him.
And so, besides these, there is the private worship of
God in the family, as morning and evening prayer, and
conferring upon the word of God, and that comely
order in thy house. And I am sure ye that use this
mean, have found the blessing of God in it.

Then, *last of all*, That communion and fellowship
with the saints among yourselves, in exhorting, comforting, rebuking, and sharpening one another, that
thou mayest cause the very mouth of such as were
with thee, to bless thee when they are departed from
thee. These things would entertain the spiritual life
among you ; then confess your sins, arraign yourselves
before the tribunal of God, and there accuse, convict,
and condemn yourself; that God, who is faithful, may
forgive you ; and then be thankful in all things, and let
never the benefits of God slip out of your mind ;
these are the means appointed by God, the which if
ye will use, I am sure ye will find a blessing in joining them all together, and in making religion a journey, that " ye must gang from strength to strength,

till ye appear before the Lord in Zion." Can it be told what blessings should be given you, if ye walk upright before God, and live such a holy and Christian conversation, as ye heard in the first, and what was told you in the second command ; " I am a jealous God, visiting the iniquities of the fathers upon the children to the third and fourth generation of them that hate me, and shewing mercy," not only to thyself, but also " to the thousand generation to come after thee," if the world were to last so long. But yet ye will ask, is there not more to do ? Yes, there is yet more, there must be laid first the foundation of faith in the Son of God, and the believing all the truths of the law and of the gospel, in his promises and his threatenings, and in his mercies and judgments. Now, upon these thou must build thy new birth, and thereafter thy sanctification, and the purity of thy heart ; and then let it bring forth these fruits of repentance and of amendment of life, as the eschewing of evil, and the doing of good. Now, these are the helps and means ordained of God to further thee in the way of salvation, and to the kingdom of heaven, as I have already taught you them ; but there is such incredulity spouted in the hearts of men and women from the fall of Adam, that they will not believe the truth of God ; and there is such an inclination to idolatry and disobedience, that they cannot submit themselves to the yoke of Christ ; and the natural eye looks upon these things slenderly, and thinks ay that the use of them is but a weak help to bring us to the kingdom of heaven. But I say to thee that it is not so ; for the strength of these means being used with faith, is stronger than the very power of angels, or all the men of the world ; therefore it remains to tell you, that ye must practice this science every day : I have been learning you this science of religion, even such a science as there is not to be had in this world, such a science that the apostle counts but *all things dung* in respect of this science, which is no other thing but the excellent knowledge of Christ ; an excellent knowledge indeed, for it ex-

cels all other sciences that can be devised : And what
is this science ? Even a science to teach you how ye
shall turn to God, and save your souls, and how ye
shall glorify God in this world, and how ye shall get
endless glory in the life to come, how ye shall live well
here, and get eternal life hereafter : Is not this an excellent science ? Now, how ye shall practise it, " blessed are ye if ye know these things, and do them."
Now, as for the doing of them, as for the practice of
Christianity, through the whole course of your life,
thou shalt put on Christ, and carry him with thee continually wherever thou goest, whether thou beest at
home, or a-field, or in the city, or in the kirk, or in thy
calling; and when thy hands are filled with labours,
how thou shalt be rejoicing with the angels, and thy
heart in heaven where Christ thy head is. That is the
point to be taught you now, therefore judge ye whether ye had need of this or not ; and that this may have
some weight with you, I will let you see it here as it
is set down here in these words : I told you, before,
the meaning of this prophecy, and it was this, a thanksgiving to God, or that great benefit of our redemption accomplished by Christ, and a declaration of the
end wherefore we are delivered. But I come to the
words, *blessed be the Lord God of Israel;* that is the
first that the dumb man spoke after his tongue was
loosed, and he, filled with the Holy Ghost, *blessed be
God.* What was the ground of it ? *That salvation:*
Ay, if a man knew what it were with the glutton to be
tormented in hell for evermore, and then heard tell of
a Saviour and a Redeemer to be sent to the world, he
would say, from the bottom of his heart, *blessed be the
Lord God of Israel;* now, there is never one of you
but ye should be as thankful to God for the glad tidings of salvation offered unto you in the gospel, as if
ye had laid in hell these five thousand years, as Cain
has been now near five thousand years : And why ?
Because the Lord might have made you to have fallen
that same time that he fell, and in the same sin that he
fell in, for ye have the same seed of sin within you that

he had. "Because he has visited and redeemed his people;" that is the only matter of his rejoicing, and is the cause of this thanksgiving, the visiting and redeeming of his people; he had to rejoice and to be thankful for the receiving his tongue again; but he counts nothing of that in respect of salvation, neither was the one comparable to the other.

But I leave this, and come to the words read, wherein he tells the end wherefore the Lord sent a great blessing to Israel, which was, "that they being delivered out of the hands of their enemies, might serve him without fear:" These enemies are the devil, sin, hell, death, the grave, and all the rest: Then they are said to have hands that grip the heart of their prisoners, and so fast as man or angels cannot loose it; for it is the justice of God that grips the heart and soul of man severely; and that justice says, I shall feed upon thee for evermore in everlasting wrath; but when the blood of Christ comes, it says, sinner, I will loose thee, and thou shalt go free, "go in peace, thy sins are forgiven thee, sin no more." What is the end then of thy deliverance? *That thou mayest serve him without fear.* Mark here, without deliverance there will be no service to God, and thou who art redeemed and loosed from hell, thou wilt desire no more but thy master's service, and to be as a hired servant with the run-away son, and serve him without fear; for thou needest not to fear with a slavish fear, and therefore David says, Psal. xxvii. 1. "The Lord is my light and my salvation, of whom shall I be afraid? The Lord is the strength of my life, of whom shall I be afraid?" And the apostle says, Rom. viii. 13. "If God be on our side, who can be against us? It is Christ that justifies: Who can condemn us?" Who dare lay any thing to the charge of God's elect? Shall the Father do it? No; we have him to be our wisdom, and our justification, and sanctification, and redemption. Shall the Son do it? No; for he has given his precious blood for a ransom for our sins. Shall the angels do it? No; for they are reconciled to us by him that reconciled all things to

himself in heaven and earth. Shall the saints do it?
No; for they are our brethren in Christ, and redeemed with the same price from the same misery. Shall
the devil do it? No; for he is but a chained traitor, a
bound up thief, a naked enemy. Shall thy conscience
do it? No; for God has spoken peace to thy conscience. Shall the reprobate do it? No; for they shall
be made speechless, and shall not get leave to speak a
word for themselves, but shall be flung into hell; and
being bound hand and foot, shall be cast into utter
darkness, where there is weeping and gnashing of teeth.
So thou needest not fear to serve God, for there is no
cause of fear. Then he says, *for all the days of our
life.* Now, is the time of our serving, and hereafter
shall be the time of our reigning. Wilt thou postpone thy service till thou beest sick, or cast into prison, or stricken in age, on thy death-bed, and then
think to come to heaven? No, no; it is a wonder if
thou gettest leave to say, God be merciful to me, if
thou delayest thy serving of God till thy old age:
"Balaam said, Oh! that I might die the death of the
righteousness:" but because he never lived the life of
the righteous, therefore he died miserable; therefore
ye should begin to serve God in time, and ye should
continue and hold on, if ye would have the reward and
the crown, even to your life's end; and I will say
more to thee, thy service on earth shall aggrege thy
crown in heaven; therefore it should not be any pain
to any of you to serve God, for none of you shall serve
him in vain, and none of you shall faint nor weary in
the service of God, suppose ye live as long as Methusalem lived; and therefore ye should count long days
a precious thing; for so it is, or else God would never have put it in among the rest of his promises as a
blessing: this should make you never to think long;
for every day thou risest, thou should say, Blessed be
my Lord for this, that I have yet gotten this day granted me to serve thee in it. David says, "doubtless,
loving kindness and mercy shall follow me all the days
of my life, and I shall live a long season in the house

of my God." So well is the man or woman that gets many days to serve the Lord in his house with him. Now, I know thou that art the child of God, redemption will be more precious to thee, than so to think it overmeikle to serve God all the days of thy life for it; no, thou wilt say, it is too little to serve the Lord, with all my heart, all the days of my life, for that unspeakable benefit of my redemption; and therefore thou wilt not in thy heart set down proper times for to worship God in. So then, I have these two things to speak of.

First, That all the days of your life ye are bound to serve God, and that is but a little thing: For what is our life but as a weaver's shuttle, that being in at the one end is out at the other? And what is that to give God a short time to serve him, to get an eternal weight of glory.

The next point is, wherein we should serve God every day, and how ye shall walk before him in righteousness and holiness, and when thou risest every morning, thou mayest be in the presence of God all the day till the evening. The apostle says, *let our conversation be in heaven,* and so it should be. Now these are the two things which I have to tell you.

First, That all the days of your life ye should serve God without fear. Next, how ye should get a heart to serve him uprightly every day, and after what manner thou shalt behave thyself in the morning after thou wakens, and all the day in thy calling, and when thou art alone, and when thou art in company, and when thou liest down at even, that thou mayest have peace in thy conscience, and thou mayest lie down in that manner, as thou wert never to rise again quick, or as Christ were to come in the clouds ere the morning. But I leave these things until the next time; and I commend this which has been spoken to the grace of God in every one of your hearts, through his Son Jesus Christ: To whom be all praise for now and evermore. *Amen.*

SERMON XXXIV.

UPON THE FREEDOM OF THE SAINTS.

Luke i. 74, 75.

That he would grant unto us, that we being delivered out of the hands of our enemies, might serve him without fear, in holiness and righteousness before him, all the days of our life.

THERE were two things left at with you before. The one was, that all the days of our life should be a service to him, who has redeemed you out of hell, and delivered you out of the hands of your enemies.

The other was, after what manner every day of your life, so far as it is possible, should be spent and passed over, that peace may be kept between God and your souls. For this cause, I will read some places of scripture to confirm you, and give you some light in this. That place in Luke i. 74. ye heard it in the morning, and in the opening of it, ye heard a deliverance must be, before ye can do any service to God; for thou that art not instructed and taught in the mystery of thy redemption, and thou that findest not, in some measure, thy heart set at liberty, and the blood of Christ cleansing thy heart, thou canst never serve God without fear as thou oughtest to do; therefore ye that would have your hearts established in the service of God, ye must often meditate upon this, that the blood of the Son has ransomed your souls from hell, from death and from the justice of God; for so long as thou doubtest, so long as thou art halting between these two, whether Christ be thy Saviour or not, thou canst not thrive in religion, and so thy comfort lasts no longer than thy sense and feeling lasts; therefore I remember it is said, "Stand fast therefore in the liberty wherewith Christ has made you free ; be ye stedfast in the faith :" So if ye mint to serve God without fear, ye would ay keep faith in the Lord Jesus, and the hope of salvation in his blood ; for whenever ye let the ground of your faith go away, then thou hast no courage to serve the Lord thy God : This ye heard already, and it follows, how long should this service be? All the days of your life, and yet they are not many, and suppose they were many, yet what are they in recompence to eternal life? Jacob his old and long age, he called it but a *few days and evil.* I told you in the morning, that ye should not defer the service of God till the end of your days, but ye should say, with David, " Lord teach me to number my days, so that I may apply my heart to wisdom ;" and this is the only wisdom, that in all the days of thy life, thou settest thy heart to serve the Lord thy God. If any of you were to go a journey on a weighty matter that ye had on hand, ye would think it no small matter to tyne one day by the way ; even so here is your journey upon so weighty a matter as salvation and condemnation ; therefore ye should think a great matter to tyne one day in this your journey ; many indeed think to get a better time afterward to serve God, therefore I may pass by this day as I please ; but they are deceived, for every day has enough of its own to do ; therefore, why will ye cast over till the morrow the thing that ye should do to-day, seeing to-morrow has enough to do with itself? Forsooth, I see the children of this world wiser in their own generation than the children of light are ; because they take account of every day's labour, and look what they have done, and what they have to do ; but we are not so wise that lets one day come and another go: So I say, ye should not cast over the worship of God to the Sabbath day, or solemn days, but should worship God every day, and ye should take account of every day's service, and not cast all in a mass together. Now, we are all far behind in this; therefore I beseech you to establish your hearts more and more in this truth, that you are bound to serve God all the days of your life in holiness and righteousness; ye should not be profane at one hour in the day nor of the night before him: that is, thou shouldst present thy heart and thy life every day and every night, and every hour of the day; for it will never be well with thee till it be so. And what is the cause that thou art so careless to serve God, and bring glory to him, and comfort to thy own soul every day? What? Because thou rememberest not that thou art before God every day, and all the hours of the day. What would ye do, if every day ye were before men of authority? and suppose thou wert before the prince every day, would not the prince see what ye were doing before him every day? Now, ye will think this hard to do, to remember that God is always forenent you, and he is ay looking upon thy thoughts, thy words, and thy deeds; but wilt thou try it, and thou shalt find that yoke easy, and that burden light; for one day spent under the yoke of Christ, that is when thou endeavourest all the day long to please God in all things, and to keep a clean conscience towards God and man, suppose thou hast not done the thing thou art bound to do, yet this day being spent to God, shall be sweet and pleasant to thee.

Now, I will read another place of scripture, Heb. iii. 11. "So I sware in my wrath that they shall not enter into my rest:" In the sixth verse he bids, "hold fast the confidence, and the rejoicing of the hope firm unto the end." And to persuade them to do this, he brings in the exhortation of the Holy Ghost, saying, "to-day if ye will hear his voice, harden not your hearts." And then he brings in the example of their fathers in the wilderness, and lost their confidence and the rejoicing of their hope, when they tempted God and proved him, notwithstanding they saw his works forty years long; and then he tells what came of that, to wit, "the Lord was grieved with that generation, and said, they err in their hearts, and they have not known my ways; therefore I sware in my wrath that they shall not enter into my rest:" that is, they shall never enter into my rest : then he subjoins his own exhortation in the 12 verse, saying, *take heed, brethren*, (for if any of you saw a ship on the sea, perishing on a rock before your eyes, would ye not take heed to yourselves, that ye perish not likewise ?) Even so here, *lest at any time,* not only in the day, but any time in the day ; I know it will be hard to any of you, who have been strangers to God this long time, to take heed to yourselves every day, and all the hours of the day, because ye have never been acquainted with this ; but yet will ye acquaint yourselves with it, and be no longer strangers from the life of God, and ye will think it nothing ; if there be in any of you an evil heart, ye will think now, Lord, may I no time have an evil heart, not yet, this is a sweet yoke and easy to be born ; and what profit or pleasure wilt thou have in sin, when thou feelest the judgment of God upon thee ? And when thy heart is evil, what canst thou do but sin ? For tongue, and hands, and all will go wrong. *In any of you,* says he, for an evil heart may poison a thousand, and put them in company with it ; *and unfaithful*, for then comes the evil heart, whensoever thou lettest Christ go, and lettest the promises go, and when the devil comes in their stead. Now, I grant thou wilt not ay get Christ, but yet thou mayest have ay the promise in thy heart not to depart away from the living God. Why, nothing can hold thy heart upon God but faith ; and when thou losest faith, then thou departest away from the living God, and then thy life and thy sense will go. See ye not now what Christianity is ? Even a taking heed to your life at all times, that ye depart not from God. Trowest thou, that Christianity is the keeping of certain proper times and hours in the worship of God ? No, thou that art bought with the blood of Jesus, art bound to take heed to thy heart all the days of thy life. Now this follows very well, " but exhort one another while it is called to-day :" God would have you have such a love one to another, that when ye meet, your mouths may be filled with grace and consolation, " lest any of you be hardened through the deceitfulness of sin." What is the cause that induration comes so oft upon you? What? But because ye exhort not one another, therefore sin slips in and deceives you, and through custom of sin induration comes on; because it is written, 1 Pet. i. 16, 17. " Be ye holy, for I am holy. And if ye call on the Father, who, without respect of persons, judgeth according to every man's work, pass the time of your sojourneying here in fear. Forasmuch as Christ has suffered for us in the flesh, arm yourselves with the same mind; which is, he that has suffered in the flesh has ceased from sin," ch. iv. 1, 2. verses, he says, " that ye henceforth live as meikle time as remains," and God only knows how meikle time remains; and therefore it is God's will, that as meikle time as is left unspent, it should now be spent in the fear of God: For we should think the time that is already spent in vanity too meikle; and therefore we should labour to redeem mispent time; and, " we should not live after the flesh, but after the will of God." Now, this should not be burdensome unto you, for he that bids the weary and heavy laden come to him, he would be loath to burden with an unnecessary burden; so that the yoke of Christ is easy to the inner-man; and all that shall be burdened therewith, it is but the old man that thou art burdened with, that thou hast nothing to do with; for it must go to the grave, and turn dust there; that says, that the yoke of Christ is not a burden to thee. How many of you have entered on in your pilgrimage, and have been going on in your journey, and running your race as ye dought, but yet ye might have made further progress in Christianity than ye have? How shall ye spend the rest of your time, then, that yet remains? I will tell you shortly.

First, Your heart would ay be kept in a right order all the day long, or else all that ye do will not stand well with you. I remember what Solomon says, " ponder the paths of thy feet, and let all thy ways be ordered aright." Now how shalt thou order thy ways aright?

Take heed, *first*, it is said, "God delights to dwell in a humble heart; therefore thou must have thy heart humbled every day, and how shalt thou get that? I will tell thee, thou must look upon thy grossest sins every day, and see if they can humble thee. Again, thou must look in the law every day, and see how thou hast broken it, and how the curse of God is above thy head for sin; this made David say, Psal. li. "My sin is ever before me," and so should thou say. That is the first *to be humbled.*

Secondly, Thou must keep thy faith, if thou wouldst have Christ dwelling in thy heart, and look ay to the infallible truth of God, and the unchangeableness of his promise, and as long as Christ is dwelling in thy heart, thou shalt ay find a virtue coming from him, and thou shalt ay get new grace. That is the next, *be stedfast in the faith.*

Thirdly, Because our communion with God must be through Christ, therefore thou must endeavour that God be the only delight of thy soul every day; and then thy heart is in good order. But who has looked to these things? No, none I trow, or, at the least, very few have looked to them. So this is the third point, that the infinite majesty of God, in the Son, by the Father, be dwelling in thy heart, and that thou set thy whole delight on the presence of God. Now this will bring other two things.

First, It will bring fear, that thou darest not offend, because it will grieve him.

Secondly, It will bring love: Why shouldst thou not have loved him, who is love itself? And then this fear and love will make thee an armed man to resist evil, and make thee ready to please God in all things, and be zealous in every good work. What more? Because there is never an hour in all thy life, but God is loading thee with new benefits; therefore thou wilt be thankful to him in all things, and thou wilt rejoice to serve him in the truth of thy heart. What more? Because the heart is a deep thing, that it cannot be searched by man, for there will ay remain some evil in it, and some secret sins that thou seest not; therefore there would be continual prayer, and watching, and spiritual meditation, and many good thoughts would be sent up to heaven. If thou wouldst do these things, then mightest thou say, O! *there* is a new soul, and *there* the long white robes, and the fair linen garments washen in the blood of the Lamb, which the Spouse has given to his Bride; and therefore it is not wonderful that he call her beautiful; then this will make thee in all the companies thou comest in, either to do good, or receive good; this will make thee in thy calling careless, however it fall out; and in thy family this will make thee gracious and comely, and thou wilt be thankful to God that he has given thee a family, and wife, and children, and servants, and a house to be in. Then in the evening before thou goest to bed, thou wilt take a reckoning of all thy doings all the day, and see wherein thou hast failed, thou wilt resolve to mend it the next day. Now, I say no more, but will ye try yourselves with this one day, and ye shall find it the sweetest life that ever ye led in the world, even this Christian state of life. The Lord grant it to every one of you, for Christ his Son's sake: To whom, with the Father, and the holy Spirit, be all praise and glory, for now and ever.

SERMON XXXV.

UPON THE FREEDOM OF THE SAINTS.

Luke i. 74, 75.

That he would grant unto us, that we being delivered out of the hands of our enemies, might serve him without fear, in holiness and righteousness before him, all the days of our life.
And some other scriptures.

YE know what was behind, viz. after what manner ye should spend your life in doing the will of God; but I fear it be not far from many from saying in their hearts, suppose they speak it not with their mouths, " it is a vain thing to serve God :" and all souls, for the most part, have made a covenant with death and hell; and they think that the Lord is so far from them, that he cannot see them. I beseech God to have mercy upon you, and to waken your consciences, that ye may be persuaded that there is a day of the manifestation of your naked souls before the tribunal of God; but, for your instruction in this point, I will read some places of scripture; and, first, that of Gen. xvii. 1. " Abram was ninety and nine years old when the Lord appeared unto him, and said, I am all-sufficient, walk before me, and be upright." Abram was well stricken in years when he got this command, even fourscore and nineteen years; therefore if thou hadst but one year to live, it is good for thee to hear the word of the Lord, " I am God all-sufficient, walk before me;" it is true, he was walking before God before, yet not so straightly as he should have walked: therefore the Lord descends from heaven, and commands him to walk before him all the days of his life; and lest that men should think this too meikle to give all the days of their lives to walk before God, as if this were a thing impossible for men to do; therefore the Lord says, *I am all-sufficient;* so that when thou shalt look into thy own wants, thou shalt find in me whatsoever thou wantest. Is it wisdom, honour, riches, and length of days, righteousness, or whatever thou wouldst have in this world, or in the world to come? Thou shalt find it in this Lord, if thou walk before him. This walking is taken from a man going on in a journey, and has his eye bent upon the place he would be at; then this should learn us in all our life, in words, ways, and all our thoughts and deeds, we should cast our hearts in heaven, look up to him that looks down to thee; and this shall make thee look into thyself, and take order with all thy doings. Moreover, he says, *and be thou upright.* The heart of man is crooked by nature, and nothing can make it straight and even, but walking before God, and the looking upon the Lord continually. Now, this integrity and uprightness is a great thing, and this may bring thee great joy, when thou mayest say, this is in my heart, that in all things I would please God. Now follows the promise in the next verse, " And I will have my covenant between me and thee, and I will multiply thee exceedingly." So ye have fair promises and excellent prerogatives, and great privileges belonging to you that walk before God, and are upright in heart, and in his sight. And lest ye would think this impossible to walk before God, ye may see the example of it in Enoch, Gen. v. 14. for it is said, " Enoch walked before God, and he was no more seen ;" and the saints before have won to this, and the grace of God is able to make man to do it, and win to it; for God who has given thee his greatest thing, his own Son, how meikle more is he not able to give thee all things with him ? The apostle also, telling his own walking, says, " but this I confess unto thee, that after the way which they call heresy, so worship I the God of my fathers, believing all things which are written in the law, and in the prophets. So worship I the God of my fathers; but how, says he, believing all things that are written in the law, and in the prophets?" For there will be no worshipping of God without faith : I said before, your faith must reach to all things that are written in the law, and in the gospel ; for if the promises and threatenings be not both believed, there will be no walking before God ; therefore your faith should be as large as the word of God ; thou art bound to believe, that God is bound to write his law in thy heart ; as thou art bound to believe the remission of thy sins, so thou art bound to believe all the promises of God, how large soever they are ; therefore ay when ye read the word of God, or when ye hear it, ye should hear it, and read it with faith ; walk before me, saith the Lord. Ye see your conversation what it should be, even an adoration with faith and hope in thy soul and conscience in the divine majesty of an infinite God, and with an endeavour that in nothing thou defile thy conscience ; see that thy conscience never be made a party to thee, either in thy duty to God, nor in thy duty towards man. The apostle, speaking of his own conversation, and of the conversation of his fathers says, "And now I stand and am accused for the hope of the promise made of God unto our fathers, whereunto our twelve tribes, instantly serving God day and night, hope to come," Acts xxvi. 6, 7. Mark, they were serving God day and night. Ye see what is required of you, even the same that they did ; the scraps and bits of Christianity are not that instant serving of God that he craves of you, and that the saints gave before unto him. O! how few have yet given their heart thoroughly to serve God instantly, to serve God both day and night. Many think a little thing may serve the Lord, suppose he get not all thy heart ; but the Lord says, by Solomon, " My son give me thy heart," Prov. xxiii. 27. and though the heart be little worth, yet it is all that the Lord craves of thee ; my son, says he, I am thy father, and thou art my son, and I have given thee life and light, and all that thou hast thou hast it of me, and I have provided for thee an heritage

in heaven; and now, for all that which I have done to
thee, I desire no more of thee, but that thou mayest
give me thy heart, and I will give thee delight in my
ways; for thy eyes and all thy members will soon tire
of the service of God, if thou givest not thy heart to
God; and therefore he says, in the 17th verse, " Let
not thy heart be envious against sinners, but let it be
in the fear of the Lord continually," or else it is not
possible that thy heart can be kept in a right order;
and therefore, in another place he says, " keep thy
heart with all diligence." These places of scripture
would be kept in remembrance all the day long, " keep
thy heart with all diligence, for thereout comes all life."
The heart is the fountain of life, and if it be foul, all
the streams will be foul also: And a little after he says,
" ponder the paths of thy feet, and let all thy ways be
ordered aright;" thou shouldst not give a step, but
thou, Christian man, shouldst be looking where thou
art going, and thou shouldst ask at thy heart, what
way is this that I am in? Whether is it in the broad
way to destruction, or in the narrow way to life? For
indeed it is but a narrow road that tends to eternal life,
therefore the gate would ay be looked to; wherefore
he says, " ponder the paths of thy feet." Now, what
pains would ye ware on a Christian life? And it is all
well wared if thou considerest how dear it has cost,
and thou that art in Christ wilt think the time spent
too long in vain, and that thou hast been too long in
beginning to serve God. " Ponder the paths of thy
feet;" that is, turn not to the right nor to the left hand,
but keep thy feet from evil. Now, *last of all,* " My
son, keep thy father's commandments, and forsake not
thy mother's instructions, bind them always upon thy
heart, and tie them upon thy neck;" that is, let them
be chainzie to adorn thee. Now, what advantage shalt
thou have by this? It shall lead thee when thou walkest, wait for thee when thou sleepest, and when thou
wakest it shall be with thee; that is, begin thy journey
with it, and it shall never leave thee till thou beest at
thy journey's end; it shall watch for thee when thou

art sleeping, and thou shalt be continually under a sweet protection all the night over; and when thou awakest in the morning, it shall be ready to give thee counsel how thou shalt spend all the day following. Now, if ye would do this, what joy and consolation should ye have, what peace in your conscience both with God and man, and what a cheerful walking, and what a pleasant life mightest thou have. But I leave this. Ye see this sort of walking is commanded you, and that ye may be the more able to do this,

First, Ye would remember your sins daily, for to keep thee under, and to humble thee; therefore look that thy heart swell not.

Secondly, Ye must reach up your hand to Christ, and be ay eating his flesh, and drinking his blood daily, and the consideration of thy sins, and of the miserable state wherein thou standest through sin, will constrain thee to esteem more of his blood.

Thirdly, Look that in Christ thou grippest to that glorious majesty of the divine and infinite essence, that thy walking may be with God; for thou wilt find him in Christ, and as long as thou abidest in him, he will abide in thee, and if thou believest in him, he and his Father will come and dwell with thee.

Again, Let the fear of God be in thy heart continually, for this fear is the beginning of wisdom, and this fear will gar thee arm thyself against all temptations, that nothing enter into thy heart which may grieve the Lord, and thou wilt " adjure the daughters of Jerusalem, that they waken not thy beloved, who is in thy arms, until he please." Again, when thou wantest him, this will make thee rise out of thy bed to seek him, and when ye have found him, ye may love him, and ye may be ready to please him in every good work, and to keep a clear conscience towards God and towards man. Again, this will bring thee another thing; that is, to make thee with joy look upon all the creatures of God with the eye of faith, and to take all his benefits out of his hand with thanksgiving: then thou wilt see the necessity of the command of our

Lord, "watch and pray continually :" so thou wilt always let down the bucket to the fountain, and ay thou wilt be drawing out of him grace upon grace.

Now if ye would do this, it should make thee in all thy ways to have thy eye upon God, that when thou liest down thou wilt take a particular account of all thy bygone ways all the day bygone, and when thou risest thou wilt address thyself to the service of God all that day; and this shall make thee to have the less ado in the time of thy dying, that when thou rememberest thou put up an account of every day's labour to God, or ever thou dost go to thy bed; therefore thou hast the less ado now. If thou gettest a discharge before thou liest down, of every sin that thou hast committed all the day long; then thou mayest defy the devil, hell and the grave, and death, and the justice of God, for they can have nothing to lay to thy charge, seeing thy ransom is paid, and thou hast gotten a discharge through that blood, subscribed by the Spirit. Now, the Lord grant you this for Christ's sake; to whom, with the Father, and the Spirit, be all praise for now and ever.

SERMON XXXVI.

UPON THE FREEDOM OF THE SAINTS.

2 Corinthians vi. 3, 4.

But if our gospel be hid, it is hid to them that are lost: In whom the god of this world hath blinded the minds of them which believe not, lest the light of the glorious gospel of Christ, who is the image of God, should shine unto them.

THERE rests two things to inform every conscience of you, who mind to go forward to that heavenly kingdom : ye heard how ye should pass the time of your pilgrimage here, and what are the grounds ye should lay, whereupon ye may build your house, to wit :

Faith in the Lord Jesus, and in all the truths of God.

Secondly, A renewed and a clean heart, and a constant persevering in the worship of God unto the end.

Thirdly, What helps God has given you, ye heard them, and all the saints experience has found them to be the power of God to salvation.

Fourthly, Ye heard how ye should spend every day, and how ye should be resolved when ye lie down : even that when ye are lying down it may be a watchman over thee, all the night ; and when ye waken in the morning again, it may be your counsellor all the day long : Your faith must be holding a grip of the promise of salvation, and all the day long ye must be waiting for Christ's coming in the clouds, and the fear of God must always be before your hearts, and the love of God must constrain you to every good work, and ye must serve him without fear all the days of your life, and that his glory may be your principal care, and the only thing that ye shoot at. Now, this shall make you ready to please God in every thing, and set a watch over your heart and lips, that ye offend not God. I know ye will not get these things done in an instant, but yet ye must know them, and ye must strive to practise them ; and this glorious conversation, suppose ye cannot get it in perfection, yet if ye strive to attain it, this very striving of yours shall make you glorious in the sight of God, and it shall make others to glorify God, when they see that there is such a glorious power in the gospel, that it can save all that believe in it.

The two things, I say, remain to be spoke of are,

First, To let you know what impediments will be cast in your hearts by Satan, to hinder your course in Christianity.

And, next, to let you see what glorious prerogatives ye have, that if ye knew what were in the Lord's mind to give thee, thou wouldst run thy race with joy and consolation, and this would make thee with all boldness and constancy to persevere unto the end.

As for the first, I have chosen this place to open it up to you, and for the better understanding, I will repeat some things. In the chapter before, he is telling what a ministry he was put into, a ministry that gives life to a dead soul, a ministry that opens the eyes of the blind sinner unto the glorious image of the Son of God ; and he tells in the preceding verses, how he used his ministry. Now, in the third verse he answers an objection, for some might have said, if thy ministry be so glorious, what is the cause that it is hid from so many? He answers, " if our gospel be hid, it is hid to them that are lost," as if he would say, speer ye wherefore it is hid? I answer, if it be hid, it is hid to the man or woman that is ordained to perdition ; but if thou beest of the number of them that shall be saved, this gospel must shine in thy heart. Then, in the fourth verse, he tells what is the cause of it ; he says, " whom the god of this world has blinded the eyes and minds of these that are infidels, that the light of the glorious gospel of Christ should not shine unto them;" the god of this world, and not of the world to come ; this is a strange thing, that the devil is the god of them to whom the gospel is hid ; and yet it is true, for he is in them, and reigns and rules in them : This is a fearful thing that the devil reigns in as many of you upon whom the gospel has not shined, and he blinds thy eyes, that thou mayest not see the glory of God revealed in the gospel ; and there are two sorts of men and women in the world, he deals so with both the sorts after divers manners. Such as are not renewed, he strives to keep them so, that they never give their heart with their will to serve God ; and if he cannot hinder thy calling, he will lay impediments and stumbling blocks to hinder thy progress : Therefore such of you as were never renewed, and this gospel never shined on you, that ye have never seen your misery, nor the value of that blood, nor the hope of that glory, ye shall know that the devil stands in your gate to hinder you to see the way that ye are in, that ye may never see that endless misery whereunto ye are going, until the time ye fall into it : Such of you as are so, I know not how long ye will be so, but I leave you to the Lord : Only this I say unto you, rest not easy, see that ye take no rest till ye be sure that ye be in the compass of the blood of Jesus ; for the time of grace will not last long, therefore deprive not yourselves of endless glory for the pleasures of a short time : Why will any of you be shut out of the doors of heaven, and see others going in ? Wherefore ye should all take heed to yourselves, for it stands weighty upon you, and the devil blinds many of the minds of you, that ye should never look into that everlasting joy, not yet into that everlasting pain, until ye have lost the one, and fallen into the other ; therefore, I say, ye had need to take heed to yourselves : And here I charge you before God, and before his Son Jesus Christ, who shall rend the heavens, and come down with his mighty angels, in flaming fire, and shall sit on his throne, and judge both the quick and the dead, rest not till ye get this true and lively faith, which may bear you out in that great day; and such of you as have gotten it, and are renewed, I must tell you the stones and stumbling-blocks that lie in your way to hinder you in your journey now, that ye may know them when ye see them, and not stumble at them, but leap over them. I know many of you have been hindered to believe, and ye knew not what hindered you, and if ye have known them, ye have not resisted them; many of you have made fair resolutions, but ye have not kept them, because ye got impediments by the gate, and ye knew not who cast them in; therefore it were good to know who hindered you to believe, and who hinders you to make progress in religion: Who does this, think ye? Even the devil your enemy, the god of this world, who has helped with thy unrenewed part; therefore there is never an impediment laid in thy gate, but thou mayest say, I know the envious one has laid this in my gate. O! these are temptations of Satan, therefore I will arm me against them. So then, in particular, ye must have two things, to wit, faith in the Lord Jesus, and repentance towards God; we shall speak of the temptations to hinder both these.

And, first, to hinder your faith, he makes some of you believe, that it is impossible to thee to get faith; and some he makes so secure, that heaven and hell are but fancies to them; and if they get glances and lightnings by the word, he makes them think it enough and so lets them never search their hearts to see whether they be rooted in Christ or no: And for thee that hast gotten faith in Christ, he labours to make thee trow that thou never hadst it truly, or else if thou hadst it once, now thou hast lost it: But assure thyself, if ever thou hast found Christ in thy heart, and working peace and joy in thy soul by the promise of mercy and salvation, and hast thy heart renewed by the same promise, thou mayest hold thee with it, and it shall never be taken from thee; " For the gifts and callings of God are without repentance:" Therefore rest upon it, and stir up thy faith again, and the grace of God in thee; therefore let him not beguile thee in this point. Was thy heart ever humbled? Was thy heart ever cast down with the sense and sight of thy misery? Wast thou ever comforted in the blood of Jesus? Felt thou ever a change wrought in thy heart thro' that blood? Then remember that thy faith rests upon that blood, and that blood shall never rest to speak for thee; therefore if once thou beest truly ingrafted into Christ, thou art never to be pulled out of him.

Again, When he cannot make thee consent to say, that thou never obtainest that precious gift of believing, from that shift he will go to another, and will say to thee, thou art the child of God, and thou art chosen to eternal life, thou art redeemed with the blood of Christ, and thou hast gotten faith an salvation, and what more wouldst thou have: Take thy liberty in this and that sin; what needest thou to pain thyself any more in praying, and in thanksgiving, or in watching, or in hearing the word? Thou art but a fool in doing of it: And so he would make thee loose the bridle to sin, that thou mayest take thy pleasure, and he may get thee in his grips: Therefore beware of that, that he prevail not against you in this, and that ye say not, we will abide in sin, "because the grace of God does abound; God forbid;" but rather think with yourself, seeing I have gotten grace, I will be the more earnest in prayer, in thanksgiving, in watching, in hearing the word, than ever I was. So, I say, let him not beguile you in the first point, and be sure thy faith shall never fail thee; for suppose the child stir not in the mother's belly, yet he may be living; even so, suppose thou findest not Christ stirring, yet he may be living in thee.

Again, Let him not prevail against thee in the second point, that thou presume not of grace, but labour to entertain Christ begun in thee, by using the means.

Thirdly, If he cannot prevail in none of these two things, he will bid thee sit down and rest upon the truth of God's promise, and content thyself with the present comfort and persuasion that thou hast gotten by the means in the morning, that all the day long thou mayest not worship the sweet God conceived in thy heart: Therefore beware of this, that when thou hast gotten Christ conceived in thy heart, give him room, that he may grow in thee and thou in him; and thou must daily renew thy faith, and thou must daily feed upon his flesh and upon his blood, and thou must have a new meal of him every day, and thou must grow from faith to faith, and "from strength to strength, till thou appearest before the Lord in Zion:" For if he hinder thee to make progress in thy faith, thou wilt lose thy comfort, and faith will decrease; for thy faith is either increasing or decreasing. So, I say, beware of all these temptations which the devil rolls in thy way of believing. This for the first point I took in hand to speak of.

Now the second point I will but touch it: What are the temptations he has to hinder thee in thy Christian life, and this repentance towards God? He has three sorts of them,

First, He will see if he can keep thee back from doing that good whereby God may be glorified and thy soul comforted.

Next, He will labour to press thy heart down with one sin or other, that he may hinder thee to serve God with joyfulness.

And, *3dly*, He will see if he can make thee use very lawful things to be a snare to thee.

Now, the good things that he would keep thee from are four: I speak this for this end, first, To discover the by-gates that Satan would have the children of God go in, that they may not go in the right way to heaven with consolation; that they should not shine as lamps in the world, "that men seeing their good works might glorify their Father in heaven." And, next, To let you see the right way, that ye may say, here is the way, and we will walk in it. Take heed to these four things.

First, He will see if he can make thee to be loose in religion, that he may hinder thee that thou study not in all things to please God every day; so whensoever thou hast not a purpose to please God every day; then thou art hindered by the devil; therefore so many days as thou passest not over in joy and peace with God, so many days the devil gets advantage of thee, for he envies thy joy and peace: Wherefore thou shouldst resolve, that the more he hinders thee to please God, thou will do it the more. This for the first.

The *second* good thing that he would hinder thee from, is the love of God, either in thy first calling or afterwards; thou mayest lose it when thou hast had it, and so that thou mayest be kept at under with doubtings all the days of thy life; therefore if ever God softened thy heart with the sense of that love, then hold the grip fast, and let not the bow slack, no, not for an hour; and when thou losest thy sense of his love, run to the fountain again, for the Lord has as much in readiness to give thee, as at the first hour thou knewest him, and he can restore thee again to thy first love, and he can make the latter works more than the former. So thou must do as a man that has lost meikle gear, who will begin his pack with small wares, and so go forward piece and piece, till his riches be increased and doubled; even so do, when ye lose the sense of the love of God, begin at smalls, and go forward, and get you riches till ye get it doubled to you.

Thirdly, He will labour to hinder thee from the private and public worship of God, or from the use of one mean or other, that so thou mayest neglect thy duty to God, and by so doing he may perturb thy peace.

Last of all, The grace that is in others he will make it a sword to pierce thy heart, and to wound thy soul, that when thou seest in others their faith, their fastness of heart, their repentance, their religion, thou wilt say, Surely I wan never to yon, and therefore I see the grace of God in me is but in vain: And yet they that have all that that thou seest, they know their own wants, and they are cast down as well as thou: Therefore when thou seest this, acknowledge the meanest measure of the grace of God in thyself, and be thankful for it, and pray that it may increase and grow daily. This for the good that he would keep thee from.

Now, the evil that he will keep thee in, that he may press down thy heart with one sin or other, it is of two sorts. *First,* The unrenewed affections of thy heart, he labours to keep them still. What are these? 1*st,* A servile fear. 2*dly,* A spiritual pride, and a lofty conceit of the blessings of God. 3*dly,* A slothfulness and sluggishnesss in the service of God. And, 4*thly,* All the worldly affections within thee; as pride, anger, envy, malice, grudging, murmuring, and all the rest of these. Now he does all this to obscure the light of God's Spirit, that it shine not in thy heart. Now, the other sorts of evil he labours to retain within thee, are these worldly lusts that John speaks of in his first epistle, ii. 16. As, " the lusts of the flesh, the lusts of the eye and the pride of life:" And this he does, either to defile thy heart with uncleanness (for he is an impure enemy) or else to move thee to desire vain glory, and the pleasures of this world. Now, the third sort of temptation, to hinder the Christian's life, is to make the very lawful things of this life to be a snare to thee; as the love of riches, or of any other thing that is lawful in itself. If he steal away thy heart, and make thee set thy affections upon the riches of the world, it is not possible but thou must fall into temptation. Now, I say no more, but I commend that which has been said to the blessing of God in Jesus Christ; to whom be all praise for ever.

SERMON XXXVII.

UPON THE FREEDOM OF THE SAINTS.

1 Thess. ii. 18.

We would have come unto you (even I Paul) once and again, but Satan hindered us.

THIS is a thing hardly believed by the world, that Satan can bind the child of God hand and foot, and can hinder him that he go not to the place where he would be at, nor to the worship of God; yet ye see here that he hinders the apostle that knew the will of God. And therefore would ye know all this, that when God gives thee a calling, and an open door to do that which God has commanded thee to do, it is Satan that hinders; and as he hinders thee to do good, so he entices thee to evil, as he enticed David to number the people; so he both hinders the good that should be done, and provoketh thee to do the evil that should not be done: Therefore remember that the hand, the tongue, the heart is never hindered to do good, nor enticed to do evil, but it is Satan that does it: This ye should think then, that ye have not only to wrestle with flesh and blood, but against principalities and powers, and against wordly governors, the prince of the darkness of this world, against spiritual wickedness which are in high places; therefore ye had need to take unto you the whole armour of God, that ye may be able to resist in the evil day: but, alas! this is gone with the most part of men and women now-a-days, for they give place to the devil wittingly and willingly. As he hindered the apostle to come to the Thessalonians, so upon thy present measure of faith, it is he that gars thee that thou grows not from faith to faith, it is he that does that; and when thy unruly affections overcome thee, it is he that does that ; therefore, to eschew this temptation, ye should hold fast the profession of your faith constantly to the end; and therefore Peter says, " the devil, our adversary, goes about like a roaring lion, seeking whom he may devour; whom resist, being stedfast in the faith." Likewise James i. 5. says, " if any man lack wisdom, let him ask of God, that giveth to all men liberally, and reproaches no man, and it shall be given him ; but let him ask in faith, and waver not ; for he that wavereth, is like a wave of the sea, tossed of the wind and carried away : neither let that man think that he shall receive any thing of the Lord." This is the first.

Secondly, Hold the grip when thou hast gotten it, and remember it is not of nature but of grace, for it bred never in thy heart ; and if God waken thy conscience, and let thee see and feel the terror of his wrath, then thou mayest say, it is the gift of God to believe. Therefore let him never bereave thee of thy faith, but be thou strong, and unmoveable, and stedfast in the faith ; for he knows that when thy faith is gone, thy love is gone too ; for "the just shall live by faith." Beware of that other temptation also, that when we have gotten faith and consolation in that blood, then look that ye fall not asleep, and become secure then, as the spouse in the Canticles, who sleeped, but her heart waked, and yet he could not gar her rise out of her bed to open the door to him, therefore he went away ; so this is the drift of the devil, to see if he can get thee on a slumber, that he may bereave thee of thy present Lord, and of great consolation. Therefore, I pray you, beware of security after ye have gotten consolation.

Thirdly, Grow from faith to faith, and from strength to strength, so long as thou art in this life, and always till thou appear before the Lord in Zion. Ye see that one meal of meat will not gain you always, but ye must have meat every day that ye have your health ; even so one bit of the flesh of Christ, and one drink of his blood, and one application of the promises will not serve thee, but there must be a plaister after a plaister, as ye see in a body that is deadly wounded ; even so, it will not be one application of the promise of salvation that will heal the wound of thy soul, but there must be a renewing of the application daily. I know not if any of you needs this doctrine, but always I must be telling you it. In this hindering thee from good, he will see if he can keep thee from a daily studying to please God in all things ; and sometimes he prevails wonderfully in this, even with the dear children of God ; for many know not that such a necessity lies on them, to endeavour to please God daily in all things, and if they know it, they resolve not to do it, and if they resolve, yet they get daily discouragements and great impediments in the way. Now, because many of you, I trow, if ye were laid on your bed, and to render an account of your bygone life, I say, I trow, there is not many actions, words, and cogitations, that could render you consolation in your whole life ; for none shall bring thee comfort but such as thy conscience will bear thee record that thou didst them in the honour of God: Therefore ye had all need to prepare you in time, that whenever ye come to the use of means, or to any company, ye may leave this stamp to them, be ye witnesses, here and there, that I sought the Lord, and here I found him. But I fear many of you, when it comes to reckoning, that all places shall bear you record, that this was never the purpose of your heart to glorify God, wherever ye came ; then, at least, all these places shall bear thee record of a lost and mispent time which cannot be recovered : therefore, every one of you, live as ye would have your conscience clear toward God and man, and as ye would have all the places that ever ye have been in, bear you witness that ye sought God in the integrity of your heart.

Now, there are two things I was speaking to you : And, *first*, To arm you against these temptations offered to you by the devil to entice you to commit sin ; for ye have need to take heed to that subtle serpent, that will creep in quietly, and give thee a deadly sting ere ever thou wit of thyself: Can any man walk in the fire and not be burnt? Even so, can any man walk in the lusts of the flesh and not be entangled therewith? Now, the things ye should think on to slay sin, are these,

First, The infinite and everlasting love of God, in so great a measure warming thy heart with the sense of it: and, through that love, think on it, how it has kythed itself, 1*st*, In loving thee, in chusing thee in Christ. 2*dly*, In sending his Son to redeem thee with his precious blood. 3*dly*, In making thee a man or woman according to the image of God, 4*thly*, In calling thee, and letting so many die in their sins. 5*thly*, In justifying thee freely, and forgiving thee so oftentimes so great sins: and, in the end, think on that endless glory which he has prepared for thee in heaven, and shall be revealed one day. Therefore, art thou tempted to anger, to envy, to distrust, and neglect of the means; then remember of the infinite deepness of the love of God toward thee, and let it constrain thee to refrain from sin.

Secondly, When thou art tempted, think that thou art always in the presence of an all-seeing God; and she is a vile strumpet that will commit adultery in the sight of her husband. So what art thou doing when thou sinnest? Thou art in the sight of Christ thy husband continually, and thou art in the very way to the tribunal of his justice. Now, to sin against him before his face, and now in the very way when the serjeant is leading thee to the very gallows; who will not say, that is a vile knave that will pick pockets when he is going to the gallows?

Thirdly, When thou art tempted, think upon that, with whom thou hast to do, even with a just and a severe God, that pursued sin so in his own Son, that he never leaves till his blood slockens his wrath, for all his torments did not satisfy his justice till his heart's blood was casten in the fire: so then, look what sin has done: sin wapped the angels, without recovery, out of heaven; cast Adam out of paradise, and he, nor none of his posterity, to come there again; the old world drowned for sin; Sodom and Gomorrah burnt with fire and brimstone for sin; Jerusalem twice destroyed; therefore, what will it avail you to hide your sin here? Remember that day of manifestation, when all shall be made manifest, and ye shall all be brought mother naked before the tribunal of God, where thou must render an account of every idle word that thou speakest: therefore arm yourselves against the devil by these and these cogitations, for he is crafty, and he will gar thee trow, that God is merciful; but when he has gotten thee into his snare, he will say then, there is no mercy for thee. Wherefore the pleasure of sin is gone, and the glory of sin is done, but the sting of it is not so soon done; for he has many things to discourage thee in the doing of the thing that is good.

First, He will say, there is such a mass of corruption within thee, that it is impossible to thee to press to this Christian life: therefore, to arm thyself against this, remember that it is the Lord's work and God's glory that thou seekest; and it stands him on his glory not to let his honour go down.

Secondly, Remember that " there is no condemnation to them that are in Christ, who walk not after the flesh, but after the Spirit," therefore thou mayest be sure thy sins shall never hinder thee.

Last of all, Suppose there be but a will to serve God, yet it is acceptable to him; and the meanest grain of uprightness in thy heart, he allows it, because it is not thy work, but his own work, and the work of his Son, therefore he accepts of it, and the little thing that thou offers he will accept of it.

The *next* thing, because Satan will gar thee trow, that thy course was never right, therefore remember, that thou art going forward as long as thou mislikest the thing that hinders thee in thy course, and as long as thou art humbled daily, and as long as thou esteemest mair and mair of the blood of Christ; then, thou art continually going forward, as long as thou art learning this lesson, that it is that blood only must bring thee to heaven, and it is grace that must lead thee forward.

Last of all, Remember though thy sanctification be imperfect, yet thy justification is perfect; and this he does first for his own glory, that ay the more thou seest thy own weakness, the mair does God clear to thy conscience, that it is the Lord's power that must bring thee forward: and besides all this, if thou gettest all thy sanctification at once, thou wouldst sit down on it; therefore the Lord will give thee new grace every day, that so thou mayest stir up thy thankfulness every day and in the end to have thy heart humbled continually, and to keep thee exercised in prayer, and in all the rest of the means. The Lord would not cast out all the Canaanites at once, but he would let some abide there, lest the land should be filled with wild beasts; and this was more profitable for the Israelites than if they had all been cast out at once. So the Lord will not cast out all thy enemies, and all thy sins at once, and at an instant, but he will let some remain in thee, to be as so many pricks and thorns in thy side, to stir thee forward to seek the heavenly Canaan, even the kingdom of heaven. The Lord grant that ye may all make this profit of your temptations, that the very weapons that Satan uses against us, we may turn them into his own belly. Again, the Lord grant this for Christ his Son's sake; to whom with the Father, and with the Spirit, be all praise for ever. *Amen.*

SERMON XXXVIII.

UPON THE BELIEVER'S PRIVILEGE.

1 Pet. ii. 9.

But ye are a chosen generation, a royal priesthood, an holy nation, a peculiar people, that ye should shew forth the praises of him who hath called you out of darkness into his marvellous light.

YE know it was the last thing we promised to speak of to you, even to tell you of our liberty, and of these glorious prerogatives, that as many of you as has truly believed, you have your right and title to them all. Now, I would ye knew them all; for without the knowledge of them, it is but hooly speed that ye will make in your journey to heaven, and a little thing will cast you down and discourage you, a little thing will feeble thy knees, and weaken thy hands, and faint thy heart, if thou knowest not thy prerogatives; for thy battles are set in this straight and narrow gate, full of thorns and briers, and wherein there stands many lions for to hinder us to go on: therefore it is good that ye know them, for this would comfort your hearts, and should make you to run your race with joy and gladness; and if ye knew what these fair privileges were that the blood of the Son has bought to you, and has given the right of them to you, and has given you a charge to stand fast in all your freedoms and liberties, unless ye will grieve him to the heart; what comfort then can the poor sinner have in his tribulation, and wearisome journey, and irksome way, if ye have not his heart cheered up and strengthened with all the liberties that his blood has bought to thee, who art a citizen of that new Jerusalem? Ye heard what your conversation should be, and what grounds ye must lay to build your house upon, viz. a saving faith, gripping to mercy in a Saviour, gripping to the blood of the second person of the Trinity, even God made flesh, then, upon that, ye must believe all that is written in the law and the prophets, and all that is written in the gospel, then, upon that, ye must have the heart cleansed, and ye must be born over again; then ye must eschew evil and do good; then ye must have your eye upon all these ten laws, that thereby ye may know what is the evil forbidden, and what is the good commanded; and then because ye are redeemed with the blood of God, for so I may call it; therefore ye must endeavour to please God in all things, and to give him obedience in all things that come out of his mouth, and in all that is written in the whole truths; then I told you what helps God has appointed for you; there is enow of them, for there is plenty and store of means whereunto God gives his presence and his blessing in the faithful use of them; and then having learned the science of religion, and the excellent knowledge of Jesus Christ your Lord, and that ye begin and put that knowledge in practice, not at set times, to keep your religion till the Sabbath day, and certain times and places; but ye should practise it at all times, in all places, and in all companies, and there must be an endeavour to please God in all things, and to keep a clear conscience toward God, and toward man, as the apostle says, "I endeavour, for the hope sake, to serve God always," that is, I rax out all the strength of my soul and heart continually for the hope of that glory which one day shall be revealed, and to keep a clear conscience, that it be not defiled nor hurt with any spot of iniquity; for, seeing God has put it within me to be a judge, therefore I have no will to make it my party; and because there will be oft wrestlings and faintings here, and sundry falls, yet ye must not give it over the more of that; therefore ye must remember this, that they are the battles of the Lord, and that the glory of these battles will be the Lord's: so that when thou fightest thou art not fighting thy own battles, but the battles of the Lord, therefore ay the weaker thou findest thyself, the glory of the Lord will be the greater, when he gars thee that art but a feeble soldier set thy feet upon the dragon's craig, and stamp him under thy feet; therefore ye have to comfort yourselves with this, that ye shall get the victory in the end.

There are many that God never puts in his warfare; therefore since he has put thee in it, only stand and look on, and thou shalt see thy salvation; and only keep thy conscience from sin, so that, suppose thou beest led like a slave to sin, yet thou mayest say, thou doest the thing that thou wouldst not do, and therefore thou consentest not unto the evil that thou doest. O! well is the soul that can count the state of their captivity to be their only misery, and cries, in the inner man, O well were the man that could deliver me from this body of death; but yet I know " there is no condemnation to them that are in Christ Jesus, that walk not after the flesh, but after the Spirit." But I will not insist any more to speak or repeat to you what was spoken of your daily conversation; for if ye practise it, ye will remember it: Therefore essay it, and let not this discourage thee because thou canst not come to it at the first; for as the sun has a time to come to his light, and as Samson had a time for his hair to grow before he came to his strength again; so thou must have a time given thee ere thou can practise this holy life and Christian conversation; therefore thou must not cast away thy confidence the more that thou canst not win to this in an instant; but if thou keepest the purpose in thy heart, to please God in all things, and to serve him always every day, it is enough; and when thou wast in thy mother's womb there behooved a time to be given thee ere thou couldst be born, and when thou wast born, there behooved a time to be given thee ere thou couldst come to the strength of a man: even so, in this new birth, thou must have a time given thee ere thou canst be a strong Christian: Therefore, I say, be not discouraged, but be ay eating and drinking the flesh and blood of Jesus, and so thou shalt grow daily; and when thou sinnest, remember, that God by these means, will have all flesh humbled; for he does it for his own glory and thy well, that not only thou mayest glorify God in thy salvation, and so put up his blessings in a heap together, but that thou mayest take all the steps of the ladder, and give glory to God for every one of them, and to learn thee that all is of grace, and all is of God, and all comes through the blood of Jesus; therefore thou must learn to be thankful for it, and to be humble and lowly in his sight. O! what a glorious garment then should there be on thy soul! First, Humbleness of heart; then thy arms ay about Christ Jesus, thy Lord; then a hope of the glory to come; then a cheerful walking before God continually: So suppose thou seest that thou canst not practise this the first day, yet step to it, and step to it again, and God shall be with thee.

Now, I go forward: The last thing I say is, to tell you your privileges; therefore it is casten in by the apostle Peter for to comfort them to whom he writes this epistle; for after he has exhorted them to drink in the sincere milk of the word, having laid aside all maliciousness and guile, dissimulation and envy, and evil-speaking; and, after he has exhorted them to come to Christ, as unto a living stone, disallowed of the Jews, but allowed of God, and precious, to whom? to you only that believe it is precious; but unto them that be disobedient, a stone to stumble at, and a rock of offence. Now, lest they should be discouraged with this saying, therefore he brings in this to comfort them; and he says, *but ye are a chosen generation*, that is, a generation of mercy and grace; he not only waled thyself out, but also thy seed, and therefore ye are a generation that is chosen and ordained for life; *a royal priesthood*, ye are all crowned kings and set at liberty, ye are not under the tyranny and slavery of the law: Now, ye are not under the slavery of that sentence, do this, or else thou shalt die for evermore; "Cursed is he that abides not in all things that are written in the law to do them." Ye are loosed now

SERMON XXXVIII.

from under that bondage and misery of that terrible law, proclaimed with a terrible voice, out of a terrible fire, out of mount Sinai; but now ye have a sweet voice out of mount Zion, spoken out of the mouth of our own husband and Lord, and what a voice is that, " Believe and thou shalt never perish: Come unto me, all that are wearied and heavy ladened, and I will refresh you;" So ye are kings loosed from the bonds of sin, and freed from the slavery of the devil, and from the curse of the law, and from the severity of that pedagogue who keeps us in so, that we durst not look out at the door for fear of that consuming fire, that whenever a thing of our heart ran wrong, it was ready to devour us. *A royal priesthood;* ye are priests; so that, not only may ye step into that sanctuary, and offer there with your own hand, and for the sins of the people, but also ye are his priests, that may not only step into the holy of holies, but into the highest heavens, not at set times or once in the year, but at all times every day, not with the blood of bullocks and goats, but with the precious blood of Jesus Christ, that immaculate Lamb, who has been slain from the beginning of the world, and takes away the sins of the world. So not only are ye priests, but ye are highpriests, who may step into heaven where Christ is, and there present not only yourselves, but every one of you may bear the twelve tribes of Israel upon your breast, and so present the whole bodies and all the members of Christ Jesus in thy arms before God, and intercede for them. Ye are a holy nation, that is, ye are the people of God, whom he has appointed to be holy as he is holy, " for without holiness no man can see God." Now, what is the end of all this? that ye might shew forth the virtues of him that " hath called you from darkness to his marvellous light;" but what virtues has our calling? peace, joy, humility, patience, meekness, love, zeal, strength, and all the rest of the graces of the Spirit; for thou that believest in Christ, and hast him in thy heart, thou hast all the graces of the Spirit with him: Therefore thou that hast them, bring them forth, and shew them to others ; for it is not good to hide them. Well, I see I must leave this ; for I will not have time to go through it, as I minded to do. Always, for the present, to give you something to be thinking upon ; ye shall remember that the privileges are of two sorts, the first are in this life, the next in the life to come ; for thou that hast once believed has as sure right to these privileges, as the surest heir in the world has to his heritage. Now, what are the privileges in this life ?

First, Thou art not only loved of God, chosen to eternal life, redeemed by the blood of Jesus Christ, and ordained to eternal glory, but also thou hast this privilege, that thou mayest know it is so ; and this is more than all the world is worth, that eating or drinking, waking or sleeping, going or sitting, or whatever thou beest doing, thou mayest know assuredly, and thou mayest say freely I am beloved, I am chosen to eternal life, I am redeemed by the blood of Christ, called, justified, and shall be glorified. Now, what comfort mayest thou have, who knowest this, that nothing can scrape thy name out of the book of life, when thou mayest say, I am the child of God, I am the brother of Jesus Christ, and I shall get a part of all my elder brother's heritage : Mayest thou not heart thee with these ? What more ? Thou hast in this life the same which was spoken to Mary, hail, freely beloved ! God is with thee. This may be said to all that believe, and are beloved, and God ay with them ; for God has a special care of thee ; it is true God is called the Saviour of all the world, because of his providence he prevails therein, and by his power he governs them ; but especially he is the Saviour of the elect, because he will let none of his sheep perish. What more ? *I will honour them that honour me*, says Christ, the true wisdom of God ; so honour belongs properly to the children of God, and no man is honourable in the sight of God, but his own children that honour him ; he will keep thee as the apple of his eye, for he thinks thee as dear to him as any man thinks the apple of his eye dear to himself. What more ? " If God be on our side, who can be against us? Who can lay any thing to the charge of God's elect? It is God that justifies us, who can condemn us ? The Lord is my light and salvation, whom shall I fear ? He is the strength of my life, of whom shall I be afraid? Though a thousand fall at my right-hand, and ten thousand at my left hand, yet it shall not come near me," Psal. xci. 7. What more ? Thou art his servant, and thou mayest come into the chamber of his presence when thou wilt ; yea, thou art his friend ; for he has told all his counsel to thee, and has hained nothing from thee that lies in his own heart ; therefore thou mayest go boldly and ask counsel of him when any thing troubles thee, seeing thou art his son. What can be beyond that ? Yet I remember that of Isaiah lvi. 5. says he, " I will give a place, and a name better than that of sons and of daughters ; I will give them an everlasting name that will not be cut off." And what name is better ? I will tell you, the name of a wife is better than the name of a son, and thou art his wife ; yea, thou art more than a wife ; for thou art his flesh and his blood ; and that is most of all, thou art his chief treasure : But is this all ? No : What more then ? Thou hast this privilege, that thou mayest believe God is bound (and therefore thou mayest ask it boldly of God) " to take away the stoney heart, and to give thee a heart of flesh." What more yet ? Thou hast Christ not only to be thy wisdom, and redemption, and justification, but also to be thy sanctification. What more ? When thou fallest God hath given thee means to rise again, and if thou usest them, God hath promised a blessing to them. What more ? God hath given thee a right and interest to all these means, that thou mayest step to them when thou wilt ; thou mayest hear the word, receive the sacraments ; thou mayest pray, thou mayest sing, thou mayest meditate, thou mayest confer upon the word, and thou mayest use all the exercises of religion when thou wilt ; yea, oftentimes God gives thee strength to use them all, when thou had little strength to thyself in the use of them. What more? He can teach thee how thou shouldst behave thyself in whatsoever estate thou beest in, whether in prosperity or in adversity. What more? If thou believest, thou mayest seek, that thy rising may be like the rising of the sun, and thy departing may be as the going down thereof; and thou mayest pray, that thou mayest get grace to grow from faith to faith, and from strength to strength, *till thou appearest before the Lord in Zion :* And so thou mayest ask grace upon grace to be poured out, and to be multiplied upon thee. What more? Thou hast this privilege, that thou shalt never depart away from the Lord finally and totally. What more? Thou hast this privilege, that, as thou hast lived in the Lord, so thou shalt die in the Lord; then after this life shall be ended, and the angels shall carry thy soul, not into the bosom of Abraham, but into the bosom of Jesus Christ, and they shall keep the very mools of thy rotten carcase in the grave, or in whatsomever part of the earth, or of the sea; that, although they be scattered pickles, ten thousand miles sundry, yet they shall keep them there until the day of the resurrection, and then they shall gather them together, and, soul and body being conjoined together, thou shall be caught up in the air with the Lord into the chamber, where thou shalt follow the Lamb wherever he goes; then thou shalt be a citizen of that " new Jerusalem descending out of heaven from God, having the glory of God, whose shining is as a most precious stone, as a jasper-stone, clear as crystal; which has a great wall, and high; which has twelve gates, and at the twelve gates twelve angels, and the wall thereof has twelve foundations, and in them the names of the Lamb's twelve apostles; and the building of the wall is of jasper, and the city is pure gold, and garnished with precious stones, and the twelve gates are twelve pearls, and every several gate is of one pearl; and the streets of the city are of pure gold, clear as shining glass. And there is no temple therein, for the Lord God almighty and the Lamb are the temple thereof. And the city has no need of the sun to shine in it, for the glory of God does lighten it, and the Lamb is the light thereof. And thou shalt walk in the light thereof, and kings shall bring their glory to it. And thou shalt drink of the pure water of life, clear as crystal, proceeding out of the throne of God, and of the Lamb. And you shall eat of the tree of life, which is on either side of the river, and bears twelve manner of fruits every month, whose leaves serve to heal the nations. And there shall be no more curse, but the throne of God and of the Lamb shall be in it ; and there thou shalt serve him day and night, and thou shalt see his face continually, and his name shall be on thy forehead, and thou shalt reign for evermore."

These are fair prerogatives, and great privileges ; therefore I beseech you, my hearts, oftentimes think on these privileges, even of this life ; for they shall transform thy soul into the glorious image of Jesus Christ, and they shall make thee partaker of the very divine nature. Now, I say no more, but the Lord give you faith to believe, and grace to apply all these things to yourself, that thereby ye may live the life of Christ your Lord : To whom, with the Father, and the Spirit, be all praise, and honour, and glory, for now and ever.

SERMON XXXIX.

UPON THE BELIEVER'S SECURITY.

John x. 27. 28.

My sheep hear my voice, and I know them, and they follow me. And I give unto them eternal life, and they shall never perish, neither shall any pluck them out of my hands.

THERE remains the last thing that I had proponed to have informed and grounded you into, and without the which your joy cannot be full, and your comfort cannot be great; and that is, your perseverance to the end; that as many as the Lord your God has called to the hope of that glory, and has brought them into his fold, may be assured that they shall never perish, but shall get eternal life: For this is one of the fiery darts of the devil, wherewith he uses to wound the hearts of many of them that belong to Christ, that when they look to their own frailty and weakness, and when they see their own corruptions and manifold falls, how that they cannot stand for an hour; and when they look to others, that have made fair professions in religion, and have seen them fall away again; and when they begin to think what can keep them from falling finally away, when others that had greater graces than they have, or can get for the present, yet have made defection; then they are deprived of their joy, and hope of that eternal glory. So then this is very needful for you to know your perseverance in faith: Therefore as many of you as God has brought into the kingdom of his Son, and have believed the remission of sins in the blood of Jesus Christ, it is very needful to you to know that none of his sheep shall perish; for this shall be matter of great consolation to sinners, when they know that God has begun that good work in them which he shall establish and perfite in his own time; this must bring great consolation to believers, when they know that this is the Lord's decree and purpose, not only to chuse them, redeem them, and justify them; but also it is his purpose that the called chosen child of God shall get grace to persevere to the end. Therefore, this is the last thing I mind to speak of anent your Christian warfare; for, having gone through the rest, I thought it needful to ground you in this also; that ye might, with greater consolation, pass your pilgrimage with fear and trembling here, seeing that it is not left in your hands to tyne yourselves. Adam was left to himself, therefore he lost himself; but it is not so with thee that art in Christ, and art the child of God, for the Father has given thee to the Son, and he holds a grip of thee with his own hand; and he that was willing to give his own life for thee, will not let thee perish, for there was never man nor woman, who ever got this saving faith, and this repentance unto life, that shall ever perish; and there was never man nor woman that heard the word of Jesus, and believed it, that ever perished. Now, if ye knew this, that it were not possible that ever thou shalt perish, with what joy might thou run thy race! And for grounds to sustain you in this, because I purpose to call to your mind again the grounds of religion and of Christianity, that ye must lead and lay: As 1*st*, Saving faith. 2*dly*, A new birth of regeneration. 3*dly*. The fruits of repentance, and the exercise of religion in your daily life and conversation. 4*hly*, To tell the manifold impediments that the devil casts in to hinder thee to grow from faith to faith; either to make thee presume, or else to hinder thee to grew from faith to faith; and then to tell the impediments he casts in to hinder thy repentance in like manner. *Last of all*, To tell your privileges again, because I mind to go through these things again: therefore, for the present, I will tell you what are the grounds to underprop you in this assurance, that ye shall never perish, and that your perseverance is as well concluded in the counsel of God, as your election, redemption, and justification, and calling is concluded therein, that ye may think upon this, that it is not in your hand to lose yourselves, no more it was in your hand to save yourselves; therefore I will now repeat them unto you shortly.

The ground to assure you that God shall give to you to persevere unto the end, are some of them taken from the Lord and from his nature, and other some of them are taken from the quality of the gifts of God that are given you. They that are taken from the Lord himself, are these,

First, God's unchangeableness of the decree, that heaven nor hell cannot alter, that thou art chosen to eternal life; as God has decreed to call thee, redeem thee, and to justify thee, and to forgive thee; so has God decreed to give thee grace to persevere to the end; therefore Christ says, "none of my sheep shall perish;" and the apostle says, "the foundation of God stands sure." Now, the foundation were not sure, if the perseverance were not decreed in the counsel of God.

The *next* ground is taken from unchangebleness of the love of God; for, *whom God loved, he loves to the end:* and he says himself, *with everlasting love I have loved thee.* So if God has once set on thee his heart's love, as God is unchangeable, so his love is unchangeable; and as his unchangeable love moved him, first to chuse thee, next to redeem thee, and then to call and justify thee; so his unchangeable ground is taken from his faithfulness in his promise. Now, God has sworn, and will not alter nor profane his holiness, "that he will put his fear in thy heart, that thou shalt never depart away from him." It is true there will be very great falls in the children of God; but such a fall as can never be recovered again that is not competent to any of the children of God.

Now, the 4*th* ground to sustain you in this, is taken from this, the Son has taken thee in his own hand, and "the Father that gave thee to him is greater than all, and none is able to take thee out of the Father's hand;" for all the powers that he has he will ware them on thy defence, ere thou perish, so to speak, that is his child; therefore he is able to save thee, so that all the powers in heaven and hell shall not be able to gar thee perish.

Now, the other grounds are these shortly, the meditation of the Son, who is at the right hand of the Father, and makes continual intercession for thee; "if any man sin, says John, 1 Epist. ii. 4. "we have an advocate with the Father in heaven, even Jesus Christ." Again, there is an inseparable conjunction betwixt thee and him; thou art one member of that body, whereof Christ is the head; and there is never a member of that body, whereof he is the head, that ever shall perish. Again there is "the Spirit, who shall abide with thee for ever;" for the spirit of adoption and sanctification being once sent from God to any man or woman, shall never be taken from him again.

Last of all, "The gifts and calling of God are without repentance." It is true, the gifts that make us with joy to serve God, may be sometimes taken from thee; but these gifts, without which thou canst not be saved, the substance of them shall never be taken from thee: therefore ye must think upon these grounds, ye must think upon them, and especially upon this main ground, "God is faithful who has promised that none of his sheep shall perish:" I am one of his sheep, therefore he will not let me perish. Now then, as many of you as the Lord has ever shined in your hearts, and to whom he has ever given the gift of believing, and whose faith has been sealed by the Spirit of God, and has found the Holy Ghost opening your eyes, and letting you see clearly the love of God was the fountain of all, remember that your names are put up in the book of life, and never to be scraped out again; ye are loved freely; ye are chosen in Christ; ye are called from darkness to a marvellous light; ye are justified by faith in the blood of Jesus: ye are sanctified and purged from dead works, to serve the living God ; and therefore ye shall never perish : for that hand of faith, once gripped to the Son shall never let thee go ; and suppose thou shouldst let him go, yet the grip that the Father and the Son has taken of thee by the Spirit shall never let thee go. Therefore whenever the devil would deprive you of the hope of that glory, by the consideration of your own frailty and weakness, then let this be the ground to sustain you, the Father has me in his hand, and none is greater than he, therefore none can take me out of his hand ; the Son has sent his Spirit to take a grip of me, and that Spirit which has gripped me will not let me perish ; " the gifts and calling of God are without repentance ;" therefore he that has given me faith, and repentance, and hope, and patience, and meekness, and long suffering, and all the rest of the graces of the Spirit, he will not repent that he has given them to me ; therefore they shall never be taken from me : so long as he has grace I must persevere ; " for his grace is sufficient for me, and the power of God is made perfect through my weakness ; therefore I will rejoice in nothing but in my infirmities."

Now, the Lord grant ye may believe these things, and, in believing, ye may get eternal life, and glorify God in his Son Jesus Christ ; to whom, with the Father, and with the Spirit, be all praise, and honour, and glory, for now and evermore. *Amen.*

SERMON XL.

UPON THE BELIEVER'S SECURITY.

John v. 24. and vi. 39.

Verily verily I say unto you, he that heareth my word, and believeth on him that hath sent me, hath everlasting life, and shall not come into condemnation; but is passed from death unto life.

And this is the Father's will, which hath sent me, that of all which he hath given me, I should lose nothing, but should raise it up again at the last day.

WHAT should be dear to you but this eternal life? For if ye would gain the whole world and lose your own souls, I assure you, your gain would be very little. Now, in the time of your life here, what should ye be thinking on, but upon these two eternities, the eternity of joy, and the eternity of pain; ye see the grounds of this here, it is sworn by him that is truth itself, and who came out of the Father's bosom, and it is said by him that would not beguile you, for if it had been otherwise, he would have told you by him whose word is spirit and life, for he has the words of eternal life; he has sworn here, and the Son knows well enough what is in the Father's mind, for he was upon the council of God at the beginning, and he was in the Father's bosom, and he that honours the Father will not falsify or break his oath; and because no less would gain to persuade you than his oath, therefore the Son of the everlasting God swears; what swears he? *Verily, he that hears my word* (ye do well that ye hear the words of God, for without hearing there is no faith; ye that come to hear, will count this time well spent, that ye abide in the kirk, when ye shall be caught within the heavens, and be there for evermore; *and believes in him that sent me*, that thou hearest and believest his word, (thou believest the author of it;) he has eternal life, he has eternity of peace and joy begun in his soul that shall never have an end, and shall not come into condemnation; *he is past from death to life;* he is gone over the back of death, and made it a stepping stone to heaven, and he has come within the marches and limits of eternal life; he that believes shall get a new heaven and a new earth, and shall dwell in the tabernacle of God for evermore: and if ye believe not, the wrath of God abides upon you for evermore, and ye are already condemned, John iii. 17.

I have told you, how ye shall try unfeigned repentance. Now, I would tell you, if ye have a true saving faith, and this is very needful for you to know; for thou that wantest faith, there is nothing betwixt thee and hell, but the small thread of thy life. I told you about repentance, that whosoever has repentance in truth begun in their soul, they have faith; therefore call these things to your memory that I have spoken concerning repentance. I refer them to your memories, I will not repeat them. Now, there are four things whereby ye shall know whether ye have true faith or not: *first*, Ye shall know true faith by the manner by the which God wrought it in your hearts. 2*dly*, If ye were sealed by the spirit of promise, ye shall know your faith by the seals or stamps of faith. 3*dly*, Ye shall know true faith by the fight, for faith has a fight and a battle joined with it. The apostle says, "I have fought a good fight, I have kept the faith, I have finished my course." *Last of all*, Ye shall know the faith by the train it has following it. Now, if ye have faith, and the works of it in your hearts, ye may rejoice then, for Christ says, "that your names are written in the book of life:" thou mayest rejoice that art within the love of God; thou that hast faith art within his love; thou mayest rejoice that art within the election, redemption and calling,

SERMON XL.

justification and sanctification, and perseverance. Now thou that hast faith, hast all these, and thou believest them all in thy heart, therefore thou mayest rejoice.

Now, as for the marks, and if ever ye have gotten true faith, it has been on this manner; I grant, some get it more clearly, and some more obscurely; some can point out the day, with Zaccheus, Luke xv. 5. that they may say, "this day salvation is come to my heart." Some get it easily, as Lydia, Acts xvi. 4. *whose heart was opened* in an instant, at a preaching of Paul's; and othersome get it more hardly, and are longer in coming to it, as Saul, Acts ix. 4. " was casten to the ground, and was led by a hand to a city, and for the space of three days was blind, and neither eat nor drank, but prayed all that space," till Ananias came to him, and preached the gospel, and he got faith and comfort. Now, if ye can remember that glorious day wherein thou wast wounded and bound up again, and wherein thou sawest clearly that thou wast in darkness all thy lifetime before, but there came a light from heaven and shined in thy heart; wherein thou sawest that thou wast lying bathing in thy blood and filthiness, and wast pricked in thy heart, and cried out, " Men and brethren, what shall I do to be saved?" And then there came glad-tidings to thy soul in such a day. Ye should remember that day; for kings will remember their birth-day. Some can tell with how great difficulty they have gone to the throne of grace, and how long they were holden, ere ever they could get faith and consolation: therefore look to the manner of working of faith in your hearts; look if thou thoughtest the past time of ignorance a lost thing; and look if thou wouldst fain have had the time redeemed, and if thou wouldst have given ten thousand worlds (if thou hadst them) to any to let thee know if ever there were mercy for thee in the blood of Jesus. Now all men get not faith in a like measure: but that ye may understand, if ye have gotten it in any measure, ye shall wit, that there are three degrees of faith; there is the weakest, the midmost, and the strongest faith. Now the weakest faith that any of you must have, it is this, he sees his conviction; he sees there is nothing for him but wrath, if he be not clad with the righteousness of the Son; he sees that that blood is able to pacify the wrath, and slocken that fire; he desires no more, but to be ducked in that blood; and would ye speir at him, what was his special desire? He would answer you, I desire to be at yonder blood, and to be at yonder Lord, and to have him in my arms, and to have my soul washen in that fountain; but yet I cannot get him, and yet I will wait on; and suppose I have not gotten that full persuasion, yet he is my Lord, and I will not admit a contrary cogitation; and suppose I want the true Comforter, I will not admit another in his room and stead. Thou that hast this meikle, thou hast true faith; and this is the *bruised reed* that every wind shakes, and yet it is *not broken*, and like the *smoking flax*, or reiking tow, that a little water would put out, yet *he will not quench it*, Isaiah xlii. 3. this is true believing, and thou that hast it cannot perish; for it is not the measure of thy faith that will save, but it is he whom faith grips. I grant thou wilt never have peace nor rest in thy conscience, until thou beest at that full measure of faith, to that full persuasion, to these exulting joys, when thou art ravished within the third heavens; therefore suppose thou canst not be content with this least and weakest measure, that is a token that thy faith is true, if thou labourest more and more to make it sure; yet the present measure is true faith.

Now, because there lies great things on it, therefore I will confirm it to you by scripture. Can any be blessed without faith? Psal. xxxii. 1. Hence says David, "Blessed is the man whose sin is forgiven." Can any have their sins forgiven them, but these that believe? And Christ says, Matth. v. 4. " Blessed is he who hungers and thirsts for righteousness;" thou that art hungry and thirsty art blessed, and therefore thou must have true faith, suppose thou seest it not: For it is easy to persuade thee that art full of these heavenly joys, and of the Holy Ghost, as Stephen was, Acts vii. 55. I say then, it is easy to persuade thee that thou hast faith, because thou feelest it within thee; but when thou art hungry and thirsty, and thou feelest thy heart toom and void of all grace, when thy soul is withered for want of Christ's blood, it is hard then to persuade thee to believe; yet if thou hast this hunger and thirst, thou art blessed : Why ? Because thou shalt get a fill. It is not the quantity of thy faith shall save thee : Why ? A drop of water is as true water as the whole ocean sea : So a little faith is as true faith as the greatest, suppose it be not so strong ; as a child of eight days old is as really a man as one of 60 years ; a spark of fire is as true fire as a great flame or bonfire; a sickly man is as truly living as a whole man, suppose his life be not so comfortable to him ; so it is not the measure of thy faith that saves thee, it is the blood that it grips to that saves thee, as the weak hand of a bairn that leads the spoon to the mouth, will feed as well as the strongest arm of a man will do; for it is not the hand that feeds thee, albeit it put the meat into thy mouth, but it is the meat carried into the stomach that feeds thee ; it is not the hand that clothes thee, suppose it put on thy garment, but it is the garment itself; it is not the gold ring that stems the blood, but it is the pearl set in the ring ; so it is not thy faith (suppose it be precious) that will heal thy wounds, but it is Christ the precious pearl, set within the ring of thy faith : So if thou canst grip Christ ever so weakly, he will not let thee perish. All that looked to the brazen serpent, never so far off, they were healed of the sting of the fiery serpent ; yet all saw not alike clearly, for some were near hand, and some were afar off ; now these that were near hand behooved to see more clearly than these that were far off ; nevertheless these that were afar off were as soon healed of the sting, when they looked to the serpent, as these that were near hand ; for it was not their look that made them whole, but he whom the serpent did represent, (and then believed he was to come ;) so if thou canst look to Christ ever so meanly, he can take away the sting of thy conscience, if thou believest; yet know, the weakest hand can take a gift as well as the strongest. Now Christ is the gift, and weak faith may grip him as well as strong faith may grip him; and Christ is as truly thine when thou hast a weak faith, as when thou hast come to these triumphant joys through the strength of faith. So comfort yourselves with the meditation of these things. *Amen.*

SERMON XLI.

UPON THE BELIEVER'S SECURITY.

Isaiah xlii. 3.

A bruised reed shall he not break, a smoking flax shall he not quench.

I will open up the text to you. The purpose wherefore this testimony is brought in, it is to verify that this man, Jesus the Son of Mary, that wrought wonders, and healed every disease, and how weak soever their faith was that came to him, he accepted of them, and would not send them away again without comfort: It is verified, I say, that he is the foreknown and foretold Saviour, and that great prophet which was to come; and this place is brought in here to bear witness, that he of whom the Father spake, should be such a man, that should have such and such marks and tokens; that the man, I say, in whom the tokens are found, should be the Saviour of the world; and, among the rest of these tokens, this is one, that he shall be so merciful and meek, that *a bruised reed he will not break, nor a smoking flax he will not quench.* Now, Jesus the son of Mary had such mercy and meekness, that never man had the like before him or after him: therefore he must be the Saviour.

I come to the words: Would ye know him that is the Saviour? The Father points him out after this manner, saying, *Behold my servant,* and he comes as a servant and like a meek lamb. I wot well, that Lamb Jesus Christ, he that is the head and master of the house; his humility and service was such: What should be the humility of the men that should be servants, and yet they would come like lairds and lords?

Well, I let them alone, but I wot well they are not the servants of God. Jesus he is my servant, says the Father; this is great consolation, the love that the Son has for you in the accomplishment and perfecting of your redemption, it is done as good servise to the Father, and the Father is well pleased with that work; *whom I have chosen*, and was chosen and waled out of the same race whereof ye came. My beloved, the Father loves him well, and all the Father's love is in the Son, but he has no love but that, that which is in the Son; then thou canst not be loved except thou beest in the Son; *in whom my soul delights*, this is another thing then to be loved; he said from heaven, *my soul is well pleased with him*; as if he would say, not only I loved him, but also I love the soul that is clad with him; well is the soul that is found in him, for my soul is well pleased with them for his sake, because I look on neither man nor woman but as they are members sticking to his body. " I will put my Spirit on him;" that is, " he shall be anointed with the oil of gladness above his fellows, and shall be filled with the Spirit above measure: He shall shew judgment to the Gentiles;" that is, he shall judge the nations and give light to them that sit in darkness: " He shall not strive nor cry, his voice shall not be heard in the streets." (Here is a lesson to you whose voice is oft heard in the streets: Ye are not like Christ that innocent Lamb, that spake not a word loud in the streets) *a bruised reed will he not break:* It is the heart that is broken through sorrow and grief, for want of the persuasion of the love of God the Father in his Son Jesus Christ. It is *bruised;* that is, it is beat in a mortar with an iron-pestle, for want of that sweet conjunction with the Lord Jesus, who is only life and light, and liberty; the broken heart is a reed, and it is shaken, yet it has a root, and it sticks fast by the root; so the broken heart is destitute of consolation, it is comfortless, it wants rest and joy, for if it had a joy, it would be soon healed, for the wound of the soul is the want of the Lord; therefore the spouse cries,

" my love is gone away, therefore I am sick of love;" but when he is come again, and has taken her within the chambers of his presence, and to his wine-cellar, where she is refreshed with flaggons of wine, and with apples of pleasure, and so she is healed ; so thy heart is sticking to a root, even when it is wounded for want of thy husband and head, the Lord Jesus ; thou art a reed, and thou hast a root, and thou art even grounded on himself, suppose thou perceivest it not, nor feelest it not. Now, let be that he will not pull thee up by the root, he will not do so meikle as break a bruised reed, he will not wip thee sundry, but he will sustain thee by that longing desire; yet thou wilt have no ease till thou gettest him again, and until thou seest thou art fast rooted and grounded in him. A bruised reed is soon broken ; so the soul that pines for want of the refreshing of the fountain of living waters, the Lord knows how little a thing would wip it in two; the tenderest thing in the world is a broken heart, and the Lord knows this, and yet he will not break it ; this is great consolation. Now, are there any of you whose soul laments the absence of the Lord, and would fain seek him, and follow after him with tears, as the Israelites did ? And are any of you saying, Lord, why goest thou away ? Our light, our life, our liberty goes away, when thou departest and goest away ; "therefore turn, Lord, unto us, and hide not thy face from us." Are any of you following him with brokenness of heart, and crying unto him, stay, Lord ? If ye be doing so, then there is your comfort, the Father points out to you so merciful a Lord Jesus, that will not break a bruised reed. This for the first mark.

Now the second, *a smoking flax he will not quench :* of flax, or lint, or tow, where it has a spark of fire in it, and a spunk that neither has light nor heat with it, but only is smoking and sending out a reik with it, he will quench any little thing that would put it out, but he will not let it be put out; even so, where there is a very little spark of faith and love, and the meanest kindling, if it be in thy soul and in thy heart, suppose it give thee not light to look to the love of God, and to look to thy election, redemption, calling, and justification, thy sanctification and endless glory, only it smokes; this is the administry of thy Saviour towards thee, that he will not put out the little thing begun in thy heart; so hold thee by the meanest measure of faith, if it were no more but a waiting on with patience, until the Lord blow at the spark that lies lurking in thy heart, that same very spark shall grow to a flame at last, and it shall get all the joints of thy soul loosed and all the hardness of thy heart melted, "till he bring forth judgment unto victory." What a judgment is this, when the judge sits down, and all parties are called on, and they are all heard, then the sentence is given out, and the party absolved gets the victory; even so the bruised reed shall not be broken, nor the smoking flax shall not be quenched, till thou gettest the victory over hell and death, over sin and Satan, over all thy enemies, and till thou beest brought to this gloriation that shall make thee to say, who dare condemn my soul for whom the Son has died, and is now risen and gone up to heaven, and is pleading for me, saying to the Father, give remission to yon soul for whom I died; then comes that full persuasion and assurance of the love of God towards thee, which is the highest degree of faith, and this shall make thee cry, Now, "I am persuaded, that neither death nor life, nor angels, nor principalities, nor powers, nor things present, nor things to come, nor height, nor depth, nor any other creature, shall be able to separate me from the love of Christ Jesus, my Lord." Now then, wouldst thou know thy Saviour, what an one he is? Such an one as *will not break the bruised reed, nor quench the smoking flax*. Now, wait the time, then thou shalt get this full persuasion, that thy absolution is pronounced, and the sentence given out, that he is thy Lord, and thou art his; therefore thou belongest to the promise, because he died for thee, and he shall never leave thee, and one day thou shalt be put into the peaceable possession of that glory in heaven (which now thou but hopest for and lookest for) to remain for evermore.

Now the question ye should all spier, and the thing ye should all spier, is this, Whether is Christ thy Saviour, thy Redeemer, or not? For if he be thine, thou mayest with boldness step in to the throne before the Father, and lay claim to all the promises made to thee in Christ; if thou beest not his, thou darest not come into his presence. Now, there will be sundry doubts here, which Satan will cast in to hinder thee to apply Christ to thy soul; the one is, thy soul is destitute of all consolation. Now where Christ is, there is comfort enough. The other is, where faith is, there must be conveyed to it a triumphant persuasion following on it; but I feel none of these things in my heart, therefore how can Christ be mine, or how can I apply him to myself? Hear the answer, The Father gives thee this ground to build thy faith upon, assure thyself, that he is a Saviour so merciful, that "he will not break a bruised reed, nor he will not quench a smoaking flax." Mark then, if thou seest thy heart is broken and wounded, because thy Lord is away from thee, and thou hast caused him to depart, and thou art sorry because thou canst not apply him, and there is a spark or spunk of love left in thy soul, and if it were no more than this, thou wouldst rise and seek him wherever thou mayest have him, and thou wilt not rest until thou gettest him, thou hast this meikle. Then hear the Father speaking of those that have weak faith, *a bruised reed he will not break, and a smoaking flax he will not quench, till he bring forth judgment to victory*. Mark next, the wounded soul, and the broken heart, suppose it be bruised, yet it has a root in Christ, and let be that he will not pull thee up by the root, he will never break thee; and have thou but a smoaking flax, he will not quench that, and he will never leave thee, *until he bring forth judgment to victory*, the which victory shall bring such peace of conscience, as shall make thee triumph over all thy enemies. Ye see the Lord will be content with a little wee thing, and of so small a thing he will make a great. This should encourage us to come to him.

Mark, 3*dly*, As the bruised reed he will not break it, so he will not let the devil break it with his machinations, nor thou wouldst not break it thyself with thy incredulity; and so, of the smoking flax, beware that Satan quench it not with his manifold speats of temptations, and beware that he bring not foul water, and pour it on thy heart to quench it. Therefore keep thee from two extremities; the one is, keep thee from incredulity, and look that there be not " an unfruitful heart of unbelief in any of you, to depart away from the living God;" and beware that ye forsake not the promise at any time, but hold ay thy heart open by believing: Incredulity will toom thy heart of him that made the heavens and earth, and of him that gave his hands to be bound for thee; so if there be no more but a broken heart, and a desire to believe, suppose thou hast never experience of effectual calling, but meikle more when thou art called, it is enough to encourage you to come to so merciful a Lord, because ye have a right to him: For, when ye were born, ye were within the covenant, he has bidden you be baptized, and in your baptism, he has promised and bound himself to be your God, and to forgive your sins; and ye have bound yourself to believe. Remember, these that were the natural branches were cut off through unbelief. Thou art born within the covenant, and art ingrafted in Christ, thou standest in the root; wilt thou then cut off thyself through unbelief? Beware of that; stand fast rooted and grounded in him, and never rest till thou findest thyself established and grounded on the Rock, that the gates of hell shall not prevail against thee. Remember, thou that misbelievest, deniest God's mercy, thou deniest his justice, thou deniest his truth, and so thou deniest God himself; the misbelief of Judas was beyond the treachery of him; for that blood was able to save him, if he had run to it, and craved mercy. So, of all sins that ever thou canst commit, incredulity or unbelief is the greatest; therefore believe, suppose thou hast no feeling, and hope above hope, suppose thou seest little appearance, and thou shalt glorify God, and save thy own soul. To him be praise for evermore. *Amen.*

SERMON XLII.

UPON GOD'S EVERLASTING LOVE.

John iii. 16, 17.

For God so loved the world, that he gave his only begotten Son, that whosoever believeth in him should not perish, but have everlasting life. For God sent not his Son into the world, to condemn the world, but that the world through him might be saved.

IN this chapter our Lord gets a visit from Nicodemus, a ruler of the Jews, a man, as it appears who wanted not wit in law, but very ignorant of the mysteries of salvation. It is much to be lamented, that men of learning and knowledge, whose wit will go very far in the law, and other matters concerning things of this life, and, in matters of salvation, are but like babes. Nicodemus wants to pay our Lord a visit, but it appears that he did not want that it should be known; therefore he comes at night; he is afraid to confess Christ publickly to the world, lest he should suffer loss of other things; it being enacted by a law, "That if any men confessed Christ, he should be cast out of the synagogue." But whatever was his fears, our Lord who went always about doing good, takes the opportunity to converse with him about the great mysteries of salvation, and tells him, in the 3d verse, "That, except a man be born again, he cannot see the kingdom of God." Nicodemus discovers his great ignorance of the new birth, and asks a question at Christ, "How can a man be born again when he is old? Can he enter the second time into his mother's womb, and be born?" Jesus answers his question, and tells him, that the new birth was of another nature, namely, "that he must be born of water and of the

Spirit;" and tells him further, that this new birth is not visible, like a natural birth; but, "as the wind bloweth where it listeth, and we cannot tell from whence it cometh, or whither it goeth, so is every one that is born of the Spirit." In the 12th verse, Jesus upbraids him with his unbelief, and tells him, that his errand to the world was, to lay down his life for sinners, ver. 14. "As Moses lifted up the serpent in the wilderness, even so must the Son of Man be lifted up; that whosoever believeth on him, should not perish but have eternal life." And, in the words of our text, he tells the reason of all this, viz. The love that God the Father had to the elect world: And, my dear friends, here is one of the greatest wonders, that ever appeared in this lower world, *God so loved the world, that he gave his only begotten Son:* He is the greatest gift that ever were given to either men or angels. What are all other gifts that ever were given to this great gift?

First, In the words we have the giver, *God the Father.*

Secondly, The cause of the gift, *God so loved the world that he gave——*

Thirdly, The gift itself—*his only begotten Son.* God the Father had no greater gift than this, his only Son, who lay in his bosom from everlasting, and a Son that never offended him, but was always his delight; yet, for his love he bore to the elect world, he parted with him for a time, that he might accomplish the great plot of infinite love for mankind sinners. Hence we may see what is the effect of all his love, *that whosover believeth in the Son shall not perish but have everlasting life.*

First, Then, O sinner thou must believe that Jesus Christ is the only begotten Son of God, clothed in our nature, and that it is through the virtue of his being God as well as man, that this everlasting life is to be had.

Secondly, Thou must believe, that he died for thee, he rose again for thee, he was humbled for thee, and glorified for thee; yet for all this there will be darkness; as a man in prison, there a wimble bore where the sun shines, and he once sees the beams of the sun, and yet there is nothing but darkness round about; even so it is here, faith lets thee see the light of the Son of righteousness so overshadowing thy soul, and yet there is nothing but darkness within thee. Next, there is a consent and approbation of that light; thou seest, allowest and esteemest of that light, for it is the precious pearl that thou seekest.

And *thirdly*, There is a judgment and tribunal decreeted in thy soul, wherein there is a judge, a party, a decreet, and a process, and absolution made: the judge is Christ, the guilty rebel is thy own soul, wherein there is a judge, a plea, a decreet; the accuser is the law, the devil and your wicked conscience, and the justice of God; thy dittay; a rebel from thy mother's womb, or from the beginning: now, faith is thy advocate, he makes answer, I grant all, but I have enough in Christ to answer you all; then upon this defence comes in the sentence, which is this, "he that believes in the Son shall never perish." Thy conscience answers, I believe in the Son: the law and the gospel gives out the conclusion, "therefore thou shalt never perish." *Last*, There is the use; when the sentence is pronounced; then thou makest forward in thy journey with a full main-sail, and so runnest into thy Lord: yet this is not the highest degree, but faith goes forward; for thou art not yet content, suppose thou seest thy name put up in the book of life, which is in Christ coming down to thy soul, that thou wilt say, O blood, come and fill a toom heart; I hunger and thirst, for thee, come, come, to fill me: then faith brings him down to thy soul: then when thou hast gotten him he will say, I will give thee but a taste and a prieving of me; and I will give thee a ring with fine jewels in it, to be a token to thee, therefore thou must long for my appearing, because thou must go up to heaven with me. I told you from that, that faith will gar thee go with thy burden, and lay it on him; it will gar thee go with a hungry and thirsty soul, to eat him, and drink him; it will gar thee go with a naked soul, to put him on thee: Faith is defined in Heb. xi. 1. "Faith is the ground of things hoped for, and the evidence of things not seen;" the Greek word is, *hypostasis*, it signifies three things.

First, It is a ground whereupon thou layest no less than the endless salvation of thy soul; so the believer sees a condemnation, then he sees no remedy in the law, but in the gospel he hears that the believer shall never go to condemnation; faith then takes thy soul and says to it, thou art undone for evermore, except thou believest. The heart answers, hereon I lay my salvation, on the certainty of this promise. Then faith answers, and says, I dare pledge the glory of God, that thou shalt never perish. *Next*, Faith will take thee to hell, and make it present to thee, to heaven, and it will make it present to thee, it will take thee to the decreed counsel of God, and make it present to thee; faith never casts thee off his word; the word says, thou, thou wast loved before all eternity; faith says, I believe. I see that the word says, the believer is justified; and faith says, I believe. The word says, there is a crown of glory laid up for the poor sinner; faith says, I see that, and I will wait patiently for it. Faith will lead thee to the very incarnation of Christ, and make it present to thee: faith will do more for thee, for it, *first*, Will make thy ground sure. 2*dly*, It makes things eternal present. 3*dly*, It makes thee stand, and set thy foot as an armed man, against all the speats of the terrors of God against thee; so it gars thee stand, for it is the buckler that quenches all the fiery darts of the devil: thou hast that jacket that will bide the proof of the cannon, suppose thou shouldst say, "the Lord has set me up as a mark to shoot at," suppose thou shouldst say with David, Psal. xxii. 1. *The Lord has forsaken me*, and suppose thou shouldst say with Heman the Ezrahite, Psal. lxxxviii. 15. "I suffer the terrors of God from my very youth:" yet faith will gar thee stand against all these, for it will say to thee that the love of God is unchangeable, "suppose thou shouldst slay me, yet I will trust in thee;" for a man that believes may have strong battles, and he must *fight a good fight;* for the winds will blow, and the storms will set on the house, and faith must hold it up. Besides this, faith is called, *the evidence of things not seen;* it is the character and evidence of our inheritance; I have that blood sealed up to me, I have the Spirit within me, therefore I know this heritage belongs to me; as for the author, it is evident, it is given to you freely to believe, so it is the gift of God; God opens the heart of Lydia, and she believes; faith is the work of God, "look up to him who is the author and finisher of your faith. He believed, and therefore he spake;" so it is the Spirit, sent from the Father and the Son, that works faith: this is the thing that makes a man to believe. Thou wilt say, if thou hadst faith, thou wilt never doubt; but when thou lookest into thyself, and missest the power of believing, thou doubtest: but thou shouldst not do so, but thou shouldst look up to heaven; for it is as impossible for thee to believe, as it is to thee to open the eyes of the blind; for this power of believing is not within the compass of nature; for it was a mystery to the angels till it was revealed in the gospel; by faith, says the apostle, "which is according to the operation of God, that raised up Jesus from the dead to life; so that same power must work in the power of believing. The law will say, *do and thou shalt live,* but it will never give thee power to do: but the gospel says, *believe, and thou shalt live,* and, with the same breath, it draws down the arm of God to thy soul, and gives thee power to believe. Next, the law requires perfection; but the gospel requires no more but faith in an honest heart, believing in sincerity, suppose it be mixt with doubtings, and suppose there be a hell in the nook of thy heart, as the apostle says, Rom. vii. 24, "who shall deliver me from this body of sin?" This was his misery; but he had not sold himself to sin; therefore he said, he consented not to it. What more? The gospel descends to thy infirmity; that if thou hast no more but a reiking tow, and if thou hast no more but an earnest desire to believe, and if thou hast no more, but that thou canst pray for faith, then thou hast the same consolation of the believer.

Now, I go forward: faith has three marks, 1*st.* A certainty of the promise. 2*dly,* Perseverance. 3*dly,* The life of Christ dwelling in the heart. That it has a certainty I need not prove it; for faith can make thee sure, and it does make thee sure, but yet only the renewed part; it only makes the law of thy mind sure, and the law of thy members sure ; it makes Jacob sure, and not Esau; for he counted no more of the promise than of a mess of pottage ; for there is an Esau within thee, that will make thee to count no more of the promise than of a mess of pottage ; but there is a part within thee that makes thee like the merchant, that found a pearl, that he went and sold all that he had for it ; so that no man can tell what unspeakable joy will be in the heart of the believer ; upon this certainty comes the battle, after a particular fall and security. Now, what is the ground of this certainty ? If thou beest a true believer, thou canst tell me a reason wherefore thou believest ; thou canst render me a reason of thy hope, and thou canst tell me what things can bereave thee of thy hope, and cut away thy anchor : it may be in the time of calmness ye will not take meikle thought for an anchor to your ship ; but ye should know there is a storm coming on, therefore ye should make your ship sure with cables and anchors. There your ground,

First, Ye lean upon the unchangeable strength of God ; *he is faithful that has promised.*

Secondly, Ye have the power of God ; Abraham gave glory to God, for " he believed that he that had promised, was able to perform."

Thirdly, Ye have the sworn testimony of God, that cannot be altered ; by these two unchangeable things thou mayest have strong consolation.

Fourthly, I look to the blood of Christ, his humiliation, his glorification ; therefore it concludes, no more can I be rugged from Christ, than he can be from my flesh and blood ; no more can I go to hell, than Christ can go to hell ; and no more can I be banished from heaven, than Christ can be rugged out of heaven.

Fifthly, Thou hast the testament of Christ sealed with his blood ; thou hast more, thou hast the King's seals in baptism and the Lord's supper. What more ? " there are three in heaven that bear witness, the Spirit," that is, all the graces and marks of the Spirit that God has given thee, as mainly, faith, love, patience, and all the rest. Next, the water, that is, the cleansing of the heart that was once foul.

Thirdly, There is the blood, that is, all the comfort and consolation that thou hast found in Christ, and the virtue which thou hast felt to proceed and come from him. More, this faith shall never fail thee, thou shalt never tyne it, suppose it were overshadowed for a time with clouds. Now, because all have not a like measure of faith, I will tell you the meanest measure that ye must have : wot ye what it is ? It is a broken heart, and that hunger and thirst in a soul that dare not apply and yet dare not cast away ; and that dare not call God his father, and yet dare not say the contrary ; that has no sense of the love of God, and yet dare not admit a contrary cogitation : there the meanest degree of faith : now, yet the strongest faith and the weakest faith will have the wrestlings of it ; for God will wrestle and strive with thee to get thee off thy feet, and faith's wrestling will be such, that the child of God thinks that there is not a straw broad between him and condemnation, and he will say, I see the angry face of God against me, I see hell open to swallow me up, I see the devils ready to devour me, what shall I do ? Now a little thing would put thee over the brae ; and yet in this wrestling thou art sustained by a secret power of God, for he wrestles against thee with one hand, and holds thee up with the other ; but the believer will set to his feet as he dow, and he will hope above hope, and he will believe above his feeling, and so he gets the victory, and overcomes at the last; and when he gets the victory, he gets unspeakable joy, that he will cry out, " Death, where is thy sting ? Hell, where is thy victory ?" Devil, where art thou now? What canst thou say against me ? " Now I am persuaded that nothing can separate me from the love of God in Christ Jesus my Saviour ;" so faith has its own growings and sometimes its own decayings; as ye see the trees in Summer have their leaves and flourishes, and their fruit, but in Winter they are, as it were dead ; even so, faith will sometimes bear fruit, and have life, and sometimes none ; but faith once given can never be taken away, for this link of salvation cannot be broken, " whom he has called, he has predestinate ; and whom he has predestinate, them he has adopted ; and whom he has adopted, them he has justified; and whom he has justified, them also shall he glorify." So thou art persuaded, that this link shall never be broken.

The *third* property of faith, it is lively ; for there is a dead faith spoken of by James ; but the true believer he lives by faith, and he will ay lay hold on Christ ; so if Christ be in thee, he will make thee live ; and if thou hast never gotten life from him, thou hast never believed ; faith will take thee to the cross, and nail thy sins to the cross, and lay thee in the grave with him ; faith will raise thee out of the grave again, and by the same power that he raised himself from the dead to life, he will raise thee from death to life, and set thy heart in heaven with himself, and by the life of Christ thou livest ; so faith has life with it, and the life of faith stands in these eight points.

First, It speaks unspeakable peace that passes all understanding, and this peace guards thy heart about, that all the powers of hell are not able to bereave thee of it ; then thou walkest with confidence and boldness, having thy heart in heaven ; because thou art reconciled to God, and thou hast thy peace confirmed to thee and sealed.

Secondly, From this peace the gates open to thee in heaven, and thou wilt say, well is me, I am not a stranger in heaven, having peace with God thro' our Lord Jesus Christ.

Thirdly, There is unspeakable joy, that a sinner can wade through a thousand hells to step into that glory in heaven, to that crown which he has set before me.

Fourthly, Faith brings love, for it makes a golden spout through the riven side of Christ Jesus, and brings down the rivers of love upon thee ; then arises thy love to him, and thou desirest no more consolation, but to get leave to love God, and to sound his praise all the days of thy life.

Fifthly, A hope and expectation that makes thee lift up thy head, and shoot it within the kingdom of heaven; and there thou seest a crown of glory laid up for thee, which thou lookest for patiently, so thou hopest to come by it at the last.

Sixthly, Thou seest Christ so sweet to thee, that thou countest all things but dirt and dung, so thou mayest win him, and thou countest all things but loss, that thou mayest gain him.

Seventhly, Thou desirest no more but to know Christ, and him crucified.

Eighthly, and last of all, It makes thee change thy company that thou wilt say, all my delight is with the saints, this will make thee to have a desire that all were as thou art, and thou wilt pray for them thou never sawest ; it makes thee spread thy love to all the saints in the earth, and thy love will reach to the very saints in heaven, and thou longest to be with them, and thou knowest that the fellowship and communion of the saints it is the life of thy faith, and therein stands thy joy here beneath. This living faith will make thee bring forth living works ; then there will be life in thy prayers, then there will be such delight in the word of God, that thou canst meditate on that law both day and night ; then in thy calling thou dost thy work chearfully and willingly, because God has set thee in it, and thou dost it diligently, because thou hast thy heart in heaven, and thou knowest it pleases God and he allows of it; because it is done in faith, it must please God.

Now, faith has two companions, love and hope, and faith fills thy soul with the love of God, and the hope of that glory; and love lets thee see his to thee again; Faith brings the bowels of God's mercy on thee, and love makes thee spread thy love and pity on his saints; Faith bids thee believe, and thou shalt see great things, and hope says, I believe, and I hope to see the thing that never eye saw, nor ever ear heard, nor ever entered into the heart of man, they shall be clearly revealed one day as I hope. Now follows the first degree and manner how God works faith in the souls of men and women. 2*dly*, The benefits of faith, if a man offer a gift to thee, what canst thou do less than to take it out of his hand; so when God reaches out his blessings to thee, mayest thou not take them out of his hand. Now it is not thy faith that gets thee these blessings, but it is the rich pearl in the gold-ring that stems the blood, and not the ring itself; therefore the benefits of faith come from the jewel that it grips, and Christ gripped by faith, works all these things. There are nine or ten several benefits that faith brings thee. *First*, It pulls thee out of nature, and plants thee in Jesus Christ the tree of life; there thou tynest thy nature, for thou art made one with Christ; so that thou renouncest the rotten stock of Adam, and thou claimest to a better lineage; thou renouncest thy wisdom, and thou wilt learn thy wisdom of God; thou renouncest thy own understanding, and reason, and thou wilt understand nothing but that which God's word bids thee understand. 2*dly*, When it has set thee in Christ it makes thee the son of God, for Christ is the only Son and heir of all things, so through him thou art adopted to be the heir of him, and with him of eternal life; and this is no small gift to make thee that wast the son of perdition to become the Son of God, and heir of all things with him. 3*dly*, It brings remission of all thy sins, both of original and actual, before thy calling; and after thy calling, it gets thee pardon of thy evil words, or thy evil deeds, or evil thoughts, were they never so great, or never so many. *4thly*, Faith, it justifies, it lets thee see that thou art naked, and it makes thee put on the garments of the innocency and righteousness of Jesus Christ, and being clad with him, thou art justified in the sight of God, and counted as righteous as if thou hadst never sinned. *5thly*, It opens the door of heaven to thee, and thou wilt say, I will go into my Lord's chamber, and I will sup with him, and I will rest under the wings of my Saviour; I know he will deny me nothing that I will ask of him in the name of his Son in whom he is well pleased. *6thly*, When he has led thee in there, thou seest thy foul heart, then faith says to thee, go into yon blood, and it will cleanse it, suppose thy soul be as red as scarlet, yet he is able to make it as white as snow. *Objection*, I am foul and ugly, I dare not lay my hands on him; it will say to thee, thou must lay hold on him, for he came to seek and save sinners. *7thly*, Faith will give thee this confidence, may I not pray and be homely with God, seeing he is become my father through Christ, I will be bold now to go to him, because I am reconciled to him; before I was his enemy, and durst not go near him, but now he has made me his friend. *8thly*, Faith makes all things possible to thee, for nothing is impossible to the believer. O! What is it that faith will not do? Faith saved Noah and his household in the ark, when all the world was drowned: Faith clave the Red Sea, and drowned Pharaoh and all his host: Faith shut up and closed up the heavens, that it rained not for three years and six months, and faith opened them again, and, in a word, will make thee accomplish that saying, I will have no fellowship with the unfruitful works of darkness, I have no delight in the things of this world, I take no pleasure in these things beneath; my conversation and haunting is in heaven, my treasure is in heaven, my life, my glory, and my crown is in heaven.

Now for the obtaining faith, there must be first a distinct knowledge of thy in-born corruption, and that there is nothing for thee by nature but remediless condemnation, and thou art meet for nothing but to be a faggot for hell's fire; and thou must know that thou bearest about with thee the things that will be thy own condemnation, and thou must know that thou art worthy of the curse and malediction of God. 2*dly*, Thou must know a remedy for it, which is only the blood of the Son of God, and except that thou knowest a remedy for thy misery (thou wilt be the worse to know it) and the knowledge of thy misery is the first step to grace; but when thou hast known thy misery, then thou must know the remedy, 3*dly*, Thou must know that there is no way to salvation, but by believing in the only begotten Son of God; for faith is the hand that grips Christ, and lays him to the wound of thy soul, and so he heals it. 4*thly*, Thou must know that thou must appropriate him to thyself, or else he will do thee no good; for what avails it thee to know that there is a Saviour, unless thou knowest that he is thy Saviour, and what good will it be to thee to know that Christ died for sinners, except thou knowest he died even for thee? So the first degree of a gracious faith is a believed torment of pain in hell, that the voice of God will be like a roaring lion, an iron-sceptre, a heavy burden pressing thee down.

Secondly, When thou seest thou wilt stand on the brae, thou wilt say, what will I do, is yon prepared for me, shall I go back to my life again? I cannot, for I will but sin more and more, and increase the wrath of God, I dare not go forward, lest I be consumed in yon fire I wot not what to do, I will stand still and wait, and see what the Lord will do with me, I will wait upon the Lord's good will. 3*dly*, Thou wilt begin to be sober, and thy heart will soften, and the hard clods thereof will break, then thou wilt say, Lord, wilt thou speak some comfort to my silly soul, I long to be reconciled with thee, now thy blood shall be sweet to me, I desire no more in this world, but a blink of thy sweet face, and thy loving countenance to shine upon my soul. 4*thly*, Thou wilt resolve never to go back to thy former ways, because they have beguiled thee, therefore thou wilt say, I promise in the presence of God, if he will reach out the golden sceptre to me, I will take my hazard, and if I die I shall die praying, and if I perish let me perish on, for I shall ay look to thee, suppose thou shouldst thrust me down to hell, and suppose thou shouldst slay me yet I will trust in thee. 5*thly*, Thou wilt have a hunger and thirst that nothing will fill, but the flesh of Christ, and nothing can slocken thee, but this blood allenarly; all things on earth cannot satisfy thee, till thou gettest Christ in the arms of thy soul, till thou beest sure of him. 6*thly*, Thou will count so meikle of salvation, that thou wilt bid all sin and the pleasures thereof farewell; and thou wilt not give thy Lord for ten thousand worlds, and thou wilt not lose his favour or lose thy peace and joy thou hast in his presence, for all the pleasures under heaven. Last of all, comes in thy glory and thy peace; then God at the last gives thee to believe, when he says, come, poor sinner, wilt thou not want me, come to me, thou shalt get me, I will be loath to bide from thee, thou art wearied and tired with the burden of thy sins, I will refresh and ease thee, I will not let thee perish; then the Lord says, thou art naked, come and I will put on robes on thee; then the soul will say, and thou hast said, " blessed are they that mourn," Lord, I would fain mourn if I could; thou hast said, " blessed are they that hunger and thirst for righteousness:" Lord, I would fain hunger and thirst, I would fain have a bit of thy flesh, and drink of thy blood, and I would fain believe if I durst, and if I saw any appearance or token of thy love to me. Jacob supposed never to have seen his son Joseph, and when his sons told him that he was living, he could not believe them; when they told him, there the chariots he has sent to thee, then he considers, wherefrae come these? O! know I now my son is living. Even so it is with thee that art a believer; at the first time thou trowest that thou art lost, and all light and life is away, and thou thinkest it is not possible that thou canst be saved, and so great a sinner as thou art can be pardoned. But when thou gettest any token from the Lord, and seest any appearance of his presence, then thou believest and grippest to the promise made to thee in Christ's blood; so look to the means, and if ever God has taken such a dealing with thy soul in any true measure, then thou mayest be glad, for thou hast the seed of true saving faith sown in thee, and thou mayest be sure the Lord will never leave thee, nor he will not let thee perish. Amen.

SERMON XLIII.

UPON GOD'S EVERLASTING LOVE.

John iii. 16, 17.

God so loved the world, that he gave his only begotten Son, that whosoever believeth in him should not perish, but have everlasting life, &c.

THE Lord's love and care to us has declared itself many ways, and especially in this point, that this privy conference with Nicodemus, spoken at this time for our consolation, it hath pleased the Lord to put it up in register, that it may be the consolation of many; and suppose it was privy and in the night, yet it has pleased the Holy Ghost to bear record of it, that all the believers to the end of the world may have their consolation in it. Now in these verses read, is, *first,* The fountain of our salvation, *the love of God.* 2*dly,* There is the means whereby he has uttered it, which is, *by the sending his Son,* to be humbled and glorified. 3*dly,* The means to get Christ that is, *by faith only.* 4*thly,* The benefit and conquest of our faith, which is, *salvation:* For this end did the Father love us, that he might save us, and give unto us eternal life; for this cause came the Son down from heaven; and for this cause was he humbled and glorified; and for this cause he went to heaven, that he might give us eternal life; and for this cause the Father causes us believe, and this is the fruit and end of all believing, to wit, eternal life. So it remains to tell what are the benefits that the believer gets in the Son. Now leaving all that has been spoken concerning this mystery of faith, as for the benefit that faith gets, in a word, it is salvation. I know it gets more benefits before it will plant thee in Christ, and make thee one with him; it will make thee flesh of his flesh, and bone of his bone; it will make thee sit in heaven with him; It will crucify thee with Christ, and it will justify thee in Christ; it will get thee remission in his blood; and it will cleanse thy heart; for it is that bush of hyssop that will sprinkle that blood on thy soul, Exodus xii. 22. Faith, in a word, will make thee to live in peace at the last, and it will put thee in the peaceable possession of that endless glory. If ye get not the former benefit, ye will not get the last, and when thou gettest the last, then thy faith shall cease: so except the conjunction be made between thy soul and Christ by the Holy Ghost, and unless thou gettest the Spirit of adoption, faith will never bring thee to the last point, and if it bring thee to the first, it shall bring thee to the last. So faith begins in this life, but it makes nothing complete till the resurrection, when soul and body shall be caught within the clouds; so look what faith works in thy heart, for if thy living faith have not a work of grace here in thy soul, it shall never have a work of glory hereafter. Now, the last thing which faith brings, which is salvation, it stand in two points.

First, In an immunity and freedom from perdition. 2*dly*, In the fruition and possession of eternal life; and both these we have here. Now I will tell you what both these are: What is the cause that makes the world count so little of Christ, and of the love of God in Christ? It is this, They know not what it is to perish for evermore, and what it is to live for evermore; so if ye knew this, ye would esteem more of Christ, and of the love of God than ever ye did: *Whosoever believes shall not perish*, then it is certain, that there is a perdition, there is a hell wherein is endless perdition; *Whosoever believes shall not perish;* there is a life after this, there is a hell and a heaven, howsoever it be that the God of this world has blinded the most part, and the devil has bewitched men and women; yet it is certain that there is a God, that there is a hell and a perdition, so it is certain that there is everlasting life; the generation before, if ye could hear them, they would all tell you this; some in an endless pleasure, some in an endless torment; for they are all gone before you to be preachers to you.

Now, wherein stands this perdition and perishing, for it is the first point I am minded to tell you. 2*dly*, Wherein all life stands.

As for the first, there are three things in it; 1*st*, The want of joy. 2*dly*, The presence of pain. 3*dly*, The eternity of the loss of joy, and the eternity of the presence of pain: Think on them all.

First, It is the loss of the presence of God, that the saints and angels have in heaven, within the gates of the New Jerusalem: Thou mayest not eat of that tree of life; thou mayest not drink of the rivers of the waters of life; thou mayest not drink in that company of saints and angels, that hast not believed in the Son of God here: So if there were no other hell, but to be deprived of the blessed society of the glorified saints and angels with God, it were hell enough.

Secondly, Consider that no excuse will be admitted that day: Friendship will do thee no good, prophesying and preaching will do thee no good. The other thing that augments it, is the loss of happiness. An unknown benefit when it is lost shall not bring meikle pain with it, but a seen benefit, a joy which ye might gave gotten, if ye could have believed, shall augment your pain wonderfully: As the pain of the rich glutton had not been so great, if he had not seen Lazarus in Abraham's bosom; so the exclusion and the barring of the gate on the misbeliever, on the soul and carcase for evermore, this is the first in the perdition; therefore the tribunal must be in the air, for thou shalt never win in at the gate of that kingdom; and if there were not another torment but the want of these joys in heaven for evermore, it were torment enough: But if there were no more, what rack of all this want of joy, and rugging and separation of the soul and body from the presence of God and his saints, in whom is all-sufficient joy? How grievous shall that be to thee? How ill-will had Peter to come down from the mount, trow ye? Ye would think it hard to be rugged and separated from a friend, and more from your own children; O! but what is that in comparison to be separated from so loving a God; but this is not all, the depriving of endless joy, (now this should cause you know the necessity of believing,) but, besides this, there is an eternity of pain; to lose heaven is a great matter, but to be cast into hell is greater; to want the palace is great, but to be flung into prison is greater; to lose the pleasure of heaven is great, but to be cast into the lake of fire and brimstone, " where the worm never dies, and the fire never goes out;" into such a fire, that the violence thereof is such, that there is no patience to bear it; for it is so great and painful, that if thou hadst ten thousand worlds thou wouldst give them all for one drop of cold water to cool thy tongue; a fire that shall never be slockened, for it shall burn as long as God lives. Again, That fire shall not consume the carcase and soul, but it is a furnace that shall burn for evermore, and thou shalt have none to keep the flames of that fire from thy conscience and carcase, and there shall be the wrath of God, and the vials full of his indignation, poured out continually upon thy soul, that it shall never get leave to look for mercy, and put off all hope of help, or ending of that pain. Besides this, there are these particulars and circumstances that aggrege this perdition; there is nothing there but a consuming fire, no company but devils, no light but a mirk prison and darkness, bound hand and foot, a death ay beginning, but never shall have an end, a worm that ay shall gnaw thy conscience. Again, It were some ease if any part of the soul or body were free of torment; but there shall never be a part of thy body free that shall not be filled with torments, and never a faculty of thy soul but it shall have its own torment; an eye that thou wouldst not open to behold the glory of God, it shall be compelled to look on that ugly sight; thy ear that thou wouldst not apply to hear the voice of God, it shall be compelled to hear the howling and blaspheming of devils and reprobates; thy mind and understanding, which thou abusest in this life, shall have their own torments.

Thirdly, There is an eternity of pain, and an eternity of loss; ye know, were the traveller or mariner never so wearied, yet the hope of an end will bring him consolation; but here there is no hope of an end; therefore there can be no consolation; but when thou knowest thy pain is endless; and when thou rememberest the eternity of time, and they know, as long as God lives their pain shall last; this spoils them of all consolation.

The next point is, what it is to have eternal life, and wherein it stands. It stands in thee things shortly. I know it is a thing that cannot be understood, none can measure the glory of that kingdom, and the joys of that life; for he that was ravished and saw it, he said he saw things unutterable. Always there are three things in it;

First, The glory of the place, *not an house made with hands*, but that new Jerusalem that has twelve ports that are of precious stones, the streets of gold, the temple of it God himself.

Secondly, The fruition of it, God himself, that shall be all in all to thee; and as ye see a drop of water mixed with a hogshead of wine, it taints the taste; so all our infirmities being flowing in the ocean-sea of God's glory shall be swallowed up.

Thirdly, and *last of all*, There is an unspeakable peace and joy for evermore; no more sin there; no more trouble there; no more tears there; but contemplation and joy for evermore, and thou occupied in beholding God eternally, and running to the fountain of the love of that blessed God, and wondering thereat eternally.

Now, ye see the first benefit ye shall get by believing;
First, A freedom from endless perdition.
Secondly, The fruition of eternal life.
The ends wherefore I have spoken of these two, are,
First, That ye may see the necessity of believing, and that ye that will not believe may quit you of eternal life, and make you for that endless pain.
Secondly, To set before you how highly ye should count of the Son of God; that when there was nothing that could redeem thee from hell, and conquer heaven to thee, but only his blood, and that thou mayest be acquainted what thou shouldst count of the love of God to thee, that sent his only begotten Son to die for thee.

Now I will apply, and so I will end. Why should word or work, ordinary or extraordinary; why should it run to your hearts; for if less things could have done the turn, it would have been done? I know the Lord is merciful and loath to destroy his own buildings, and to pluck up the plants which his own hand planted; so if the word had done it, the work had not been done: These things that are fallen out are not only warnings to you, but they are warnings to make you believe; and therefore think not that they were greater sinners than ye; "but except ye repent, ye shall perish also with the like judgment."

I have not now time to commit to you how many things I designed. Since I came here, God has added to his word for our walking; it is not long since there was not an house among you, but there were some of you bed-sick, and some of you have been restored from the very death again; and I know some of you had rather laid down your life than have convoyed them to the grave. Now the more this be old, yet it is not the less. What need was ye in, when ye would be content to have wanted your whole stock for half a year's provision? I leave this to your own conscience. Likewise, how the Lord has guarded you round about, and gave command to the pest that it should not come near to your ports, when he scattered it over other congregations, and made men and women cry, I have no more but one hundred merks, take it all, and give me leave to take one hatful of water: Their skallet-boards, and skallet-trenchers in Glasgow and Edinburgh, they may bear you witness. I wot well ye had as great sins of incessant whoredom as they had. What other extraordinary things fell out, I have not will to tell you; but if I would shew you it, ye would say, He will spare one, and shew severity to another; and if there be no more but that mad woman, she might be a preacher to us all: May not God soon bereave us of our wits, and make us as beasts, as he did Nebuchadnezzar? And those two works that have fallen out this week, one in the night, and another in the noon-tide of the day, he will have all these to cry to you, that ye should cry to the Lord, and say, Lord, keep me and my children, that we get not a doleful wakening; thou mayest rise in the morning, but who can tell with how doleful a heart thou mayest lie down in the evening, that ye may know what need ye have of a protection. I cannot tell what these thick spurring warnings mean; I wot well God has a warning for you in this congregation and town, as well as your nearest neighbours: So I see the Lord will have us either renewed to God, by true repentance in time, or else it will be all wrong with us. Now, I beseech you, wit well that you reconcile you and your children to God ere you lie down, and let them not step out of the door in the morning, till ye have commended you and them to God; trow ye not that these have been fearful warnings to the mother that bare them, and to the father out of whose loins they came; and as they are fearful preachers to them, so let them be to you; and I lay this necessity on every one of you, that ye hold up your hands to God evening and morning.

Now to him that is able to protect you in soul and body, Father, Son, and Holy Ghost, be praise, honour, and glory for evermore. *Amen.*

SERMON XLIV.

THE UNBELIEVER CONDEMNED.

John iii. 17.

For God sent not his Son into the world to condemn the world, but that the world through him might be saved.

THERE are three things that every one of you that would look for eternal life, and to be saved from condemnation, that of necessity ye must believe: The one is, that ye must know that there is such a necessity laid on you, *that except thou beest born again,* and except the Holy Ghost renew your soul, ye *shall never see the kingdom of God;* and if thou hast but the stony heart when thou art going to the grave, which thou hadst when thou wast born, and die so, thou shalt never step into the gates of the kingdom of heaven.

Secondly, Ye must know there is no way to get your hearts cleansed, but only by believing in the Son of God; if thou hast the Son thou canst not perish.

Thirdly, Ye must believe in your hearts that there is a decreed condemnation, and remidiless vengeance abiding the soul that believes not in the Son of God. Thou mayest eat, and drink, and sleep, and lie down with dool and dolour, for thou goest about with thy condemnation on thy back. There are three points that the good Shepherd informed Nicodemus of, and he takes him into his school, and gives this to him as the first lesson; that thou, nor no man, except thou beest born again, shall ever tread on the floor of heaven. The second lesson he gives him is this, heaven is closed on all sinners, how wilt thou win in then? I am the way, I rave the heavens at my down coming, and I will rive the heavens at my up coming, come thy way to me, and I will lead thee in. The third lesson we are commanded to it, and it is this, "he that believes not is condemned already; the halter is about the neck of him, the doom is given out, the sentence is past, God has decreed, and it shall be put in execution, and this shall be the cause of their condemnation, "because men loved darkness better than light."

The last day ye heard, "Whosoever believes not shall perish." What is that to perish? To be cast from God, from the air, and from the earth, and be flung in that bottomless depth of utter darkness, where there is nothing but weeping and gnashing of teeth, and in a fire that eternity of time shall not put an end to it; as the Lord lives, there is an endless perdition abiding men and women; "I speak the truth in Christ, I lie not," there are many millions of reprobates crying out of that endless darkness; and as there is eternal perdition, so there is eternal life; but I leave this. There are three things in this speech here:

First, The confirmation of the certainty of salvation to every believer, that is in the 17th verse: the certainty of endless glory to thee that believest in the Son of God.

Secondly, There is answer to that which the man had in his heart to cast up to him, which is this, if that be true that God sent his Son into the world to save it, what is the cause that all the world is not saved, but the most part go to hell? Thou hast said, "many, are called but few are chosen; the way is broad that goes to destruction, and many go in it; the way is narrow that leads to life, and few there be that enter in thereat: How is it then that thou sayest, God sent his only begotten Son, not to condemn the world, but that the world through him might have been saved?" He answers this, "he that believes is not condemned, but he that believes not, is condemned already;" and this is the cause, that light is come into the world, but men love darkness better than light, because their works are evil." These are the heads; I will come back and handle them severally. He said before in the 16th verse, (I would ye understood the words of Christ, that they might have the greater weight in your hearts, for I am sure they shall either be the words of life, or else the words of death to you.) He has said before, I say, "that God so loved the world, that he sent his only Son into the world, that whosoever believeth in him should not perish, but have eternal life." Now, he says, "for God sent not his Son to condemn the world, but that the world through him might be saved." Now this is above nature, and contrary to all light within thee; this had been incredible to Adam in his integrity, and incredible to the angels, if the Spirit had not persuaded them, that the justice of another can justify a sinner, and the blood of another bring another to heaven. The light of nature tells all men, if I can pay my debt, I shall be free of the prison; but this is above nature, and this is a mystery that nature cannot understand, nor yet believe; but he that is taught of God, he will believe that the Father will take the justice of the Son, and will impute it to thee that wilt believe, and take that blood for a sufficient ransom for so many as will run to the Son; this is hard to us, that sin daily, to believe it, such sinners, by believing, shall get eternal life; therefore he confirms this, and takes his ground from the purpose of God, "for he sent not his Son to condemn the world, but that the world through him might be saved."

O! if it had been the purpose of God to condemn the world, he would never have sent his Son, but thou that art the profane dog, lest that thou take thy advantage of these words, I will take this cloak from thee, that thou shalt not go to hell but with a convicted conscience; except thou amendest, thou shalt be condemned; but thou that believest shall never be condemned, says our Saviour: he speaks here of such a believer, that has his soul washed in the blood of Jesus, that suffers himself to be led by the Spirit of Jesus, and lets his word renew his heart daily; it is of such a believer that he speaks here, and not to thee that liest still in thy sins, and yet sayest, thou believest in the blood of Christ Jesus. The argument is taken from the sending of the Son; mark here, the Son is a sent Saviour; he had his Father's commission, and came at his Father's command; for he came not till he was sent; *this is the will of him that sent me;* this may make thy conscience to be at peace, that the Son is a sent Saviour, that he has his commission from the Father; thou wilt not get comfort enough by believing, but thou must look to him as a sent Saviour, authorised by the Father and by the Spirit; *the Spirit of the Lord is upon me,* says the Lord; he is sent to be a Saviour to thee that believest. Now, if God had been minded to condemn a sinner that believes, he would never have sent his Son into the world; that was not the purpose of God to condemn the world; but this is his purpose, to save all that believes. Would he have made him thy brother, and to have taken flesh and blood from thee; would he have slain him, and taken his blood, if he had been minded to condemn thee that believest in the Son? So, for the certainty of this, that thou that believest shalt never perish, there thy warrant God would never have sent his Son into the world, to take thy flesh and thy blood, and to be humbled to the very death of the cross, if he had been purposing to condemn a believer; but the cause wherefore I speak it, is this, that the Papists teach not the truth of God; thou art a liar that wouldst teach the believer and the people, that it is not possible that a man can be sure in this life that he shall never perish; thou liest, for the believer is as sure that he shall never perish, as the very angels are sure they shall never perish; God knows if their conscience were wakened to see God wapping infants into hell for their in-born corruptions, they would never have joy nor peace until they were persuaded that they shall never perish. I leave them, and speak to you. What greater argument could the Father give to you of the certainty of salvation, than to send his Son into the world, and to take your nature, and to become your brother, and be obedient to his Father's will unto the very death of the cross, and be so far humbled as to be laid in the grave? So this may comfirm thee, that thou shalt never perish, that believest in the Son.

Now, the next point is the answer to the objection. If this be true, that this is the Father's purpose to save the world, what is the cause, then, that there are so many called, but few are chosen, and waled out in the counsel of God to get eternal life? I grant there shall be many saved, "I saw multitudes standing with palms in their hands, clothed in long white robes, and crying with a loud voice, saying, Salvation comes of our God that sits upon the throne, and of the Lamb," Rev. vii. So, I grant, there are numbers that cannot be told, compare them with themselves, he that has the secrets in numbering, he said, that "broad is the way that leads to destruction, and many enter in thereat; but straight is the way that leads to life, and few there be that go in there." What is the cause then that so many perish? He answers, the cause is not in him, but the wyte is in men themselves; for never a believer yet perished: there the gloriation of Abraham, and the fathers, we believed, and are saved: He says, *he that believes is not condemned.* How is that? May he not be condemned? No; for in the very moment of his believing, he is absolved from all his sins, and in that hour that he touches the blood of the Son, the Father absolves him; therefore the Apostle says, "Now, therefore, there is no condemnation to them that are in Christ Jesus, who walk not after the flesh, but after the Spirit;" so there the mark of them that are past all peril of condemnation, they walk not after the flesh, but after Spirit; he says, *he that believes is not condemned;* he speaks in the present time, and he says not, he shall not be condemned, but he is not condemned; so there is a present remission, a present justification, a present absolution to thee that believest; thy sanctification is wrought out by degrees; thy calling is by degrees; thy glory is by degrees; thy justification is done in an instant; therefore he says, *he that believes is not condemned;* for he is past peril, for the gates of hell cannot prevail against him that is in the Son, there is no perdition to thee that art in the fold of Jesus: *none of my sheep shall perish,* says he. Why? the Lord Jesus has set thee in a precious stone, and is wearing thee upon his heart; and not only that, but the Father takes thee in his own hand; therefore he prays, *Father, keep them:* so, thou that art in Christ, not only hast thou the Son to be thy shepherd, but also the Father to be thy keeper.

Now, again he says, *but he that believes not is condemned already.* Mark the words in these two sentences; I need not winter this, but I may proclaim it a verity surer than the covenant with Noah; here I proclaim, that the believer that has his heart washen in the blood of the Son, his justification is as sure, that the heavens are no surer, and there is not a possibility that he can perish; but let none look to be saved but a believer; as for the unbeliever, he bears already in his conscience condemnation, sealed up in his heart; so, eatest thou, drinkest thou, thou mayest take many doleful meals, for thou that believest not, thy doom is given, thou shalt never see heaven; therefore, if thou wilt not believe, make thee for the devil and his angels; for life mayest thou not see with thy eyes; the jailor has put the cord about thy neck, that he will hang thee with; the jailor has already covered thy face, that thou shouldst not see the son, nor the light of God no more, and thou art ready to die for evermore. Why? Let's see, he says, not because thou hast broken the law, but he says (it is true, thou shalt be flung into hell for thy sins) but this shall be the principal cause, that thou wouldst not let the gospel renew thy heart. I see of all my sins this is the greatest, the contempt of the gospel, and this infidelity that thou wilt not give credit to the verity thereof. I see there is no sin against the whole law proclaimed out of the mount, and out of the midst of a terrible fire, that is comparable to the contempt of the gospel.

Why? In the breach of the law thou breakest two lights, and one bond, but in the breach of the gospel, thou violatest three rights, and two bonds: in the breach of the law, thou violatest the light of nature, and the light of the law, but thou violatest but one bond between God and thee, as he is thy Creator; but, in the breach of the gospel, thou violatest another light, which is the essential light of the gospel, come from the Father; and, as thou violatest the greatest light, so thou violatest the greatest bond, thou tramplest under foot the blood of Jesus; thou upbraidest the Spirit of grace, that would renew thy heart, and thou wilt have none of him; this gospel is the power of God to turn a sinner; so thou that will not believe, fightest and repinest against the Spirit that would renew thy heart.

The Lord teach me how, and after what manner to speak unto you: I beseech God to keep both you and me from that fearful thing; I have been over long in beginning to tell it, always I dare not omit it altogether. Ye are fallen in the fulness of time, that it is no condemnation to love this light, and it is condemnation to love darkness; I will say here before my Lord, ye are fallen in this time, that if this light heal you not, and convert you not, and put life in you, think on, I tell you, the contempt of this light shall make your damnation to go beyond the damnation of all ages gone before you; the damnation of Cain, of the old world, of Sodom and Gomorrah, of the Jews that crucified Christ, the damnation of the Turks and Barbarians, and wild Americans, shall all be nothing to thine. I know the congregation was never, but there were some in it fore-ordained to condemnation, as there must be here also; whom it is, I leave it to the Lord; but whether is the light contemned or not? Every one of you run to your own heart, let your deeds be with you, either to justify, or else to condemn you; there is a security fallen upon us, a sound and deadly sleep; and I confess to the Lord, your security and mine goes both together, and this is now fallen upon us all; and except the Lord blow the coal again, and put to his hand and waken us, I dare not speak of all that I am persuaded is to come; I see a fearful darkness and shadow of death drawing on every soul, what shall we say of this proclaimed imprecation!

The Lord knows I have holden up these hands of mine to God, that he would not suffer his kingdom to fall down among us, and that he would regard the glory of his own name.

Now the second thing I would say, so many of you as have left off your watching one over another, I would exhort you, and obtest you, by the Lord Jesus, that ye open your eyes again, and watch over one another.

Next I proclaim a malediction upon them that use not the worship of God in their houses, morning and evening, and live not according to this gospel, and as men and women that profess themselves to be bought by the blood of Christ, that they bring not an evil name to the house of God. What know I, if there be any of you that entertain secret whoredoms in your house? Some of you have lost your authority, ye are not like men that dare command sin out of your houses: Shall the worship of God be mocked now with these things? It is hard to wit but very visible judgments shall fall upon their carcase; and because it is not in vain to call upon God, let this be one of your petitions, that God would discover the actor, the Lord make thee known either in mercy, if thou beest his, or in judgment in this world, the Lord make thee known. Again, ye that are young damsels, your sitting under stairs together, and your vain tattling and talking when ye meet, ye should sing Psalms together when ye meet, or speak the word of grace together; for it may be your meeting is the ground of this; away with you that make pastime of the worship of God; these are the two things I crave of you; God knows there is cause of lamentation among us. Is this the thankfulness that God craves of you? What ado had ye with these filthy speeches among you? The thing that God graves of us, truly, I think God would have us to renew our repentance; therefore ye must begin again, and I must begin again; for I see that otherwise the wrath of God cannot be averted.

The next thing I crave of you, is, that such of you as with your madness, fury, and whoredoms would profane this town and place, I would request you to live more soberly and godly, and renew the morning and evening worship of God in all your houses, and let not evil be suffered among you, for holiness should be written on the very lasses that dights out the ashes, and dresses your house.

I say no more; but I pray God to amend all your misses, and heal all your faults, for his Son's sake. To whom, with the Father, and with the Spirit, be all praise for evermore. *Amen.*

SERMON XLV.

THE UNBELIEVER CONDEMNED.

John iii. 18.

He that believeth on him is not condemned, but he that believeth not is condemned already, because he hath not believed in the name of the only begotten Son of God.

THERE are three things that every one of you must know that would have eternal life; the one is, the necessity of a new birth, and of a new creation, (understand ye me all) the necessity that ye must all be born again, and that there must be a marvellous change made in all your souls by the Holy Ghost, or else ye will never see the kingdom of God. Next, ye must know the way how ye shall get your souls cleansed, and how ye shall get your eternal life begun here; and how to get the full possession of it hereafter: and this way is Jesus Christ honoured and glorified, by faith in him only. 3*dly*, Ye must know that there is such a necessity of believing, that there is nothing but merciless condemnation to the soul that *believes not in the only begotten Son of God.* These were the three lessons that our Lord, in his speech to Nicodemus, teaches him.

First, He tells him, "except thou beest born again (for as old as thou art) by the Spirit, thou nor none, shall enter into the kingdom of heaven." Next, he tells, *that he was the way*, for sin had steiked the gate of heaven upon all flesh; therefore he was the way, and the door, and the ladder to step up to heaven upon; that whosoever he be that *believes in me shall never perish.* This he makes out,

First, By the type of the brazen serpent; then he sends him to the fountain and spring, which is the love of God the Father, and that because however it be that profane sinners make it the easiest thing in the world to be persuaded of salvation: (and he will say, he is but a fool that doubts, and he is worthy to be hanged that doubts, for he never doubted, and therefore he thinks he will never pain himself for salvation) yet it is not so with the true believer; for of all things that pain him most, is, because he doubts of his faith, and cannot be persuaded enough that he has truly believed; he dow not get the skirfens and hardness of his heart taken away, that he may get a fill of Christ, and of his blood; and that thing that is weightiest on a true believer is, the fear of condemnation; and because he gets sweet blinks of mercy, therefore he would fain be out of doubt, that he shall get leave to be in heaven with Christ. Now, because Christ is willing to put them out of doubt, he says, *whosoever believes shall not perish.*

Now, from the second point, he goes to the third, and this is as needful to know. All of you would hear of eternal life, but ye must hear of condemnation also: It is not heaven only that must be preached, but hell also; therefore he tells him, "as he that believes shall never perish so he that believes not shall perish and be condemned:" As there is undoubted life to the believer; so there is undoubted wrath to the unbeliever. This is the sum; the particulars are these; *First,* He answers to a secret doubt, that seeing God has sent his Son into the world, what is the cause that all the world is not saved, but the most part condemned? He answers, *he that believes is not condemned;* but the cause that so many are condemned is not because of the purpose of God, but because they *believe not in the only begotten Son of God;* for the purpose of God stands sure: And, as in the drowning of the old world, when all the world was destroyed, yet Noah was saved; so it shall be in that great day of the Lord's appearing in the cloud's to render vengeance to them that are ignorant of God, and have disobeyed the gospel of our Lord Jesus, and when millions shall be condemned, yet there shall be a number saved, and shall go in with him into eternal glory; so ye must not stumble at this, that there are many condemned.

Next, I see the cause whereof many perish. I grant the love of God is great, and that blood was sufficient to redeem a thousand worlds; yet the cause why so many perish is not for want of virtue in the blood of the Son of God, but the cause is, *because they believe not in the only begotten Son of God;* so, thou that shalt perish, the cause of thy perdition shall be found written in thyself, and thy incredulity and misbelief, and the contempt of the gospel, shall be registrate in the gospel and thy conscience, as the cause of thy condemnation, and this shall be his glory ; Miserable wretch! thou mightest have been saved through my blood, but thou wouldst not; therefore he says, *he that believeth not is condemned already;* for he has done, the doom is already put upon his heart; and in that great day, when the books of conscience shall be opened, and it shall be found written there a secret sentence of condemnation, which thou carriedst about with thee whilst thou wast living, thou wouldst not come and get life in the Son of God when thou mightst have had it.

Now I go forward to the next verse, where he opens up and aggreges that sin of incredulity, that brings condemnation: And, first, he says, " This is the condemnation of the world, that light is come into the world, and men love darkness rather than light;" he tells the cause why, " because their deeds are evil;" then he tells the reason why they do so, to wit, " he that does evil, he hates the light, and comes not to it ;" Why ? " lest their deeds be reproved." Then he tells by the contrary, whoever does sincerely, and have their heart right, they dare not only come before men, but also before God, because their works are good, and according to God; therefore the tribunal of God will not affright them, because he allows their deeds.

P 3

Now there are some words that I will open up to you, that ye may understand the rest the better. In the 19th verse there is a *condemnation* spoken of, and next there is a *light* spoken of; and 3dly, There is a *darkness* spoken of. I would ye understood all these three words. What is meant by *condemnation?* When one is condemned to die, when a sentence and doom is given out (by a sure assize) and past upon the life of a guilty man, that has broken a law; therefore they give out the doom upon him; that is, he is worthy to die, and not to live any longer; even so it is here, when a guilty sinner is set upon pannel before Jesus Christ the judge, the doom is given out on him, that he shall never live, but be with the devil and his angels; ye have the doom in Matth. xxv. "Go your way from me, ye cursed of my Father, into the everlasting fire of hell, with the devil and his angels;" I judge thee from me and my angels, and from God; away to endless torment with the devil and his angels: upon the which follows the execution of the sentence, so soon as it shall be pronounced. Now this condemnation has three degrees: the *first* is in this life; the next is at the parting of the soul and body: and it shall be the *last* degree at the resurrection. It has the first degree here; for no man shall be condemned, but he that has lived condemned. The *first* degree ye have it in the verse before, "He that believes not is condemned already," where there is a present condemnation of the reprobate here, that whether he eat, or drink, or sleep, he bears about with him his condemnation. I grant this is not ay felt; for there are numbers that never feel this condemnation, either living or dying, till they feel themselves flung into that endless fire. So the *first* degree of condemnation is in this life. The next degree is, when the life goes out, as it was said of Judas, *he went to his own place;* and of the rich glutton, it is said, *he was in hell in torment;* so there is the next degree of condemnation. The third degree shall be in the resurrection, when body and soul shall be joined together, as it is said, "some shall rise to the resurrection of life, and some shall rise to the resurrection of damnation." Now, by the contrary, as this condemnation has three degrees, so the absolution of the godly has three degrees, *first*, They have it in this life begun here, and they have the possession when this life is ended ; and then at the great day, they shall be solemnly absolved, and have the full fruition of joy with men and angels.

Now, the next word is *light*, by the which is meant himself, *I am the light of the world;* it is the truth, he was in the world before in all the ceremonies, and in all these sacrifices, and prophecies, and shadows ; but here he means that he " is come unto the world, when that Word was made flesh."

The third word (and that is opposite to the light) is *darkness*, whereby is meant this wilful ignorance of the Son of God, that the world takes no pleasure to know Christ. Now ye may see what is this condemnation, (to wit) the contempt of this light, ratified by God ; therefore would he say, justly is the unbeliever condemned, because he contemns the light : But mark here, was there no condemnation before the coming of Christ ? What means this ? Did not all the Gentiles go in their own ways ? Did not they who never had a law, perish by a law ? (Lord give his Spirit, I wot well the matter is beyond the word) I wot well there was condemnation before ; Why takes he the name of condemnation from all former ages, and ascribes it to that age only ? I will tell you, scarcely is it worthy the name of condemnation, if put into the balance with the condemnation of them that perished in that age : I grant eternity is common to both ; I grant the rich glutton had an intolerable wrath, and torments ; but yet it is nothing, if compared with the condemnation of them that were condemned in that age. Why ? Because there is no light comparable to this light that the Son of God brought with him from heaven ; no, not that light of Adam in his integrity ; the one was but the image of man, but the other is the image of the Lord, which as far surmounts this light of Adam, as the image of God surmounts the image of a natural man; when Adam had sinned against that first light, he had a regress to this last light which was to come: But the man that sins against this light, (and gets no life in this light) he shall not have regress to another light. Indeed the light of the prophets was a great light, but no more comparable to this light, than the light of a star is comparable to the light of the sun shining at noon-day. Now, seeing this light is so great, that no other light in the world is comparable to it, and scarcely worth the name of light, in comparison of this light, why may we not say, no condemnation (being put in the balance with this condemnation) will be comparable to this? But mark this, "they love darkness better than light;" now, if darkness be loved better than light, shall not this be condemnation? And if this light be not principally loved, is not this matter enough to condemn a world? But I leave off here, and come to the application. The grounds have been laid, and the believer is not condemned, the unbeliever is already condemned: the cause of their condemnation is, the greatness of the light; the less that thy light be, the less shall be thy condemnation; "they that sinned without a law shall perish without a law;" the same light of the gospel has its own degrees also. It was great when he was in his humility, it was greater when he was risen and glorified, and ay it grew greater, but afterward it was obscured and hidden under the darkness of Popery and Mahometanism; but now it is broke out again, and this is the last light, when time shall be no more, and also the greatest light. It is greater than the light of nature, greater than the light of the law, and it is greater than the light in the time of Christ's humility, yea greater than that light in the time of the apostles, after his ascension. Why speak ye this? Ye have the last light, and that everlasting gospel preached to tongues and nations, ye have it preached to you. (Now, know ye what the little book means.) So we are all fallen in the time when all the prophecies of the Old Testament are fulfilled, and made clear to us. Now what gather I of this? I laid this ground else, that the greatest light was the greatest condemnation; in the days of the prophecies many prophecies were not understood; for little knew they what these prophecies meant, because they were not fulfilled; so the light is greatest now; then it is clear, whosoever be condemned in this age, his condemnation is greatest. Judas's condemnation that betrayed the Lord in his humility, the condemnation of the Jews, the condemnation of the whole old world, shall be nothing to the condemnation of this age; look then that ye perish not in this age; look that ye hate not this light; and look that your works be not evil. What shall I say? There is the sorest condemnation abiding these united kingdoms for the contempt of this light. O light, light! How art thou contemned in this land? How is it that no man stands in awe to sin in the face of this light? Well, desolate land, the day shall come that thou shalt say, O! if we had the light we once had, we should be loath to contemn it; and this shall be the doom of this land, even the contempt of this light. I think in the Lord's judgment it is decreed, that he is minded to take away his visible presence from this land, and he shall never leave flitting, until we be seen to seek him after another manner than ever we have done yet; therefore do no ill, but let this light renew you; wrestle not against it; do no evil, since this light looks on you; why should ye get the greatest condemnation? (because of the contempt of the greatest light.) There is yet time of mourning and repentance, but ye know not how long this time will last; therefore I beseech you let not this time get a refusal, but run to get mercy as long as the door of mercy stands open; for there is a time when it shall be steiked, and ye shall not win in, albeit ye stand and knock, ye shall get no entrance, but a woful sentence shall be pronounced against you, " depart from me, ye cursed, unto the devil and his angels:" therefore repent, and turn unto the Lord your God, for Jesus Christ's sake; to whom with the Father, and with the Holy Ghost, be praise and honour for now and ever. *Amen.*

SERMON XLVI.

OF ATTAINING UNTO THE RESURRECTION OF
THE DEAD.

Philippians iii. 11, 12.

If by any means I may attain unto the resurrection of the dead.

BECAUSE I would end this at this time, therefore I would but expound the words shortly. Ye know the purpose we had in hand; it was to set down to you for what end ye should lead a Christian life and conversation: so many of you as mind to get salvation, and look for the crown of glory which is laid up in heaven for you, the pattern whereof is set down here, whereunto as many of you as look to get the blessing in that great day, ye would conform yourselves unto it. The first thing in the pattern is the reverend estimation he had to the Son of God, that he " counted all things but dung in comparison of the excellent knowledge in Christ;" the course of Christianity will be a burden to you till ye get this ground laid in your heart, that nothing could smell in your nose but that that comes through Christ; therefore it is no wonder that ye are so oft bigging, and so oft casting down again the thing that ye have bigged; and this is the cause why we are so oft running backward, and not forward, because we lay not Christ as the ground-stone of our souls, and we build not upon the reverend estimation of him; for till we get him this gate, that we count him the only pearl and jewel of our souls, our walking in Christianity will never be with joy and delight, till Christ be first the delight of our souls, and then I am sure all our race in Christianity should be with joy and gladness; and if ye would have your building sure, this must be the first and ground-stone that ye must build upon, even this reverend estimation of Christ.

Next, it was the desire of his soul to be found in him, that is, in the very heart out of which blood and water came, he might be found there; and then he knew that that tribunal should not be terrible to him. What canst thou fear whilst the Son has satisfied the justice of God, and therefore his wrath cannot overtake thee. Now after he is found in him, there are other two things that he desired, *first*, He sought his righteousness to cover him; for it will never be thy inherent righteousness, nor the begun work of grace in thy soul, that can bring thee to this solid joy and consolation; but it is that imputed righteousness of Christ only, that only can bring true peace and joy to thy heart; therefore thou must first believe in thy heart, that the justice of the Son is thine, ere thou canst find any joy and peace in thy soul; and when thou believest this, it shall be unto thee as thou believest, and this shall bring joy and peace to thy soul. It cannot be told what joy and consolation is in the soul that may say, I am in Christ, and Christ is in me, his righteousness is covering my soul from the consuming fire of the wrath of God; therefore there is no condemnation for me. When thou hast this persuasion, then all that is within thee, or without thee, cannot bereave thee of peace.

The next thing he desired in Christ, was this, not only desired he his righteousness covering him, but also he desired to have a lively and perfect knowledge of Christ, not by the letter, but by the experience of the Spirit; not by speculation, but by practice; such a knowledge as might make him partaker of his resurrection, and conformable to his death.

Now the *first* ground being laid, all the rest shall

SERMON XLVI.

follow on ; so labour then to get Christ and his righteousness imputed to thee, then thou canst not look upon his death, but thy sins must die with him, and there is never a stripe that his back kepped, but it will be an healing salve to thy soul. So there are none that have been found in Christ, and are in him, but when they look upon his death, they must be made conformable thereto, and this will gar them say, shall my hands and feet be loose to sin, and he bound for me ? Shall my Lord be dead, and my sins living in me ? Shall he be laid in the grave, and my sins going on earth, as lively like as ever they were ? What is the cause, trow ye, that so many sins are living, and ramping redwood as beasts within them, but because they lay not this crucified Lord to their hearts, that the savour of his death might give sin a deadly wound in them ? But so many as have lively knowledge of Christ, they never rest till they find a lively virtue coming from his death, and slaying sin in them. Here an excellent knowledge, and well may it be called an excellent knowledge ; for he that has gotten it, has gotten a fine craft, and has learned a brave art and heavenly science. Well is that soul that gets this heavenly knowledge, that makes it know the virtue of his resurrection, the fellowship of his afflictions, and the conformity of his death. Now here he goes to a further mark than either his justification or his sanctification, which is this, the mark of his glorification, even the hope of eternal life ; therefore he says, " if by any means I might attain to the resurrection of the dead," as if he would say, suppose I be in Christ, and suppose his righteousness be covering me, and suppose I be partaker of the virtue of his resurrection, and of the fellowship of his afflictions, and suppose I be conformable to his death ; yet I will never rest till I be within the clouds, and there get a visible armful of the Lord of glory ; *if by any means*, says he, I care not how difficult or hard a thing it be to me to come by it, so if I can by any means come by it ; therefore I care not to trample all things under

my feet, that they may be like as many footstools to
help to lift my heart to heaven : I care not to bear all
the crosses and afflictions on my shoulders, so be I
may win in to yonder glory ; for the sight of yonder
glory has ravished my soul, that I care not how difficult and hard, and how rough the way be, for I must
be at it, I must be within that New Jerusalem, the city
of the everlasting God ; I must sing that new song,
and that hallelujah, which the saints and angels in heaven do sing to God continually. I know that the way
is hard, but I care not how hard it be, if I can any
manner of way win to it : indeed the way is narrow
and strait, and therefore it must be hard ; but it is
hard only to flesh and blood, and it is hard only in the
beginning ; yet it is called the new way, because it has
new and fresh joys at every mile's end, that shall not
let thee tire ; it is called the living way, because it
makes thy soul ay to live, as long as thou art going in
it. *I might attain to the resurrection of the dead ;* the
word attain signifies to meet with, as if he would say,
I know the Lord is coming, and I know the dead must
rise ; therefore I desire to go out and meet him : even
so should ye ay think upon this, the Lord is coming to
judge both the quick and the dead, therefore all must
rise and compear before him : some shall be forced
to rise against their will, others shall rise joyfully to
meet him in the clouds, and these shall be caught up in
the air with him, but the rest shall be left on the earth
by themselves ; therefore I desire to be of the number
of these that rise to meet him gladly, and I desire the
hope of that joyful meeting to be more and more established and confirmed to my soul. Well, I see I must
leave it to another time, for I will not fash you ; therefore I commend to the blessing of God the things that
have been spoken hitherto, and I beseech God to sanctify your memories, that ye never forget this reverend
estimation that ye should have of Christ your Lord ;
that ye never want that blessed fruition, and happy conjunction with your Lord ; that ye never want his
righteousness to cover you, and his blood to justify and

sanctify you; that ye may so know him, that ye may daily draw life out of him; that ye may be conformable to him, both in his death and resurrection; and that ye may continually be more and more confirmed in the hope of that glory. *Amen.*

TWO

NOTABLE SERMONS,

PREACHED BY

Mr. JOHN WELCH,

AT AIR,

UPON THE TWO LAST TUESDAYS IMMEDIATELY BEFORE

HIS IMPRISONMENT;

AND THE FIRST OF THEM

UPON TUESDAY THE 16TH DAY OF JULY, 1605.

SERMON XLVII.

NO CONDEMNATION TO GOD'S ELECT.

Romans viii. 1, 2, 3, &c.

Now therefore there is no condemnation to them that are in Christ Jesus, who walk not after the flesh, but after the Spirit. For the law of the Spirit of life in Christ Jesus hath made me free from the law of sin and death. For what the law could not do, in that it was weak through the flesh, God sending his own Son, in the likeness of sinful flesh, and for sin condemned sin in the flesh, &c.

BECAUSE, in this chapter, there is a compend of all the comforts and consolations that the wearied and tired sinner, in the day of his pilgrimage, has mister of to sustain him, that he may stand fast in the ill day, and, because we are not certain how long the day of mercy will last; therefore I hope this is from the Lord, who knoweth how to dispose of every thing, and who has led me in this, that I desire to open to you the comforts contained in this chapter, that ye may want nothing that may bear you out with joy and comfort, to run your race unto yon kingdom. I will leave it to the Lord to work in every one of you, by his own truth, as it shall please himself; and, in simplicity, as I can, I shall open this to you in that measure of light that it shall please God to distribute unto me for your comfort.

Now, that ye may the better understand this, I will speak somewhat of the chapters going before. He has told, in his letter here written to the saints at Rome, he has told us, I say, three things. The first is, that all flesh, both Jew and Gentile, are under condemnation by nature; and that all the world is shut up under unbelief; and that "the wrath of God is revealed from heaven against all ungodliness;" and that no flesh need ever to look for righteousness, life, or salvation, by the law. This is the first.

The next thing is this, he tells them, that there is not a way under heaven to a sinner who is lying under the wrath of God, and subject to condemnation, there is not a way for him to win out, but only to run out of himself, and into the blood of the Son of God, and to lay his heart in that blood, and to believe, that remission of sins and eternal life is purchased to him through that blood; for God justifieth every sinner that believeth. Therefore he says, Rom. v. 9. "And being justified by his blood, we shall be saved from wrath through him." And he tells them, verse 12th, "That as by one man sin entered into the world, and death by sin;" verse 18th, "And as by the offence of one the fault came on all men to condemnation ; so, by the righteousness of one, the benefit hath redounded towards all men to the justification of life;" verse 19th "And as by one man's disobedience many were made sinners ; so, by the obedience of one shall many be made righteous."

Thirdly, He tells, that all that have faith in the Son of God, all that have gotten pardon in his blood, and all that are reconciled unto God freely through Christ, all these are justified by faith, and sanctified by grace, and the death of Christ is effectual to slay sin in them, that it reign not in their mortal bodies : And the resurrection of Christ is effectual in them, to work righteousness and a new life in them; that, whereas before they gave their members as weapons of unrighteousness to sin, now they give themselves unto God, and their members as weapons of righteousness to please him in all things. But here is the difference, our justification, by grace is perfect even in this life, but our sanctification is imperfect. Therefore upon this ariseth two things to every Christian; the one is this, when he looketh to a perfect Saviour, then he has peace that passeth all understanding, and he has free access to him, that he may go to the throne of grace when he will, to find mercy and grace in time of need, and he has joy unspeakable in the Lord Jesus. The other is this, when he looketh to himself, and seeth that he is yet in bonds, and he is led captive like a slave, so that he cannot get leave to do the thing that he would do, but he is compelled to do the thing he would not; and this maketh him to cry out, Rom. vii. 20. "O miserable man that I am, who shall deliver me from this body of death? So, when he looks to the one, to wit, his justification by faith in the Lord Jesus, then he has consolation his fill; but when he looks to the other, and sees that he is daily offending the sweetest God, and the most merciful Father that ever was, then he has sorrow and dole at his heart, and he longeth for the day of his dissolution, and to be with the Lord.

Now, when he has done this in the seven chapters going before, he tells now, in this chapter, the happy case of the man that is justified by faith, and sanctified by grace; and it is this, *there is no condemnation to them.* And, because there are two things that hinder the very chosen child of God to get his full comfort in this world; the one is sin that dwelleth in him, that in-born corruption wherewith he came into the world; the other is, the manifold crosses and afflictions that follow him in this life, and are laid upon his back; and because these two deprives him of much comfort; for when he looketh to himself, he sees a body of sin within him, and when he looketh to his back he sees many crosses and afflictions laid upon him, which he is not able to bear without an extraordinary strength, and therefore he has not many hours to rejoice in, because of these two temptations wherewith the child of

God is continually assaulted; therefore the Holy Ghost, who is upon the secret counsel of God (for he searcheth the deep things of God, and he knows the thoughts of thy heart, and what are the discouragements of the child of God) therefore here he giveth sufficient consolation to every one of them, and he ministreth to them comfort enough to sustain them against both these temptations. For suppose thou beest a miserable sinner, sold under sin, and led captive as a slave, and suppose there be many crosses and afflictions laid upon thy back, yet there is no condemnation to thee, and this is comfort enough to thee: So because there are two things that trouble the child of God, and hinder him to run his race with cheerfulness, to wit, the burden of sin, and the burden of crosses and afflictions; and therefore he furnishes sufficient consolation against both these. The one he doth from the beginning of the chapter to the 18th verse, the other from the 18th to the 31st verse; then he concludeth all with a comfortable disputation, wherein he proveth, that nothing can do against the child of God; "for nothing shall be able to separate thee from the love of God in Christ Jesus."

Now what consolation mayest thou have who art in Christ? for suppose thou hast a body of sin within thee, yet thou mayest thank God, "that in thy mind thou servest the law of God, but in thy flesh the law of sin, and there is no condemnation to thee." And suppose thou beest full of troubles, crosses and afflictions, yet all the afflictions of this present time are not worthy of the glory which shall be shewed and revealed to thee one day. So, poor sinner, why art thou discouraged and out of heart, partly for the evil that is within thee, and partly for the crosses and afflictions that are upon thy shoulders; for, if God be upon thy side, who dare be against thee? Who shall lay any thing to the charge of God's elect? If God do justify thee, who shall condemn thee?" Thy sins shall never be able to condemn thee. And as for the crosses and afflictions, "who shall separate thee from the love of God that is in Christ Jesus? Shall tribulation or anguish, &c. in all these things we are more than conquerors." Then he tells his own persuasion in the two last verses, "For I am persuaded that neither death nor life, principalities nor powers," &c. So there is the sum of this chapter.

Now, that ye may think upon it, there are two things that dishearten thee who art God's child; the one is, that in-born corruption that is within thee, which is left to exercise thee, lest thou grow sluggish or idle; the other is, the manifold crosses and afflictions that God layeth upon thy back to hold thee down, lest thy heart be swelled up puffed and with pride.

Now against both these two the Spirit of God ministreth comfort enough to them both. As to the first, thy sins shall not condemn thee; as to the other, there is a fair glory to be revealed one day to thee, if thou sawest it, thou wouldst think that all the afflictions of this life are not comparable to that infinite weight of glory that is laid up for thee in heaven. Wherefore seeing the Lord is with thee, and seeing all the crosses in the world shall never be able to separate thee from the love of God that is in Christ Jesus; therefore thou hast matter enough of consolation.

But now, to come to this particular, 1*st*, There is set down here the comfort itself. 2*dly*, The persons to whom it belongeth, to wit, to them that are in Christ Jesus, who walk not after the flesh, but after the Spirit. 3*dly*, There is the ground of this comfort to warrant it to thy soul, that it is sure and certain; and that is set down in the 2d, 3d, and 4th verses. The ground is this, that man or woman shall never be condemned that is freed from the law of sin and death, by the Spirit of life; but thou that art in Christ Jesus art freed from the law of sin and death; therefore thou shalt never be condemned. Now I would ye marked this, for there is a fair building to be bigged on this ground, even the comfort of thy soul, the hope of eternal life, and the full assurance of salvation. That man or woman that is in Christ, thou mayest go blythly to bed, yea thou mayest go blythly to the grave, and blythly mayest thou take death in thine arms, and thou mayest blythly send out thy spirit, knowing that thy spirit shall never go to the spirits beneath, and to that blackness of darkness; but it shall enter into everlasting glory: Therefore, I say, the ground must be sure on which so fair a consolation must be builded. What would a poor sinner give to know that he was ransomed with so precious a blood, which is able to ransom ten thousand worlds, if there were so many. Wouldst thou not be the merchantman, to sell all that thou hast to buy this one consolation, that thou mightest know it is the purpose of God that thou shalt never perish, and that there is no condemnation to thee? Wouldst thou be sure of this? There the ground then which thou must lay; they that are freed from the law of sin and death shall never perish; and thou who art in Christ and justified by faith, and walkest not after the flesh, but after the Spirit, thou art freed from the law of sin and death: therefore thou shalt never perish: for there is no condemnation to thee.

But yet thy conscience will not rest here; for it is much that will put the conscience of a poor casten down sinner out of doubtings, because he sees that it an everlasting wrath that he has to do with. Now then to confirm thee in this, he tells thee the ground of it in the 3d verse, as if he would say, The cause why all that are freed from the law of sin and death by the Spirit of Jesus shall never perish, nor there is no condemnation to them, it is even this, because Christ the Son of God, in the similitude of sinful flesh, was condemned for sin in the flesh; now the justice of God cannot condemn twice for one fault, therefore the severity of God's justice cannot strike upon thee who art in Christ Jesus. Again, The severe justice of God cannot condemn him who has fulfilled the law; but thou who art in Christ Jesus, and walkest not after the flesh, but after the Spirit, thou hast fulfilled the law; therefore the severe justice of God cannot condemn thee who art in Christ Jesus. But how hast thou fulfilled the law? I answer, That which Christ has done in the flesh is imputed unto thee, who art justified by faith; but Christ in the flesh fulfilled the law; therefore the fulfilling of the law by Christ is imputed unto thee. Thus much for the meaning of this text.

Now, we will come back again; and before that we come to the words, mark the dependance, and how this hangeth on the things that are said before in the former chapter. The sight of his misery gart him cry out in the end of the viith chapter, "O miserable man that I am, who shall deliver me from this body of sin!" He longed for any person in the world, or elsewhere, that would deliver him from his misery. Yet in the end he takes comfort to himself, and he says, " I thank my God, through Jesus Christ our Lord; then, I myself, in my mind, serve the law of God, but in my flesh the law of sin." Now, here he subjoineth the ground whereupon his comfort ariseth, to wit, " there is no condemnation to them that are in Christ Jesus." Mark this, I pray you, the sight of thy misery will never bring thee comfort, except, with the sight of it, thou knowest there is no condemnation to thee, because thou art in Christ Jesus. Therefore, if God waken any of your consciences, and if he spread the bill of the law, and read your dittay, and let you hear your own doom, except thou get this comfort that there is no condemnation to thee, the sight of thy misery will either gar thee despair, or seeing thyself out of hope of recovery, thou wilt run further on in sin than ever thou didst before; therefore, my hearts, when ye are wakened, hold your eyes upon God, and on the Mediator Jesus Christ, and if thou dowest not win within the vail, and unto the throne of grace, yet look back to Gethsemane, and there look on that Lord sweating blood in the garden for thy sake, that when thou seest the sight of thy sins, which are ready to bring down a consuming fire upon thee, and when thou seest that these same sins made the Son of God heavy, and his soul sorrowful to the very death; then thou mayest say, I am a miserable man, but yet, God be thanked, I serve God in my mind; therefore there is no condemnation to me. I grant the sight of thy sins is very needful to thee, and therefore God has given thee two eyes to look upon both these, that thou mayest never hold the one eye off thy misery, lest thy heart swell; and that thou hold thy other eye ever upon God's mercy, and be thankful for the one, but mourn for the other.

Look on thy misery, but look also within the vail, and see the Son of God who has delivered thee from thy misery; then sweet shall be thy comfort which shall arise upon this sight. Then shalt thou say, O loving Father! what shall I render unto thee, who hast sent thy Son to die for me? O sweet and loving Saviour! what shall I render unto thee, for coming willingly to die for me? O sweet Comforter! what shall I render to thee, who hast brought these glad news to me from heaven? So this first shall make thee humble, and make thee comfortable.

Next again, mark before I come to the words. He says, "I thank my God, through Jesus Christ our Lord;" then, "I myself serve God in my mind, but in my flesh the law of sin." These are the words of the last chapter.

Mark here, except thou knowest thou art freed from misery, and that thou shalt never be condemned in hell; in the sight of thy misery, thou wilt never lift up thine heart to say, "I thank my God, through Jesus Christ my Lord?" Why? because as long as the darkness of hell covereth thine eyes, so that thou seest not thy doleful estate and condition by nature, it may be that thy temporal comforts and refreshments of meat and drink, will lift up thy heart, and make thee to say, for that time, God be thanked; but take me a sinner that is chained, and bound in the fetters of Satan, and ready to be cast into hell, except he get this comfort given him, that there is no condemnation to him, he will never say, God be thanked, from his heart, for any thing in this world. But take thee this comfort and apply it to thyself when thou art in this case, thou mayest say, Lord this is the chiefest sinner that ever the earth bore ; yet, I thank God I have consolation, that I know if I be a great sinner, the mercy of God shall appear so much the more clearly in giving me mercy ; and this will make thee to say, let other men say what they will, but I will say, that I have gotten the greatest mercy that ever man or woman got, and therefore, I thank God, through Jesus Christ our Lord.

But now, perhaps, ye will speir, Whether may I say, there is no condemnation to me ; for I know I shall never be condemned ; I will tell you belyve whether ye may say it or not : But before I come to it, mark this, so many of you as have ever gotten this comfort, ye know that there are two things that have hindered you to praise God ; the one is, the bondage that ye have been in would never suffer you to praise God so heartily as ye would have done, if it had been otherwise with thee ; therefore learn this lesson, if this comfort belong to thee, that there is no condemnation to thee, if thou wert the most miserable sinner in the world, let never the sight of thy misery bind up thy tongue from the praises of God, or hinder thee to say, God be thanked in Jesus Christ. And I know many of you are hindered to praise God, because ye have not gotten your hearts loosed yet ; and therefore thou thinkest that thou canst not praise God : But I say, let this be sufficient to thee, that thou knowest there is no condemnation to thee, and that thou shalt never come into that blackness of darkness ; if thou hadst so many miseries on thy back as ever man had, let this be sufficient, I say, that thou mayest say, well is me, I know there is no condemnation for me. Now, God be merciful to me and you both ; for when we have gotten this consolation many a time offered, yet our sin within us has bound up our hearts, that we could not say, God be thanked for this ; therefore we have been injurious to God, and injurious to our own souls. I remember the mountains are bidden rejoice, because the Lord hath redeemed his people ; how much more then should we ourselves rejoice of that redemption who are partakers thereof? O that ye knew what it is to be freed from hell and condemnation! For then should ye cry to all the creatures of God to help you to praise the Lord, for that unspeakable benefit of your redemption.

But now I come to the words. I say, he subjoineth here the matter of his comfort in these words, *Now then there is no condemnation to them that are in Christ Jesus.* There the ground of his comfort: What now? Wot ye that the word is, *No condemnation to them;* thou who art in Christ, shalt stand before the throne, the books of thy conscience shall be opened, and the judge shall judge thee, but he shall never pronounce doom against thee; he, who is the judge, shall condemn others; but such as are in himself, he will no more condemn their souls, than he will condemn himself. I remember the apostle says, *Who shall condemn?* He speireth at man, angel, and devil, where will the person be found in heaven, in hell, or in the earth, that shall condemn thee who art in Christ? Where shall the judge be gotten to do this? Will the Father do it, who of his own good will and free love sent his Son to die for thee, when thou wast his enemy? Will the Son do it, who bought thee with his own precious blood, and died for thee? Will the Holy Spirit do it, who is sent from God to tell thee that the blood was shed for thee? Will the angels do it, who are made thy servants to minister comfort to thee? Will the saints do it, that are saved by the same blood which has saved thee? Will the devils do it? No, for they may well be the accusers of the brethren, but they are not the judges, for they themselves shall be judged; for the apostle Peter saith, 2 Pet. ii. 4. " God has delivered them into chains of darkness, to be kept there unto damnation." Will the reprobate do it? No, for Jude says, Jude 13, " they are reserved to that blackness of darkness for ever." Where shall a judge be found then? Will the heavens or the earth do it? No, for we know that (Rom.

viii. 22, 23.) "every creature groaneth with us also, and travaileth in pain together, until this present; and not only the creatures, but we also who have the first fruits of the Spirit, even we do sigh in ourselves, waiting for the adoption, even the redemption of our bodies." Will the law do it? No, for the mouth of the law is stopt, because he has fulfilled the law. Will the justice of God do it? No, for that were against justice to condemn twice for one fault. Will thy conscience do it then? No, for the blood shall be louder than thy conscience. This much for the comfort. *Now then there is no condemnation.*

But to whom? That is all that we should be about to know, to whom this comfort belongeth; *to them that are in Christ Jesus;* to be in him, that is a great word, for thou canst not be in him till thou beest rugged out of the old stock of Adam; thou wilt say then, how shalt thou know whether thou beest in Christ or not? I answer, if thou beest in him, he is in thee.

But thou wilt say, that is as hard yet to know, whether he be in me or not; for if I wist that he were in me, then my soul should get comfort and ease there; how shalt thou know if thou beest in Christ, and Christ in thee! For if thou beest out of Christ, there is nothing but condemnation for thee, and the fire of God's wrath will tumble on thee. Dool to the soul that is found alone, and wo to the miserable conscience of that man or woman, that is not planted in Christ! How shalt thou know then? I will tell thee thou shalt know by the way thou art walking in, and the guide that thou art following: so then, is thy course toward yon glory to be revealed in heaven, and toward the blood, and toward that everlasting habitation, and toward that New Jerusalem in heaven. Then thou art in the way to Christ.

Now, look whereunto thy heart has the course, and where is thy treasure laid up? Is thy course toward heaven? Is thy heart and treasure there? And wouldst thou fain have thy soul filled with joy, peace, and righteousness in Christ? Then thou art in the way that leadeth to life.

Next, look to the guide that convoyeth thee, for there are two guides within thee, there is both the flesh and the Spirit in thee; and the flesh will guide to thy gain, and to thy pleasure, and to thy profit; and the Spirit will guide thee to thy sins, to thy miseries, to the blood, and to the man Christ Jesus made flesh, conceived in the womb of a virgin, laid in a crib, subject to all infirmities without sin, sweating blood in the garden, hanged on a tree, laid in the grave, risen and gone to heaven. The Spirit will lead thee in through heaven, and he will guide thee to the love of the Father, which is the fountain of thy salvation, unto the unchangeable decree of thy election, and unto that everlasting glory. But I must leave this. But to give you some ease in your minds to go away with, I will give you but these two marks to know whether thou beest in Christ, or not? The one is, if thou beest in Christ, then the Spirit of Christ is in thee; and if the Spirit be in thee, then Christ himself is in thee; and if Christ be in thee, then thou art the Lamb's wife; and therefore he will never condemn thee.

But yet thou wilt say, I follow the flesh oftentimes. I answer, but thinkest thou that thou art out of the way, when thou art going another course than the Son of God, or the Spirit of Christ would lead thee in; yea, Will not the sheep wander? And will not the penny put up in the purse be lost? Now then, would ye know what is the mind of God towards you? I am here to testify it to you, and would ye know if there be no condemnation to you? Then answer thou me, and I shall pronounce the testimony of God to thee. Tell me what way thou art going, wouldthou fain believe in Christ? And wouldst thou fain live the life of Christ? And would ye fain be in heaven, where Christ your head is? And long ye to dwell with God? And doth the Holy Ghost come in whiles within thee, to speak to thy soul, and to say, here is the way, walk in it? This is no false Spirit; this is no beguiling Spirit;

that leads thee first to thy misery; next to the blood of Jesus; and thirdly, to the love of the Father; for this is the Spirit of God.

But yet thou wilt say, the flesh ay mastereth me, and gets oftenest the victory. I answer, there are four differences betwixt them that walk after the flesh, and them that walk after the Spirit.

First, He that walketh after the flesh, his course is as one, and is never changed; but he that walketh after the Spirit findeth a change wrought, and he is turned out of the broad way into the narrow way, and his general course is towards heaven, howsoever it be that he is oftentimes driven off his course.

Secondly, He that walketh after the flesh committeth sin with greediness, for he thinks he dow not get a fill of sin; but he that walketh after the Spirit, thinketh his sin his misery, and therefore it is a burden to him.

Thirdly, He that walketh after the flesh, remembereth his sin with gladness and joy; but he that walketh after the Spirit, remembereth his sins with grief and sorrow of heart.

Fourthly, He that walketh after the flesh, sin reigneth in him, and he followeth it whithersoever it leadeth him; but he that walketh after the Spirit, he is loath to sin, and wo is him when he is compelled to sin, and when he has sinned he weepeth bitterly.

Now to conclude, as many then as at this time may arraign their hearts and consciences before God, and there may protest, saying, Lord, thou art witness to my soul, that I would fain walk after the Spirit; I would fain turn to thee with my whole heart, soul, mind, and strength; I would count sin my greatest misery, and a burden to me; I would fain remember my sins with grief and sorrow, and with a heavy heart; and I would fain have sin slain, that it reign not in me; so many of you as may say this, in the truth of your heart, here I bear you record, that there is no condemnation to you; and therefore blythly may ye go home to your house, and blythly may ye go out at this church door, and ye may say, when ye are come home, this day salvation is come into my house, I am made the child of God, and the brother of Jesus Christ, for I am in him, and he is in me; and therefore there is no condemnation to me. Now the Lord grant you this for Christ his Son's sake; to whom with the Father, and Holy Ghost, be all praise, honour, and glory, for now and evermore. *Amen.*

SERMON XLVIII*.

NO CONDEMNATION TO GOD'S ELECT.

Romans viii. 1, 2, 3, 4—18—37, &c.

There is therefore now no condemnation to them which are in Christ Jesus, who walk not after the flesh, but after the Spirit. For the law of the Spirit of life in Christ Jesus hath made me free from the law of sin and death. For what the law could not do, in that it was weak through the flesh, God sending his own Son, in the likeness of sinful flesh, and for sin condemned sin in the flesh: that the righteousness of the law might be fulfilled in us, who walk not after the flesh, but after the Spirit. For I reckon, that the sufferings of this present time, are not worthy to be compared with the glory which shall be revealed in us. Nay, in all these things we are more than conquerors, through him that loved us, &c.

THERE are but two things especially that dishearten and faint the child of God in the time of his pilgrimage here; *first*, There is the corruption of nature within him, which hindereth him to honour the Lord in the strength of his heart, and with freedom of Spirit, as he desireth to do, and which gars him weary of

---

* The last Sermon preached at Air by Mr. John Welch, the 23d of July, 1605, on a Tuesday before noon, when he was to take journey to Edinburgh that same day; and, immediately after his coming there, was commanded to ward by the council of Scotland, and conveyed by a guard to the castle of Blackness.

Now let the Lord give his blessing to his word, and let the Spirit of Jesus, who is the author of this verity, come in and seal up the truth of it in your hearts and souls, for Christ's sake.

his life, and compels him to cry out of his misery, and to wish for a deliverer that would make him quit of his natural life, which is a body of death, that he might be dissolved, and that sin might cease in him, and here the example of it: a man sold under sin, that he could not get leave to do the thing he would do, but was compelled to do the thing he would not; a man who had a law in his members rebelling against the law of his mind, and leading him captive a gate which otherwise he would not have gone. And this is a part of all the saints case, and ye who are in Christ both see and know this; but as many of you as were never yet brought up in Christ's kingdom, ye know no such thing; for ye feel not the sin to be a burden, ye see no misery, nor ye feel no battle within you; but it is otherwise with the children of God; they feel a battle within them, betwixt the flesh and the spirit, and this maketh them to weary of their life, because they cannot get leave to serve God as they would, nor in the truth of their heart they dow not glorify God. This is the first and principal thing that discourages the child of God, and hinders him most to run his race with joy and gladness.

The next thing is, the many crosses and afflictions of this life that follow upon the back of the children of God, and this made the Spouse to cry, Cant. i. 4. "I am black and sun-burnt, O daughters of Jerusalem." This was the case of the Head, and this is the case of all his members, that through many tribulations they must enter into the kingdom of heaven. Therefore it hath pleased the Lord to set down here two consolations, opposite to these two discouragements. The one is, there is no condemnation to them that are in Christ Jesus. The other is, I count all the afflictions of this present time not worthy of that glory which shall be revealed unto us. Suppose thou sinnest daily, yet there is no condemnation to thee who art in Christ, because the Son of God speaketh for thee, because he has died and risen for thee; and as for troubles and crosses the saints are more than conquerors over them, through him who loved them before the world was; and they are persuaded that nothing in heaven or earth shall be able to separate them from the love of God in Christ Jesus. And this is shortly the sum of this chapter.

Ye that were present here the last day, heard that there were two things in this chapter. 1*st*, A consolation to hold thee up, that thou faint not under the burden of thy sins; and 2*dly*, A consolation to sustain thee, that the crosses and troubles of this life make thee not to weary in thy pilgrimage, or tire in thy journey towards heaven.

As to the *first*, It is in these words that I have read, where, first, there is the consolation itself; and next, the persons to whom it belongeth. Thou hast need of comfort who feelest the burden of sin, and the bondage which thy in-born corruption brings thee into, and the Spirit knoweth this well enough; therefore he who knoweth the mind of God, and who searcheth the deep things of God, he telleth to thee what is God's mind towards thee, and there thy comfort, that the remanent corruptions within thee shall never be able to condemn thee. There the comfort which the Spirit takes from the Father and the Son, and bringeth it to the law of thy members rebelling against the law of thy mind; suppose it gar thee lead a miserable life, suppose it lead thee captive to sin; yet it shall never condemn thee into utter darkness.

Now I grant this consolation is not for every one; for what needeth he comfort who never was troubled? Because there is a law in thy members rebelling against the law of thy mind, and leading thee captive to sin, and gars thee dishonour God: But this comfort is only for thee who feelest thyself bound in fetters, and thou wouldst fain run the ways of God but thou dowest not. And if thou wert without sin, then thou needest not his voice proclaimed to thee from heaven; for it is only sin which bringeth the fear of condemnation: But because there is sin pressing thee down daily, therefore thou hast daily need of the consolation of the

Spirit. And as for thee that has tasted of a wrath, and who knowest what it is to be deprived of the presence of God for evermore, no other consolation will content thee than this of the Spirit revealed in the word. But as for thee who wast never burdened with thy sins, nor with the sense of wrath for sin, other news will stake thee, suppose thou never hearest a word of a heaven or hell, of an eternal life, or of an everlasting condemnation.

Mark then: Tell me, what is thy only consolation in this life? Is the news of eternal life, and that thou shalt never be condemned, the only matter of thy consolation? This is a sure token that thou art the child of God. But if thou canst be content to hear news concerning the estate of the court and commonwealth, or of the affairs of the country, or of matters touching thy own calling, and thou wilt never speir a word of the estate of the church, or of thine own soul: This is a token thou wast never in Christ, and there is nothing but condemnation to thee, except thou be changed and become a new creature. But I leave this.

The next thing ye heard was the persons to whom this comfort belongeth. This might be blyth news to a world if it belonged to all; for then might they say, what recks it what life I lead, seeing there is no condemnation to me. No, no, there are marches and meithes set down, and there are marks of them to whom this comfort belongeth, and they that want these marks and are without the marches, they may make them for the wrath of God; and if they die so, they are already condemned; for there are numbers foreordained to condemnation. And trow ye then to step into heaven so easily? No, ye shall be beguiled; for as there are sheep, so there are goats; as there are vessels of honour, so there are vessels of dishonour; and as there are vessels of mercy, so there are vessels of wrath: As there is wheat, so there is chaff; and as the blessing shall be given to some; so the malediction and curse shall be given to other some.

Now the persons to whom it belongeth are they that are in Christ Jesus. So then, if thou beest not in Christ, and within the compass of that blood, and a member of that body which was slain on the tree, and in that heart which was pearced with a spear, and in that flesh which bore the curse of the law on that tree; if thou be not rugged out of nature, and translated out of the rotten stock of Adam, and planted in the Son of God, Christ Jesus; so that his blood is daily washing thee from thy sin, and feeding thy soul, and quenching thy thirst: If thou have not these things, then there is nothing but condemnation for thee; but if thou be in Christ, then all the rest must follow, and there is a decreet given out from the throne of God, that there is no condemnation to thee.

But how shalt thou know if thou be in Christ? I told you, that ye shall know by the Spirit that guideth you. Thou who art in Christ, hast that Spirit of Christ leading thee: By the contrary, thou that art not in Christ, thou hast not the Spirit of Christ; and they who are not in Christ, have no guide but the flesh allenarly, and they follow that guide. Now, if thou beest led by the flesh, it will never lead thee to heaven, it will never lead thee to the tribunal of God's justice, it will never lead thee to the sight of thy sins, nor it will never lead thee to the blood of the Son of God, for to wash away thy sins, nor it will never lead thee to the Spirit of Jesus to comfort thee; for the flesh (as it is within thee) so it will never lead thee out of thyself, nor to the way of holiness. So thou shalt know by this whether thou be in Christ or not; even this, if thou be in Christ, then thou hast the Spirit of Christ. And how shalt thou know the Spirit of Christ? I will tell thee how that is: He will take thee, and lead thee to a clear understanding of thyself; and he will let thee see, that by nature thou art a lost sheep and a forlorn son; that thou wilt say, I will die, except I go home to my father, and I will perish, except I get the sweet balm of the blood of Christ, to heal the deadly wound of my soul. Oh that every one would mark the work of the Spirit, when he entereth into their heart : For, who led thee to the sight of thyself ? and who did let thee see thy miserable estate by nature ? None but the Spirit of Jesus, which the Father sent to thee with this commission, saying, break in, and open the eyes of yon blind sinner, and let him see what he is, as he is indeed. This is the first mark of the Spirit.

Next, he will lead thee out of thyself, and he will take thee to Christ, and he will gar thee fall down at his feet and cry, " have mercy upon me, thou Son of the everlasting God." So, wast thou ever led by the Spirit with a bleeding soul to the blood of Christ, and to the well of life ? Who led thee there but the Spirit of Christ ? And wast thou ever led to the sheep-fold of Christ ? Who led thee there but the Spirit of Jesus ? What more.

Thirdly, When he has led thee to the blood, then he will lead thee out through the heavens, and through the blood, and in through all to the love of the Father, which is the fountain, and to the ocean sea of the love of God : and there thou shalt see the Father loving thee for the Son's sake, or ever the world was made. There thou shalt see the Son loving thee freely, because the Father made choice of thee, and delivered thee to him. There thou shalt see that the Father sent his Son to die for thee, even when thou wast his enemy, and reconciled thee to himself, by the death of his Son ; and therefore thou dost conclude, seeing that " while we were yet sinners, Christ died for us ; much more then being justified by his blood, we shall be saved from wrath through him." Rom. v. 10. and therefore there is no condemnation to me. Oh ! how blyth mayest thou be, who has gotten this sealed to thine heart, that there is no condemnation to thee, because thou art in Christ.

Fourthly, Thou shalt know the Spirit by the fruit and effects of the Spirit. Now, what are the fruits of the Spirit ? They are set down to you in that fifth chapter of the epistle to the Gallatians, 22d and 23d verses.

The first is *love*. And who moved thee to love God, and his saints, but the Spirit of love himself.

The next is *joy*. Gottest thou ever, then, an unspeakable joy to thy soul? Who could lead thee to it, but the Spirit of joy, the Comforter himself?

The third is *peace*. So gottest thou ever peace in thy conscience, that peace which passeth all understanding? Then it was the Spirit of Jesus that led thee to it.

The fourth is *long-suffering*. So didst thou ever bear the cross patiently? And wast thou ever content to suffer for his name? And didst thou ever esteem the rebuke of Christ greater riches than the treasures of Egypt? Who could give thee grace to do this, but he who is the Spirit of all grace?

The fifth is *gentleness*. Who made thee meek and lowly of mind, that thou canst willingly put thy neck under the yoke of Christ? None but he who is the Spirit of meekness.

The sixth is *goodness*. Who moved thee to eschew evil and do good, and to be ready to every good work? None but the Spirit of Jesus who is goodness itself.

The seventh is *faith*. So, who gave thee to believe in Christ's death and resurrection? None but the Spirit of Christ which raised up Jesus from the dead.

The eighth is *meekness*, and the *ninth is temperance*. Who gave thee these graces, but the Spirit of Jesus who is the author of all grace? So ye shall know the Spirit by the fruits of the Spirit. Now because the time has overshot me; therefore I will but open the rest to you, and so conclude.

Ye see to whom there is no condemnation; ye see the mark that they have, is the Spirit of Christ; and ye see the work of the Spirit, is first to rebuke; and next, to lead thee out of thyself unto the Mediator, and to his blood.

Thirdly, To convoy thee through that blood unto the love of the Father, and to the everlasting decree of thy election and redemption.

Fourthly, It is the work of the Spirit which bringeth forth these fruits in thee, as *love, joy, peace, longsuffering, gentleness, goodness, faith, meekness, and temperance.* But the flesh will lead thee, to *adultery, fornication, uncleanness, wantonness, idolatry, witchcraft, hatred, debate, emulation, wrath, contention, sedition, heresy, and envy, murder, drunkenness, gluttony, and such like:* And so by the fruits, thou shalt know which of these two does guide thee, whether the flesh or the Spirit.

But you will say sometimes I have had love, and joy, and peace, and patience, and gentleness, and faith, and all the rest; but oftentimes I find that the flesh has the upper hand in me, and I am forced to follow it.

I answer, thou needest not this consolation, if thou wert quit of the flesh; but because thou wilt not be quit of it, so long as thou art in this life, for it will ay lie in thy bosom, to hinder thee from doing good, when thou wouldst do it; therefore, this consolation is sent to thee who fightest against the flesh; so if thou followest not the flesh, thou followest the Spirit as thy only guide. This is a token that there is no condemnation to thee.

Now, because it is hard to ground this into the heart of man, which is so subject to incredulity; and because thou who art the child of God, if thou hadst but one desire granted to thee in this world, I trow, thou wouldst ware it upon this, to have this consolation grounded and established in thine heart; therefore the apostle, in the second verse, applieth it to himself, as when he speaketh of his misery, he speaketh of it in his own person; so when he speaketh of his freedom, he speaketh of it in his own person also: Even so thou who art the child of God, canst speak of these two things, thou canst speak of the bondage and slavery of sin that led thee captive unto it; and thou canst speak of the freedom of the Spirit who set thee at liberty; thou canst tell that thou hadst terrors, and fears, and torment of conscience; and thou canst tell that thou hast gotten such joy, and such peace of conscience, that thou couldst step out with it, and take thy life into thine hand, and go to the grave; and thou couldst say with Simeon, "Lord, lettest thou thy servant depart in peace; for mine eyes have seen thy salvation," that's a token that thou art the child of God.

Now, the Spirit which lets him see his misery, the same Spirit lets him see his freedom; therefore he saith, "For the law of the Spirit of life, which is in Christ Jesus, hath made me free from the law of sin and death:" a law is a commanding power, grounded upon the authority of the law-giver? So by the law of the Spirit of life, he meaneth the virtue and power of the crucified and risen Lord, who now is living and reigning in glory; he calleth it a law because it commandeth, and it gets obedience in the hearts of God's children, and it commandeth with authority, and under this penalty, that I shall die except I give obedience to it.

Again, *The law of the Spirit of life,* (for there is Spirit and life in yon risen Lord that died on a tree, and there is virtue enough in him to free me from sin and death) *which is in Christ Jesus;* there is no life in angels nor saints that can quicken me, and there is no spirit that can bring life to my soul, but the Spirit of Jesus who once was dead, but now is alive, and reigneth now in glory *has freed me.* I was a slave to sin and Satan before; but now the Spirit of life, which is in yon crucified and glorified Lord, which I have apprehended by faith, has freed me from this slavery; so that now I am made a free burgess of that New Jerusalem, *from the law of sin.* The law of no prince got never such obedience of no subject in the land, as sin got of me in all the members of my body, until I looked to yon crucified Lord, and to his death and resurrection; then it commanded me, and I obeyed it: it promised, and I believed; it threatened, and I left off: So, I was before a slave sold unto sin; but now, sin, thou mayest well be a tyrant over me, to gar me give obedience unto thee, against my will; but thou shalt never get the willing obedience that thou hadst before. *And death:* There are two deaths, brethren, the first and second death; he spake of it in the first verse, where he says, *There is no condemnation to them that are in Christ Jesus:* that is, the souls of the elect shall never go where the souls of the reprobates go; because the angels shall wait on the elect when they die and shall carry their souls into the bosom of Christ where they shall lie under the altar, and shall rest there while the number of their brethren be fulfilled: but the evil spirits shall wait on the reprobates when they die, and they shall take away their souls to these endless depths in the bottom of hell, where they shall be tormented for evermore.

Now then, thou who art in Christ shalt never taste of the second death; but as to the first death, how art thou freed? I answer, Thou art freed from the curse, and from the sting of death, so that thou mayest step on the back of death, and go into that endless glory: Therefore, this first death is no death to thee who art in Christ, but rather an entry, or passage, or port to eternal life. I will say but this to you, if thou wouldst be sure to be freed from death, then thou must first be freed from sin, by the law of the Spirit of life; and thou must know who it is that brings this freedom to thee, to wit, the Lord Jesus only. Now I shall end.

But this I leave with you, even my testimony of this truth, written and sealed here by the Holy Ghost; and what is that? Ye are all of two sorts, and ye are all going two ways and ye have but two guides, and ye will all come to two sundry places. I will make this more plain to you; some of you are in Christ, and ye are walking in the way to heaven, and to the Son of God now reigning in heaven, and at the right-hand of his Father's majesty; and some of you are yet in yourselves, and in nature, for ye were never in the Son. Now, ye who are in Christ, and walk toward heaven, you have the Spirit of Jesus to be your guide, and the gate that he guides you is, 1*st*, To the sight of thy sin and misery. 2*dly*, He will lead thee unto the blood, and to the Mediator, and to the throne of grace, that there thou mayest find grace and mercy in time of need. 3*dly*, He leads thee in through the blood, to the love of the Father, who sent his Son to die for thee, when thou wast his enemy ; to the love of the Son, who by his death, reconciled thee unto God, and saved thee from wrath ; to the love of the Holy Ghost, who came from heaven to thee, to tell the glad tidings of salvation to thee. *Last of all*, He bringeth forth good fruits in thee, as, love, joy, peace, long-suffering, &c. and ye, who are in yourselves have nothing to guide you, but the wisdom of the flesh, which is enmity to God ; take no thought for the flesh, saith the Spirit ; but the flesh will say the contrary. So the Spirit draweth thee one gate, and the flesh draweth thee another gate. Now, these two gates will have two sundry ends, far different from other ; for as there is a great difference betwixt thee who art in Christ, and thee who art in the flesh, thee who art in the way to heaven, and thee who art in the way to hell ; now, as there is a great difference in all these, so there is a greater difference betwixt them in their ends, in their resurrection, and in their future judgment which is to come in the end.

Thou who walkest after the Spirit, as thou livest in Christ, so thou shalt die in Christ. Therefore I leave with thee this testimony, which I have from God in his word, that thou who art led by the Spirit of Jesus in the course of thy life, thou shalt die in Christ ; thou that art in thyself if thou abidest so, (for God forbid that I should conclude the reprobation of any of you) thou mayest turn to God, and the Lord may soon, and in an instant, change thine heart, and a voice of the Son of God can, at a word, raise thee from death, and out of the grave of sin ; and thou mayest be in thyself, in nature, and in the flesh, now this morning ; yet who can tell but thou mayest be in Christ ere the evening ; therefore far be it from me to say of any of you peremptorily that ye shall be condemned. And suppose ye have never yet tasted of the sweetness of that blood, yet far be it from me to conclude or say, that ye shall go to condemnation.

But this I testify to you, and here I open the gates of the kingdom of heaven to thee who art in Christ, and walkest not after the flesh, but after the Spirit. But to thee who art not in Christ, but in the flesh, I testify to thee, that as long as thou art in the flesh, the gates of heaven are closed upon thee, and the gates of hell are open to thee. Therefore, my brethren, I say, there are numbers of you who never yet knew what the Spirit of Jesus is : I say, I will judge none of you, but I would have you judging yourselves that ye be not judged. But here I bear you witness, that if you live in the flesh, and die in the flesh, thou shalt never see heaven. And that ye may not say in that great day, that ye wanted warning, therefore here I take the heaven and the earth to record, I take these walls and pillars of stone to record, I take this sun that shineth yonder, and your own consciences, to be witnesses betwixt you and me, that I have told you the whole counsel of God, so far as he has revealed it unto me, and that now I speak the truth in Christ, and lie not : Thou that livest and diest in the flesh, thou shalt lie in hell for evermore. Here I bear you witness of this, that none of you may say, that I have been a traitor to your souls, that I told you not your danger while I was with you : For why should be I guilty of any of your bloods ? Therefore suppose ye had never gotten more warning than at this day's preaching, I take heaven, and the earth, and this house, to be witnesses, that I am free of your blood. For I have told you, that if you be not in Christ before ye depart this life, and if ye remain in yourselves, in nature, and in the flesh, ye shall never see life, but shall come unto condemnation. By the contrary, I say to thee who art in Christ, and walketh not after the flesh, but after the Spirit; suppose there be a body of sin within thee, which leadeth thee captive many a time, and suppose there be a law in thy members, rebelling against the law of thy mind, and suppose thou beest sold under sin, and forced to do the thing that thou wouldst not do, and to leave undone the thing that thou wouldst do ; yet I bear thee record, and take this consolation to thee, that if thou desirest to walk after the Spirit, and not after the flesh, I assure thee, thy inherent corruption shall never be able to condemn thee.

Now, such of you as were never in Christ, nor walked never after the Spirit of Jesus, I beseech you come to him, and say, sweet Lord, give me a drink of thy blood to quench the thirst of my scorched soul, and to save me from the wrath to come ; give me a fill of thy flesh, that I die not eternally ; send down thy Spirit to lead me in that strait and narrow way which leadeth unto life ; turn me, Lord ; and I shall be turned, convert me, and I shall be converted, Lord, if thou wilt, thou canst make me clean.

Now will ye come to him, my hearts, for I assure you, he is a merciful Lord, and he came to save sinners and he has forgiven great sinners, and he will say to thee, if thou hast been a great sinner, I will have great mercy upon thee ; and if I have forgiven thee much, then thou wilt love me much.

Now, as for you who are in Christ already, I beseech you be thankful to God, in that he has shewed thee great mercy, and rejoice in that free grace of his Son Christ Jesus, who hath bought thee from sin and hell, and walk worthy of that calling of his whereunto thou art called ; abide in him, and he will abide in thee ; and study daily to make thy election sure. Use all the means of his worship daily ; as these, namely, hear the word gladly, meditate on it day and night ; let the words of grace be in your lips, watch and pray continually, and in all things be thankful ; for this is the will of God in Christ Jesus towards you. Go often unto prayer, and run with joy to the Father, and to the Mediator, and to the blood of the new covenant, and to mount Zion, and to the Lamb Christ Jesus : For if thou knewest how pleasant thou wert to him, I am sure thou wouldst take pleasure to talk with him oftener and longer than thou dost. So thou mayest come when thou wilt, and I know the Father can deny thee nothing that thou wilt ask of him in the name of his Son Christ Jesus.

And last of all, Forget not the poor church of God; but thou, who art a member of that body, I beseech thee to take care for the rest of the members of that body, pray for it; for I crave nothing of you but prayer, and we have no other weapons but prayer. And pray, that the Lord would arise, and manifest himself from heaven, and defend his poor church, and overthrow his enemies. Now, I say no more, but I commend you all to the blessing of God in Christ Jesus; to whom, with the Father, and Holy Spirit, be all praise, honour, and glory, now, and for evermore. *Amen.*

F I N I S.

www.ingramcontent.com/pod-product-compliance
Lightning Source LLC
Chambersburg PA
CBHW071219290426
44108CB00013B/1221